of

DISCOVERY&DESTINY

AN ANTHOLOGY OF AMERICAN WRITERS AND THE AMERICAN LAND

FULCRUM inc.

EDITED BY ROBERT C. BARON AND ELIZABETH DARBY JUNKIN

Copyright © 1986

Fulcrum Incorporated

Cover and Book Design
by Bob Schram

LIBRARY OF CONGRESS CATALOGING-IN-PUBLICATION DATA

Baron, Robert C.
Junkin, Elizabeth Darby

Of Discovery and Destiny

Bibliography: p. 432
1. American literature. 2. Nature – Literary collections.
3. Landscape – Literary collections.
I. Baron, Robert C. 1939 -   II. Junkin, Elizabeth Darby 1958 -

PS509.N304 1986   810'.8'036 86-15006
ISBN 1-55591-004-1

FULCRUM, INC.
GOLDEN, COLORADO

Acknowledgements

Beyond the Wall by Edward Abbey. Copyright © 1984 by Edward Abbey. Reprinted by permission of Henry Holt and Company, Inc.

The Land of Journey's Ending, Mary Austin, Tucson: University of Arizona Press, © 1983.

Seven Half-Miles from Home by Mary Back, published by Johnson Books, Boulder, 1985.

Aaron C. Bagg, from the December 1947 Bulletin of the Massachusetts Audubon Society.

Selected Works of Stephen Vincent Benét, Holt, Rinehart & Winston. © 1922 by Stephen Vincent Benét, © renewed 1950 by Rosemary Carr Benét. Reprinted by permission of Brandt and Brandt.

The Gift of Good Land, Copyright © 1981 by Wendell Berry. Published by North Point Press and reprinted by permission. All Rights Reserved.

The Outermost House by Henry Beston. Copyright 1928, 1949, © 1956 by Henry Beston. Copyright © 1977 by Elizabeth C. Beston. Reprinted by permission of Henry Holt and Company, Inc.

High, Wide and Lonesome. Hal Borland. Copyright © 1956 by Hal Borland. Copyright renewed © 1984 by Barbara Dodge Borland. Permission of Marie Rodell-Frances Collin Literary Agency.

You May Plow Here, the Narrative of Sara Brooks, Edited by Thordis Simonsen, reprinted by permission of W. W. Norton & Company, Inc. Copyright © 1986 by Thordis Simonsen.

Wildlands in Our Civilization, edited by David Brower. Copyright © 1965 by David Brower. Reprinted with permission of David Brower.

Canadian Spring. Sheila Burnford. Copyright © 1962 by Sheila Burnford. Reprinted by permission of Harold Ober Associates.

Summit of the Years by John Burroughs. Copyright 1913 by John Burroughs. Copyright renewed 1941 by Julian Burroughs. Reprinted by permission of Houghton Mifflin Company.

One Day at Teton Marsh, by Sally Carrighar. © 1947 by the Curtis Publishing Company. Copyright 1945, 1946, 1947 and renewed 1975 by Sally Carrighar. Reprinted permission of Alfred A. Knopf, Inc.

The Sense of Wonder by Rachel Carson, Copyright © 1956 by Rachel L. Carson. Reprinted by permission of Harper & Row, Publishers, Inc.

O Pioneers! by Willa Sibert Cather. Copyright 1913 and 1941 by Willa Sibert Cather. Reprinted by permission of Houghton Mifflin Company.

From The Orange Mailbox: Notes From a Few Country Acres pp. 178-180. Reprinted © 1985 by A. Carman Clark, by permission from The Harpswell Press.

The Prairie, James Fenimore Cooper, New American Library, 1633 Broadway, New York, NY.

The Course of Empire by Bernard DeVoto. Copyright 1952 by Bernard DeVoto. Copyright renewed © 1980 by Avis DeVoto. Reprinted by permission of Houghton Mifflin Company.

The Poems of Emily Dickinson, Reprinted by permission of the publishers and the Trustees of Amherst College edited by Thomas H. Johnson, Cambridge, Mass.: The Belknap Press of Harvard University Press, Copyright 1951, 1955, 1979, 1983 by the President and Fellows of Harvard College.

The Complete Poems of Emily Dickinson edited by Thomas H. Johnson. Copyright 1914, 1942 by Martha Dickinson Bianchi. By permission of Little, Brown & Company.

Pilgrim at Tinker Creek pp. 15-23 by Annie Dillard. Copyright © 1974 by Annie Dillard. Reprinted by permission of Harper & Row, Publishers, Inc.

This House of Sky, © 1978 by Ivan Doig. Reprinted by permission of Harcourt Brace Jovanovich, Inc.

Of Men and Mountains pp. 316-329 by William O. Douglas. Copyright © 1950 by William O. Douglas. Reprinted by permission of Harper & Row, Publishers, Inc.

The Immense Journey © 1953 by Loren Eiseley. reprinted by permission of Random House, Inc.

The Portable Emerson, edited by Carl Bode in collaboration with Malcolm Cowley. © 1946, copyright renewed The Viking Press, Inc., 1974. Reprinted by permission of Viking Penguin, Inc.

The Poetry of Robert Frost edited by Edward Connery Lathem. © 1934, © 1969 by Holt, Rinehart and Winston. © 1962 by Robert Frost. Reprinted by permission of Henry Holt and Company, Inc.

Table of Contents

The Authors Vital Statistics

Edward Abbey	1927	"Agrarian Anarchist"	381
Mary Hunter Austin	1868 - 1934	Historian	309
Mary Back	1905	Artist	94
Aaron C. Bagg	- 1947	Teacher, Naturalist	370
Katherine Lee Bates	1859 - 1929	Teacher	155
Stephen Vincent Benet	1898 - 1943	Poet, Novelist	360
Wendell Berry	1934	Farmer	274
Henry Beston	1888 - 1968	Writer	98
Hal Borland	1900 - 1978	Writer	30
Sara Brooks	1911	Farmer	316
David Brower	1912	Environmentalist	269
William Cullen Bryant	1794 - 1878	Poet	379
Sheila Burnford	1918 - 1984	Writer	204
John Burroughs	1837 - 1921	Naturalist	372
Sally Carrighar	1905	Wildlife Writer	110
Rachael Carson	1907 - 1964	Biologist, Writer	91
Willa Cather	1873 - 1947	Novelist	195
A. Carman Clark	1917	Writer	107
James Fenimore Cooper	1759 - 1851	Writer	173
Bernard DeVoto	1897 - 1955	Historian	5
Emily Dickinson	1830 - 1886	Poet	352
Annie Dillard	1945	Writer	118
Ivan Doig	1939	Writer	235
William O. Douglas	1898 - 1980	Supreme Court Justice	386
Loren Eiseley	1907 - 1977	Anthropologist	130
Ralph Waldo Emerson	1803 - 1882	Minister, Essayist	301
Robert Frost	1874 - 1963	Poet	354
Zane Grey	1875 - 1939	Western Writer	180
John Hay	1915	Nature Writer	338
William Least Heat Moon	1939	English Teacher, Author	62
Brewster Higley	1823 - 1911	Doctor, Song Writer	56
Edward Hoagland	1932	Writer	217
Thomas Jefferson	1743 - 1826	3rd President of the U.S.	305
Peter Jenkins	1951	Student, Writer	254
James Kavanaugh	1934	Former Priest, Writer	368
Richard Ketchum	1922	Editor	250
Joseph Wood Krutch	1863 - 1970	Writer	126
Aldo Leopold	1886 - 1948	Forester	335
Abraham Lincoln	1809 - 1865	16th President of the U.S.	348
Jack London	1876 - 1916	Writer	200
Henry Wadsworth Longfellow	1807 - 1882	Teacher, Poet	71
Barry Holstun Lopez	1945	Writer	134
James Russell Lowell	1819 - 1891	Editor, Poet	22

Norman Maclean	1902	Professor, Writer	279
C.W. McCall	1928	Songwriter	158
John McPhee	1931	Writer	243
Wallace McRae	1936	Montana Rancher	347
Farley Mowat	1921	Explorer, Storyteller	79
John Muir	1838 - 1914	Naturalist	223
Margaret Murie	1902	Biologist, Teacher	231
William Cotter Murray	1929	Teacher	40
Roderick Nash	1939	Professor	329
Charlton Ogburn, Jr.	1911	Writer	85
Sigurd F. Olson	1899 - 1982	Ecologist, Writer	67
Francis Parkman	1823 - 1893	Historian	26
John Wesley Powell	1834 - 1902	Explorer, Army Officer	189
Rosalind Richards	1874 - ?	Writer	139
O.E. Rölvaag	1876 - 1931	Teacher, Novelist	167
Theodore Roosevelt	1858 - 1919	26th President of the U.S.	213
Carl Sandburg	1878 - 1967	Poet	357
Mari Sandoz	1896 - 1966	Historian, Naturist	226
Robert William Service	1874 - 1958	Poet, Naturalist	76
John Steinbeck	1902 - 1968	Novelist	259
Bill Stockton	1921	Montana Rancher, Artist	240
George Miksch Sutton	1898 - 1982	Artist, Ornithologist	364
Bayard Taylor	1925 - 1878	Historian, Writer	163
John Teal	1921 - 1982	Anthropologist/Writer	14
Edwin Way Teale	1899 - 1980	Naturalist	54
Ten Bears	1792 - 1872	Comanche Chieftain	314
Henry David Thoreau	1817 - 1862	Writer, Philosopher	144
Frederick Jackson Turner	1861 - 1932	Historian	324
Mark Twain	1835 - 1910	Writer, Humorist	342
William W. Warner	1920	Writer	48
Walt Whitman	1819 - 1892	Poet	73
Nancy Wood	1936	Writer	350
Ann Zwinger	1925	Teacher, Writer	104

INTRODUCTION

Of what importance is nature and the land to us, as American people? This is a land of vastness, ranging from the mountains of Appalachia to the Rockies and on to the Sierra Nevadas. Consider the large rivers. Hold in your mind's eye the slow, grand movement of the Ohio River, or the Missouri and Mississippi, or the Rio Grande, or the Columbia. Think of the sections of the land that create this country – the Great Plains of the United States and Canada that challenged and bewildered us, the mountain peaks that promised wealth, the river valleys which invited homesteading, the stark and curious deserts of the Southwest.

Now ponder for a moment what the effect would have been upon us as a people had the North American continent ended at the Ohio River. By 1800, we would have known all of the unknown about this country — essentially within the space of one man's lifetime after our formation as a country and two centuries after the first settlements. There would have been no Yellowstone to discover and amaze us that such a place could actually exist. No Yukon to fascinate us in its subtle yet terrific northern beauty. No West to pin our hopes on and to offer us dreams. The challenge of the unknown, of the frontier, of the wilderness would have had limits which we understood rather than which we continue to explore four hundred years after the initial settlements in North America.

The American character is forged from our learning about and contending with the vastness of the land that makes up our country. We have looked to the land to draw and forge our independent character as a people and as a country. Our experiences with the vast amounts of nature that exist in the North American continent redefined our experience of ourselves, and our perceptions of limitation, boundaries, possibility, and opportunity. The land provided the answers for our concerns about a goal for our lives and piqued our curiosity. We dared to think and dream about what we might make of ourselves, individually and as a society.

This experience on this vast land is simply what has given us a character that is American, different from any other character of any other country in the world. Through the process of discovery, we learned about ourselves as well as what lay in the land of this continent — what we wanted, what we could do, and what we couldn't. During the four centuries of development of us as a people, there was never a limit to the land, just to our imaginations and to our strength. The land challenged us — sometimes with life and death situations, sometimes to persevere, sometimes to simply open our eyes a little more and let the land touch us in new ways outside our specific control. Because, in the end, nature, like the span of our lives, is out of our control. The land offers us a sense of place within this world, and thus a sense of peace. Nature to us is immortal, for its cycles continue while our own life ends.

Through this interaction with the land, we have sought our own reflection — our own and that of nature itself. We see beauty, we are in awe, and yet we are in conflict with nature and with ourselves as we function in it. We cherish it and feel about it all the values that a work of art — our own creation — inspires within us: comfort, sadness, fantasy, suffering, happiness, curiosity, inspiration, gain and loss, a sense of proportion, resolution, affirmation and self-definition, and peace.

This anthology is a sampler of man's celebration of nature. It is an exploration of man's search for himself in nature and through his experience with the land. In this anthology we have included what we think are whispers of the creation of this peculiar American character, this character that has always looked outside of itself for peace and in hope of ever more possibility. Each of these selections speaks of a different experience with nature, ranging from observations to feelings, reflective to analytical, philosophical to practical, religious to humorous.

We have divided the readings into three sections — nature and discovery, nature and challenge, and nature and the peace of self-definition. These reflect the major theme of the author's experience, but are but a part of the whole American experience of this continent. We have also included two short interludes between these legs of our journey: Songs of the American Spirit and 450 Years of Discovery, containing excerpts and quotes about the land. At the end of the book, there is a bibliography listing several works of each of the authors in the book.

This is a book we have intended to be read often. It offers the reader an introduction to unfamiliar writers, and it reintroduces old favorites. Authors and passages have been selected not only by the editors but also by others who offered contributions and suggestions of writers who captured the sense of importance of the land to the American people.

We chose writings in several ways. There are certain writers who almost by definition must be included: Thoreau, Emerson, Beston, Krutch, Teale, Leopold, Carson, Borland and Burroughs, to name but a few. There are others who are not normally considered strictly nature writers but who wrote about America and the American land: Lincoln, Longfellow, Cather, Twain, Steinbeck, Dickinson, Cooper, Sandoz and DeVoto. And some are writers who are likely to be unfamiliar names to all but the most dedicated of readers, such as Wally McRae, a rancher from Montana; Mary Back, an artist from Wyoming; A. Carman Clark, a weekly columnist from Maine; and Sara Brooks, a farmer originally from North Carolina.

The land has always been a place of discovery for man. William O. Douglas in his book *Of Men and Mountains,* says: "Discovery is adventure. There is an eagerness, touched at times with tenderness as one moves into the unknown. Walking the wilderness is indeed like living

The horizon drops away, brings new sights, sounds and smells from the earth."

The land has always been a place of challenge. Francis Parkman, in his book *Pioneers of France in the New World,* says: "A boundless vision grows upon us; an untamed continent; vast wastes of forest verdure; mountains silent in primeval sleep; river, lake and glimmering pool; wilderness oceans mingling with the sky. Such was the domain which France conquered for civilizations." Such was also the world the English, Spanish, and other early explorers found and that later Americans faced for 300 years. If we are lucky, we shall have the opportunity to face such an experience for another three centuries.

The American land has also been a land of emotion, a place of peace, contentment, and self-awareness. Christopher Columbus noted to his essay in the *Journal of the First Voyage:* "The Admiral says that he never beheld so fair a thing: trees along the river, beautiful and green, and different from ours, with flowers and fruits each according to their kind, many birds and little birds which sing very sweetly."

"We need the tonic of wildness . . . We can never have enough of nature . . . In wildness is the preservation of the world." Henry David Thoreau in his Journals

Why is nature and the land important? It is ultimately because we are all part of nature and the land. We gain understanding; we are challenged; we find peace through nature. Mankind is transitory; the land is permanent. And in studying nature we are ultimately learning about ourselves.

"What is life? It is the flash of a firefly in the night. It is the breath of a buffalo in the wintertime. It is the little shadow which runs across the grass and loses itself in the sunset." The last words of Crowfoot of the Blackfoot.

We hope that you enjoy this journey through the American experience of the land and that it takes you on a journey of your own in understanding nature and the land. Share it with your friends. Let us know if there are other favorite writers and selections that should be shared with other readers.

We would like to thank all those who made suggestions for this book and the publishers who allowed us to include these selections. A book like this requires much attention to detail, and we would like to thank Cara Smedley for so carefully typing and assisting us with this manuscript.

But most of all, we would like to thank the writers who saw, felt, and loved the American land and shared their experiences and feelings with others.

Robert C. Baron & Elizabeth Darby Junkin
Colorado, 1986

Nature and Discovery

Discover: To obtain
knowledge of; arrive at
through search or study.

There are two kinds of discovery: the discovery of the
world around us and the discovery of the world within us. Each
of us throughout our life is continuously exploring both worlds. And
the more we study, the more we
search, the more we know, the more
interesting the world is and the more
interested we become.

America was a land made for discovery. Where so much of Europe
had been known for centuries, America was the great unknown, a place
where people settled on the coast
and wondered what was in the interior. America became a nation of explorers, with people questioning and
searching for what was perpetually
across the river or over the next hill.
Over the last four centuries, Americans moved across the continent,
searching, studying, and learning.
This process of discovery never
really ends; it is still important to
Americans as we continue the exploration of the corners of our continent,
solar system, outer space, and internal spaces of our hearts and minds.

Courtesy of the Buffalo Bill Historical Center, Cody, Wyoming

This section opens with a selection by Bernard DeVoto about the discovery of parts of North America by the Spaniards in the early 16th century. It includes other types of discovery, at other times, by other people including Francis Parkman's personal study on the Oregon Trail, James Russell Lowell's experiences in Maine in the 19th century, as well as the young Hal Borland learning about the land in eastern Colorado early in this century.

One does not have to go, however, to strange places or be in olden times in order to experience discovery. Life, nature, and understanding are all around us. We have but to open our eyes and feel the world, as Rachael Carson writes in *The Sense of Wonder*. Henry Beston experienced discovery on a beach on Cape Cod; Ann Zwinger on a lake by her home; Carman Clark in her backyard in Maine; and Mary Back, on short walks near her Wyoming home, when her doctor suggested she start to exercise. As people began to discover the world around them, they also learned about the world inside of them.

Some people bring the curiosity they had as children and the excitement of learning and experiencing with them throughout their lives. These people are on a continual voyage of discovery. Others lose this curiosity, tune out the world around them, and turn off their minds. These people have lost their sensitivity, their excitement, and their potential as thinking and feeling creatures.

Nature is around us, and we are a part of nature. The more we discover about nature, the more we discover about ourselves. Enjoy the writings of Teale, Whitman, Ogburn, Dillard, Mowat, Krutch, Warner, Eiseley, Thoreau, and the others. And then go outside, look, hear, feel, and discover the wonder, the beauty, the excitement, and the joy of nature.

Bernard DeVoto

The Course of Empire
"The Children of the Sun"

The story of Cabeza de Vaca is incredible and would have to be considered myth except that it is true.

By 1527 the entire shoreline of the Gulf of Mexico had been coasted and, after a fashion, mapped. Portions of the map on paper and in men's minds were misconceived; in particular there were serious condensations of distances. The Atlantic coastline of Florida and in fact the entire coast of North America as far as Newfoundland had been investigated more carefully than the Gulf coast. In some areas the results were already amazingly accurate but the preconceptions behind the investigations affected all results. The errors of thought that followed were inevitable but they were also enormous.

In 1527 the Spanish usually applied the name Florida to the vague, misconceived, unknown extent of North America westward from the peninsula to the unknown northern reaches of Mexico. No one knew whether the peninsula of Florida was an island or part of the continental

mainland which, by then, North America was widely thought by no means universally believed to be. The extent and shape of the continental mainland, if such it should turn out to be, were unknown but variously conjectured. That continental North America was a peninsula of Asia was widely, perhaps generally, believed. Its relation to Asia was of first concern to all who were concerned with the Americas, but arbitrary acts of logic or guess were the only means of determining what the relation was. The Spanish had penetrated the peninsula of Florida inland from both coasts a little way. They had done the same in the Carolinas and Virginia and perhaps in Maryland. Several perfunctory efforts to establish colonies, or rather bases for conquest, on the Atlantic seaboard had been wrecked by ignorance, disease, Indians, or the lust for gold. Many slave-hunting raids, from Cuba or Santo Domingo, had acquainted the coastal Indians with metal and the white man's artifacts, and had flashed along the Indian underground word that these pale, bearded beings might be gods and were as dangerous as the evil gods.

Of the interior: nothing. Nothing was known for there was no experience. The mind will not tolerate a vacuum. When there is no knowledge there will be data; wish, desire, fear, and deductive thinking will provide them. Variously as people thought about the interior, everyone thought it far smaller than it was, thought it but tenth or a hundredth of its real size. Whatever size and shape it might have, no one doubted that it was cut across somewhere by a strait or some other kind of water passage that led from the Atlantic of the Gulf to the Pacific Ocean. (To the South Sea; the Pacific was called that not because Balboa had first seen it from the north, as is sometimes thought, but because it was visualized as south of Asia.) No one doubted that it contained many marvels and much gold.

In 1527 Pánfilo de Narváez got himself named governor of the elastically bounded big unknown called Florida, which meant that he was licensed to conquer and exploit it. He had had some experience at conquest but more at administering conquests others had made. In the islands he had displayed the requisite treachery and barbarity and had made himself rich. He was arrogant, vain, red-bearded, and one-eyed. He had lost an eye when the governor of Cuba sent him to steal the conquest of Mexico from Cortés. Cortés easily parried the double cross, bribing and exhorting more of Narváez's force away from him, then defeating the rest of it. Now he was staking his fortune on the unknown . . . Cabeza de Vaca was appointed treasurer of the expedition, the king's agent to make sure that the crown got its stipulated percentage of the take.

Preliminary disasters were an omen that the dark star which shone on so many ventures in the New World would govern this one. In the islands treachery, betrayal, disease, and a hurricane reduced the expedition by a third. But in 1528 Narváez set out for Florida with four hundred men and eighty horses. (Horses were by far the best weapon for offensive warfare that the Spanish had.) He understood that he was sailing for the southern and western boundary of his domain, which, though without stated location, would be somewhat north of the northernmost outpost town on the east coast of Mexico, Pánuco. (It can be located on a map near Tampico.) Storms drove the ships off their course and nearly half the horses died. When they made a landfall the pilots knew that they were still east of Pánuco but not how far. They decided that they were only a few days' sail from it, say two or three days. They were in fact just south of Tampa Bay and so erred by the width of the Gulf of Mexico.

This was April of 1528. As soon as they landed they met Indians but they killed none yet and in fact the conquest of Florida did not last long enough to be very bloody. At once they saw, or thought they saw, minute quantities of gold — the focus of desire. They could talk to the Indians only by gesture.[1] Desire translated gestures to mean that people to the north and west — a numerous and populous people who lived in big towns — had gold in bulk. The Indian pastime and expedient of getting rid of visitors by waving them on begins here. Well, there was gold in Georgia and Carolina but these peninsula tribes knew nothing of it — and the white men would not exploit it for nearly three centuries yet.

They were in the New World. The European mind had as yet but few concepts for dealing with it, and such as it had were based on the conquest of the islands, Mexico, and the littoral of the Caribbean. Here even the most accurate of those ideas were unrealistic to the verge of fantasy. Thinking made incapable by assumption of dealing with the realities at hand was fully as responsible as the climates, diseases, and

§ 7 §

strange food of the New World for the disasters that overtook Narváez and many who came after him. Learning of Indian towns which were temporary aggregations of a few bark huts, they expected them to be like Spanish cities, Seville, say, or Cadiz. News of a chief who held together a small band of underfed neolithic savages meant (and could only mean) a prince or a king, which implied a court, nobles, ceremony, and an economy which could produce the wealth required to maintain them. And the Spanish had come here to find great cities, such as they had found in Mexico. These cities must be close to the South Sea or on the water passage that led to it. They would therefore always be west or northwest, and not much farther on. They had come to find at least such quantities of gold as they had found in Mexico. They knew, they expected, they wished, they dreamed, and so they always found confirmation or would find it a few days from now. Finally, the mind was stretched taut by dealing with the strange landscape and terrain, the strange weather, the strange world. Strangeness was everywhere and it was roofed over by the unknown. Among whose components have always been mirage and fear.

Narváez was without inner substance; he lacked the steel a conquistador must have. Two weeks of swamps, rivers, forests, and strangeness crumpled him. His logistics were so fantastic that there were only a couple of pounds of food per man: Was not Florida the land of plenty? He ordered the ships, with a quarter of his command aboard, to find the big harbor which his chief pilot thought must be near at hand while he marched the expedition overland toward it. The decision insured his ruin and his nerve had already broken. They set off by land and for two months marched, waded, forded, and swam. They had no notion where they were going, except that Pánuco on the east coast of Mexico could be only a few days farther on, and no plan but to get to the salt water on their left flank and then work west. They captured the town they had heard of and got food but not gold.

This was the end of June and now they reached Indians who were better fed, more developed, and more warlike. They had to fight the rest of their way, learning that neither cuirasses nor shirts of mail would turn an arrow. They knew nothing about living in the wilderness and so never had enough to eat. By August a third of them were sick from malnutrition and swamp fevers. They had traveled a wavering course through fearful country, from a little north of St. Petersburg to the Apalachicola River (in the western extension of Florida) somewhat above its mouth. They were sick, hungry, frightened, licked, and in despair. The ships on which they had counted for food and rescue were gone forever. They could get out of this country, Cabeza de Vaca thought, "only through death, which from its coming in such a place was to us all the more terrible."

They did a tremendous thing: they made boats. Almost all of the condemned were hidalgos, gentlemen, whose pride it was to be incompetent at everything but fighting. But a carpenter and a smith taught them to make woodworking tools from their arquebuses and swords and belt buckles, sails from their shirts, and rigging from horse hair and palm fibers. They ate the forty-two horses that were left. Two hundred and forty-two conquistadores who had survived so far embarked in five indescribable craft. It was the end of September and they intended to follow the Gulf coast to Pánuco, near Tampico. They would reach it in just a few days.

The sun against which they had no shelter was as bad as the storms that blew them out to sea. The thirst was worse; once they had no water for five days. When they landed, the Indians were almost always hostile; in one attack they wounded all forty-nine of the boatload that Cabeza de Vaca captained. They were traveling toward their deaths but one day destiny burned bright. Cabeza de Vaca's boat rounded a promontory at the mouth of a wide river whose current swept them out from the shore, and two and a half miles out they "tooke fresh water within the Sea, because the River ranne into the Sea continually and with great violence." So he and his crew saw the Mississippi thirteen years before De Soto.

They may have been the first white men who ever saw it. The chart of this coast, for what it was worth, had been made by a navigator named Pineda who in 1519, having been blown into the Gulf when he had intended to go up the east coast of Florida, coasted all the way to the mouth of the Pánuco River, which he named and where the presence of Cortés frustrated his designs. (Like everyone, Pineda wanted gold and hoped to find the water passage to the South Sea.) The map showed the mouth of a big river somewhere in the vicinity, allowing for the condensed distances, of where Cabeza de Vaca unquestionably saw the Mississippi. Either he or his chief named it the Espíritu Santo, the River of the Holy Ghost. Thereafter the Spanish knew that a big river reached the Gulf somewhere in these parts, but no one can tell now whether Pineda had seen the mouth of the Mississippi or the estuary of the Mobile.

Four days after they took fresh water within the sea another storm separated the boats. Cabeza de Vaca's caught up with one, lost it, and after an undeterminable time but probably early in November, was driven ashore by a storm. Hunger, thirst, disease, apathy, and despair had so worn them down that only he and another had been able to stand to an oar; none were far from death. They thought that they were near Pánuco; it was more than five hundred miles away along the coastline but in comparison with the route by which he eventually reached his countrymen they were near it. Their landfall was Galveston Island, off the northeast coast of Texas.[2] By an amazing chance another of the boats was wrecked near by. (Even more amazingly, they were able, eventually, to make sure that the other three had been lost.) Eighty naked, unarmed men, already dragged into death's undertow by the failure of their culture, then, were here the last muster of the expedition of Pánfilo de Narváez "to conquer and governe the Provinces which lye from the River of Palmes [the Rio Grande] unto the Cape of Florida."

The Indians of the region, good-natured but of so wretched an economy that half the year they could barely hold starvation away, took them in. Soon all but five of them were dead: some drowning in an heroic effort to go on to Pánuco, some killed by the Indians for a few remaining personal trinkets or just idly, some executed in Indian revulsion for eating corpses of their companions, some of starvation, more of an epidemic, even more of the fading-out of the soul that may occur in the wilderness when hope has failed. In five the will to live prevailed but in one of them not quite enough. When the time came this one made the start with Cabeza de Vaca, in whom the will was absolute, but fled back to the comfort of slavery in terror of the unknown.

That was in 1532; Cabeza de Vaca, the king's treasurer, had been the slave of a small band of Indians for four years. So, with other bands, had the man of broken will and the other three whom he eventually found and who dared to make the cast with him. The bands moved with the seasonal food supply — they had no agriculture and little game — and sometimes came together to conduct a miserable trade in trinkets, holy objects, and a small surplus of weapons and clothing. They met once a year for gluttony when the cactus (*Opuntia*, the flowering prickly pear) was ripe for eating and there was enough food for everyone. At one of these annual feasts Cabeza de Vaca met the other three, at the next one they made their plans. Meanwhile his owners worked him sorely and with the caprice of Indians alternately beat or tortured him and treated him as one of themselves, which was not much better than torture. But he had two periods of ease. For a time he was a healer, curing the sick and the possessed. At another time he was an itinerant peddler making long journeys, perhaps as far as Oklahoma, trading such shells, feathers, flints, ochre, and sinews as he could collect and prepare. He kept his manhood firm in this squalor of heat, cold, mud, sickness, insects, reptiles, semistarvation, and hope deferred. And three times he saw buffalo, the first white man who ever saw them in the area of the United States.

In early fall of 1534 the four fled from slavery, going south for a space in hope of finding their countrymen at Pánuco. They knew neither where they were, nor how far their island was from their starting place of their destination, nor what the lay of the land was. Almost to the end of their journey they supposed that the Gulf of Mexico was at their left.

The names of Cabeza de Vaca's two white companions do not matter here but that of a slave who belonged to one of them does. He was called Estéban; Cabeza de Vaca says he was "an Arabian black," which means that he had once been owned by Moors. For the last six years he had been the slave of a slave. Now he was to become a god.

Cabeza de Vaca understood that the four had survived by miracle, for the expiation of their sins and for some other, still unrevealed purpose of God. He believed that he had been saved so that he could lead the others; his was certainly the dominant intelligence and will and without him they would have succumbed to the wilderness. Not long after the beginning of their journey the favor of God was manifest and they began to work miracles. They were strangers to the tribes they met, as strangers they were given welcome, and their strangeness was strong magic. The demented, the sick, and the dying were brought to them and they healed them of divers diseases. They thought they healed by prayer and faith, but as word ran ahead of them the Indians knew that they were children of the sun.

Their suffering was over now — except for marching that never ended, bloody feet, backs cut by pack-straps, long thirst, desert sun, mountain cold, tempest, and hurricane. But a pillar of cloud went ahead of them by day and the tribes came to pay homage and be healed.

They reached the Colorado River of Texas, which empties into Matagorda Bay halfway down the state's long coastline, and turned inland up its valley, traveling north of west. Sometimes they were by themselves but there was always an Indian trail and, if they had no notion where they were going, they were never lost. (Almost always when white men are crossing the American wilderness for the first time, they are following an immemorially old highway system of Indian trade, hunting, and war.) More often there were reverent guides, embassies coming out to meet them, and other embassies to take them on when they would stay longer. When cold weather came on they were nearing the West Texas hills. They met a tribe who were better fed than any they had known before, though still half starved in the winter time, and spent eight moons with them. Here Cabeza de Vaca learned another language — he knew six by the time he reached Culiacán and Estéban knew even more. Here too they were able to check off the last two of the original company whose deaths they had not heard about.

But the radiance begins in the summer of 1535, when they set out again. They traveled on up the valley of the Colorado, then left it and turned toward the Pecos River, marching west into the fourth house of the sky, where their father slept at night. Since Cabeza de Vaca was living a myth, his account is majestically unregardful of landmarks and geography but eventually they saw wraiths of peaks on the horizon and these must have been the Davis and Guadalupe Mountains of New Mexico. He thought that they came down from the North Sea . . . Another judgment from the geography beyond men's knowledge, and a revealing one. The North Sea was the one that hypothesis said must lie above Asia. So the continents drew together and the world was small.

Cabeza de Vaca thought that the mountains walled them off to the southward and he understood the Indians to say that the coast, the Gulf of Mexico, was only a short distance to the south. There were many tribes in that direction and the Indians who were charging high fees in native goods for the miracles worked by their guest-divinities, wanted them to turn eastward long enough to reach these untouched fields. But the coastal tribes they had met had been cruel: best avoid them. Moreover, the apathy of lost, starved, enslaved men had ended; they were proud and expectant. Who knew what they might find beyond this new horizon? The children of the sun would keep to their westward bearing. The Indians told them, truly, that this meant harsh mountains and canyons, worse deserts, and long stretches between tribes. No matter: "We ever held it certain that going toward the sunset we would find what we desired."

In four centuries no one ever said it more fully.

BERNARD DeVOTO was born and raised in Ogden, Utah and educated at Harvard. He was a writer, an historian and one of the more influential literary figures of the 20th Century. He spent over two decades writing *The Easy Chair,* a monthly column for *Harper's Magazine.* He was the author of numerous books including *Mark Twain's America, The Year of Decision-1845, Across The Wide Missouri.* This selection is taken from his book, *The Course of Empire,* which is the story of the amazing discovery of the North American continent by the early explorers who first saw the vision of this wild and opulent land.

John and Mildred Teal

Life and Death of the Salt Marsh
"Invasion"

ne day into the marsh came a man, an Indian. He hunted by himself for a day and then brought other hunters the following day for the abundant game he had discovered in this virgin territory. There was no nearby village. Food had been short for the Indians that summer and hunters had ranged farther and farther from the home village. But that winter all that remained of the hunting expeditions were a few duck feathers and the black remains of a wood fire at the edge of the marsh.

Later, a hunting village was established only a short distance inland from the marsh in the bay. The early men, few in number, were content to live with nature. They took what was necessary for survival. There was more than enough production for all and the marsh was but little affected by the invasion of this new animal species. But it was visited more and more regularly. Trails were worn into the high parts of the marsh. At the end of the trails lay rich clam beds.

The Indians were little more important to the marsh than were the bears which came to fish the upper end of a freshwater creek nearby. Deer came onto the marsh to catch the breeze when flies swarmed into the woods and browsed the vegetation along the landward marsh edge.

An occasional wolf prowled through the *Spartina* in his wide-ranging search for prey, looking especially for muskrats which lived in the fresher, cattail areas. Foxes looked for young ducklings in the creeks. Cougars, weasels, bobcats, skunks, raccoons, and mink wandered out onto the marsh, preyed and were preyed upon.

The Indians left in the winters but returned the following springs. They fished the creeks when the sun warmed the inland freshwaters before the sea lost its chill. Alewife, a herring, came up through the marsh in large numbers on their way to spawning grounds. The Indians made their way to the herring runs guided by clouds of gulls interspersed with ospreys and eagles, screaming and fighting over captured fish. The Indians bailed large numbers of alewife into woven twig baskets which they carried back to the village. They feasted on the fish. More were used to fertilize their corn to encourage a decent crop from the poor sandy soil.

Paths of trampled grass leading to the alewife creeks grew up again during the year after the herring had stopped running. New paths were worn through the grass the following year which were then obliterated by time and disuse.

In the shallow parts of the water in front of the marsh the Indians built fish traps constructed of long lines of brushwood stuck into the sand. When fish, swimming along the edge of the grass at high tide, met the barrier of brush, they turned into deeper water, moving along the brush row. At the end of the row they were caught in an enclosure in which they milled around until the tide fell. Then the Indians scooped them from the shallow water as they did the alewife.

The fish trap remained in the same general location for generations, several hundred years. Brush was replaced as it was washed away or broken. In time, when sediment filled the shallows which led into the trap, it was abandoned and marsh grass colonized the area. The brush remained in the sand for several years and helped to accelerate the marsh growth by slowing the passage of water so that sediment was deposited. The inner brush circle of the trap was finally buried and preserved for hundreds of years in the mud. This first important effect of man on the marsh was constructive.

As well as the alewife, the Indians took large numbers of shellfish from the pools in the growing parts of the marsh where *Spartina* roots had not yet changed the soft mud into firm ground. These collecting efforts destroyed bits of marsh grass and made slight erosion but the damage was quickly repaired by the robust *Spartina* plants.

The effects of the several thousand year tenure of the Indians were exceedingly slight. There were not many Indians and there was a lot of marsh. At the height of the Indian population there were still only a few hundred individuals living in the village. To us the environs would have seemed completely wild. Yet it was not altogether wild.

A bit of civilization crept in when the Indians cleared land for crops and instituted a system of crop rotation allowing the fields to lie fallow alternate years. Corn, squash, and beans were fertilized with fish and seaweed gathered from the marsh. There was little erosion from the cultivated land. Because of the crop fertilization and rotation, it was possible to harvest the same fields for generations. The Indians did not exhaust the fields as did the Englishmen who later grew tobacco in the central Atlantic colonies.

When winter came the Indians moved from their summer residence near the marsh to permanent winter villages up in the river valleys. The seasonal migrations were quite like they are today, except for the time necessary to cover the ground between the two villages. Some families stayed late in the fall, for the lingering warmth of the sea kept their gardens green longer than the vegetation in the river valleys. There was also the fall hunting of marsh birds.

Hunting began when the earliest shorebirds came through in July on their way south after a quick nesting trip in the north. Flocks of trusting dowitchers probed the mud vertically with their long bills. Pectoral sandpipers stalked crickets in the *S. patens* marshes. Other shorebirds followed. The greatest flocks and best hunting came late in summer when the migrations were in full swing. The migrant birds settled on the marsh to feed and rest. When the shorebirds flew on, they were replaced by rafts of ducks and gaggles of geese.

It was on the marsh creeks that the first Europeans to invade the area met the Indians. The Europeans were fishermen who came to the New World to seek the wonderful fishing grounds that had been reported. They found the shelter of the bay by the marsh and anchored there to mend their boats and fishing gear. A party of sailors went up in the marsh creeks to look for freshwater and meat. They came face to face with the Indians who were coming down the marsh creeks to look at them. After a few uneasy moments on each side, each decided the other was friendly. The Indians had meat and vegetables. The Europeans had knives and fishhooks. Negotiations for an exchange began at once.

Later fur traders came. When they could, they traded beads and worthless trinkets. The wiser Indians demanded iron tools for their valuable furs. The fishermen continued to come at irregular intervals. These hardy sailors, dark-complexioned men from Spain and Portugal, sailed their small ships across the Atlantic Ocean for fish. They visited the bay and marsh only when beset by troubles.

About a hundred years after Europeans had been coming regularly to trade with the Indians, and shortly before the first colonists were to arrive, serious trouble arose. The Indians and the English, who were by then doing most of the trading along the coast wherein the marsh was located, were in dispute. Differences intensified and boiled up into war. Perhaps the Indians ran out of furs or the English out of trade goods. Perhaps there was deception on both sides. But the merits of the two sides as fighting teams were never really tested. Between the time of the beginning of hostilities and the coming of the first colonists, a disease, probably one of the communicable diseases of childhood to which Englishmen were immune, killed a large number of the Indians. They thought the disaster to be the result of a curse put upon them by the foreigners. The few Indians left alive fled from the coastal villages. For a time men, both Indian and European, disappeared from the marsh.

As soon as the first settlers came from Europe, the uncorrupted epoch of the marsh ended. From that time on a major force shaping the life of the salt marsh was the activities of men.

The shores of the bay marsh were occupied very early in the settlement of New England. To men coming from a well-gardened country with neat, one-crop fields, the salt marsh presented a favorable sight in the untamed landscape. Here was cleared pasture. Here was a hay field waiting to be cut.

Among the earliest arrivals on the shore near the marsh were a hard-working, wiry Englishman, John Deacon, and his wife Abigail. The Deacons chose a likely spot for their homesite on a creek with depth enough to float a small boat. They had easy access from the water on one side but only rough land access from the other.

Since it was the main and most landward creek in the marsh, it carried freshwater from land runoff as well as tidal water. Except for the muddy banks of the main creek and its equally muddy but smaller tributaries, the marsh had developed into high marsh, drier than wet. John Deacon decided early that this excellent pasture should be used. He had been a smith in England and had brought tongs and hammers. He traded his skill for a cow with calf. The cow was a tired skinny animal just arrived from England, but she and the heifer she dropped grew sleek on the marsh grass. John simply let them wander at will where there was available food.

The Deacons were too busy building, clearing and trying to get gardens started in those first years to fence in the growing cattle herd, soon five head, as they had lost no time breeding the calf when she reached the age. There was little need to build fences. The animals moved from pasture to greener pasture. In those years the greener pastures were the marshes. The cattle spent considerable time in the woods browsing, but for hearty grazing they always moved back to the salt hay flats. It was soon apparent that the unrestrained cattle damaged the surface soils of the marsh but not dangerously so.

One day the old cow slipped on the soft sides of a tidal pool. She tried to regain her footing but slipped farther and farther into the soft ooze. John Deacon, unable to move her, was finally forced to shoot her. There were a few dark days in the Deacon household. The old cow had been their first and she was still good for a few more calves. Even worse, John had been forced to waste ball and powder with nothing to show for it on the table.

Other farmers were having the same difficulty. Cattle had to be kept off dangerous marsh but there were no fenced pastures in which to confine them. Fences were time-consuming to build. Time spent building fences was less time spent doing the multitude of jobs necessary to keep a family alive in the harsh new world. So fences were built only around gardens, to keep cattle out, not to fence them in.

By now twenty farms were strewn along the rise bordering the marsh. The boys took turns acting as common drovers to keep cattle off the marsh and to bring them back to owners for milking in the evening.

With the cattle off the marsh, the grass grew undisturbed again. More hay could be cut for the winter and more was needed as the numbers of farms and cows increased.

John Deacon and two other men, close neighbors who would call on him for a similar service, took scythes out to mow the marsh in August when the grass was tall but not yet mature. At this season it made the best fodder, as the men knew from their experiences with upland grasses. They chose neap tides for their work when the salt hay marsh was not flooded. The men moved along, three abreast, and cut the high marsh grasses. After the hay was cured the men gathered it by pitchfork and piled it onto stacks. They also cut what they could of the tall *S. alterniflora*, thatch as it was called. Some areas along the banks of the creeks were difficult to cut but on the flat new growths of marsh it was easier.

On the lower reaches sure to be flooded, the salt hay was cut and carried to the upland, perhaps to be put in the barn. On the high marsh, the hay was piled on small poles driven into the surface of the soil in clusters about two feet high and two feet apart. On these groups of small piliings, called staddles, the hay was safe from high tides. The hay was collected in the fall if necessary, but usually it was left until winter came and the frozen marsh surface could support an ox team and sledge.

Sometimes an unusually high tide occurred when a regular high was made higher by strong winds in an autumn storm. Then the carefully piled haystacks floated off the staddles intact and finally lodged up against the land somewhere. The farmers went out, tried to locate and identify their own. One, less generous than his neighbors, put a marked stick into his stacks for identification and was accused of putting similar sticks into any lost stack he came across.

The house John and his neighbors built contained three rooms at first, snug and tight. Its heavy wood frame was surfaced with clapboards. The roof of thatch was put on in the old style carried over from English thatchers but the thatch came not from an upland corn-field as it had in England, but from the rugged *S. alterniflora* especially selected from the lush growth along the tidal creeks.

The thatched roof caught fire on two occasions from flying chimney sparks. Both times John and Abigail were lucky enough to discover the fire in time to climb to the roof and pitch the burning thatch to the ground.

In time there were quite a number of Deacon children surrounding the hearth and small hands helped with the farm and marsh chores. John Deacon had borrowed a little lore from the Indians. Fishing and shellfishing did not stop because one group of men supplanted another. The food gathering continued but the methods changed. Men still waited for the warming in spring to herald the coming of the alewife, now also called sawbelly. They went down, entire families together with nets, to catch the fish. They dammed the creeks and waited for the dammed area to fill with fish. Then they harvested. Like the Indians the colonists carried the fish back to the fields where they planted them along with the corn for fertilizer.

Alewife season was one of feast. Some of the fish were eaten fresh or pickled and some salted for future use. The herring were a welcomed item in a diet which was beginning to bore after the long winter of living on stored foods from last year's harvest.

John and the children watched bald eagles with fully developed white heads, soaring over the creeks to get their share of the alewife bounty. They watched flocks of gulls pick up the silvery fish from the water and carry them to nearby dry spots where they slit the belly of the fish open with their beaks and extracted roe. The Deacons took a lesson from the birds and gathered only roe to fry for a meal when they had already preserved as many fish as they needed.

The marsh continued to grow and now it extended for miles up and down the bay from its original beginnings. More land was cleared and more farms built along those miles. Roads were cut through the wilderness but they remained rough and often rutted. Travel was still difficult inland.

Farmers, seeking the easiest means of transport, turned to boating through the marsh creeks on their way to market at the village which was growing midway along the marsh. The village was only a small cluster of houses early in its existence, but it boasted a town landing consisting of a crude ramp of stones and logs. A roadway was built across the high marsh to the landing. Eventually the creek was dug out and enlarged and a small pier built.

Soon coastal schooners sailed up the creek at high tide. The schooners, if they were caught between tides, waited out the hours with their bottoms in the mud. If it took a certain amount of time to get the schooner up the twisting creek, it was of small concern to the townsmen. However, it was of concern to the schooner's crew and the new merchant class developing in the village. The pier was often crowded with loads of lumber and foundation stones from northern New England. Some schooners brought cargo from old England too, dishes, furniture, and tools, When empty, the boats were loaded with farm and fishing produce. The lumber and stones were used to build more houses in the village, which grew vigorously.

JOHN TEAL (1921-1982) was an anthropologist, ecologist, arctic research-er, geographer, educator, and author. He founded the Institute of Northern Agricultural Research in 1954 to domesticate the arctic Musk Ox for agricultur-al use. He was a Professor of Human Ecology at the University of Alaska from 1964-1977. His wife, Mildred, collaborated with him on this book. In this selec-tion they describe the changes to the salt marsh brought by man – Indian and European – and witness the sometimes permanent change man causes upon his environment.

James Russell Lowell

from *White Pine and Blue Water: A State of Maine Reader* "The Moosehead Country in 1853"

Friday the 12th. — The coach leaves Waterville at five o'clock in the morning, and one must breakfast in the dark at a quarter past four, because a train starts at twenty minutes before five — the passengers by both conveyances being pastured gregariously. So one must be up at half past three. The primary geological formations contain no trace of man, and it seems to me that these Eocene periods of the day are not fitted for sustaining the human forms of life. One of the Fathers held that the sun was created to be worshipped at his rising by the Gentiles. The more reason that Christians (except, perhaps, early Christians) should abstain from these heathenish ceremonials. As one arriving by an early train is welcomed by a drowsy maid with the sleep scarce brushed out of her hair and finds empty grates and polished mahogany, on whose arid plains the pioneers of breakfast have not yet encamped, so a person waked thus unseasonably is sent into the world before his faculties are up and dressed to serve him. It might have been for this reason that my stomach resented for several hours a piece of fried beefsteak which I forced upon it, or, more properly speaking, a piece of that leathern conveniency which in these regions assumes the name. You will find it as hard to believe, my dear Storg, as that quarrel of the Sorbonists, whether one should say ego amat or no, that the use of the gridiron is unknown hereabout, and so near a river named after St. Lawrence, too!

Today has been the hottest day of the season, yet our drive has not been unpleasant. For a considerable distance we followed the course of the Sebasticook River, a pretty stream with alternations of dark brown pools and wine-colored rapids. On each side of the road the land had been cleared, and little one-story farm-houses were scattered at intervals. But the stumps still held out in most of the fields, and the tangled wilderness closed in behind, striped here and there with the slim white trunks of the elm. As yet only the edges of the great forest have been nibbled away. Sometimes a root-fence stretched up its bleaching antlers, like the trophies of a giant hunter. Now and then the houses thickened into an unsocial-looking village, and we drove up to the grocery to leave and take a mail-bag, stopping again presently to water the horses at some pallid little tavern, whose one red-curtained eye (the bar-room) had been put out by the inexorable thrust of Maine Law. Had Shenstone travelled this road, he would never have written that famous stanza of his: had Johnson, he would never have quoted it. They are to real inns as the skull of Yorick to his face. Where these villages occurred at a distance from the river, it was difficult to account for them. On the riverbank, a saw-mill or a tannery served as a logical premise, and saved them from total inconsequentiality. As we trailed along, at the rate of about four miles an hour, it was discovered that one of our mail-bags was missing. "Guess somebody'll pick it up," said the driver coolly: " 't any rate, likely there's nothin' in it." Who knows how long it took some Elam D. or Zebulon K. to compose the missive intrusted to that vagrant bag, and how much longer to persuade Pamela Grace or Sophronia Melissa that it had really and truly been written? The discovery of our loss was made by a tall man who sat next to me on the top of the coach, every one of whose senses seemed to be persecuting its severe investigation as we went along. Presently, sniffing gently, he remarked: "'Pears to me's though I smelt sunthin'. Ain't the aix het, think?" The driver pulled up, and, sure enough, the off fore-wheel was found to be smoking. In three minutes he had snatched a rail from the fence, made a lever, raised the coach, and taken off the wheel, bathing the hot axle and box with water from the river. It was a pretty spot, and I was not sorry to lie under a beech-tree (Tityrus-like, meditating over my pipe) and watch the operations of the fire-annihilator. I could not help contrasting the ready helpfulness of our driver, all of whose wits were about him, current, and redeemable in the specie of action on emergency, with an incident of travel in Italy, where, under a somewhat similar stress of circumstances, our vetturino had nothing for it but to dash his hat on the ground and call on Sant' Antonio, the Italian Hercules.

There being four passengers for the Lake, a vehicle called a mud-wagon was detailed at Newport for our accommodation. In this we jolted and rattled along at a livelier pace than in the coach. As we got farther north, the country (especially the hills) gave evidence of longer cultivation. About the thriving town of Dexter we saw fine farms and crops. The houses, too, became prettier; hop-vines were trained about the doors, and hung their clustering thyrsi over the open windows. A kind of wild rose (called by the country folk the primrose) and asters were planted about the door-yards, and orchards, commonly of natural fruit, added to the pleasant home-look. But everywhere we could see that the war between the white man and the forest was still fierce, and that it would be a long while yet before the axe was buried. The haying being over, fires blazed or smouldered against the stumps in the fields, and the blue smoke widened slowly upward through the quiet August atmosphere. It seemed to me that I could hear a sigh now and then from the immemorial pines, as they stood watching these campfires of the inexorable invader. Evening set in, and, as we crunched and crawled up the long gravelly hills, I sometimes began to fancy that Nature had forgotten to make the corresponding descent on the other side. But erelong we were rushing down at full speed; and, inspired by the dactylic beat of the horses' hoofs, I essayed to repeat the opening lines of Evangeline. At the moment I was beginning, we plunged into a hollow, where the soft clay had been overcome by a road of unhewn logs. I got through one line to this corduroy accompaniment, somewhat as a country choir stretches a short metre on the Procrustean rack of a long-drawn tune. The result was like this: —

"Thihis ihis thehe fohorest prihihimeheval; thehe murhurmuring
    pihines hahand thehe hehemlohocks!"

At a quarter past eleven, P. M., we reached Greenville, (a little village which looks as if it had dripped down from the hills, and settled in the hollow at the foot of the lake,) having accomplished seventy-two miles in eighteen hours. The tavern was totally extinguished. The driver rapped upon the bar-room window, and after a while we saw heat-lightnings of unsuccessful matches followed by a low grumble of vocal thunder, which I am afraid took the form of imprecation. Presently there was a great success, and the steady blur of lighted tallow succeeded the fugitive brilliance of the pine. A hostler fumbled the door open, and stood staring at but not seeing us, with the sleep sticking out all over him. We at last contrived to launch him, more like an insensible missile than an intelligent or intelligible being, at the slumbering landlord, who came out wide-awake, and welcomed us as so many half-dollars, — twenty-five cents each for bed, ditto breakfast. O Shenstone, Shenstone! The only roost was in the garret, which had been made into a single room, and contained eleven double-beds, ranged along the walls. It was like sleeping in a hospital. However, nice customs curtsy to eighteen-hour rides, and we slept.

JAMES RUSSELL LOWELL was an American poet, critic, and editor. He was the first editor of *The Atlantic Monthly* and, later, *The North American Review*. In 1877 he was appointed American Minister to London and remained there for eight years. His literary influence on the country, especially New England, was immense. Among his books are: *The Bigelow Papers, Fireside Travels,* and *Lowell's Poems and Democracy* .

Francis Parkman

The Oregon Trail
"Jumping Off"

The creek where the wagon had stuck was just before us; Pontiac might be thirsty with his run and stop there to drink. I kept as near him as possible, taking every precaution not to alarm him again; and the result proved as I had hoped, for he walked deliberately among the trees and stooped down to the water. I alighted, dragged old Hendrick through the mud, and with a feeling of infinite satisfaction picked up the slimy trail-rope, and twisted it three times round my hand. "Now let me see you get away again!" I thought, as I remounted. But Pontiac was exceedingly reluctant to turn back; Hendrick, too, who had evidently flattered himself with hopes, showed the utmost repugnance, and grumbled in a vain manner peculiar to himself at being compelled to face about. A smart cut of the whip restored his cheerfulness; and, dragging the recovered truant behind, I set out in search of the camp. An hour or two elapsed, when, near sunset, I saw the tents, standing on a swell of the prairie, beyond a line of woods, while the bands of horses were feeding in a low meadow close at hand. There sat Jack C ——, cross-legged, in the sun, splicing a trail-rope; and the rest were lying on the grass, smoking and telling stories. That night we enjoyed a serenade from the wolves, more lively than any with which they had yet favored us; and in the morning one of the musicians appeared, not many rods from the tents, quietly seated among the horses, looking at us with a pair of large gray eyes; but perceiving a rifle levelled at him, he leaped up and made off in hot haste.

I pass by the following day or two of our journey, for nothing occurred worthy of record. Should any one of my readers ever be impelled to visit the prairies, and should he choose the route to the Platte (the best, perhaps, that can be adopted), I can assure him that he need not think to enter at once upon the paradise of his imagination. A dreary preliminary, a protracted crossing of the threshold, awaits him before he finds himself fairly upon the verge of the "great American desert," — those barren wastes, the haunts of the buffalo and the Indian, where the very shadow of civilization lies a hundred leagues behind him. The intervening country, the wide and fertile belt that extends for several hundred miles beyond the extreme frontier, will probably answer tolerably well to his preconceived ideas of the prairie; for this it is from which picturesque tourists, painters, poets, and novelists, who have seldom penetrated farther, have derived their conceptions of the whole region. If he has a painter's eye, he may find his period of probation not wholly void of interest. The scenery, though tame, is graceful and pleasing. Here are level plains, too wide for the eye to measure; green undulations, like motionless swells of the ocean; abundance of streams, followed through all their windings by lines of woods and scattered groves. But let him be as enthusiastic as he may, he will find enough to damp his ardor. His wagons will stick in the mud; his horses will break loose; harness will give way; and axletrees prove unsound. His bed will be a soft one, consisting often of black mud of the richest consistency. As for food, he must content himself with biscuit and salt provisions; for, strange as it may seem, this tract of country produces very little game. As he advances, indeed, he will see, mouldering in the grass by his path, the vast antlers of the elk, and farther on the whitened skulls of the buffalo, once swarming over this now deserted region. Perhaps, like us, he may journey for a fortnight, and see not so much as the hoof-print of a deer; in the spring, not even a prairie-hen is to be had.

Yet, to compensate him for this unlooked-for deficiency of game, he will find himself beset with "varmints" innumerable. The wolves will entertain him with a concert at night, and skulk around him by day, just beyond rifleshot; his horse will step into badger-holes; from every marsh and mud-puddle will arise the bellowing, croaking and trilling of legions of frogs, infinitely various in color, shape and dimensions. A profusion of snakes will glide away from under his horse's feet, or quietly visit him in his tent at night; while the pertinacious humming of unnumbered mosquitoes will banish sleep from his eyelids. When thirsty with a long ride in the scorching sun over some boundless reach of prairie, he comes at length to a pool of water, and alights to drink, he discovers a troop of young tadpoles sporting in the bottom of his cup. Add to this, that, all the morning, the sun beats upon him with a sultry, penetrating heat, and that, with provoking regularity, at about four o'clock in the afternoon, a thunderstorm rises and drenches him to the skin.

One day, after a protracted morning's ride, we stopped to rest at noon upon the open prairie. No trees were in sight; but close at hand a little dribbling brook was twisting from side to side through a hollow; now forming holes of stagnant water, and now gliding over the mud in a scarcely perceptible current, among a growth of sickly bushes, and great clumps of tall rank grass. The day was excessively hot and oppressive. The horses and mules were rolling on the prairie to refresh themselves, or feeding among the bush in the hollow. We had dined; and Deslauriers, puffing at his pipe, knelt on the grass, scrubbing our service of tin-plate. Shaw lay in the shade, under the cart, to rest for awhile, before the word should be given to "catch up." Henry Chatillon, before lying down, was looking about for signs of snakes, the only living things that he feared, and uttering various ejaculations of disgust at finding several suspicious-looking holes close to the cart. I sat leaning against the wheel in a scanty strip of shade, making a pair of hobbles to replace those which my contumacious steed Pontiac had broken the night before. The camp of our friends, a rod or two distant, presented the same scene of lazy tranquillity.

FRANCIS PARKMAN was born in 1823 in Boston. In 1846, he journeyed along the Oregon Trail with his cousin and wrote a book about his experiences. His excellent literary style and his careful historical research made him one of the best American historians, focussing on the history of France and Britain in North America. His other books include: *Pioneers of France In The New World, The Discovery of the Great West, Montcalm and Wolfe,* and *A Half Century of Conflict.*

Hal Borland

High, Wide and Lonesome

When father and I started out, that late April morning, it was like the dawn of creation, so sweet and clean and crisply damp-cool. All along the first two miles south from town the blackbirds in the big cottonwoods *ka-cheed* among the jade-flake leaves, leaves no bigger than a ground squirrel's ear. The blackbirds themselves were like gems, jet set with ruby and gold, the red-wings and the yellow-heads, all *ka-cheeing* in the sun not half an hour high. And in the roadside alfalfa, silvery blue-green in new leaf and dew, was a jack rabbit in from the sand hills for breakfast, the sun making his long black-tipped ears pink as rose quartz. It was all spring and new beginnings, a morning to be alive and laughing.

I wanted to laugh and shout when the jack rabbit in the alfafa swiveled his ears, stood on his haunches, knee-high to a tall man, and wriggled his nose at us. Then Father did laugh, and Dick and Shorty broke into a trot, snorting and eager and full of life, and the rabbit hopped away. The wagon, loaded with lumber and roofing paper and sections of galvanized well casing, jolted on the gravel road, creaking and rattling.

Father let the horses trot a little way, then drew them down to a walk again and handed the lines to me while he rolled a Bull Durham cigarette. Already Nebraska was "back east" and we were Coloradoans. Father, who had been a printer since he was fourteen, was going to be a ranchman, or at least a farmer.

"If I'm ever going to make a change," he'd said two months ago, "I'd better make it now, or I'll wake up some morning and find that I'm an old man." Father was almost thirty-two years old. So he came to Colorado alone, from the little Nebraska town where he was born less than thirty miles from the Missouri River, and he found the land he wanted and filed on it as a homestead. He went back to Nebraska, sold his share of the weekly newspaper, sold the house where we lived, and told Mother and me we'd move just as soon as winter was over.

Winter began to break up in March, hurried as though just for us by an early spring. Mud and melt crept along the Missouri River bottom lands and up Nemaha Creek, and Father helped us with the first packing. Then he left the rest of the packing to Mother and me and came to Colorado, to rent the little green house in Brush for a temporary home, to buy a team and wagon and a couple of cows and a dozen chickens. He even set two broody hens so Mother would have a flock of chicks for summer frying. And, ten days ago, Mother and I came out to Brush, eighteen hours on the cindery green-plush train, eating from the big box of picnic food, napping in the stiff-backed seats, talking to the friendly conductor and brakeman. The brakeman said to me, "Why, at almost ten, you're big enough to ride a bronco and shoot a coyote!" And I couldn't wait to get to Colorado.

Now we were on the way to the homestead, Father and I. Mother had seen us off, breakfasted and eager. Father had said, "We'll be back within a week or so, ten days at most. We'll get a house up and dig a well; then we'll come back for you." And she had kissed us both and waved goodbye, slim and dark-haired and a little misty-eyed. Mother would be twenty-nine in the fall. She was still standing there in the dooryard, watching, her hands wrapped in her apron, when we turned the corner at the depot and waved. She waved to us, then turned and went back to the little green house, and we headed south along the road lined with tall cottonwoods just leafing out.

Two miles from town we came to the end of the cottonwood lane. Ahead was the first range of sand hills. We turned east, skirting them. We were climbing out of the Platte valley, going toward the high flatlands. Behind us the valley was lush with trees and irrigated fields. Ahead, where we were going, the hills rolled gently all the way to the horizon without a tree in sight. We skirted the sand hills another mile to the east, then turned south again, and the hard road ended. The horses began to strain as the heavily laden wagon's wheels bit into the sand track.

I watched the front wheel on my side, the left, as it turned in the sand, felly-deep. The sand lifted with the wheel and fell back in a little cascade that glistened in the sun and made a soft, singing hiss. The hub rattle was muffled. Only the puffing of the horses and the creak of harness were louder than the singing hiss of the sand at the wheels. I looked south and asked, "Is that where we're going, to that hill?"

"Farther than that," Father said. And when we had crossed the next hollow there was a new farthest hill. We were going farther than that one too, much farther.

We crossed the sand hill strip and were on hard road again. The sun was halfway toward noon. The horses were sweating, and the smell of sweat and warm leather was a Nebraska smell. It was a Grandpa smell, Mother's father, who was a farmer and teamster. I would always remember him for the smell that was upon him, a clean farm smell of hay and horses, not a barn smell. Grandpa was a gentle man, a man who never had a cross word for horses or dogs or small boys. The other grandfather, Father's father, I never knew. He died before I was born. He was a blacksmith and a millwright. There was a profile picture of him that hung in an oval frame in Grandma Borland's house. It showed only one side of his face, and one eye; he lost the other eye as a boy. He had a face like Father's, except that Grandpa Borland had a full black mustache. All grandfathers had mustaches. Grandpa Clinaburg had a brown one, except when he had been hauling flour for the mill; then it was white, and so was his hair. Sometimes Father told stories about Grandpa Borland, but not this morning.

We topped another rise and I pointed again to the farthest hill in sight. "Farther than that one?"

Father laughed. "That hill is this side of Gary, and Gary's just about halfway there."

So I watched the meadow larks on the fence posts at the side of the road, saw the yellow of their breasts and the spotted brown of their backs and the lengths of their bills. I watched the funny way they flew on their stubby wings. As I listened to their songs it seemed they were saying, "This is the time to see the world!" and "Hello there, boy!" And I watched the striped-backed little ground squirrels and asked Father what they were. He told me and I said they couldn't be squirrels because the squirrels along Nemaha Creek back in Nebraska had long, bushy tails. These, I said, were squinneys, and Father said, "You'll see lots of squinneys."

It was eleven o'clock when we reached Gary. Gary wasn't really a town; it was a store and post office, a big, rambling frame building with a wide porch and a long hitch rack. Father tied the team at the hitch rack and we went inside. It was dark and cool and smelled of coffee and leather and calico and coal oil. Tom McDowell, the tall, lean, leisurely storekeeper, wore a blue work shirt and a vest open down the front. He drawled when he said, "Warm morning for April, ain't it?" Then he glanced out the big front window, saw our wagon and its load, and he asked, "Homesteaders?"

Father said, "Yes. We're going down in the corner of the county. Just going out to build the house."

Mr. McDowell said, "Well, good luck. That's down on John Gerrity's range, isn't it?"

I was edging down the long brown counter, looking at the yellow coils of lariat rope, the leather work gloves, the bibless overalls, the high-heeled boots hanging in pairs from the ceiling. At the few bolts of calico on the shelves, the rolls of table oilcloth, the square, slant-topped, lacquered bins of coffee and tea, the glass-topped bins of ginger snaps and pink-iced cookies. There was a glassed case with boxes of cigars and bags of smoking tobacco and a pile of long brown slabs of chewing tobacco. And at the back of the store, in the corner, was a cubbyhole of a post office with its barred window and its squares of mailboxes. Beside the mailboxes stood big burlap bags of Mexican beans and white hundred-pound sacks of sugar.

Father was buying cheese and crackers and sardines. Mr. McDowell was saying, "That's down south of Gerrity's main camp. Up at the head of Ketchem Holler."

"I don't know that name," Father said.

"That's the big valley just west of the school section," Mr. McDowell said. "They used to use it to hold the herd when they had roundup, the big ranches."

"I guess that's it," Father said. "We're just west of the school section. On section seventeen."

Mr. McDowell nodded and put the things in a paper sack. "Good hay land in there. Well, I'll probably be seeing you some more. Expecting any mail?"

"Not yet," Father said. He paid the bill and we went back to the wagon. There was a watering trough beside the store, so we watered the horses before we drove on.

Three more miles south, past a few farms and alfafa fields, and we came to another range of sand hills. We drove to the top of the first hill, pulled out of the main track, and unhitched the horses. Father slipped the bits from their mouths and set out a tin pail for each of them with a couple of quarts of oats.

We sat in the shade of the wagon and Father opened the package of cheese. He cut a slice with his pocket knife, laid it on a big square cracker, and handed it to me before he opened the can of sardines. I took a bite, caught the cracker crumbs with my tongue, and sucked the warm, tangy cheese and felt the crispness of the cracker. I held it in my mouth, just tasting it, before I chewed it. Father cut another slice of cheese, put it on another cracker, and lifted a mustard-drippy sardine on his knife blade. He put the sardine on the cheese and handed the whole wonderful thing to me.

Crisp cracker, tingly cheese, and mustardy sardine! It was even better than Nemaha Creek catfish and bread and butter! The oozy mustard filled your mouth, there was the crunchy taste of cracker and the warm sardine taste, and there was the clinging cheese taste, all combined. Cheese and crackers are good food on any hilltop; cheese and crackers and mustard sardines are a banquet.

We banqueted till there wasn't a crumb of cheese left or a drip of mustard in the sardine can. Then we lay in the shade under the wagon and watched two sand lizards no longer than my hand, lizards with green and sand-colored backs and yellowish white bellies and white throats that pulsated as they breathed. The horses snuffled, there was a breath of cool air in the shade, and somewhere in the distance a hawk on the wing screamed a faint, echoing challenge.

Off to the south was another high hill, faint green and gleaming sand-gold in the sun. I sat up and pointed, and Father smiled and said, before my question came, "Still farther than that, son." We hitched the horses to the wagon and went on.

There were no more fences, now. On a distant hill there was a house, a lonely house without even a barn. Then, as we drove on and on, that last house was out of sight.

The road had become a trail, two faint ruts in the greening sand grass. Then we came to the far edge of the sand hills and hard land was under us again. There we left the wagon tracks, turned southwest onto a high flatland. We climbed a long gentle slope and were alone in a vastness and a distance that were like nothing I had ever seen or imagined. In all directions I could see the horizon, not a hill between that interrupted the smooth, round bowl-rim of blue. It was like being a very tiny ant on a table under Mother's very biggest mixing bowl, a blue and silver bowl and a tablecloth all greeny-tan and full of little wrinkles.

Father drew up the horses for a moment and just sat and looked. There was an expression on his face that I had seen only once before, the first time he came home from out here and told Mother and me about the homestead he had filed on. But now it was even brighter, that look, and it had a kind of smile deep inside that didn't show on his lips but only in his blue eyes. I looked at him, and I looked again at the distance, and I felt a kind of smile, inside myself, and a sense of awe that made me not want to say a word. It was so big, so vast, so new, so wonderful.

Father took a deep breath and we drove on. It was like driving into a world nobody had ever seen before except God, a world God had just made, like the world in the Bible before there was an Adam or an

Eve. Even the sounds were all new. The hub rattle of the wagon was muted in the deep mat of curled buffalo grass. The creak of the harness was not much louder than the squeak of a cricket in your pocket.

We went on across the upland and came to a prairie dog town where the grass was thinned away and there were hundreds of pock-mark holes and pimple mounds where the brown little prairie dogs, fatter and bigger than Nebraska squirrels, sat and yipped at us and jerked their skinny tails and dived down their burrows when the wagon came near.

We came to a broad, shallow lake, melt from the winter snow and drain from the spring rain, that would shrink to a little mudhole in another month or two. It hardly looked like water, it was so clear, and under the water the grass was growing, much greener than the flat all around it. Ducks were there, scores of teal and mallards and even canvasbacks, swimming on the clear water over the green grass as though they were swimming in the air. And around the edges were brown curlew and snipe, with their long grotesque beaks and fat stubby bodies. And killdeers, with their black coats and white shirt fronts, running along in the shallows and bobbing and leaping into the air and crying *kill-deer, kill-deer, kill-dee, dee* as they flew a little way and settled again.

We came close to the water and the ducks quacked in excitement and flailed the water and rose on beating wings, dripping so much that for a moment there was a flash of rainbow in the spray. They rose and circled and came back to land with outstretched feet and cupped wings, in a new rush of spray.

Then the lake was behind and the meadow larks were singing, " Hello there, boy!" And little horned larks went spiraling up, right under the horses' noses, singing as they flew high in circles. And when we came down a little slope into hidden hollow there was a rush of small hoofs and a flash of white rump patches as a herd of pronghorn antelope, surprised at their grazing, bounded away, stiff-legged and breathtakingly swift. They ran to the next hilltop, circled, came back behind us and, full of curiosity, followed the wagon for half a mile.

Midafternoon and we saw another wagon coming toward us. Just the sight of it was startling. I felt the way Robinson Crusoe felt when he saw the footprints in the sand. We had been all alone in this tremendous world, and now there was someone else.

The wagon was drawn by a black team, a shiny, black, archtailed team of horses, and on the wagon seat was a little man with a round face and stocky body and a grin that was a welcome itself. He drew alongside and stopped and shouted, "Hello, strangers! Where you heading?"

Father said we were going out to our homestead to build a house.

"Where you located?" the little man asked.

"Section seventeen," Father said. "North half of seventeen."

"Good!" the little man exclaimed. "I'm just a couple of miles from you. My name's Farley, Jake Farley." He reached in the pocket of his bibbed overalls. "I've got a house built and you can stay there till you get a roof up. I'm going to town a week or so. Here's the key." He tossed it over and Father caught it. "Make yourself at home!" and Mr. Farley relaxed the lines and his black team took off at a fast trot, the empty wagon rattling over the grass.

We drove on, now following Mr. Farley's wagon tracks, the only mark on that whole expanse of grass.

The hills were covered with buffalo grass or buffalo mixed with grama, and the draws, or valleys, were carpeted with bluestem. Here and there were clumps of yucca with their stiff, evergreen, bayonet leaves; and now and then we came to a hollow where sheep had grazed the grass away and cut it out with their sharp hoofs and sagebrush had taken over, sage and greasewood. And here and there were big beds or scattered clumps of cactus, the flat-leafed gray-grizzly ones full of vicious thorns and the greener, less spined prickly pears. But even the yucca and the sagebrush and greasewood and the cactus were lost in the vastness of grass, the highest sagebrush wasn't as high as the hubs on the front wheels of the wagon.

"Good soil," father said. "That grass has been here forever. Even the sagebrush doesn't do too well, because sage likes poor soil. The grass takes over even from the sage, when it gets half a chance."

At last we came to a hill that sloped down to Mr. Farley's house, and we were at the end of the day's journey.

Mr. Farley's house was set on the gentle hillside above a valley of bluestem already ankle-high with new growth. It was a long low building still new-pine yellow and smelling of pitch. Just down the hillside was a pump on a little wooden platform, a green pump so new the paint was still on the handle.

We unlocked the door in one end of the house, the end with two windows. There was a partition across the middle. One end, the end we went in, was the house. It had a cookstove and an iron bed with brown blankets over a blue-striped mattress and a bench built under one window to eat from and a bench beside it to sit on. The other end of the building was the barn, with big doors and no windows and no floor and a manger built against the partition.

We unhitched the horses and put them in the barn. Father took our box of groceries into the house and I went for a pail of water. Father built a fire in the stove with cow chips, dried cow dung, from the pile in the corner behind the stove. He opened a can of beans and fried a pan of bacon, and we sat down at the bench beneath the window and ate our supper.

The sun set. We grained the horses. We walked to the top of the hill west of the house and Father pointed to the third hill beyond and said,"It's over there, son. That's where our homestead is."

We stood there several minutes, looking. Father undoubtedly was thinking of Nebraska, of the job he had given up, the home town he had left, the warnings spoken and unspoken that had accompanied the goodbyes. A man with a job was supposed to stick to it, and a man in business for himself was honored and respected. For a man who left school at the age of thirteen, Father had done well. One of his brothers, I learned long later, had said he was a fool to pack up and leave. But then, he had been called foolish to quit the blacksmith shop and become a printer. He had gone his own way, following his own dream; and now that dream had turned to the land, to land of his own in a new country. He had worked nineteen years for someone else. Even as part owner of the paper back home he had been under a boss, the editor who taught him the printer's trade and who would, as long as they worked together, always be the boss. He wanted to own himself, be his own boss, work out his own destiny. These things must have been heavy in his mind, as well as a sense of responsibility for a wife and a son, who had been uprooted from home, friends and security. He had moved from one job to another the eleven years he had been married, had lived and worked in half a dozen places including Omaha and

Nebraska City before he returned to his home town. But always it had been a move from a good job to a better one, and always there had been a weekly pay envelope. Now he had quit a job to move to a new land, to take his chances there. But it was his choice, his and Mother's.

We watched the flare of the sunset and we looked out over the endless rolling plains. Then we went back down the hill, and even I felt that Nebraska was a long, long way from there. I looked at the horizon to the east, but I couldn't see beyond the plains. In the eastern sky, maybe half as far away as Nebraska, was a long thin cloud all pink and lavender with reflected sunset. I wondered if they could see that cloud in Nebraska.

HAL BORLAND is the author of over two dozen books including *When the Legends Die*, *Hal Borland's Book of Days*, *Twelve Moons of the Year*, *Countryman*, and *The History of Wildlife in America*. For many years, he wrote a weekly outdoor essay for the Sunday *New York Times*. This selection is taken from *High, Wide and Lonesome*, describing Borland's experience in 1910, when as a nine-year-old boy he moved with his family to the eastern Colorado plains. It is a selection as much about discovering life as it is discovering a new place to call home.

William Cotter Murray

from *American Heritage*,
April 1968
"Grass"

As far as the eye could reach, in every direction, there was neither tree, nor shrub, nor house, nor shed visible; so that we were rolling on as it were on the bosom of a new Atlantic, but that the sea was of rich green grass and flowers, instead of the briny and bottomless deep." Thus James Silk Buckingham, a British traveller, described America's Great Plains in 1837. This was the same "Atlantic of grass" that the homesteaders saw, and the longhorns when they spread over the open range up from the South — an ocean of grass to be grazed. There were homesteads to be developed, cattle empires to be expanded, and wheat fields to be plowed deep and combined. The grass grew naturally; it did not need to be cultivated. Who could imagine the broad green ocean drying up?

The Great Plains used to be one of the richest natural grasslands of the world. From the Saskatchewan-Manitoba line it extended south along the ninety-eighth meridian to the Gulf of

Mexico and all the way west to the Rockies, taking in eastern Montana, Wyoming, Colorado, and New Mexico, the western part of the Dakotas, Nebraska, Kansas, and Oklahoma, and the Texas Panhandle — "The Great American Desert," it was designated on the maps of the early 1800's. And it was all public domain. We owned the grass and had a rich heritage, but within a century after Buckingham's visit we had almost destroyed it.

The grass kept the Plains in place, kept them from becoming a real desert. It was as simple as that. In an environment with a maximum annual rainfall of only twenty inches and an evaporation rate as high as sixty per cent, there was a hairline balance between sun, water, rivers, soil, wind, and grass. The grass — putting down its roots four, even six feet into the soil, improving its structure, ventilating it, letting water penetrate it, keeping moisture loss low — held the balance of power and kept the environment from destroying itself. During the summer months the rain fell in thunderstorms, hailstorms even; water rushed in torrents down from the Rockies, carried by the Red River, the Platte, the Missouri. Against that force of water nothing could stop the erosion of the soil, nothing but a good thick carpet of grass to hold it down.

Through the ages, nature had laid down such a carpet — native grasses capable of withstanding the special conditions of the environment. They lay dormant through drought and came back above ground when water came again. Some grasses grew in the warm seasons, others in the cool. They could grow with little moisture, hoarding what they got. Over the centuries they had struggled for survival in the Great Plains, adapted to the environment, and thrived.

The environment is diverse. The Great Plains are not all on one level: from an altitude of 5,500 feet up against the Rockies they flatten out going eastward at ten feet per mile. They embrace sand hills, loessal plains, buttes, "badlands," depressions, and rolling flatlands treeless and without protection from the sun except for the grass. The precipitation is uncertain. Temperatures range from 60 degrees below to 120 degrees above. The Plains were formed when the great Cretaceous seas withdrew along the continent and the Rocky Mountains were uplifted, preventing moisture from the Pacific from penetrating eastward. The area gradually dried up; mountain streams cut valleys and ridges through it and grew into rivers that spilled out onto the Plains. There evaporation was so high, rain so scarce, and the land so flat that the rivers lost their force, deposited their burden of mountain soil in aprons over the land, and dribbled on into shallow streams and mudholes or buffalo wallows, where many a settler's wagon got stuck up to its axles.

The grasses that took root and kept the soil from washing away were of several types. In the Northern Plains (roughly Montana, Wyoming, and the western Dakotas) and in the High Plains (the eastern third of Colorado and New Mexico and the western part of Oklahoma) there were the short grasses: buffalo grass, blue grama, three-awns, curly mesquite. Farther east, the longer mid-grasses took root: little bluestem, needle grass, wheat grasses. In the Low Plains — the region's eastern third, along the twenty-inch rainfall line that runs from the eastern Dakotas southward to western Texas — big bluestem and other tall grasses thrived. The plainsman will recognize minor grasses in the kingdom with colorful names like bottlebrush, red ray, fool hay, pancake, jungle rice, panic grass. The environment created these grasses; they are natives — the original natives, which were there even before the buffalo and the Indian came.

Coronado saw the grasses in 1541 in his abortive search for gold in the Seven Cities of Cibola. He and his army almost got lost among them; as soon as they passed, the grasses straightened. Men who wandered away from the army train got lost. Finally Coronado gave up on the Plains; there was no gold there, and it was too cold. The grass was good for the expedition's cows, but there was no civilization there to conquer.

The Indians inhabited the Plains before Coronado came and remained after he passed. Thirty-one tribes held sway there, each somehow able to read the landscape so that they recognized one another's territories. We can order the succession of invaders of the Great Plains like this: first, the soil came from the Rockies, then the grasses grew, then the buffalo came down from the north for the grasses, then the Indians followed the buffalo. The tribes themselves — Blackfoot, Crow, Cheyenne, Pawnee, Arapaho, Apache, Comanche — had an ideal relationship with their environment: the Indian lived off the buffalo; the buffalo lived off the grass. Colonel Richard Irving Dodge reported seeing a herd of buffalo numbering over 500,000. The grass could sustain herds that big without danger of being overgrazed, for by instinct the buffalo moved with the seasonal growth of the grass.

Sometimes, to make their hunting easier, the Indians burned the grass, but the homesteaders, who began to come in 1862, were the first to break the sod. They had to, first to make their sod houses and then to cultivate their 150 acres. Pioneers came in great numbers from the East, from Europe, even from Australia, encouraged by Congress and the railroads. A small registration fee and a five-year occupancy were all Congress required before giving away the land. And the homesteaders plowed away.

The first sight of the tall grasses waving over an expanse of rolling land often inspired the newcomers with a kind of "seasickness," or fear, or exhilaration, or loneliness. In 1837, Buckingham had noted: "I never felt so strongly the sense of loneliness as here."

For the homesteaders it was the same. Beret Hansa, in O. E. Rölvaag's *Giants in the Earth,* exclaimed: "Why there isn't even a thing that one can *hide behind!*" From the door of her sod house the plainswoman looked out on grass whispering in the wind, scorched by the sun, and if she dared go out herself she would get lost. Or the wind would turn her face to leather, as it was turning her man to leather as he plowed up the land around the sod house. The walls of that house were held together by the roots of the grass, and the mud floor was strewn with grass. Sometimes, twisted into hanks and tossed into the stove, the grass even heated the house. The homesteader's wife worried about water; soon the windmill would bring her water from deep below the topsoil. But what would bring water to the soil?

This was in the eighteen sixties. In 1873, the settlers were hit with the first bad drought. In 1874, the locusts came, Rocky Mountain grasshoppers which ate the leaves and stems of the grasses — and not only every green thing but even the clothes off the line. The settlers panicked; some left, convinced that it would take a special kind of human being to stick it out here in an environment they themselves knew nothing about.

Meanwhile, in southwest Texas, longhorn cattle, originally raised on the old Spanish missions, now roamed wild. The North, hungry after the Civil War, was screaming for beef. Northward cattle drives had begun as early as the mid-1830's, but those herds were small compared with these that were now beginning. As the buffalo was killed off (and the Indian with him, practically), the longhorns, the cowboys, and the cattle ranchers took over as much open range in the Plains as they could manage. But unlike the buffalo, the longhorns did not move with the seasonal growth of the grasses. They were either fenced in by the ranchers near water, or fenced out by homesteaders protecting their farms. Overcrowding of the range began. Ranchers, finding the grass cheap fodder, let their longhorns graze all year round, and fought for water rights with the homesteaders — who now, under the Desert Land Act of 1877, could have an entire section, 640 acres, provided only that they would irrigate it. (The irrigation provision, alas, was often met by throwing a bucket of water on the grass.)

By the mid-1880's, cattle ranches had spread north into the short-grass country, into Colorado, Wyoming, and Montana. In his pioneering survey of the Plains presented to Congress in 1878, John Wesley Powell had pointed out that this vast area of public domain was not being properly used. In an arid and sub-humid climate most of the soil does not contain enough moisture to permit farming by the usual methods. Most of the region, Powell felt, was not suitable for farming at all; grazing was its best use. But not the kind that was then going on: letting the cattle graze all through spring, summer, autumn, and winter, never giving the grass a chance to renew itself. Powell recommended that pasture lands be parcelled out in lots of 2,560 acres and held in common, with all the participating ranchers responsible for the right use of them.

But western politicians in Congress, land speculators, and cattlemen, all of them in a hurry to profit from the bounty of the region, could not halt for planning. Cattle grazing was causing more injury to the land than farming, Powell said. And then there were the sheep. Both the farmer and the rancher turned on the sheepman; they said his animals' thin muzzles and sharp teeth cropped the grass to the ground, while their spiky hoofs pockmarked the soil.

All — homesteader, rancher, sheep farmer — were busy destroying the grass.

Then, in the eighteen nineties, the sod was really stripped away as huge wheat farms were established in the Red River valley in Minnesota and North Dakota — farms sometimes as large as 65,000 acres.

Drought struck in the 1890's, and again in 1900, in 1910, and in 1917. But the World War I years were good for the wheat farmer, and he survived. By 1924, in spite of the dry spells, Plains farmers were growing seventeen million more acres of wheat then they had grown in 1909. Arid, short-grass regions of Oklahoma, Texas, New Mexico, Wyoming and Montana, where plow should never have furrowed a sod, were being farmed.

The day of reckoning had to come.

The story of the Dust Bowl is well known. There had been dust storms in the Plains before, but never anything like those that began to darken the sky in the early nineteen thirties. Black clouds of prairie soil were blown as far eastward as Washington, D. C. And farther: the dust was visible two hundred miles at sea.

The grass was gone, and there was nothing to prevent the dust from blowing. Farmers and cowboys, trying to work in dust, got only failed crops, thin and dying cattle, and mounting debts. Nearly four and a half million people lived in the Plains in the early nineteen thirties before the drought; within five years, forty thousand families moved out, leaving vast areas of the land not only denuded but uninhabited.

Finally, where individuals had failed, Washington took a hand. With the Bankhead-Jones Act of 1937, the federal government reacquired some of the lands that had been vacated, and made loans to farmers who stayed on, to begin soil conservation measures.

Biologists like F. W. Albertson and ecologists like J. E. Weaver now began to help in the study of what had been ignored, for the most part, all along: the grasses themselves. Many of the recommendations in the Great Plains report of 1936 were aimed at one end: restoring the grasses. But that was a big job: nature had taken ages to put them there. Scientists — and the Department of Agriculture, with its Soil Conservation Service and Forest Service — set to work. First, surveys were made. Next, the government acquired large areas of range and granted use of them, under rules of controlled grazing, to permittees. Water resources were developed through a series of dams and irrigation projects. Finally, Washington sought the co-operation of local governments and private owners in projects to control erosion and promote proper grazing.

The program put into motion by the government — and by the private agencies and individual landowners whose co-operation it enlisted — had three objectives: converting essentially nonarable cropland back to range or natural grassland; re-establishing the native grasses on depleted and killed-out range areas or on worked-out farm land that had simply been allowed to go back to whatever vegetation developed; and encouraging the people of the region to adopt improved methods of land management.

For the conversion and reestablishment processes the first requirement, of course, was a supply of seeds. In special Plant Materials Centers set up by the Soil Conservation Service throughout the Great Plains, various strains of native grasses — such as the gramas, bluestems, switchgrass, and indiangrass — were produced. The process was far from simple: strains of little bluestem which thrived in Texas, for example, might not survive in the Dakotas. The Agriculture Department's Agricultural Research Service, notably the center under the direction of Dr. L. C. Newell at the University of Nebraska, made a major contribution in discovering which grasses would grow best in various Plains areas. Then, special machines were developed to plant the seed.

Finally, farmers were encouraged to stop plowing land that was not meant to be plowed, and to put it to its proper use: grazing. The Soil Conservation Service also suggested to them — and to ranchers as well — how the land ought to be grazed: rotationally, with grazing deferred on some grasses until early summer so that they could get a good spring start. Typically, a conservation plan for an entire farm or ranch would be developed, with the government sharing the costs of reestablishing the grasses.

The recovery of the Great Plains and the bringing back of the grass were not accomplished by human measures alone. Nature herself helped out. Beginning in 1941 with the coming of wet years again, the land itself began to go through its almost miraculous, age-old cycle. Weaver and Albertson observed and documented this recovery of the native grasses: first the primeval weeds came back — goosefoot, tumbleweed, and common sunflower; then a second weed stage began — little barley, peppergrass, and stickseeds; thereafter, early native grasses began to return — sand dropseed, western wheat grass, false buffalo grass; finally, the mature native grasses — the gramas, buffalo grass, three-awns — were seen again.

Today, driving through the Great Plains region, the traveller will often pass signs bearing the initials "U.S.," with a bunch of grass between the "U." and the "S." This sign indicates he is travelling through National Grasslands. On June 20, 1960, nearly four million acres of federal lands were so designated. They are managed by the Forest Service and are set up as outdoor recreational areas, range land, wildlife habitats, and fishing preserves. These lands are public domain. Artificial lakes have been created for water sports and for conservation purposes; thirty campsites now dot the Plains and more are being prepared; hunters flock to the Dakotas each year for the ringneck pheasant, to Wyoming and Montana for geese, duck, and Barbary sheep. There are over three million acres of unposted land to which we have free access, and it is all covered with grass. The names of the new grasslands are old and familiar: the Comanche in Colorado, the Cimarron in southwest Kansas, the Pawnee in northeastern Colorado, the Oglala in Nebraska, the Kiowa in New Mexico.

But the National Grasslands are only the most visible results of what will go down in history as one of the major conservation efforts of modern times. Thanks to the cropland-conversion, range-reseeding, and land-management programs, the grasslands of the ten Great Plains states are in better condition today than they have been for seventy-five years. The environment has come full cycle: once more a rich carpet of grass holds the Plains in place, letting the land fulfill itself — and the men who live on it and draw their sustenance from it.

WILLIAM COTTER MURRAY was born in Ireland in 1929 and became a naturalized U.S. citizen in 1952. He has taught English and written novels. This work is from a 1968 *American Heritage*. It is a work about the plains, but it is also a work about exploring in order to understand all of the facets contained within the rolling hills that have been seen as alternately beautiful, dangerous, and desolate.

William W. Warner

Beautiful Swimmers
"The Bay"

t is so known through the length and breadth of its watershed. The Bay. There is no possible confusion with any other body of water, no need for more precise description. It is, after all, the continent's largest estuary. Its waters are rich, the main supply of oysters, crabs, clams and other seafoods for much of the Atlantic seaboard. Its shorelines cradled our first settlements. It is the Chesapeake.

North to south, from the choppy wavelets of the Susquehanna Flats to the rolling surges of the Virginia Capes, the Bay measures almost exactly two hundred miles. Alone among its vital statistics, its breadth is not impressive. The extremes are four miles near Annapolis and about thirty miles near the mouth of the Potomac River. In all else the Bay is champion. Its shoreline is prodigious. Put together the great rivers on its western shore: the York, the James the Susquehanna and the Potomac. Add the labyrinthine marshlands of the Eastern Shore, always capitalized, since it is a land unto itself. The combined shorelines string out to about 4,000 miles, or more than enough to cross the country at its widest. Some say the figure doubles if all tributaries are followed beyond the reach of the tide. The Bay's entire watershed extends north through Pennsylvania to the Finger Lakes and Mohawk Valley country of New York, by virtue of the Susquehanna, the mother river that created the Bay in Pleistocene time. To the west it traces far back into the furrowed heartland of Appalachia, but one mountain ridge short of the Ohio-Mississippi drainage, by agency of the Potomac. To the east the flatland rivers of the Eastern Shore rise from gum and oak thickets almost within hearing distance of the pounding surf of the Atlantic barrier islands. To the south, Bay waters seep through wooded swamps to the North Carolina sounds, where palmettos, alligators and great stands of bald cypress first appear.

To qualify as an estuary, a body of water must be well enclosed, provide easy entry and exit for open sea water and enjoy a vigorous infusion of fresh water from one or more rivers. These are minimum requirements. The fiords of Norway are estuaries, but they are uniformly rocky, deep and thus biologically impoverished, which is why Norwegian fishermen spend most of their time on offshore banks. A good estuary with high biological productivity requires other things. Shallow water, for one, which the sun can penetrate to nourish both plankton and rooted aquatic plants. Extensive marshland is another. An estuary without it lacks the lace-work of tidal creeks and shallow coves which traps nutrients and protects and feeds the larvae and juveniles of a host of fish and invertebrates.

Also, to be summa cum laude in estuarine productivity, there must be circulation. A good mix, one is tempted to say, is almost everything. Not just in one direction. There should be two-layered or horizontal circulation in which heavier salt water from the ocean slides under the lighter and fresher surface water from rivers. Inexorably, that is, with a new flow upstream on the bottom and downstream on the top which surmounts the temporary effects of wind and tide. Ideally, there should also be some vertical mixing, which is not found in every estuary, since it requires significant contrasts in depths and water temperatures.

By all tests the Chesapeake does well. Its very configuration, its long north-south axis, encourages and concentrates horizontal or two-layered circulation. The result is a splendid salinity gradation or, to be more exact, twenty-five parts salt per thousand of water down near the Virginia capes, which is almost ocean, to zero or fresh water at the northern or upper end of the Bay. Fresh water infusion is constant and indeed vigorous. Often, in fact, it is too much of a good thing, as when the rivers of the western shore rise in spring floods. Mightiest of these is the Susquehanna, the longest river of the eastern seaboard. Next in order along the Bay's western shore come the Potomac, James, Rappahannock, York and Patuxent. We must note these next-in-rank carefully, because each is a considerable estuary in its own right which replicates the salinity gradients of the main Bay. The York, although at the smaller end of the scale, is a good example. Water lapping the beaches below Yorktown's historic heights is unmistakably salt, or seventeen to twenty parts per thousand. Only thirty miles upstream it is completely fresh.

Vertical mixture takes place thanks mainly to a deep channel running almost the total length of the Bay. Geomorphologically speaking, it is the fossilized bed of the ancient Susquehanna. It lies at the bottom of the Bay at depths of eighty to one hundred and twenty feet, still well defined after 15,000 years of silting and sedimentation. In its first life it was the course of an upstart river searching and scouring its way to the sea, nourished by Pleistocene glaciers not far to the north. As glaciers melted in the post-Pleistocene, rising ocean waters drowned the river valley to create the Bay much as we know it now. Today ship captains running to Baltimore know the old river well; it is the route of seagoing commerce. Trouble is in store for those who don't or who ignore the pilot's warnings. Its shoulders are sharp, and sure stranding attends any deviation from course.

To the Bay's host of marine organisms the fossil river is equally important. In late summer and early fall fresh seawater — fresh in the sense of oxygen content — creeps in along its bottom and branches up the tributaries with unusual strength, since rivers are low and their obstructting flow weak. Above it lies tired or biologically exhausted water. All summer long the surface waters have supported immense communities of plankton, not to mention sometimes harmful algae, greedily consuming oxygen. Now these waters are oxygen-starved. But it is autumn and they are cooling more rapidly than the deep water below. Being heavier, they sink. Conversely, the intruding seawater below carrying fresh oxygen slowly begins to rise. The mix is thus two-way. In the process the microscopic plant and animal plankton, heavily concentrated near the surface in summer, are swirled up and down and thus distributed more uniformly. Some of the Bay's most prominent year-round residents — the blue crab, the striped bass, the white perch — take their cue and make rapidly for the deeps. There they can feed amid the deeper groves of plankton and enjoy warmer water as autumn slowly turns to winter. (Theoretically, oysters and clams would do well to follow suit, but locomotion, alas, is not within their powers.) Crabs especially appreciate the deep water in autumn, since it prolongs the time left to them before cold water will force virtual hibernation in the post-Pleistocene ooze. The great channel is therefore a winter haven, a place for rest and limited feeding free of the temperature extremes of surface waters.

In spring vertical mixing again takes place through reversal of the autumn factors. Reoxygenation starts at the surface. In response the fish ascend and the crabs' eventual goal is the shoal areas where eelgrass abounds and where the new spring water courses over the shallows with every tide. They go there to hide and to feed and to feel the rays of the warming sun. And think about other things associated with spring.

"Feller hasn't run ashore, he don't much know this Bay," a waterman once said to me after he pulled my ketch off a tenacious sandbar. It was the nicest thing anyone could possibly say under such embarrassing circumstances and it made me feel much better. What he meant, of course, is that the Chesapeake does not lack for the shallow water that is another prime estaurine requirement. The average depth of the Chesapeake, mother river and tributary channels included, is twenty-one feet. For most of the Bay, fifteen feet or less would be a better figure.

Shallower still are vast areas along the Eastern Shore, the waters surrounding the great marsh islands of Tangier Sound, for example, which Captain John Smith called the Isles of Limbo, where vigorous sounding will fail to uncover anything deeper than five feet. Captain Smith was glad when he left, and today's less venturesome sailors shun the marshy islands like the plague. Yet these very shoal waters have their place, if not for yachtsmen. They provide an optimum habitat for such rooted aquatic plants as wild celery and widgeongrass, the choice of waterfowl, or eelgrass and sea lettuce, which although acceptable to ducks and geese, are only preferred by small fish, crabs and young seed oysters. Almost invariably the shoals supporting these water plants are bordered by marsh. The marshlands in turn support a much greater growth of plants, plants which want to have their roots covered by water some of the time, but cannot tolerate it all of the time. Dominating these, heavily outweighing all other species in sheer tonnage and outdistancing them in distribution, are the spiky *Spartinas* or cordgrasses. *Spartina patens*, that is, which ripples in windrows or lies in natural cowlicks on firmer ground, and *Spartina alterniflora*, taller and denser, which grows on the quaking mudbanks and along creek borders first invaded by tidewater.

The interaction between the two plant communities, one just below the water and the other barely above, is admirable. The marsh grasses are the storehouse or granary. The agents that mill them and their associated plant and animal life, principally algae and insects, are death and decay. We cannot readily see the crop so produced, since it ultimately takes the form of pinhead particles of detritus and bacteria-manufactured nutrients dissolved in the water, but it beggars anything that happens on dry land. Most of the Chesapeake's marshlands produce an annual average yield of five tons of vegetation per acre. Those in the southern reaches, along the lower Eastern Shore, go as high as ten. Down every tidal gut and through every big "thorofare" and little "swash" or "drain," as the breaks in the marsh islands are called, there comes an enormous and nourishing flow of silage made from this decomposing *Spartina* crop. Waiting to receive the flow, well protected by wavy forests of eelgrass, are many forms of life. First recipients are plankton and the larvae and the young of larger forms, who need it most. In the latter category are enormous infant populations of fish, clams, oysters, jellyfish and worms. Predominant among adult forms are the blue crabs, who have a fine time of it preying on the small fry, including, sometimes, some of their own.

The animals of the aquatic plant communities give something back to the marsh in return, although not as much as they receive.

Since they consume great quantities of marsh-produced nutrients, they also therefore release considerable amounts of nitrogen and phosphorous after their rapid browse-feeding and digestion. The waters so fertilized return to the marshes twice every twenty-four hours, as sure as the moon and sun make tides. The same waters, of course, also bring salt, which is what permits the cordgrasses to reign as uncontested monarchs of the marshland. Alone in the plant kingdom, the *Spartinas* thrive on it. Or, more accurately, despite it. Thus interaction.

Most of the Chesapeake's *Spartina* marsh is concentrated on the lower Eastern Shore in a broad belt extending south from Maryland's Little Choptank River. "South of the Little Choptank," the watermen tell you, "the fast land disappears." It is their way of saying that only isolated islands or small clumps of firm ground dot the vast marsh landscape of these parts. The larger islands are called hammocks; often they support whole fishing villages or a considerable growth of pine and hardwoods. The smaller ones, with barely enough soil to nourish a single bush or tree, are dismissed as "tumps." Seen from the air, the region appears very much like an Everglades of the north. It is the largest undisturbed marshland in the mid-Atlantic states, undisturbed because it is far from ocean beaches and thus largely overlooked by developers. May it remain so.

WILLIAM WARNER (born 1920) worked for the U.S. Information Agency and later as Latin American Coordinator for the Peace Corps. He was appointed Director of the Smithsonian Institute for International Activities. This selection is taken from *Beautiful Swimmers,* an award-winning book. It expresses some of the implausible, mystifying occurrences we see but rarely comprehend in an estuary.

Edwin Way Teale

North with the Spring
"May at Monticello"

ur speedometer touched 11,000 miles on that eighty-sixth day of our trip. We had been running west through Virginia where May had turned locust trees into creamy clouds of white and fire-pink blazes along em bankments and lions and ti-gers bared their teeth on bill-boards that marked the trail of the earliest circus of spring. Now, in midmorning, we were climbing the wooded mountain road that led to Monticello.

Automobiles with license plates from more than twenty states had already mounted the road ahead of us that morning. They had brought people of var-ied interests and diverse out-looks to do homage to the many-sided genius of Thomas Jeffer-son. Most were attracted by the patriot, the statesman, the hu-manitarian. Some were interest-ed by the architect, the inventor, and we — in addition to all these — by the naturalist. An often-overlooked facet in the life of this extraordinary man is his not inconsiderable contribution as a pioneer naturalist in America.

Thomas Jefferson published the first accurate and extensive list of birds in this country. He kept careful meteorological records for decades. He set down detailed facts about the trees of Virginia. He classified its animals. He recorded the comparative weights of red, gray, and black squirrels. He was the first American to make a scientific report on the fossils of the New World.

In 1787, when Jefferson published his celebrated *Notes on Virginia*, he listed all the birds known in the area. The total was fewer than 130 species. Today, according to Dr. J. J. Murray, of Lexington — editor of *The Raven*, official organ of The Virginia Society of Ornithology — the state list includes 400 species and subspecies — 344 of the former and 56 of the latter. In all the United States east of the Rockies the number of full species is well under 450. So Virginia's 344 indicates the richness of bird life in that state. Driving across it, we noted down the different kinds of birds we saw as we rode along. By the time we came to Monticello our list had reached 85.

And at Monticello, birds were all around us — wood thrushes, towhees, brown thrashers, ovenbirds, yellowthroats, rubycrowned kinglets, catbirds. We saw — to use the terminology of the Jefferson list — the lettuce bird or the goldfinch; the Virginia nightingale or the cardinal; the fieldfare of Carolina or the robin. We did not see, and no one will ever see again, two of the species on the list. Both of them — the passenger pigeon and the Carolina paroquet — have in the intervening years become extinct. But we saw two other birds not on the list and unknown in America when it was made. These were the comparatively recent introductions, the English sparrow and the starling. Jefferson, however, was one of the few Americans of his day who would have recognized them. In all probability he had seen them abroad while representing his country in Europe.

On that May morning one hundred twenty springs had passed since Jefferson died on his mountaintop overlooking the valley where he was born. One hundred sixty years had gone by since he published his *Notes on Virginia.* Yet the natural history of Monticello remained virtually unchanged. Bluebirds sang on the fence posts. Phoebes flitted in and out of the open doors of the old stables. A robin had built its nest at the top of one of the white columns of the west portico. And brown thrashers ran across the grass beneath an ancient linden tree that once provided shade for the third President of the United States.

Off to the east, beyond the mountainside where spring-clad trees stretched in a tumbling sea down the slope toward the Piedmont, a trio of turkey buzzards swung slowly, curving on the wind, hanging on the updrafts, drifting far out over the valley above tiny fields snipped from the plush of wooded hillsides, then sliding back to go riding low above Monticello. And all that morning the brilliant blue sky was filled with the metallic crackling of the chimney swifts.

Beside Jefferson's grave, we watched a chipping sparrow tilting its rusty cap this way and that as it fed on dandelion seeds. Fluttering into the air, it would alight on a bending stem and ride it to the ground. Oc - casionaly, as it plucked the seeds, it would lift its head for a quick sur- vey, with dandelion fluff projecting like a scraggly white mustache on either side of its bill. Before swallowing each seed, it clipped off the par- achute, which floated to the ground. At the end, beneath the denuded stem the accumulated fluff looked like a little windrow of foam cling- ing to the grass. How many thousand dandelion seeds never take root because of the feeding of a single sparrow!

The birds of Monticello provide one of the outstanding memories of a naturalist's visit. The trees provide another. Here, rooted where Thomas Jefferson had planted them in the eighteenth century, stood ancient tulips, lindens, copper beeches, sugar maples, European larches. Here were noble trees, patriarchs that brought to mind Sir Thomas Browne's observation of long ago: "Generations pass while some trees stand and old families last not three oaks."

In beginning one of his *Socratic Dialogues*, Plato wrote:

"Scene: Under a plane tree . . ."

Under a tree . . . That phrase recurs frequently in the history of human thought. Thinkers as diverse and as far removed as Guatama beneath his Bo tree in the Far East and Ralph Waldo Emerson under a New England pine have been associated with trees. "He spake of trees, from the cedar tree that is in Lebanon even unto the hyssop that springeth out of the wall." So the Book of Kings in the Bible describes King Solomon, whose wisdom was proverbial in his time.

Around us, on this May morning, rose trees that had been associ- ated with the thoughts of Jefferson. He had walked beneath their boughs, rested in their shade, seen them against blue sky and red sunset, watched them in wind and rain. They were part of his life when the author of the Declaration of Independence was evolving and strengthening his own eloquent philosophy of justice and human rights.

Now they were clothed in a new installment of green. For the leaves, life was new. For the trees, the events of spring represented merely an old, old sequence. One hundred twenty, one hundred fifty times, or more, a fresh mantle of leaves had taken the place of those which had fallen in autumn. Their green varied from tree to tree, almost from branch to branch. And beyond, along the mountainside, the shadings of spring were manifold. At no other time of year, except in autumn, is there greater variety of color in a woodland than in spring. A thousand and one subtle shadings of green, lost in summer, characterize the new foliage. Autumn colors are flaunting; they catch the eye. Spring tintings are delicate and often overlooked.

Every hour, under that brilliant morning sun, each square yard of outstretched leaves was manufacturing something like one fiftieth of an ounce of sugar. The broad ribbon leaves of an acre of growing corn will produce, in a single summer day, as much as two hundred pounds of sugar which is converted into the material of the plant. Leading to all the leaf factories of the trees around us was the running transportation system of the sap. Spring had increased its volume, had stimulated its flow. Coursing through the channels of trunk and branch and twig, it moved often under surprising pressures. In one laboratory experiment, scientists found that even the lowly tomato plant can produce pressures ranging up to about one hundred pounds to the square inch — sufficient to carry sap to the topmost twig of a California sequoia. Each tree at Monticello, beech, linden, maple, tulip, was being nourished by its own particular kind of sap. As in human blood groups, the fluid within tree trunks is specialized. Oak sap, for example, will not nourish a birch tree nor maple sap a beech.

From the tops of all the trees that Jefferson had planted, lightning rods project upward. This wise precaution protects them from thunderbolts in their exposed position on the mountaintop. In other ways, good sense has prevailed in keeping the house and grounds unchanged. The gardens have been laid out from sketches Jefferson made. The same fine and simple flowers he planted in the different beds — columbine, Virginia bluebells, phlox drummondi, tulips, and stock — grow there still. On this spring day — hundreds of butterfly generations after Jefferson's desire, expressed in the words: "All my wishes end where I hope my days will end, at Monticello," had come true — tiger swallowtails drifted among the garden flowers. And all along the edge of the restored fish pool, honeybees were alighting to drink the brick-red water.

We spent a long time within that noble house whose designing and building might be called Jefferson's lifelong avocation. He began it in his twenties; he was in his sixties when it was done. Everywhere we delighted in evidences of his brilliantly original mind. In turn, we became interested in his revolving study table, his "Petite Format" library, his clock that marked the days as well as the hours, his octagonal filing table with its pie-piece drawers. We had just emerged and were standing near the spot where Jefferson used to set up his telescope to watch the progress being made in building the University of Virginia, at Charlottesville in the valley below, when all the small birds feeding in the open dashed pell-mell into the bushes.

A swift gray shape skimmed past us. It was a Cooper's hawk scud - ding low among the trees. As it went by, from the bushes around us there arose a confused babel of bird voices. Instead of remaining silent in the presence of the hawk, all the hidden birds joined in a twittering crescendo. We were in the midst of that curious phenomenon sometimes referred to as the "confusion chorus."

The psychology of the bird of prey directs it toward an individual which it pursues. By flocking together in the air, small birds are able to divide the attention of the hawk, to distract it by many shapes in motion. As long as they keep together, and the hawk is unable to cut one individual from the flying mass, all escape. The confusion chorus appears to be a kind of flocking by sound. The calls, coming from all sides at the same time, apparently disconcert the bird of prey. At any rate, the Cooper's hawk swept on without pausing, reached the edge of the mountainside, and slid down out of sight. The twittering chorus ceased. The little birds, mostly chipping sparrows and English sparrows, flitted out of the bushes into the open. Their fright was over. The appearance of danger had set off a sequence of instinctive acts. Now that the danger was past there remained no visible remnant of haunting fear. Monticello in May was once more a place of sunshine and of peace.

In the Forest of Fountainebleau, which Jefferson often visited while American minister to the court of France, the green woodpecker is known by the apt name of the "awakener of the woods." An American bird deserving the same title is the familiar flicker, the "yucker" of Jefferson's bird list. Directly above our heads, as we were starting down the road on leaving, one of these woodpeckers burst into its strident, rolling cry. It filled all the space between the trees and was flung far out over the valley. Then, with that disconcerting suddenness that ends a flicker's call, the sound ceased. This was the last bird voice we heard at Monticello.

A hundred miles by road to the south and west, down the Blue Ridge Mountains, we came to Virginia's famed Natural Bridge, once owned by Thomas Jefferson. George Washington first surveyed it in 1750. Jefferson first called the attention of the world to it in his *Notes on Virginia*. In 1774, just two years before the American Revolution, he acquired it from King George III, of England.

The sum he paid, ironically, was almost exactly the amount we were charged for admission. Commercial interests have fenced in this natural wonder — which ages of running water and not commercial interest produced — and have turned the spot — intimately associated with great men of the nation's founding — into a moneymaking enterprise. Like Niagara Falls, the Grand Canyon, and the geysers of the Yellowstone, all such scenic marvels of the land are part of the country's heritage. The natural wonders of the nation should belong to the nation. They should be part of the park system, open for the enjoyment of all and not closed for the enrichment of a few.

Depressed by this commercialization of natural beauty, we wandered along the paths, past the oldest and largest arborvitae tree in the world — a 1,600-year-old patriarch with a trunk 56 inches in diameter — and under the great stone arch, higher than Niagara Falls, where rough-winged swallows shuttled back and forth and Louisiana water thrushes ran among the rocks, hunting for food in the shallow stream. Nellie compared the short call-note of the water thrush to the striking together of two pebbles and we fell to listing in our minds the birds we knew whose voices suggested sounds in their surroundings — from the liquid, gurgling notes of the redwing in the swamp to the call like tinkling icicles made by the tree sparrow that comes down from the Far North in winter. Thus beguiled, by and by we began to feel better.

That evening, outside a little Virginia town, the day ended with a pleasant adventure. Dusk was far advanced when a small boy came trudging down the dusty road outside our cabin. Bird voices seemed to accompany him, surrounding him and moving with him as he advanced. Whistling to himself, he was imitating robins, cardinals, orioles, bob whites, meadowlarks. Like Thomas Jefferson, this country boy was more alert, more observant, more richly alive than most of those around him. We envied him this springtime of his interest in wild singers. "The birds of the naturalist," John Burroughs had written half a century before, "can never interest us like the thrush the farmboy heard singing in the cedars at twilight as he drove the cows to pasture or like that swallow that flew gleefully in the air above him as he picked stones from the early May meadows."

We never saw the passer-by except as a small dark shape moving through the dusk. But we have often remembered that whistling boy. I feel asleep wondering about him — who he was, what he was like, what adventures life had in store for him — and wishing him well.

"The Longest Day"

During all the days of our travels — in the Everglades, along the delta marshes, on a barrier island, in the Great Smokies, among the pine barrens and the Lilliput forests of Cape Cod and the green hills of the border — we had wondered vaguely about this final twenty-four hours of spring. What would the day be like? Where would we be? What would we be doing? In what surroundings, bright or gloomy, would we come to the end of travels with a season?

Now we knew the answers. This was the final day, the summit of the spring.

We awoke before four o'clock. Already a clear sky was brightening above the birchtops outside our cabin window in Crawford Notch. By four, robins were singing and the wooded steeps above us echoed with the calling of an ovenbird. Then came the pure sweet strain of the whitethroat, most moving of all the voices of this north-country choir.

Long before five even the bottom of the deep ravine, where dusk comes swiftly and dawn is retarded, was filled with daylight. With this sunrise the tide of light reached its annual flood to begin the long slow rollback to the low ebb of December.

During that day — between the earliest sunrise and the latest sunset of the spring — we roamed amid the beauty and grandeur of the mountains. They formed a fitting climax for our travels with the spring. Where else except in America would that journey have carried us through such variedly impressive scenery, such altering forms of plant and animal life, such diverse events of natural history interest?

EDWIN WAY TEALE was born in Illinois in 1899. A graduate of Earlham College, he received his masters degree from Columbia University. He is the author of numerous books and articles and received the Pulitzer Prize in 1966 for his series of books about the seasons in America: *North with the Spring, Journey into Summer, Autumn Across America,* and *Wandering Through Winter.*

William Least Heat Moon

Blue Highways
"South by Southwest"

Somewhere out there was the Colorado River perfectly hidden in the openness. The river wasn't more than a mile away, but I couldn't make out the slightest indication of it in the desert stretching level and unbroken for twenty or thirty miles west, although I was only fifty miles above where it enters Grand Canyon. This side of the Colorado gorge was once an important Hopi trail south, and, some say, the route Hopi guides took when they first led white men to the canyon. While the arid path followed the river cleft, water was an inaccessible four hundred feet down. Typically, the flexible Hopi solved the desert: women buried gourds of water at strategic points on the outward journey for use on the return.

The highway made an unexpected jog toward Navajo Bridge, a melding of silvery girders and rock cliffs. Suddenly, there it was, far below in the deep and scary canyon of sides so sheer they might have been cut with a stone saw, the naturally silted water turned an unnatural green (*colorado* means "reddish") by the big settling basin a few miles upriver called Glen Canyon Dam. Navajo Bridge, built in 1929 when paved roads began opening the area, is the only crossing over the Colorado between Glen Canyon and Hoover Dam several hundred river miles downstream.

West of the gorge lay verdant rangeland, much of it given to a buffalo herd maintained by the Arizona Game Commission; the great beasts lifted their heads to watch me pass, their dark, wet eyes catching the late sun. To the north rose the thousand-foot butt end of the Vermillion Cliffs; the cliffs weren't truly vermillion, but contrasting with the green valley in the orange afternoon light, they seemed so.

In 1776, a few months after white-stockinged men in Philadelphia had declared independence, a Spanish expedition led by missionaries returning Francisco Silvestre Velez de Escalante and Francisco Atanasio Dominguez, from an unsuccessful search for a good northern route to the California missions, wandered dispiritedly along the Vermillion Cliffs as they tried to find in the maze of the Colorado a point to cross the river chasm. They looked for ten days and were forced to eat boiled cactus and two of their horses before finding a place to ford; even then, they had to chop out steps to get down and back up the four-hundred-foot perpendicular walls. My crossing, accomplished sitting down, took twenty seconds. What I saw as a remarkable sight, the Spaniards saw as a terror that nearly did them in.

Escalante's struggles gave perspective to the easy passage I'd enjoyed across six thousand miles of America. Other than weather, some bad road, and a few zealous police, my difficulties had been only those of mind. In light of what was about to happen, my guilt over easy transit proved ironic.

I went up an enormous geologic upheaval called the Kaibab Plateau; with startling swiftness, the small desert bushes changed to immense conifers as the Kaibab forest deepened: ponderosa, fir, spruce. At six thousand feet, the temperature was sixty: a drop of thirty degrees in ten miles. On the north edge of the forest, the highway made a long gliding descent off the plateau into Utah. Here lay Kane and Garfield counties, a place of multicolored rock and baroque stone columns and, under it all, the largest unexploited coalfield in the country. A land certain one day to be fought over.

At dusk I considered going into the Coral Sand Dunes for the night, but I'd had enough warmth and desert for a while, so I pushed north toward Cedar Breaks in the severe and beautiful Markagunt Plateau. The cool would refresh me. Sporadic splats of rain, not enough to pay attention to, hit the windshield. I turned onto Utah 14, the cross-mountain road to Cedar City. In the dim light of a mountainous sky, I could just made out a large sign:

ELEVATION 10,000 FEET
ROAD MAY BE IMPASSABLE
DURING WINTER MONTHS.

So? It was nearly May. The rain popped, then stopped, popped and stopped. The incline became steeper and light rain fell steadily, rolling red desert dust off the roof; I hadn't hit showers since east Texas. It was good. The pleasant cool turned to cold, and I switched on the heater. The headlights glared off snowbanks edging closer to the highway as it climbed, and the rain became sleet. That's when I began thinking I might have made a little miscalculation. I looked for a place to turn around, but there was only narrow, twisted road. The sleet got heavier, and the headlights were cutting only thirty feet into it. Maybe I could drive above and out of the storm. At eight thousand feet, the wind came up — a rough, nasty wind that bullied me about the slick road. Lear, daring the storm to "strike flat the thick rotundity of the world," cries, "Blow winds, and crack your cheeks! Rage! Blow!" And that's just what they did.

A loud, sulphurous blast of thunder rattled the little truck, then another and one more. Never had I seen lightning or heard thunder in a snowstorm. Although there were no signs, the map showed a campground near the summit. It would be suicide to stop, and maybe the same to go on. The wind pushed on Ghost Dancing so, I was afraid of getting blown over the invisible edge. Had not the falling snow taken away my vision, I might have needed a blindfold like the ones medieval travelllers wore to blunt their terror crossing the Alps. A rule of the blue road: Be careful going in search of adventure — it's ridiculously easy to find.

Then I was on the top, ten thousand feet up. UP. The wind was horrendous. Utah 14 now cut through snowbanks higher than the truck. At the junction with route 143, a sign pointed north toward Cedar Breaks campground. I relaxed. I was going to live. I puffed up at having beaten the mountain.

Two hundred yards up 143, I couldn't believe what I saw. I got out and walked to it as the raving wind whipped my pantlegs and pulled my hair on end. I couldn't believe it. There it was, the striped center-line, glowing through the sleet, disappearing under a seven-foot snow-bank. Blocked.

Back to the truck. My heart dropped like a stone through new snow. There had to be a mistake. I mean, this wasn't 1776. The days of Escalante were gone. But the only mistake was my judgment. I was stopped on state 143, and 143 lay under winter ice.

I turned up the heater to blast level, went to the back, and wrapped a blanket around the sleeping bag. I undressed fast and got into a sweat-suit, two pairs of socks, my old Navy-issue watch cap, a pair of gloves. When I cut the engine, snow already had covered the windshield. Only a quarter tank of gas. While the warmth lasted, I hurried into the bag and pulled back the curtain to watch the fulminous clouds blast the mountain. That sky was bent on having a storm, and I was in for a drubbing.

At any particular moment in a man's life, he can say that every-thing he has done and not done, that has been done and not been done to him, has brought him to that moment. If he's being installed as Chieftain or receiving a Nobel Prize, that's a fulfilling notion. But if he's in a sleeping bag at ten thousand feet in a snowstorm, parked in the middle of a highway and waiting to freeze to death, the idea can make him feel calamitously stupid.

A loud racketing of hail fell on the steel box, and the wind seemed to have hands, it shook the Ghost so relentlessly. Lightning tried to outdo thunder in scaring me. So did those things scare me? No. Not *those* things. It was something else. I was certain of a bear attack. That's what scared me.

Lightning strikes the earth about eight million times each day and kills a hundred and fifty Americans every year. I don't know how many die from exposure and hypothermia, but it must be at least a comparable number. As for bears eating people who sleep inside steel trucks, I haven't been able to find that figure. It made no sense to fear a bear coming out of hibernation in such weather to attack a truck. Yet I lay a long time, waiting for the beast, shaggy and immense, to claw through the metal, its hot breath on my head, to devour me like a gumdrop and roll the van over the edge.

Perhaps fatigue or strain prevented me from worrying about the real fear; perhaps some mechanism of mind hid the true and inescapable threat. Whatever it was, it finally came to me that I was crazy. Maybe I was already freezing to death. Maybe this was the way it happened. Black Elk prays for the Grandfather Spirit to help him face the winds and walk the good road to the day of quiet. Whitman too:

> *O to be self-balanced for contingencies,*
> *To confront night, storms, hunger, ridicule, accidents,*
> *rebuffs, as the trees and animals do.*

I wondered how long I might have to stay in the Breaks before I could drive down. The cold didn't worry me much: I had insulated the rig myself and slept in it once when the windchill was thirty-six below. I figured to survive if I didn't have to stay on top too long. Why hadn't I listened to friends who advised carrying a CB? The headline showed darkly: FROZEN MAN FOUND IN AVALANCHE. The whole night I slept and woke, slept and woke, while the hail fell like iron shot, and thunder slammed around, and lightning seared the ice.

WILLIAM LEAST HEAT MOON (William Trogdon) was born in 1939 in Kansas City, Missouri. His pen name came from the translation of his last name from his Sioux ancestry. He is a Native American teacher and author. Finding himself separated from his wife and laid off from his job as an English teacher in a small Missouri college in 1978, he packed his van, Ghost Dancing, and headed around the country following the back highways – the ones colored blue – on the road map. This selection notes a moment of discovery and of challenge, and of self-recognition.

Sigurd F. Olson

*Reflections from
the North Country*
"Timelessness"

Our lives seem governed by speed, tension, and hurry. We move so fast and are caught so completely in a web of confusion there is seldom time to think. Our cities are veritable beehives dominated by the sounds of traffic and industry. Even at the top of the highest building, one is conscious of the hive's human busyness.

The change of season is often unobserved, the coming of winter, spring, summer, and autumn. Winter merely means an aggravation of traffic and transportation, spring the sloshiness of rain, summer dust and heat, fall the withering of transplanted flowers and the threat of cold. For one who has lived in the wilderness, it is impossible to adjust to this, and each time I come away from the city, I feel drained of silence and naturalness.

During a trip into the wilds, it often takes men a week or more to forget the frenetic lives they have led, but inevitably the feeling of timelessness does come, often without warning.

On a trip long ago, I remember the first impact of a rising full moon. We were in the open on a great stretch of water, with islands in the far distance. The sky gradually brightened and an orange slice of moon appeared; we watched as the great sight unfolded before us. At that moment, the city men in the party caught a hint of its meaning. They were entranced as the moon became clear: pulsating as though alive, it rose slowly above the serrated spruces of the far shore. Then, as it almost reluctantly paled, we took to our paddles again. We searched and searched and found a long point from which we could see both sunset and moonrise at the same time. The calling of the loons meant more after that, and as the dusk settled all were aware of something new in their lives.

I know now as men accept the time clock of the wilderness, their lives become entirely different. It is one of the great compensations of primitive experience, and when one finally reaches the point where days are governed by daylight and dark, rather than by schedules, where one eats if hungry and sleeps when tired, and becomes completely immersed in the ancient rhythms, then one begins to live.

For uncounted millennia man lived this way; only under the stress of danger and the activity of the chase was it violated, and then just for short periods. Life went along as smoothly and gradually as the rising of the moon. It is this long inheritance that governs us in spite of our supposed sophistication. No wonder we have nervous breakdowns and depend on artificial calming devices to sleep and quiet down.

It is not surprising city dwellers leave their homes each weekend and head for beaches, mountains, or plains where they can recapture the feeling of timelessness. It is this need, as much as scenery or just getting out of town, that is the reason for their escape. In the process, however, they may still be so imbued with the sense of hurry and the thrill of travel that they actually lose what they came to find. Many tour the national parks with the major objective of getting as many park stickers as possible in the short time available, and what should have been a leisurely experience becomes a race to include all the areas within reach. When such travelers return, they are often wearier than when they started.

I shall never forget a young couple who roared into a lookout spot of the Grand Canyon just at dusk when it was at its most spectacular, with the last slanting rays of the sun touching the tops of pinnacles with gold just before they darkened into the deep blues and lavenders of night. Several of us had been waiting for an hour, feasting on a panorama unequaled anywhere in the world, and over it was a silence and timelessness that gave added meaning to the scene.

Without warning, a car door slammed and the couple hurried to where we were. In a moment the girl said, "Well, we've seen this one. Let's try to make it to the next before we call it a day," and off they sped into the night. I know they were disappointed, for tension and activity were really their goal. They were doing what so many do: "killing time," as though time were inexhaustible and could be wasted at will.

In the wilderness there is never this sense of having to move, never the feeling of boredom if nothing dramatic happens. Time moves slowly, as it should, for it is a part of beauty that cannot be hurried if it is to be understood. Without this easy flowing, life can become empty and hectic.

Not long ago, as I was sitting beside my cabin, a mink came along the shore followed by three half-grown young. They were in and out of the water, slipping over rocks and between roots, and their movements were grace personified. They did not see me, nor were they conscious of my scent, for I was hidden by a clump of hazel and the wind was from the shoreline. They soon disappeared in their eternal search for food, or perhaps just for the joy of movement.

That afternoon I paddled down a river, flowing through mats of sedges, with towering hills toward the north. A golden eagle soared high above the ridges, gliding without effort on the wind currents over the valley. As I watched the huge bird, I could not help but feel I was part of its lazy movement, of the sky and the wind, looking down over its domain as eagles had done for centuries, when only Indians were there to mark its flight, or voyageurs in birchbark canoes on the way from Lake Vermilion to Shagawa Lake and the border.

With natives one is more conscious of this sense of timelessness. They look at us with puzzlement, wondering why we hurry so desperately. In Hawaii a year ago I saw a native Polynesian standing on a sandy shore where the surf came in. He was alone, bronzed and calm, just listening to the endless roar as the glistening combers struck the reefs outside. He had his surfboard and I knew he had been part of the scene for hours, possibly all day long. If he had been a white, he might have thought of taking one more ride, but he merely stayed there quietly, reluctant to leave.

In the Far North of this continent, I have known Indians and Eskimos and have sensed ancient rhythms with them, the feeling of endless time, and I sometimes think the reason we do not understand them is because they listen to a different drummer and see no purpose in the constant pushing and rush. Back of this sense of unlimited time is an entirely different philosophy of life from ours.

We cannot all live in the wilderness, or even close to it, but we can, no matter where we spend our lives, remember the background which shaped this sense of the eternal rhythm, remember that days, no matter how frenzied their pace, can be calm and unhurried. Knowing we can be calm and unhurried we can refuse to be caught in the so-called rat race and the tension which kills Godlike leisure. Though conscious of the roar around us, we can find peace if we remember we all came from a common mold and primeval background. It is when we forget and divorce ourselves entirely from what man once knew that our lives may spin off without meaning.

SIGURD F. OLSON, born in 1899, was educated at Northland College and the Universities of Wisconsin and Illinois. A professor until he devoted himself full time to awareness and appreciation of wilderness, he was president of The Wilderness Society and also The National Parks Association. He was the author of many books including *The Singing Wilderness, The Lonely Land, Wilderness Days,* and *Of Time and Place.* He spent much of his life in the Quentico-Superior region of Minnesota and Ontario. This selection is from his book *Reflections from the North Country* and is a reflection in itself of how much we miss each day, although our lives may be surrounded by nature.

Henry Wadsworth Longfellow

Evangeline

Far in the West there lies a desert land, where the mountains
Lift, through perpetual snows, their lofty and luminous summits.
Down from their jagged, deep ravines, where the gorge, like a gateway,
Opens a passage rude to the wheels of the emigrant's wagon,
Westward the Oregon flows and the Walleway and Owyhee.
Eastward, with devious course, among the Wind-river Mountains,
Through the Sweet-water Valley precipitate leaps the Nebraska;
And to the south, from Fontaine-qui-bout and the Spanish sierras,
Fretted with sands and rocks, and swept by the winds of the desert,
Numberless torrents, with ceaseless sound, descend to the ocean.
Like the great chords of a harp, in loud and solemn vibrations.
Spreading between these streams are the wondrous, beautiful prairies;
Billowy bays of grass ever rolling in shadow and sunshine,
Bright with luxuriant clusters of roses and purple amorphas.
Over them wandered the buffalo herds, and the elk and the roebuck;
Over them wandered the wolves, and herds of riderless horses;
Fires that blast and blight, and winds that are weary with travel;
Over them wander the scattered tribes of Ishmael's children,
Staining the desert with blood; and above their terrible wartrials
Circles and sails aloft, on pinions majestic, the vulture,
Like the implacable soul of a chieftain slaughtered in battle,
By invisible stairs ascending and scaling the heavens.
Here and there rise smokes from the camps of these savage marauders;
Here and there rise groves from the margins of swift-running rivers;
And the grim, taciturn bear, the anchorite monk of the desert,
Climbs down their dark ravines to dig for roots by the brookside,
And over all is the sky, the clear and crystalline heaven,
Like the protecting hand of God inverted above them.

HENRY WADSWORTH LONGFELLOW was one of the most popular American romantic poets both in the United States and in England. Educated at Bowdoin College, he taught there and at Harvard. His most famous poems include: *The Song of Hiawatha, The Courtship of Miles Standish, Paul Revere's Ride, The Village Blacksmith,* and *The Wreck of the Hesperus.* He also made a poetic translation of Dante's *A Divine Comedy.*

Walt Whitman

Songs of Myself

[14]

The wild gander leads his flock through the cool night,
Ya-honk! he says, and sounds it down to me like an invitation;
The pert may suppose it meaningless, but I listen closer,
I find its purpose and place up there toward the November sky.

The sharphoofed moose of the north, the cat on the housesill, the
     chickadee, the prairie-dog,
The litter of the grunting sow as they tug at her teats,
The brood of the turkeyhen, and she with her halfspread wings,
I see in them and myself the same old law.

The press of my foot to the earth springs a hundred affections,
They scorn the best I can do to relate them.

I am enamoured of growing outdoors,
Of men that live among cattle or taste of the ocean or woods,
Of the builders and steerers of ships, of the wielders of axes and
     mauls, of the drivers of horses,
I can eat and sleep with them week in and week out.

What is commonest and cheapest and nearest and easiest is Me,
Me going in for my chances, spending for vast returns,
Adorning myself to bestow myself on the first that will take me,
Not asking the sky to come down to my goodwill,
Scattering it freely forever.

[*31*]

I believe a leaf of grass is no less than the journeywork of the stars,
And the pismire is equally perfect, and a grain of sand, and the egg
    of the wren,
And the tree-toad is a chef-d'oeuvre for the highest,
And the running blackberry would adorn the parlors of heaven,
And the narrowest hinge in my hand puts to scorn all machinery,
And the cow crunching with depressed head surpasses any statue,
And a mouse is miracle enough to stagger sextillions of infidels,
And I could come every afternoon of my life to look at the farmer's
    girl boiling her iron tea-kettle and baking shortcake.

I find I incorporate gneiss and coal and long-threaded moss and
    fruits and grains and esculent roots,
And am stucco'd with quadrupeds and birds all over,
And have distanced what is behind me for good reasons,
And call any thing close again when I desire it.

In vain the speeding or shyness,
In vain the plutonic rocks send their old heat against my approach,
In vain the mastoden retreats beneath its own powdered bones,
In vain objects stand leagues off and assume manifold shapes,
In vain the ocean settling in hollows and the great monsters lying low,
In vain the buzzard houses herself with the sky,
In vain the snake slides through the creepers and logs,
In vain the elk takes to the inner passes of the woods,
In vain the razorbilled auk sails far north to Labrador,
I follow quickly . . . I ascend to the nest in the fissure of the cliff.

WALT WHITMAN was born in 1819 in Huntington, Long Island. He worked as a printer, as a carpenter, as a journalist, and as a hospital nurse. His first book, *Leaves of Grass*, was received with mixed reviews. He continued to revise this book throughout his life. Other books include *Drum-Taps, Sequel to Drum-Taps, and November Boughs*. His life and poetry touched many people including: John Burroughs, Ralph Waldo Emerson, and Carl Sandburg. He is considered by many to be America's foremost poet.

Robert W. Service

Best Tales of the Yukon
"The Call of the Wild"

Have you gazed on naked grandeur where
    there's nothing else to gaze on,
  Set pieces and drop-curtain scenes galore,
Big mountains heaved to heaven, which the
    blinding sunsets blazon,
  Black canyons where the rapids rip and roar?
Have you swept the visioned valley with the
    green stream streaking through it,
  Searched the Vastness for a something you have lost?
Have you strung your soul to silence? Then
    for God's sake go and do it;
  Hear the challenge, learn the lesson, pay the cost.

Have you wandered in the wilderness, the sage-brush desolation,
  The bunch-grass levels where the cattle graze?
Have you whistled bits of rag-time at the end of all creation,
  And learned to know the desert's little ways?
Have you camped upon the foothills, have you
    galloped o'er the ranges,
  Have you roamed the arid sun-lands through and through?
Have you chummed up with the mesa? Do
    you know its moods and changes?
  Then listen to the Wild — it's calling you.

Have you known the Great White Silence, not
    a snow-gemmed twig aquiver?
  (Eternal truths that shame our soothing lies.)
Have you broken trail on snowshoes? mushed
    your huskies up the river,
  Dared the unknown, led the way, and clutched the prize?
Have you marked the map's void spaces,
    mingled with the mongrel races,
  Felt the savage strength of brute in every thew?
And though grim as hell the worst is, can you
    round it off with curses?
  Then hearken to the Wild — it's wanting you.

Have you suffered, starved and triumphed,
    groveled down, yet grasped at glory,
  Grown bigger in the bigness of the whole?
"Done things" just for the doing, letting babblers tell the story,
  Seeing through the nice veneer the naked soul?
Have you seen God in His splendors, heard the
    text that nature renders?
  (You'll never hear it in the family pew.)
The simple things, the true things, the silent
    men who do things —
  Then listen to the Wild — it's calling you.

They have cradled you in custom, they have
    primed you with their preaching,
  They have soaked you in convention through and through;
They have put you in the showcase; you're a
    credit to their teaching —
  But can't you hear the Wild? — it's calling you.
Let us probe the silent places, let us seek what luck betide us;
  Let us journey to a lonely land I know.
There's a whisper on the night-wind, there's
    a star agleam to guide us,
  And the Wild is calling, calling . . . let us go.

ROBERT W. SERVICE (1874 - 1958) was an English-born Canadian poet and novelist. He moved to Canada when he was 20 and was soon assigned to the Yukon branch of a Vancouver bank in which he worked in 1904. His poetry, such as this selection from *The Spell of the Yukon*, hit many of the best seller lists, and he became one of the most popular poets of the era. "Verse, not poetry is what I was after," Service wrote. " . . . Something the man on the street would take notice of and the sweet old lady would paste in her album." In *The Spell of the Yukon*, Service transforms the tales of the Yukon's Gold Rush days into lively verse.

Farley Mowat

Never Cry Wolf
"Naked to the Wolves"

T he weeks which we spent cruising the tundra plains were idyllic. The weather was generally good, and the sensation of freedom which we derived from the limitless land was as invigorating as the wide-ranging life we led.

When we found ourselves in the territory of a new wolf family we would make camp and explore the surrounding plains for as long as was required in order to make the acquaintance of the group. We were never lonely, despite the immensity and solitude of the country, for the caribou were always with us. Together with their attendant flocks of herring gulls and ravens, they imparted a sense of animation to what might otherwise have seemed a stark enough landscape.

This country belonged to the deer, the wolves, the birds and the smaller beasts. We two were no more than casual and insignificant intruders. Man had never dominated the Barrens. Even the Eskimos, whose territory it had once been, had lived in harmony with it. Now these inland Eskimos had all but vanished. The little group of forty souls to which Ootek belonged was the last of the inland people, and they were all but swallowed up in this immensity of wilderness.

We encountered other human beings only on a single occasion. One morning, shortly after starting on our journey, we rounded a bend in a river and Ootek suddenly raised his paddle and gave a shout.

On the foreshore ahead of us was a squat skin tent. At the sound of Ootek's cry, two men, a woman and three half-grown boys piled out of the tent and ran to the water's edge to watch us approach.

We landed and Ootek introduced me to one of the families of his tribe. All that afternoon we sat about drinking tea, gossiping, laughing and singing, and eating mountains of boiled caribou meat. When we turned in for the night Ootek told me that the men of the family had pitched their camp at this spot so they could be in position to intercept the caribou who crossed the river at a narrows a few miles farther downstream. Paddling one-man kayaks and armed with short stabbing spears, these men hoped to be able to kill enough fat animals at the crossing to last them through the winter. Ootek was anxious to join in their hunt, and he hoped I would not mind remaining here for a few days so that he could help his friends.

I had no objection, and the next morning the three Eskimo men departed, leaving me to bask in a magnificent August day.

The fly season was over. It was hot and there was no wind. I decided to take advantage of the weather to have a swim and get some sun on my pallid skin, so I went off a few hundred yards from the Eskimo camp (modesty is the last of the civilized vices which a man sheds in the wilds), stripped, swam, and then climbed a nearby ridge and lay down to sunbathe.

Wolflike, I occasionally raised my head and glanced around me, and about noon I saw a group of wolves crossing the crest of the next ridge to the north.

These were three wolves, one of them white, but the other two were almost black — a rare color phase. All were adults, but one of the black ones was smaller and lighter than the rest, and was probably a female.

I was in a quandary. My clothes lay by the shore some distance away and I had only my rubber shoes and my binoculars with me on the ridge. If I went back for my clothes, I knew I might lose track of these wolves. But, I thought, who needed clothes on a day like this? The wolves had by now disappeared over the next crest, so I seized my binoculars and hared off in pursuit.

The countryside was a maze of low ridges separated by small valleys which were carpeted with grassy swales where small groups of caribou slowly grazed their way southward. It was an ideal terrain for me, since I was able to keep watch from the crests while the wolves crossed each of these valleys in turn. When they dropped from view beyond a ridge I had only to sprint after them, with no danger of being seen, until I reached another elevated position from which I could watch them traverse the succeeding valley.

Sweating with excitement and exertion I breasted the first ridge to the north, expecting to see some frenzied action as the three wolves came suddenly down upon the unsuspecting caribou below. But I was disconcerted to find myself looking out over a completely peaceful scene. There were about fifty bucks in view, scattered in groups of three to ten animals, and all were busy grazing. The wolves were sauntering across the valley as if they had no more interest in the deer than in the rocks. The caribou, on their part, seemed quite unaware of any threat. Three familiar dogs crossing a farm pasture would have produced as much of a reaction in a herd of domestic cattle as the wolves did among these caribou.

The scene was all wrong. Here was a band of wolves surrounded by numbers of deer; but although each species was obviously fully aware of the presence of the other, neither seemed perturbed, or even greatly interested.

Incredulously, I watched the three wolves trot by within fifty yards of a pair of young bucks who were lying down chewing their cuds. The bucks turned their heads to watch the wolves go by, but they did not rise to their feet, nor did their jaws stop working. Their disdain for the wolves seemed monumental.

The two wolves passed on between two small herds of grazing deer, ignoring them and being ignored in their turn. My bewilderment increased when, as the wolves swung up a slope and disappeared over the next crest, I jumped up to follow and the two bucks who had been so apathetic in the presence of the wolves leaped to their feet, staring at me in wild-eyed astonishment. As I sprinted past them they thrust their heads forward, snorted unbelievingly, then spun on their heals and went galloping off as if pursued by devils. It seemed completely unjust that they should have been so terrified of *me*, while remaining so blase about the wolves. However, I solaced myself with the thought that their panic might have resulted from unfamiliarity with the spectacle of a white man, slightly pink, and clad only in boots and binoculars, racing madly across the landscape.

I nearly ran right into the wolves over the next crest. They had assembled in a little group on the forward slope and were having a social interlude, with much nose smelling and tail wagging. I flung myself down behind some rocks and waited. After a few moments the white wolf started off again and the others followed. They were in no hurry, and there was considerable individual meandering as they went down the slopes toward the valley floor where scores of deer were grazing. Several times one or another of the wolves stopped to smell a clump of moss, or detoured to one side to investigate something on his own. When they reached the valley they were strung out in line abreast and about a hundred feet apart, and in this formation they turned and trotted along the valley floor.

Only those deer immediately in front of the wolves showed any particular reaction. When a wolf approached to within fifty or sixty yards, the deer would snort, rise on their hind feet and then spring off to one side of the line of advance. After galloping a few yards some of them swung around again to watch with mild interest as the wolf went past, but most returned to their grazing without giving the wolf another glance.

Within the space of an hour the wolves and I had covered three or four miles and had passed within close range of perhaps four hundred caribou. In every case the reaction of the deer had been of a piece — no interest while the wolves remained at a reasonable distance; casual interest if the wolves came very close; and avoiding-tactics only when a collision seemed imminent. There had been no stampeding and no panic.

Up to this time most of the deer we had encountered had been bucks; but now we began to meet numbers of does and fawns, and the behavior of the wolves underwent a change.

One of them flushed a lone fawn from a hiding place in a willow clump. The fawn leaped into view not twenty feet ahead of the wolf, who paused to watch it for an instant, then raced off in pursuit. My heart began to thud with excitement as I anticipated seeing a kill at last.

It was not to be. The wolf ran hard for fifty yards without gaining perceptibly on the fawn, then suddenly broke off the chase and trotted back to rejoin his fellows.

I could hardly believe my eyes. That fawn should have been doomed, and it certainly would have been if even a tenth of the wolfish reputation was in fact deserved; yet during the next hour at least twelve separate rushes were made by all three wolves against single fawns, a doe with a fawn, or groups of does and fawns, *and in every case the chase was broken off almost before it was well begun.*

I was becoming thoroughly exasperated. I had not run six miles across country and exhausted myself just to watch a pack of wolves playing the fool.

When the wolves left the next valley and wandered over the far crest, I went charging after them with blood in my eye. I'm not sure what I had in mind — possibly I may have intended to chase down a caribou fawn myself, just to show those incompetent beasts how it was done. In any event I shot over the crest — and straight into the middle of the band.

They had probably halted for a breather, and I burst in among them like a bomb. The group exploded. Wolves went tearing off at top speed in all directions — ears back, tails stretching straight behind them. They ran scared, and as they fled through the dispersed caribou herds the deer finally reacted, and the stampede of frightened animals which I had been expecting to witness all that afternoon became something of a reality. Only, and I realized the fact with bitterness, it was not the wolves who had been responsible — it was I.

I gave it up then, and turned for home. When I was still some miles from camp I saw several figures running toward me and I recognized them as the Eskimo woman and her three youngsters. They seemed to be fearfully distraught about something. They were all screaming, and the woman was waving a two-foot-long snowknife while her three offspring were brandishing deer spears and skinning knives.

I stopped in some perplexity. For the first time I became uncomfortably aware of my condition. Not only was I unarmed, but I was stark naked. I was in no condition to ward off an attack — and one seemed imminent, although I had not the slightest idea what had roused the Eskimos to such a mad endeavor. Discretion seemed the better part of valor, so I stretched my weary muscles and sprinted hard to bypass the Eskimos. I succeeded, but they were still game, and the chase continued most of the way back to the camp where I scrambled into my trousers, seized my rifle, and prepared to sell my life dearly. Fortunately Ootek and the men arrived back at the camp just as the woman and her crew of furies swept down upon me, and the battle was averted.

Somewhat later, when things had quieted down, Ootek explained the situation. One of the children had been picking berries when he had seen me go galloping naked across the hills after the wolves. Round-eyed with wonder, he had hastened back to report this phenomenon to his mother. She, brave soul, assumed that I had gone out of my mind (Eskimos believe that no white man has very far to go in this direction), and was attempting to assault a pack of wolves bare-handed and bare everything else. Calling up the rest of her brood, and snatching what weapons were at hand, she had set out at top speed to rescue me.

During the remainder of our stay, this good woman treated me with such a wary mixture of solicitude and distrust that I was relieved beyond measure to say farewell to her. Nor was I much amused by Ootek's comment as we swept down the river and passed out of sight of the little camp.

"Too bad," he said gravely, "that you take off your pants. I think she like you better if you left them on."

FARLEY MOWAT was born in Ontario in 1921. He began writing as an Infantryman in WWII "as a means of hanging onto my sanity . . ." He considers himself to be primarily a storyteller in the ancient sense, "a saga man." He has been a prolific writer on nature — working in mostly the non-fiction area — yet telling stories that express the challenge and inspiration taken from nature at its wildest. This selection from *Never Cry Wolf* is full of the wonder and discovery of man, himself, against a landscape of the vastness of the Arctic.

Charlton Ogburn, Jr.

The Winter Beach
"More of Maine and
South to Cape Ann"

ount Desert was not entirely without pilgrims even at this season. Occasional out-of-state cars passed on the park roads and at midday there was likely to be a couple eating boxed lunches at Sand beach or below the cliff of Newport (to give Champlain Mountain its earlier name). Schoodic Point, an outlying bit of park across Frenchman Bay, seemed to draw a light but steady traffic. It is a very exposed rocky promontory famous for the stupendous seas that crash upon it during storms. It is also well known for the sea-birds to be observed from it. All during the lunch I ate there little groups of eiders came winging in. On the water, the adult drake appears entirely white but for the rear two-thirds of his underparts and the top of his head. (The long, black-capped white head tapering to a beak put me in mind, I don't know exactly why, of pictures of scorchers from the early days of the bicycle craze.) Eiders, which breed on Arctic coasts, are big ducks, on the way

to being thick-necked geese, with a deliberate flight. They were arriving about a dozen at a time and, with feet splayed in front of them, hitting with a splash and skidding to a stop. Now and again part of the growing raft of them off the point would skitter across the water, flailing the surface with their wings and whipping up a surf, all evidently in play.

In another car a girl was also watching the eiders, through a telescope. Looping my binocular conspicuously over my neck, I went over to exchange impressions with her. To dispel without delay any doubts of my bona fides, I remarked that as far as could be seen the male eiders in the vicinity out-numbered the females by a good four to one. We speculated why this might be so. She turned out to be well informed as well as attractive. She had, she said, seen two gannets and some American scoters (the least common of the three kinds) on her last trip to Schoodic. Her greatest find there had been a Kumlein's gull. Her eyes lighted up at the recollection. Had it been any farther away than at the end of the rocks, she declared, she would never have dared claim an identification. I asked if there were any chance of our picking up (I took care to keep within the idiom, since from the way she kept pulling her skirt down every time she squirmed around to get a better view of a bird I surmised she was not yet sure of my exclusive devotion to bird-watching) any alcids. (Alcids are what the fraternity call those northern-hemisphere equivalents of the penguins: the razor-billed auks, murres, guillemots, puffins and dovekies.) She explained that it took a storm to bring them close enough in to be seen and that if the storm were just a little bit too heavy the mist of the breakers obscured them; it was touch and go.

She was, I learned, a member of the Maine Audubon Society and had driven, all by herself, down from Bangor just for the birds of the Scoodic.   She was distinctly an entry for the other side of the uneven balance sheet one draws up mentally as one travels about our country, she and the many thousands she stood for. "Whatever else America may be," said a friend of mine who had flown from New York to Washington after several years in Switzerland and been aghast at what he saw, "it is the land of the bulldozer." That is surely true. But there is another side. The national and state parks you see incorporate only a tenth part of the land they should — at least in the East — but for every acre of them men and women have sacrificed, have fought and bled in legislatures. Every living gull, meadow-lark, raven, sandpiper, hawk, heron is testimony to other battles waged in its behalf — not for gain but for love; the self-servers all are on the other side, except for those sportsmen who contribute to protection to make sure of having something to kill in the future. The country is not all gas stations, out-door movie theaters, roadhouses, wrecked-car lots, parking plazas, though it may seem to be so in places. Among them are trees, shrubs, flowers, planted and tended by people who had no other motive than a care for what is living and green.

I often wonder about the place of nature in the soul of Western man. Western literature from Shakespeare to the publications of the Sierra Club is eloquent in the responsiveness it reveals to woods, mountains and rivers, birds and four-footed animals, to the whole out-of-doors — clouds and sky and thundering sea. It leads to the belief that a feeling for nature and a sense of being integral with the natural world are deep-seated among us and have roots far back in the north-ern European past. Perhaps only in the art of China and Japan could one find comparable expression of such receptivity to nature. Yet (and this I can never fully fathom) we were led to adopt and at times have fanatically prosecuted a religion — that is to say, a view of what life is ultimately about — in which there is no fellowship whatever of man and nature. Christianity abstracts man from nature. Nature it at best relegates to subservience as man's handmaiden and for the rest stigma-tizes as the source of impulses in man which he may scarcely obey without shame or even risk of perdition. So it is with all three of the monotheistic religions that arose in the eastern Mediterranean to sweep in time over five of the inhabited continents and part of the sixth. The God of Judah, Christianity and Islam created the animals solely to be of use to mankind. This is made explicit in *Genesis*. It is put unequivocally to Noah in a pronouncement that must have been meant as a blessing but reads like a curse:

> *And the fear of you and the dread of you shall be upon every beast of the earth, and upon every fowl of the air, upon all that moveth upon earth, and upon all fishes of the sea; into your hand are they delivered.*

Why this animosity to nature? Possibly the prophets of monotheism saw in paganism their mortal foe and in man's feeling of identity with nature the seedbed of paganism. Beyond that, nature meant the world of the present life, the satisfactions of which were an impediment to the realization of those of a postulated future life of eternal duration and were accordingly condemned. The consequences were to be immeasureable. Alienated from the world they lived in, the Judeo-Christian-Islamic believers were put on their mettle to prove themselves like invaders who owe the land no fealty and are denied the comfort of a sense of participation in its being, thrown upon their own to triumph or perish. The world around them had nothing of value to say to them; the tolerant, open-minded relativity of view we acquire from observation of the natural world was not for them. Theirs was the absolutism of revelation. There is no such incentive as the conviction that one possesses the single, preclusive, comprehensive and unalterable truth — as we have recently illustrated in the dynamics of Communism, that shaky amalgam of the Judeo-Christian social aim with the supposed lessons of science.

The disciples of the monotheistic, monopolistic, antinatural religions who set out to achieve the next world unquestionably won this one. Their God had given them the world as a fief of small and transitory worth for their use. He enjoined mercy toward their fellow men, and charity, and this surely was a teaching from which humanity could draw incalculable benefit, but of mercy toward their fellow creatures, of respect for the intricate and multiform family of plants and animals of which they were a part, nothing was said. In the writings to which the peoples of two-thirds of the civilized world have for centuries been taught to look for supreme guidance there is not a word making it immoral for man to stride across the earth with rapine and slaughter — provided only that he spare his own kind — and convert it into a desert lifeless but for himself. Perhaps there was less need when man's capacity for destruction was limited. But the march proceeds apace today and if there is thunder from the pulpit against the havoc we are wreaking on the lands we occupy and on their aboriginal inhabitants it is very muted thunder. The savage American Indian — even he — asked pardon of the spirit of the bear he killed out of necessity, but we may read today how communicants in good standing with church or chapel fly airplanes far out over the icepack to hunt down the vanishing polar bears — for fun.

Indifferent to the natural world external to man and generally hostile to the nature that is in man, expressed in our spontaneous emotions and actions, our religious preceptors have left it to poets to sing of the wine that nature instills in our veins and of our kinship with the world around us in all its grandeur, its loveliness and its pathos. To the Greeks of the great age, religion and poetry were inseparable, but with us they have given rise to two distinct literatures with little overlapping between them. That this should be so seems to me symbolic of the cruel dichotomy of soul which is the price we have paid for our preeminence in the world; for Western man has been pulled in opposing directions by the governing forces of his existence.

Such being the pass he had reached, one can only give thanks for the birth of the scientific spirit among us. Science has shown us what we had been in danger of forgetting, how much we are a part of nature and how much nature is a part of us. In its exclusive concern with the apprehensible it has caused us to think more of making all we can of what this world has to offer instead of turning our backs upon it like the ungrateful dog in the parable who dropped irretrievably the bone he had been given in order to snatch at its shimmering reflection in the water. It has warned us in terms we have at last begun to heed of the consequences of impoverishing the earth. It has relieved us of much of the impossible load of guilt that an endemic puritanism had taught us to feel for being what by nature we are and must be. And its capacities for discovering us to ourselves and thus enabling us to live in greater harmony with ourselves and our surroundings may only have begun to be tapped.

At least one may hope so. But that is not to suggest that men can live by science alone. Science is only the method of rational analysis and what we have learned by it, nothing more. In all its findings there is less to warm the heart than in a single ration of rum issued on the wind-swept deck of a ship to the shivering hands. It offers no justification for or encouragement to those who in the fullness of their feeling would like to do homage to the Great Spirit in observances attuned to the gulls' cries and the sea's splash in a grove of balsams sacred to its worship. There are no shrines within its purlieus upon which we may unload the bittersweet burden that the experience of living lays upon our hearts. But if it does not enjoin reverence upon us it does not proscribe it either. And it wonderfully sharpens our observation and informs our comprehension of the Great Spirit's handiwork. Because that is its purpose, I would believe that comfortless though its uncompromising rationality may be (while being prodigiously productive of material comforts), science shows creation and hence the Creator the most genuine possible respect and deference. Those views of the universe that make creatures like ourselves its ultimate reason for being must necessarily be suspect. To see the universe as nearly as possible without regard to our own predispositions or desire, as science tries to, seems to me to approach the godly. Said Sir Thomas Browne three centuries ago:

> The wisdome of God receives small honour from those vulgar heads that rudely stare about, and with a gross rusticity admire his workes; those highly magnifie him whose judicious enquiry into his acts, and deliberate research into his creatures, returne the duty of a devout and learned admiration.

CHARLTON OGBURN, JR. was born in 1911. He is the author of numerous books; *The Winter Beach* is the story of Charlton Ogburn's voyage during the winter of 1964 from Mount Desert Island down the coast to the Outer Banks of North Carolina. One of the charms of this book is the way Ogburn swings from accurate observations of the world around him to those of the philosophy of man and nature.

Rachel Carson

The Sense of Wonder

A child's world is fresh and new and beautiful, full of wonder and excitement. It is our misfortune that for most of us that clear-eyed vision, that true instinct for what is beautiful and awe-inspiring, is dimmed and even lost before we reach adulthood. If I had influence with the good fairy who is supposed to preside over the christening of all children I should ask that her gift to each child in the world be a sense of wonder so indestructible that it would last throughout life, as an unfailing antidote against the boredom and disenchantments of later years, the sterile preoccupation with things that are artificial, the alienation from the sources of our strength.

If a child is to keep alive his inborn sense of wonder without any such gift from the fairies, he needs the companionship of at least one adult who can share it, rediscovering with him the joy, excitement and mystery of the world we live in. Parents often have a sense of inadequacy when confronted on the one hand with the eager, sensitive mind of

a child and on the other with a world of complex physical nature, inhabited by a life so various and unfamiliar that it seems hopeless to reduce it to order and knowledge. In a mood of self-defeat, they exclaim, "How can I possibly teach my child about nature — why, I don't even know one bird from another!"

I sincerely believe that for the child, and for the parent seeking to guide him, it is not half so important to *know* as to *feel*. If facts are the seeds that later produce knowledge and wisdom, then the emotions and the impressions of the senses are the fertile soil in which the seeds must grow. The years of early childhood are the time to prepare the soil. Once the emotions have been aroused — a sense of the beautiful, the excitement of the new and the unknown, a feeling of sympathy, pity, admiration or love — then we wish for knowledge about the object of our emotional response. Once found, it has lasting meaning. It is more important to pave the way for the child to want to know than to put him on a diet of facts he is not ready to assimilate.

If you are a parent who feels he has little nature lore at his disposal there is still much you can do for your child. With him, wherever you are and whatever your resources, you can still look up at the sky — its dawn and twilight beauties, its moving clouds, its stars by night. You can listen to the wind, whether it blows with majestic voice through a forest or sings a many-voiced chorus around the eaves of your house or the corners of your apartment building, and in the listening, you can gain magical release for your thoughts. You can still feel the rain on your face and think of its long journey, its many transmutations, from sea to air to earth. Even if you are a city dweller, you can find some place, perhaps a park or a golf course, where you can observe the mysterious migrations of the birds and the changing seasons. And with your child you can ponder the mystery of a growing seed, even if it be only one planted in a pot of earth in the kitchen window.

Exploring nature with your child is largely a matter of becoming receptive to what lies all around you. It is learning again to use your eyes, ears, nostrils and finger tips, opening up the disused channels of sensory impression.

For most of us, knowledge of our world comes largely through sight, yet we look about with such unseeing eyes that we are partially blind. One way to open your eyes to unnoticed beauty is to ask yourself,

"What if I had never seen this before? What if I knew I would never see it again?"

What is the value of preserving and strengthening this sense of awe and wonder, this recognition of something beyond the boundaries of human existence? Is the exploration of the natural world just a pleasant way to pass the golden hours of childhood or is there something deeper?

I am sure there is something much deeper, something lasting and significant. Those who dwell, as scientists or laymen, among the beauties and mysteries of the earth are never alone or weary of life. Whatever the vexations or concerns of their personal lives, their thoughts can find paths that lead to inner contentment and to renewed excitement in living. Those who contemplate the beauty of the earth find reserves of strength that will endure as long as life lasts. There is symbolic as well as actual beauty in the migration of the birds, the ebb and flow of the tides, the folded bud ready for the spring. There is something infinitely healing in the repeated refrains of nature — the assurance that dawn comes after night, and spring after the winter.

I like to remember the distinguished Swedish oceanographer, Otto Pettersson, who died a few years ago at the age of ninety-three, in full possession of his keen mental powers. His son, also world-famous in oceanography, has related in a recent book how intensely his father enjoyed every new experience, every new discovery concerning the world about him.

"He was an incurable romantic," the son wrote, "intensely in love with life and with the mysteries of the cosmos." When he realized he had not much longer to enjoy the earthly scene, Otto Pettersson said to his son: "What will sustain me in my last moments is an infinite curiosity as to what is to follow."

Few writers have had more influence on America in this century than RACHEL CARSON. Born in Springdale, Penn. in May, 1907, she graduated magna cum laude from Chatham College, and received an M.A. in zoology from John Hopkins University. Her books include *Under the Sea Wind, The Sea Around Us, The Edge of the Sea,* and *Silent Spring*. But it is *The Sense of Wonder,* that we turn for a sense of discovery. In it she writes about her relationship to her nephew, Roger, but also about any child's experience with his world.

Mary Back

Seven Half-Miles from Home
"Seven Walks"

Most of the year the walks are indeed before breakfast, just as the doctor ordered. For a few weeks around the winter solstice — from say mid-November into February — it's too dark before breakfast to see anything; those weeks I eat first and take off at dawn. As soon as dawn comes by 6:30, I start off then and eat when I get back.

Weather doesn't really matter. It can hardly ever be severe enough to hurt me in a mere mile stretch. Raincoat, plastic head scarf, and rubber boots take care of wet days; heavy wool pants, two pairs of wool socks, overshoes, padded jacket with hood take care of cold ones; an added scarf across my face takes care of high wind with blinding snow, and I walk within sight of a fence. My greatest safeguard is the blessed knowledge that if I'm more than fifteen minutes late, Joe will come looking for me. So what can really go wrong?

The Monday walk is northeast to east, or about two to three on a clock diagram. I go down Wind River on its south bank to the Motel Slough, around the Slough Woods, across the Bog Knots, behind the Red Rock Motel, and home by the road past the bridge. This takes me through several life zones or ecological communities: the live stream, with its bars, beaches, and islands; the slough; two springs, and a cattail swamp; bottomland cottonwood forest; heavy streamside brush; the log bridge; a brush-grown dike or levee; a single land dirt road; and some houses.

Tuesday is the southeast day, or four to five on the clock diagram. I cross the Red Rock hayfield, cross the Red Rock pasture south of the Motel Slough, go on east to the New Slough, across the gravel flats to the New Channel, then south across the highway into the Jakey's Fork moraine, then northwestward home across CM draw. The ecological communities are meadowland; fence rows; willow thickets; grazed pasture; gravel and mud flats; a new island covered with Cottonwoods; the highway and its edges; moraine hills spotted with sagebrush; sage flats; and the lawn, flower borders, brushy spots, and gravel parking space of home.

Wednesdays I go straight south (six o'clock on the clock diagram). I follow the section-line fence up CM Draw, climb steeply out of the draw up a moraine hill to the section corner (a pile of stones high on the east bank of the draw) back north down CM Ravine and through the Pole Gate, up the west bank of CM Draw, across the flat bench, through the gravel pit, down Gravel Pit Draw, and across the highway to home. This is the dry walk. Except close to our river-house, it's through only the sagebrush community, the walk with the widest views and the fewest birds. Just the same, I'm likely to be breathless with expectation, because here may be the most dramatic confrontations: like the two coyotes; like a rock wren on a boulder against the sky, tilting his head back and singing; like ten mule deer running among cabin-sized granite rocks; like a pair of golden eagles sitting shoulder to shoulder on a block of granite; a raven circling low over my head and exchanging croaking remarks with me; or a badger digging himself in under a sagebrush, facing an excited Buttons, answering her wild yelps with snarls of hair raising ferocity.

Thursday is southwest, or seven to nine o'clock on the diagram. I cross the highway, climb to the Low Bench, wander westward as far as I like (maybe to the steep canyon opposite Leseberg's bridge), down the canyon and northeast to the cattle pass under the highway to the water-gap at the river, eastish along the river bank to the bridge, then home. This is a wildly varied walk, with the lives of different ecological communities absurdly mixed. I can walk along the desert edge of the bench and look down on great blue herons fishing in the river and on California gulls beating up and downstream above it. I can study a water ouzel at close range as he walks about under water eating snails, while a raven sails over from the dry bench, lights in a cottonwood tree above me, and makes gutteral comments. In the course of this walk I study the ecology of the sagebrush flat, of piles of boulders, of canyons just beginning, of rancher's corrals, of the live stream with its brushy banks, of the bridge, the fence-row, and finally the cottonwood forest of home.

Friday is west and northwest, nine to eleven o'clock on the clock diagram. The ecological communities are the live stream and its brushy banks, two cottonwood copses, two islands with narrow shore-side water channels, the wide weed-patch spotted with barren alkali disks, the dirt road and fence row, and the grass and rabbitbrush of our open space.

Saturday, eleven to three o'clock on the diagram, is straight north to the Badlands, along and near the section-line fence. On this trip I look for horned larks and meadowlarks and a variety of sparrows over the flats; a colony of prairie dogs; hawks, ravens, and swallows in the cliffs; chickadees, nuthatches, vireos, and warblers in the cottonwood bottom; and ducks, kingfishers, sandpipers, and dippers; by and in the stream.

Sunday is the day for concentrating on our own acreage: the dirt road and the bridge; the open land, with turf, rye grass, and rabbitbrush; the buildings, with jutting logs, vines, fences, and flower beds; the cottonwood forest, with brush piles and undergrowth; and the river and its banks.

This is an embarrassment of riches. I can never get around to seeing it all.

Each walk is further complicated by the weather and by the changing seasons. Even if the route were just the same, which it isn't, the change in weather and seasons makes each walk a brand new thing. It's new, yet companionably old, as day by day and week by week I greet old friends and they greet me.

Most of the old friends, and the new ones, too, are remarkably closely tied to one kind of environment. After a while I began learning where and how to look for each one. A few species may turn up anywhere, and quite a few are at home in more than one life-zone. And even the most stay-at-home individual may find himself in a most strange location. I should be astonished to find a water ouzel on a Badlands cliff, or a horned toad on a gravel bar in the river, or a great blue heron in CM Ravine, or fifteen rosy finches on my windowsill. But things like this do happen. They add color and flavor and texture to the mystery of life.

To bring this embarrassment of riches into order without diminishing the joy of it is the purpose of this study. (What is it then, Mary Back, that you hope to accomplish? Why, Conscience, I hope to get numbers of people like me into a state of frantic curiosity about the walkable country around their own homes. I hope to get them as excited as I am by the discovery that all life is one thing, and that each of us is part of it. We are part of all life, and all life is part of us. We have a right to share the excitement of a birch tree when the new sap comes running up its stems, and a right to feel flattered when the bald eagle hovers low above us, looking us over with fierce yellow eyes, considering us as one equal to another.)

The key to this unity in diversity of life is the arrangement in ecological communities. So that will be my pattern. I'll study the communities in turn, first giving a summary of them all, from the river outward and upward. Then I'll have a chapter for each one in turn: the lay of the land, its geology, the plant life, the animal life, unusual experiences, and the mysteries that capture the imagination.

MARY BACK began her career in Illinois where she attended the Art Institute of Chicago and helped found a wildlife museum. In 1935, she moved to Wyoming with her husband, Joseph Back. She has illustrated several books and maintained an art studio ever since. In March, 1963, at the advice of her doctor, she began to walk a mile every day before breakfast. Twenty years later she wrote this book, her first. It illustrates how much beauty there is in nature, nearby, for those who observe.

Henry Beston

The Outermost House
"Night on the Great Beach"

Our fantastic civilization has fallen out of touch with many aspects of nature, and with none more completely than with night. Primitive folk, gathered at a cave mouth round a fire, do not fear night; they fear, rather, the energies and creatures to whom night gives power; we of the age of the machines, having delivered ourselves of nocturnal enemies, now have a dislike of night itself. With lights and ever more lights, we drive the holiness and beauty of night back to the forests and the sea; the little villages, the crossroads even, will have none of it. Are modern folk, perhaps, afraid of night? Do they fear that vast serenity, the mystery of infinite space, the austerity of stars? Having made themselves at home in a civilization obsessed with power, which explains its whole world in terms of energy, do they fear at night for their dull acquiescence and the pattern of their beliefs? Be the answer what it will, today's civilization is full of people who have not the slightest notion of the character or the poetry of night, who have never even seen night. Yet to live thus, to know only artificial night, is as absurd and evil as to know only artificial day.

Night is very beautiful on this great beach. It is the true other half of the day's tremendous wheel; no lights without meaning stab or trouble it; it is beauty, it is fulfillment, it is rest. Thin clouds float in these heavens, islands of obscurity in a splendour of space and stars: the Milky Way bridges earth and ocean; the beach resolves itself into a unity of form, its summer lagoons, its slopes and uplands merging; against the western sky and the falling bow of sun rise the silent and superb undulations of the dunes.

My nights are at their darkest when a dense fog streams in from the sea under a black, unbroken floor of cloud. Such nights are rare, but are most to be expected when fog gathers off the coast in early summer; this last Wednesday night was the darkest I have known. Between ten o'clock and two in the morning three vessels stranded on the outer beach – a fisherman, a four-masted schooner, and a beam trawler. The fisherman and the schooner have been towed off, but the trawler, they say, is still ashore.

I went down to the beach that night just after ten o'clock. So utterly black, pitch dark it was, and so thick with moisture and trailing showers, that there was no sign whatever of the beam of Nauset; the sea was only a sound, and when I reached the edge of the surf the dunes themselves had disappeared behind. I stood as isolate in that immensity of rain and night as I might have stood in interplanetary space. The sea was troubled and noisy, and when I opened the darkness with an outlined cone of light from my electric torch I saw that the waves were washing up green coils of sea grass, all coldly wet and bright in the motionless and unnatural radiance. Far off a single ship was groaning its way along the shoals. The fog was compact of the finest moisture; passing by, it spun itself into my lens of light like a kind of strange, aerial, and liquid silk. Effin Chalke, the new coast guard, passed me going north, and told me that he had had news at the halfway house of the schooner at Cahoon's.

It was dark, pitch dark to my eye, yet complete darkness, I imagine, is exceedingly rare, perhaps unknown in outer nature. The nearest natural approximation to it is probably the gloom of forest country buried in night and cloud. Dark as the night was here, there was still light on the surface of the planet. Standing on the shelving beach, with the surf breaking at my feet, I could see the endless wild uprush, slide, and withdrawal of the sea's white rim of foam. The men at Nauset tell me that on such nights they follow along this vague crawl of whiteness, trusting to habit and a sixth sense to warn them of their approach to the halfway house.

Animals descend by starlight to the beach, North, beyond the dunes, muskrats forsake the cliff and nose about in the driftwood and weed, leaving intricate trails and figure eights to be obliterated by the day; the lesser folk– the mice, the occasional small sand-coloured toads, the burrowing moles – keep to the upper beach and leave their tiny footprints under the overhanging wall. In autumn skunks, beset by a shrinking larder, go beach combing early in the night. The animal is by preference a clean feeder and turns up his nose at rankness. I almost stepped on a big fellow one night as I was walking north to meet the first man south from Nauset. There was a scamper, and the creature ran up the beach from under my feet; alarmed he certainly was, yet was he contained and continent. Deer are frequently seen, especially north of the light. I find their tracks upon the summer dunes.

Years ago, while camping on this beach north of Nauset, I went for a stroll along the top of the cliff at break of dawn. Though the path followed close enough along the edge, the beach below was often hidden, and I looked directly from the height to the flush of sunrise at sea. Presently the path, turning, approached the brink of the earth precipice, and on the beach below, in the cool, wet rosiness of dawn, I saw three deer playing. They frolicked, rose on their hind legs, scampered off, and returned again, and were merry. Just before sunrise they trotted off north together down the beach toward a hollow in the cliff and the path that climbs it.

Occasionally a sea creature visits the shore at night. Lone coast guardsmen, trudging the sand at some deserted hour, have been startled by seals. One man fell flat on a creature's back, and it drew away from under him, flippering toward the sea, with a sound "halfway between a squeal and a bark." I myself once had rather a start. It was long after sundown, the light dying and uncertain, and I was walking home on the top level of the beach and close along the slope descending to the ebbing tide. A little more than halfway to the Fo'castle a huge unexpected something suddenly writhed horribly in the darkness under my bare foot. I had stepped on a skate left stranded by some recent crest of surf, and my weight had momentarily annoyed it back to life.

Facing north, the beam of Nauset becomes part of the dune night. As I walk toward it, I see the lantern, now as a star of light which waxes and wanes three mathematic times, now as a lovely pale flare of light behind the rounded summits of the dunes. The changes in the atmosphere change the colour of the beam; it is now whitish, now flame golden, now golden red; it changes its form as well, from a star to a blare of light, from a blare of light to a cone of radiance sweeping a circumference of fog. To the west of Nauset I often see the apocalyptic flash of the great light at the Highland reflected on the clouds or even on the moisture in the starlit air, and, seeing it, I often think of the pleasant hours I have spent there when George and Mary Smith were at the light and I had the good fortune to visit as their guest. Instead of going to sleep in the room under the eaves, I would lie awake, looking out of a window to the great spokes of light revolving as solemnly as a part of the universe.

All night long the lights of coastwise vessels pass at sea, green lights going south, red lights moving north. Fishing schooners and flounder draggers anchor two or three miles out, and keep a bright riding light burning on the mast. I see them come to anchor at sundown, but I rarely see them go, for they are off at dawn. When busy at night, these fishermen illumine their decks with a scatter of oil flares. From shore, the ships might be thought afire. I have watched the scene through a night glass. I could see no smoke, only the waving flares, the reddish radiance on sail and rigging, an edge of reflection overside, and the enormous night and sea beyond.

One July night, as I returned at three o'clock from an expedition north, the whole night, in one strange, burning instant, turned into a phantom day. I stopped and, questioning, stared about. An enormous meteor, the largest I have even seen, was consuming itself in an effulgence of light west of the zenith. Beach and dune and ocean appeared out of nothing, shadowless and motionless, a landscape whose every tremor and vibration were stilled, a landscape in a dream.

The beach at night has a voice all its own, a sound in fullest har-

mony with its spirit and mood – with its little, dry noise of sand for-
ever moving, with its solemn, overspilling, rhythmic seas, with its
eternity of stars that sometimes seem to hang down like lamps from
the high heavens – and that sound the piping of a bird. As I walk the
beach in early summer my solitary coming disturbs it on its nest, and it
flies away, troubled, invisible, piping its sweet, plaintive cry. The bird I
write of is the piping plover, *Charadrius melodus*, sometimes called
the beach plover or the mourning bird. Its note is a whistled syllable,
the loveliest musical note, I think, sounded by any North Atlantic bird.

Now that summer is here I often cook myself a camp supper on
the beach. Beyond the crackling, salt-yellow driftwood flame, over the
pyramid of barrel staves, broken boards, and old sticks all atwist with
climbing fire, the unseen ocean thunders and booms, the breaker
sounding hollow as it falls. The wall of the sand cliff behind, with its
rim of grass and withering roots, its sandy crumblings and erosions,
stands gilded with flame; wind cries over it; a covey of sandpipers pass
between the ocean and the fire. There are stars, and to the south Scor-
pio hangs curving down the sky with ringed Saturn shining in his
claw.

Learn to reverence night and to put away the vulgar fear of it, for,
with the banishment of night from the experience of man, there van-
ishes as well a religious emotion, a poetic mood, which gives depth to
the adventure of humanity. By day, space is one with the earth and
with man – it is his sun that is shining, his clouds that are floating
past; at night, space is his no more. When the great earth, abandoning
day, rolls up the deeps of the heavens and the universe, a new door
opens for the human spirit, and there are few so clownish that some
awareness of the mystery of being does not touch them as they gaze.
For a moment of night we have a glimpse of ourselves and of our
world islanded in its stream of stars – pilgrims of mortality, voyaging
between horizons across eternal seas of space and time. Fugitive
though the instant be, the spirit of man is, during it, ennobled by a
genuine moment of emotional dignity, and poetry makes its own both
the human spirit and experience.

HENRY BESTON was born in 1888 and raised in Quincy, Massachusetts. In 1925 he built a small house on the beach of Cape Cod and in September, 1926, he went to Cape Cod intending to spend a week or two there. He spent a year living alone on Nauset Beach, Cape Cod, Massachusetts. The book, *The Outermost House*, is about that year and has become a nature classic. In 1964 when *The Outermost House* was in its twenty-eighth printing, the site was officially proclaimed a National Literary Landmark by the Commonwealth of Massachusetts and the Department of the Interior. The house was destroyed during a blizzard in 1978. Mr. Beston married the writer Elizabeth Coatsworth and moved to Nobleboro, Maine, where he continued writing.

Ann Zwinger

Beyond the Aspen Grove
"The Lake Rock"

When I need my sense of order restored, I sit on the lake rock. It sums up all I have learned about this mountain world. Connected to the shore by a narrow, somewhat unstable catwalk, the rock is just big enough to sit on comfortably. It is a pebble dropped into the water, the center of widening rings of montane life, beginning with the life of the lake itself and culminating in the evergreen forests, where the succession that is taking place is mapped in the communities that I can see. The rock is a place of order, reason, and bright mountain air.

Encircling the rock is the community of plants and animals which can survive only in the water. Small motes of existence, they float with its currents, cling to underwater supports, or burrow in the brown silt of the lake bottom. Some I can see as I sit here. Others have to be corralled under a microscope lens. I watch a fat trout lurking in the fringed shadows of the sedges. All around the edges of the lake, where water meets land, grow willows, sedges, and rushes, predicting a time when amber water will be green plant, the lapping sound of small waves the sly whisper of grass stems.

It is a busy place with a constant spin of insects, punctuated by the pursuing green arcs of leopard frogs. The south stream enters the lake through willows and cow parsnip and a pile of logs placed there when the lake was built to prevent silting. The north stream's entrance is hidden in elephant-foot-sized clumps of bulrush which change sheen in every breeze. Tangles of willows forecast spring in their catkins. Yellow or red branches identify them even in winter. The streams are the one constant in the landscape.

The circle widens. Behind the lake edge, to the north and west, the land rises into the lake meadow, drying as it slopes upward. Blue grass and brome grass crowd every square inch. I see chipmunk and ground-squirrel burrows, haloed with dandelions. Hundreds of wildflowers grow in this meadow, perennials whose coming I look for each year. A few aspens tentatively grow along its edge.

The established young aspen community between the two streams contains small slender trees, growing almost a foot a year. Still gangling and adolescent, they will in a short time obscure the view of the mature grove behind them. Leaves flicker celadon in spring, viridian in summer, clinquant in fall, tallying the sovereign seasons, graying and greening to reiterate the message of snow and sun.

Wider still, the north edge of the lake meadow steps upward over its granite base. Where it levels off, the ponderosas grow, big and sturdy and full of cones. They stand staunch, widely spaced, allowing sunlight to filter through for wild geranium and kinnikinnik and tiny wild candytuft that crosses the dusky duff.

The south slope of the lake curves away from the shore, becoming more spruce-shaded as it retreats. This area is the first to be snow-covered, the last to be clear. Shade-tolerant plants root in the precipitous hillside, from here I can see a few late orange-red Indian paintbrush and the stalks of monkshood and larkspur. Dark-red strawberry blite ties down an old log with the help of raspberry and rose bushes. A few last aspens mingle with the spruces, trunks thin and pallid, most of their branches down from insufficient light. Above them the Douglas firs and spruces grow close together, presenting a solid wall of black-green.

The ever-widening circles of montane life culminate in these evergreens which intrude visually into the lake. Even in winter, when the India-ink reflections are gone, the uncompromising contrast of black and white still commands the eye. In the spring, when the air is heavy and laden with late snows, the lake reflects their pendent spires, solid as a German expressionist woodcut. In the summer the reflections shimmer in the breeze, slotted with blue sky, an animate Monet. In the fall they form a moving mosaic with the aspen when the wind fragments the surface to create tesserae of emerald and gold leaf — a Byzantine pavement.

It is impossible to look at the land and not be aware of the evergreens. In all seasons they dominate, unchanging in color, towering in size. Their spires crenelate the sky. Their opacity of color, depth, and density create a background against which are measured the brightness of aspen leaf, iridescence of dragonfly wing, scarlet of gilia, and gleam of lake. The ponderosa, spruce, and Douglasfir are the reminders of an end point of succession for this land, for there is no other vegetation that will replace them, short of catastrophic climate change.

These trees change the environment to fit their needs, making an acid soil which is inhospitable to other plants, attracting rain by the massiveness of their own transpiration. At the beginning of succession, moss and lichen grow a few centimeters above the ground and a few below. At the end of succession, for this land, trees tower many feet into the air and send their roots through the ground, demanding the most that the environment can give. These conifers will be there in decades, in centuries, to come. They will shade out other trees and brighter flowers, intrude into the deepening soil of the meadows. Succession is an inexorable progression which may be altered or disrupted but which will eternally begin again and again to achieve the same end. No emotional pleas or moral inducements will change it; to understand this is to accept the irrevocableness of nature.

ANNE ZWINGER (born 1925) is an artist and writer. Her work is a careful yet celebratory exploration of the land around her. It is a land to which she moved and with which she became involved as one might with a new-found passion. In this selection, a sense of self-affirmation of life and living colors the world around her that she sees and in which she takes root.

A. Carman Clark

From the *Orange Mailbox*

Twenty-six robins gathered on the back lawn at sunset. At dawn thirty or more juncos appeared on the front lawn. Such a contrast. The robins hopped quietly about respecting each other's space and feeding rights like a group of well-bred senior citizens about to begin a southern cruise together. The slate gray juncos flitted about like junior high students on a field trip. Four of them played a diving, dodging game over and under my car with startling agility and speed.

Signs of the season, these arrivals and departures of the birds accent the transition into colder weather. Weed seeds, the red berries on the asparagus ferns, and the squash seeds on the compost pile provide food for the finch tribe. The blue jays seem willing to try any morsels other birds discover, making loud comments between bites.

In late October a certain number of field mice decide to winter in my cellar and shed and there are always a few bright or persistent ones who find their way into the kitchen. Before the

traps and poison pellets control this immigration, seeing a mouse head appear out of the stove burner is just another sign of the drawing in when night temperatures drop below freezing.

This year the killing frost — what some old timers refer to as "black" frost — came in the middle of the night under the cold clear light of the hunter's moon. The chill set this old house to creaking and an icy cold permeated through every room. There was a spooky quality about the invading chill which stirred thoughts of science fiction with a frozen earth.

Thick white mist hung low over the valley at dawn and every twig and leaf was crisp with frost. The icy particles caught the beams of the rising sun, turning the fields to acres of diamonds.

By noon the spinach was a sodden black mess and even the Swiss chard dropped. Only the kale and parsnips retained their crisp greenness. The cherry and yellow plum tomatoes which had looked like bright Christmas ornaments swollen from the first light frost had burst and hung limp upon the leafless stems.

In a way it's a relief to have a definitive end to the garden season. I have no yen for year-round gardening. With the produce stored, canned or frozen, it's time for a transition to other interests.

With the drawing in as temperatures drop and daylight hours lessen, an anticipation of change brings pleasure. Company around the fireplace and savory stews from the abundance of vegetables. Yeast rolls golden with shredded carrots. Squash pie. Three new cookbooks await, and clippings from last month's magazine suggest dozens of new dishes. Pork pie (*tourtiere*) and Cornish pasties are hearty autumn foods and the hot peppers suggest a Texas chili.

Although transition and change are a known factor of life, the first icy mornings are chill reminders that winter is coming. The valley begins to hum with chain saws as the grasshoppers hurry to get the firewood cut and under cover. Jacketed figures toil at hooking in storm windows and families cooperate in lugging in the lawn furniture.

The list of last chores includes oiling the handles of the rakes and spades and trundling the wheel barrows into the cellar. When the garage is free of gardening equipment so the car can fit in beside the woodpiles, there's a feeling of being ready for winter.

The transition from swimming in the pond to exercising at the pool means missing the close-up sight of geese and ducks coming in at sunset to rest and feed along the coves. From the kitchen windows I can watch the Canadas circle down to the pond, but being in the water to see their group landing adds a touch of wonder to the whole image of all birds traveling thousands of miles each autumn. Their built-in weather indicators get them up and away before our local storms.

With the time of drawing in and enjoying the warmth of the fireside, it's also time to begin to listen for the sound of the owls. At dusk and at dawn their hoots can be heard from the woods and if I watch carefully, sometimes I see them carrying off mice from the field beyond the garden. With this first autumn leisure I'm trying to learn how to identify them by the rhythm and pitch of their calls. Another sound and sign of rural autumn.

A. CARMAN CLARK lives in Union, Maine. She has written for *Country Journal, Farm Journal* and *Women's Day,* and since 1982 has been writing a weekly column for *The Camden, Maine Herald* of her observations of life in and around her home. *From the Mailbox* is her first book, a delightful set of observations and feelings about country life.

Sally Carrighar

One Day at Teton Marsh
"The Varying Hare"

 he dry shine of the moon, that night, showed that the leaves were breaking away from the boughs. They were taking flight — like the small birds who had perched among them, were off in the air, free and wild. During previous weeks a few had drifted out singly, but, released by the wind, they departed in flocks.

As the Varying Hare hopped along her paths, leaves would race by above her. Others would skitter ahead on the ground, to drop when the wind slackened and then, caught up by the next gust, whirl away through the impatient rooted grasses.

When the sun rose in the morning, the Hare was back in her form. It was a fragile home, only a space between willow shrubs, but it always had been a pocket of shadow, where she was concealed on the brightest day. Now, however, she tried to hide among streaming lights. The blowy night had torn holes in her overhead screen, and the sun found its way through them.

The wind had died before dawn, for it was veering. But a fresh breeze was swinging the willows and swinging farther and faster the scraps of sunshine below. The branches would strain to one side, with a look of agonized tension would quiver against the wind's drive, and a new little covey of leaves would escape. Then the gust would withdraw its pressure. The riven boughs would spring back, and the beams wider now, would flow over the Hare.

To keep herself smooth, she sat facing the wind. Ahead were more willows, pierced for the first time by the glare of the pond. Her eyes, at the sides of her head, could see also the water-meadow behind her. The reed-grass there had stood tall and thick until recently, but, in dying, had bent down in hillocks. On the west side of the meadow, along the backwash of the pond, aspen brush grew on a low ridge of drier ground. It was thinner this morning. In the glittering tops was the shape of the boughs' coming bareness.

The Hare had been crouching with feet beneath her and ears flat along her neck. It was her sleeping position, as smooth as a weather-worn mound of earth. But this day she could not relax. She sat back like a small bundle suddenly breaking open. First licking the dust from the hairy palms of her forepaws, she scrubbed her face 'round and 'round, rolling her head. With her paws she pulled one of her long ears down against her cheek and brushed it; and brushed her other ear, and her sides, and back; and washed her hind feet. To be clean seemed to smooth her emotions, too. She lowered her ears, pulled in her shape, that her weight had hollowed. Openings in the branches above might expose her, but nothing had changed the cozy sensation beneath her, and she would console herself with it.

Even after she closed her eyes, she could feel the new, unfamiliar lights darting over them. Soon, though, no more of them touched her lids. She looked up and imperceptibly started, shrinking lower. For a march hawk was hovering over her thicket.

The feathered cross, balancing on the wind, broke the gleams in the leaves with a shadow, one shadow she did not like. It hung in the air, swaying sliding off as the hawk let the wind push him back but swinging forward again, tilting and leveling down, a threat that waited, a silent torment that still did not strike, never quite motionless but patient with the sense of its power.

The Hare was shaken with terror. She cast a frantic glance toward the red-grass and under adjoining willows; there was no deeper gloom in which she could hide. The hawk could not drop through the branches, even if they were entirely bare, but the Hare was excitable, likely to flee in a panic. Again he rode back on the wind, for an instant was blurred by the churning of blown boughs, but he swept ahead, dropping lower, and opened his claws and beak.

The Hare's fear was now at the last bearable point of it tension. Yet she did not break. The hope of the hawk already was sagging when his eye caught a quiver of grass at the side of her thicket. He turned, dipped, and alighted, his claw clutching a mouse.

He stayed on the ground while he ate it, near the Hare but not able to reach her and not once shifting his angry eyes in her direction. When he had finished his small meal, he lifted his wings and soared up and away.

The Hare continued to crouch in her form, with no sign to reveal the decision her nerves were making. Through half the summer these willows had been her refuge. She had been born on the other side of the meadow, under the aspen brush, but one day, returning there after a little canter, she had found a very disturbing thing. It was her mother's foot, with the scent of mink all around it. She had left the aspens then, to stay under these willows. She still kept the aspens for one of her covert-nooks, into which she could dodge when she was in danger, but the willows had been her form — till this morning. She no longer could trust them, now that a hawk had threatened her through their broken screen. Whether or not she knew it yet, she had lost the sense that this hideaway was her home.

Beside the fall of the leaves, the Hare had another problem — she herself had begun to shine. Several weeks before, her brown fur had started to shed when she licked it. Beneath growing up through her undercoat, was a new kind of hairs, white, the color to her of the noonday sun.

First her feet had turned white, and the fur on her soles had become long and stiff. When she bounded over the ground, spreading her toes, she came down on thick, springy pads and left much wider footprints. Denser white fur had grown over her ears. In summer the near-naked skin of her ears had helped her lose warmth and be comfortable. A few frosty nights had proved that they soon would need coverings. Her legs, then hips, shoulders, chest, and sides had whitened. On this day of the equinox only parts of her face and a strip down her back still were brown.

From her earliest life the Hare's eyes had led her away from the revealing sunlight. And now she could not escape anywhere from her own glisten. She was luminous even, because bubbles of air in her new hairs caught every faint gleam and enclosed her in a halo. Nature, having taught her to hide, had made hiding impossible.

Her instinct was groping for some solution.

Leave the thicket here, it suggested. A push on her toes sent her up in a rounded hop. Her forepaws touched earth, one then the other, to ease her down. Her hind feet, leap-frogging over, dropped in front of them . . . springing at once in a second soft bound. She didn't stretch out at full length when she jumped; she held her legs close to her, so that she tumbled ahead like a curl of white swan's-down, blowing.

She was passing the meadow, on a path she had flattened between the reed-grass and the shoreline willows. A few times she dodged into the brush, into her own familiar cover-nooks. On all of her trails she had shelters, with clear openings under the boughs that she could enter without a pause. She knew the location of each, the angle at which to approach it, and the pattern of leaps — alighting here, here, and here — that would take her to safety most quickly. This morning the shadows in all the nooks were as shredded as in her form, and she didn't stay long in any.

Rounding the Leopard Frog's puddle, then, she came to the aspen brush. A small, slow, conclusive hop took her under, and she huddled down in soft earth. The branches above her were nearly stripped, and the sun, splashing into the shelter here, may have shocked her more than the light in the willows did. For this nook was the kindling place where she and her brother and sister had come into life. More precocious than little rabbits, the hares were born fully furred and with open eyes. Soon they had been able to swing their ears to their mother's delicate bounds approaching, and to the terrible screams of ravens, harsh as rocks breaking on rocks. Their mother had left at once and returned only to feed her leverets. It was the aspen leaves that protected them from the menacing birds above, from hawks, owls, and eagles, as well as the ravens.

The leaves silken incessant whisper had been as comforting to the Hare as the touch of her mother's tongue, licking her while she nursed. And ever since, there had been a happy relationship between the Hare, who avoided light, and the leaves, which layered themselves into a cover in order to find it. Leaves had another meaning. She had been only a week old when she crept out, with motions as unaggressive as theirs, tasted a stalk of sorrel, and found its sharp flavor as good in her mouth as milk. Her life had been filled with the ministrations of leaves. They were the lovable things to the Hare, as stones were to the marmots and logs to the salamanders.

And now suddenly they were deserting her. They were failing her neighbors too, that fall morning. The grass near the aspen brush glinted with dragonfly wings. Every summer evening the dragons had gathered, for some reason they knew, at this small part of the meadow. Clinging low on the stems, they were sheltered from wind and cold as they slept. Moose had rested here in the sunshine, but the grass always rose again when they left — until one day late in August. When the insects came home that night, they found that their grass was flat. Some had sought other perches, but many had settled onto the prostrate blades and, exposed there, had frozen. Water-shrews had eaten their bodies and discarded the wings.

On the other side of the Hare the movements of mourning doves smoothed past her gaze. The birds walked about in the bed or sorrel, selecting a seed from a stalk here and farther along another. Their heads tilted gently to examine the seeds and then nodded with each intimately touching step. The foraging was sedate and slow, although the birds must have sensed that the marsh plants, which had fed them with buds, seeds, and berries, soon would have nothing more for them.

Beyond the doves was the pond. Thirsty, the Hare left her nook and set herself down in several airy jumps to the shore. As she lapped the water, a muskrat passed, swimming home with a sheaf of cut bur-reeds in her mouth. All the floating reeds had been ice-coated this morning. Farther along the shore a pintail stood in a mat of the plants that human beings named bedstraw, because they liked to believe that the Christ child's manger was filled with something so tiny and sweet. The duck was tweaking off ends of the sprays, where seeds had replaced the little white flowers. The duck, the doves, muskrat, the Hare, and most other plant-eating creatures were a company of the harmless — almost too mild and shy, it seemed, to meet such a violent change as the coming of winter.

The Hare, having drunk, was ready herself for food. She nipped a clover stem close to the root and drew it in, bit by bit, as she chewed. Then she reached for another, forepaws hopping ahead and hind feet stepping up leisurely to enclose them. The leaves of the clover were smaller now than in summer, and she didn't find one blossom with its delectable honey taste. Whole parts of the patch were bared, for she had cropped it through many weeks, and the clover was only attempting to stay alive; it no longer was growing. As she munched along, her eyes were half-closed with dreamy pleasure, but her ears were alert, lightly turning in separate directions or swinging in unison. They were sensitive ears; when all the green plants of the marsh were expanding, they may have caught a minute murmur of growth. If they reached now for that sound, they found only silence.

The Hare came to a gentian, a march bluebell, and a lupine — all fresh, as if the season, for them alone, were spring. They were but three small flowers; when she severed a stalk of meadowsweet, the dust of its dead blooms fell over her. Her bite, jarring a silky white head of goldenrod, loosened it, and it blew away. She ate and enjoyed the fine blades of blue-grass, although they were dry; but she found that a fireweed had a coarser harsh flavor. Most of the plants had a different taste now, bitter, as if they resented what the autumn was doing to them.

The Hare turned back to the aspen nook but as soon as her meal was digested wanted to leave. No other place lured her; she had merely a sense that sitting under these boughs was no longer the thing to do. She hopped along one of her paths in the meadow, reached a moose-bed, and found herself leaping straight up and down! She was making showy white bounds higher, even, than the heads of the standing grasses! The next time she sprang in the air, she twisted herself at the top of the leap so that she came to earth faced the opposite way. She jumped again, turned about, and reversed her direction. She had done this before. It was a comic impulse that slipped through her caution occasionally, but always till now in the dark of night. And here she was hurling her dazzling new self into sunlight!

Bounding across the meadow, she came to a line of willow shrubs. She had covert-nooks here but didn't go into them. She leapt, instead, over a thicket — a great arc that brought her down on the other side, in a place new to her.

This was a flat ledge behind the bank of a river, which the Hare had avoided because she would be too exposed on its low bed of scouring rushes and moss. Now, however, she raced about over it as if she were chasing some invisible playmate. At the edge of the water she stopped, resting upon her haunches, with her forelegs straightened below her shoulders. The river's swift movement, its rush and roar seemed to excite her. She swung back, sitting upright, and whirled her forepaws in the air.

But other hares should be here. Her heart may have felt suddenly pinched by the strangeness, for she turned away from the heavy tide, rolling past, and thumped on the ground with one of her hind feet. It was a hare's way of signaling to companions, and after she pounded a few times, she would listen. No one answered. She left the river, passed the willows, and was once more in her meadow. She would return to the aspens, for uneasiness swept her.

As she was bounding along her trail, the marsh hawk swung over the aspen tops. Even before he had cleared them, the Hare's eyes had detected his smooth streaming behind the last quivering leaves. How long he hops now — and how swift! She was leaping at mad speed, sure of the entrance among the boughs. But the hawk was crossing the aspens, was swooping down, and had leveled above her with spread claws toward her back.

Into the narrowing instant dived an enemy of the hawk himself. A young Osprey, seeing a chance to torment his foe, struck out from his perch. The wings of the birds entangled, the two beat their way off toward the lower end of the pond. The Hare was safe under her brush, forgotten if not concealed.

Her heart's thumping rocked her, but not for long. At the edge of the pond the Leopard Frog thrashed about in a heron's beak. The Hare watched them, so interested that her fears began slipping away. A bull

Moose and a cow raced out over the meadow. The hoofs' pounding startled the Hare, but she turned, in order to see the huge creatures clearly, and soon was curious more than alarmed. In their chase was a weird buffoonery, like a great grotesque shadow of her own antic racing.

Something in her temperament seemed to be opening out, since she was white and almost everywhere sun-lighted, and no longer could hide. The loosening of her secretiveness had been paced with the changes of autumn. It was slow at first, now was progressing more rapidly. Inasmuch as the leaves were falling, exposing hideaways, all the animals were compelled to face each other as they had not in the summer. Others besides the Hare were darting about with new courage, or a new reliance on bluff.

She started forth again. While she was sitting among the sedges, eating a tuber, a furious gust of wind blew over the dead tree where the Osprey had perched. Even the snags and the bare boughs, as well as the grass and leaves, seemed to be coming down.

The crash of the tree frightened her, as it did all the animals, but she soon recovered her poise and went about, savoring her new sense of freedom. The tree had been part of the beaver dam, and its overturn opened the dam, letting the pond start to flow away. The lowering of the water made the Hare's neighbors, those who lived in the pond or entered it, apprehensive. Some already were suffocating in the dry air that their gills could not breathe. Surrounded by panic, the Hare jumped and tumbled in droll solitary games. She had not played as much at any time since her brother and sister left to find homes somewhere outside the marsh.

SALLY CARRIGHAR is a writer and naturalist. This extraordinary woman wrote for the motion pictures between 1923 and 1928, and then for radio from 1928 to 1938. She attributes her love of nature and her fascination with the details of how it works to the summers spent at her grandparents' house in Ohio, where most of her play was outside. She later spent several summers exploring the Canadian woods and the Rockies. She began writing books in 1937. This selection from *One Day at Teton Marsh* talks about a different kind of discovery and challenge — from a snow hare's point of view — in which every moment of life is filled with the challenge of just surviving.

Annie Dillard

Pilgrim at Tinker Creek

When I was six or seven years old, growing up in Pittsburgh, I used to take a precious penny of my own and hide it for someone else to find. It was a curious compulsion; sadly, I've never been seized by it since. For some reason I always "hid" the penny along the same stretch of sidewalk up the street. I would cradle it at the roots of a sycamore, say, or in a hole left by a chipped-off piece of sidewalk. Then I would take a piece of chalk, and starting at either end of the block, draw huge arrows leading up to the penny from both directions. After I learned to write I labeled the arrows: SURPRISE AHEAD or MONEY THIS WAY. I was greatly excited, during all this arrow-drawing, at the thought of the first lucky passer-by who would receive in this way, regardless of merit, a free gift from the universe. But I never lurked about. I would go straight home and not give the matter another thought, until, some months later, I would be gripped again by the impulse to hide another penny.

It is still the first week in January, and I've got great plans. I've been thinking about seeing. There are lots of things to see, unwrapped gifts and free surprises. The world is fairly studded and strewn with pennies cast broadside from a generous hand. But — and this is the point — who gets excited by a mere penny? If you follow one arrow, if you crouch motionless on a bank to watch a tremulous ripple thrill on the water and are rewarded by the sight of a muskrat kit paddling from its den, will you count that sight a chip of copper only, and go your rueful way? It is dire poverty indeed when a man is so malnourished and fatigued that he won't stoop to pick up a penny. But if you cultivate a healthy poverty and simplicity, so that finding a penny will literally make your day, then, since the world is in fact planted in pennies, you have with your poverty bought a lifetime of days. It is that simple. What you see is what you get.

I used to be able to see flying insects in the air. I'd look ahead and see, not the row of hemlocks across the road, but the air in front of it. My eyes would focus along that column of air, picking out flying insects. But I lost interest, I guess, for I dropped the habit. Now I can see birds. Probably some people can look at the grass at their feet and discover all the crawling creatures. I would like to know grasses and sedges — and care. Then my least journey into the world would be a field trip, a series of happy recognitions. Thoreau, in an expansive mood, exulted, "What a rich book might be made about buds, including, perhaps, sprouts!" It would be nice to think so. I cherish mental images I have of three perfectly happy people. One collects stones. Another — an Englishman, say — watches clouds. The third lives on a coast and collects drops of seawater which he examines microscopically and mounts. But I don't see what the specialist sees, and so I cut myself off, not only from the total picture, but from the various forms of happiness.

Unfortunately, nature is very much a now-you-see-it, now-you-don't affair. A fish flashes, then dissolves in the water before my eyes like so much salt. Deer apparently ascend bodily into heaven; the brightest oriole fades into leaves. These disappearances stun me into stillness and concentration; they say of nature that it conceals with a grand nonchalance, and they say of vision that it is a deliberate gift, the revelation of a dancer who for my eyes only flings away her seven veils. For nature does reveal as well as conceal: now-you-don't-see-it, now-you-do. For a week last September migrating red-winged blackbirds were feeding heavily down by the creek at the back of the house. One day I went out to investigate the racket; I walked up to a tree, an Osage orange, and a hundred birds flew away. They simply materialized out of the tree. I saw a tree, then a whisk of color, then a tree again. I walked closer and another hundred blackbirds took flight. Not a branch, not a twig budged: the birds were apparently weightless as well as invisible. Or, it was as if the leaves of the Osage orange had been freed from a spell in the form of red-winged blackbirds; they flew from the tree, caught my eye in the sky, and vanished. When I looked again at the tree the leaves had reassembled as if nothing had happened. Finally I walked directly to the trunk of the tree and a final hundred, the real diehards, appeared, spread, and vanished. How could so many hide in the tree without my seeing them? The Osage orange, unruffled, looked just as it had looked from the house, when three hundred red-winged blackbirds cried from its crown. I looked downstream where they flew, and they were gone. Searching, I couldn't spot one. I wandered downstream to force them to play their hand, but they'd crossed the creek and scattered. One show to a customer. These appearances catch at my throat; they are the free gifts, the bright coppers at the roots of trees.

It's all a matter of keeping my eyes open. Nature is like one of those line drawings of a tree that are puzzles for children: Can you find hidden in the leaves a duck, a house, a boy, a bucket, a zebra, and a boot? Specialists can find the most incredibly well-hidden things. A book I read when I was young recommended an easy way to find caterpillars to rear: you simply find some fresh caterpillar droppings, look up, and there's your caterpillar. More recently an author advised me to set my mind at ease about those piles of cut stems on the ground in grassy fields. Field mice make them; they cut the grass down by degrees to reach the seeds at the head. It seems that when the grass is tightly packed, as in a field of ripe grain, the blade won't topple at a single cut through the stem; instead, the cut stem simply drops vertically, held in the crush of grain. The mouse severs the bottom again and again, the stem keeps dropping an inch at a time, and finally the head is low enough for the mouse to reach the seeds. Meanwhile, the mouse is positively littering the field with its little piles of cut stems into which, presumably, the author of the book is constantly stumbling.

If I can't see these minutiae, I still try to keep my eyes open. I'm always on the lookout for antlion traps in sandy soil, monarch pupae near milkweed, skipper larvae in locust leaves. These things are utterly common, and I've not seen one. I bang on hollow trees near water, but so far no flying squirrels have appeared. In flat country I watch every sunset in hopes of seeing the green ray. The green ray is a seldom-seen streak of light that rises from the sun like a spurting fountain at the moment of sunset; it throbs into the sky for two seconds and disappears. One more reason to keep my eyes open. A photography professor at the University of Florida just happened to see a bird die in midflight; it jerked, died, dropped, and smashed on the ground. I squint at the wind because I read Stewart Edward White: "I have always maintained that if you looked closely enough you could *see* the wind — the dim, hardly-made-out, fine debris fleeing high in the air." White was an excellent observer, and devoted an entire chapter of *The Mountains* to the subject of seeing deer: "As soon as you can forget the naturally obvious and construct an artificial obvious, then you too will see deer."

But the artificial obvious is hard to see. My eyes account for less than one percent of the weight of my head; I'm bony and dense; I see what I expect. I once spent a full three minutes looking at a bullfrog that was so unexpectedly large I couldn't see it even though a dozen enthusiastic campers were shouting directions. Finally I asked, "What color am I looking for?" and a fellow said, "Green." When at last I picked out the frog, I saw what painters are up against: the thing wasn't green at all, but the color of wet hickory bark.

The lover can see, and the knowledgeable. I visited an aunt and uncle at a quarter-horse ranch in Cody, Wyoming. I couldn't do much of anything useful, but I could, I thought, draw. So, as we all sat around the kitchen table after supper, I produced a sheet paper and drew a horse. "That's one lame horse," my aunt volunteered. The rest of the family joined in: "Only place to saddle that one is his neck"; "Looks like we better shoot the poor thing, on account of those terrible growths." Meekly, I slid the pencil and paper down the table. Everyone in that family, including my three young cousins, could draw a horse.

Beautifully. When the paper came back it looked as though five shining, real quarter horses had been corralled by mistake with a papier-machéé moose; the real horses seemed to gaze at the monster with a steady, puzzled air. I stay away from horses now, but I can do a creditable goldfish. The point is that I just don't know what the lover knows; I just can't see the artificial obvious that those in the know construct. The herpetologist asks the native, "Are there snakes in that ravine?" "Nosir." And the herpetologist comes home with, yessir, three bags full. Are there butterflies on that mountain? Are the bluets in bloom, are there arrowheads here, or fossil shells in the shale?

Peeping through my keyhole I see within the range of only about thirty percent of the light that comes from the sun; the rest is infrared and some little ultraviolet, perfectly apparent to many animals, but invisible to me. A nightmare network of ganglia, charged and firing without my knowledge, cuts and splices what I do see, editing it for my brain. Donald E. Carr points out that the sense impressions of one-celled animals are *not* edited for the brain: "This is philosophically interesting in a rather mournful way, since it means that only the simplest animals perceive the universe as it is."

A fog that won't burn away drifts and flows across my field of vision. When you see fog move against a back drop of deep pines, you don't see the fog itself, but streaks of clearness floating across the air in dark shreds. So I see only tatters of clearness through a pervading obscurity. I can't distinguish the fog from the overcast sky; I can't be sure if the light is direct or reflected. Everywhere darkness and the presence of the unseen appalls. We estimate now that only one atom dances alone in every cubic meter of intergalactic space. I blink and squint. What planet or power yanks Halley's Comet out of orbit? We haven't see that force yet; it's a question of distance, density, and the pallor of reflected light. We rock, cradled in the swaddling band of darkness. Even the simple darkness of night whispers suggestions to the mind. Last summer, in August, I stayed at the creek too late.

Where Tinker Creek flows under the sycamore log bridge to the tear-shaped island, it is slow and shallow, fringed thinly in cattail marsh. At this spot an astonishing bloom of life supports vast breeding populations of insects, fish, reptiles, birds, and mammals. On windless summer evenings I stalk along the creek bank or straddle the sycamore log in absolute stillness, watching for muskrats. The night I stayed too late I was hunched on the log staring spellbound at spreading, reflected stains of lilac on the water. A cloud in the sky suddenly lighted as if turned on by a switch; its reflection just as suddenly materialized on the water upstream, flat and floating, so that I couldn't see the creek bottom, or life in the water under the cloud. Downstream, away from the cloud on the water, water turtles smooth as beans were gliding down with the current in a series of easy, weightless push-offs, as men bound on the moon. I didn't know whether to trace the progress of one turtle I was sure of, risking sticking my face in one of the bridge's spider webs made invisible by the gathering dark, or take a chance on seeing the carp, or scan the mudbank in hope of seeing a muskrat, or follow the last of the swallows who caught at my heart and trailed it after them like streamers as they appeared from directly below, under the log, flying upstream with their tails forked, so fast.

But shadows spread, and deepened, and stayed. After thousands of years we're still strangers to darkness, fearful aliens in an enemy camp with our arms crossed over our chests. I stirred. A land turtle on the bank, startled, hissed the air from its lungs and withdrew into its shell. An uneasy pink here, an unfathomable blue there, gave great suggestion of lurking beings. Things were going on. I couldn't see whether that sere rustle I heard was a distant rattlesnake, slit-eyed, or a nearby sparrow kicking in the dry flood debris slung at the foot of a willow. Tremendous action roiled the water everywhere I looked, big action, inexplicable. A tremor welled up beside a gaping muskrat burrow in the bank and I caught my breath, but no muskrat appeared. The ripples continued to fan upstream with a steady, powerful thrust. Night was knitting over my face an eyeless mask, and I still sat transfixed. A distant airplane, a delta wing out of nightmare, made a gliding shadow on the creek's bottom that looked like a stingray cruising upstream. At once a black fin slit the pink cloud on the water, shearing it in two. The two halves merged together and seemed to dissolve before my eyes. Darkness pooled in the cleft of the creek and rose, as water collects in a well. Untamed, dreaming lights flickered over the sky. I saw hints of hulking underwater shadows, two pale splashes out of the water, and round ripples rolling close together from a blackened center.

At last I stared upstream where only the deepest violet remained of the cloud, a cloud so high its underbelly still glowed feeble color reflected from a hidden sky lighted in turn by a sun halfway to China. And out of that violet, a sudden enormous black body arced over the water. I saw only a cylindrical sleekness. Head and tail, if there was a head and tail, were both submerged in cloud. I saw only one ebony fling, a headlong dive to darkness; then the waters closed, and the lights went out.

I walked home in a shivering daze, up hill and down. Later I lay open-mouthed in bed, my arms flung wide at my sides to steady the whirling darkness. At this latitude I'm spinning 836 miles an hour round the earth's axis; I often fancy I feel my sweeping fall as a breakneck arc like the dive of dolphins, and the hollow rushing of wind raises hair on my neck and the side of my face. In orbit around the sun I'm moving 64,800 miles an hour. The solar system as a whole, like a merry-go-round unhinged, spins, bobs, and blinks at the speed of 43,200 miles an hour along a course set east of Hercules. Someone has piped, and we are dancing a tarantella until the sweat pours. I open my eyes and I see dark, muscled forms curl out of water, with flapping gills and flattened eyes. I close my eyes and I see stars, deep stars giving way to deeper stars, deeper stars blowing to deepest stars at the crown of an infinite cone.

"Still," wrote Van Gogh in a letter, "a great deal of light falls on everything." If we are blinded by darkness, we are also blinded by light. When too much light falls on everything, a special terror results. Peter Freuchen describes the notorious kayak sickness to which Greenland Eskimos are prone. "The Greenland fjords are peculiar for the spells of completely quiet weather, when there is not enough wind to blow out a match and the water is like a sheet of glass. The kayak hunter must sit on his boat without stirring a finger so as not to scare the shy seals away . . . The sun, low in the sky, sends a glare into his eyes, and the landscape around moves into the realm of the unreal. The reflex from the mirror-like water hypnotizes him, he seems to be unable to move, all of a sudden it is as if he were floating in a bottomless void, sinking , sinking, and sinking . . . Horror-stricken, he tries to stir, to cry out, but he cannot, he is completely paralyzed, he just falls and falls." Some hunters are especially cursed with this panic, and bring ruin and sometimes starvation to their families.

ANNIE DILLARD was born in 1945. She has been an editor and a teacher of poetry and calls herself a "a poet and a walker with a background in theology and a penchant for quirky facts." *Pilgram at Tinker Creek* is the remarkable result of one year of her living in the country. It is but one year of an entire life of discovery of new ways of seeing, but the author rankles at the suggestion that it was easy to write. "The truth is your life is literature, and *Pilgrim at Tinker Creek* is the result of hard work. They think you just sit on a tree stump and take dictation from some little chipmunk." Join her in a new way of seeing.

Joseph Wood Krutch

The Desert Year
"From a Mountaintop"

In the legends of saints and the prophets, either a desert or a mountain is pretty sure to figure. It is usually in the middle of one or on the top of the other that the vision comes or the test is met. To give their message to the world they come down or come out, but it is almost invariably in a solitude, either high or dry, that it is first revealed.

Moses and Zoroaster climbed up; Buddha sat down; Mohammed fled. Each in his own way had to separate himself from men before he could discover what it was that he had to say to mankind. In a "wilderness" (Near Eastern and therefore certainly xeric) Jesus prepared himself for the mountaintop from which he would reject the world which Satan would offer. Loneliness is essential and loneliness, it would seem, is loneliest where the air is either thin or dry and nature herself does not riot too luxuriously. If Plato was satisfied with no more than a grove in Athens, that was because he was already halfway to the mere college professor.

Yesterday, when I stood on a peak and looked down at an arid emptiness, I felt on my shoulders an awful responsibility. Under such circumstances as these, said I to myself, other men have grown wise. Only a few before me have ever had the double advantage of mountain and desert. It is now or never. If THE ANSWER is ever to be whispered into my willing ear, this should be the moment.

No awful presence — I hasten to add — handed me any tablets of the law. Neither did Satan appear to offer me the world, and if he had done so I might, for all I can really know, have taken him up. Yet it did seem that I saw something with unusual clearness and that I came down not quite empty-handed.

From where I stood there was no visible evidence that the earth was inhabited. Like some astronomer peering through a telescope at the planet Mars, I could only say, "It might be." It was thus the world must have looked at the end of the fifth day, and I found myself wondering whether the text of Genesis might not possibly be garbled; whether, perchance, it was really after the fifth, not after the sixth day, that God looked at his work and saw that it was good. Would not I, in His place, have stopped right there? Would I have risked the addition of a disturbing element? Was the world ever again so obviously good?

But God's decisions are, by definition, wise, and presumably He knew what He was doing. Perhaps, as some have fancied, He wanted one more projection of Himself to contemplate. Perhaps, as the deists supposed, man is an essential link in that Great Chain of Being which stretches unbroken from the most imperfect up to perfection itself. But in any event, here we are! And here, too, are others, sometimes exasperatingly like us, sometimes exasperatingly different. With ourselves and with these others we must somehow deal.

If one could stay on the mountaintop there would be no problem. To be wise there would be easy. Poetry and philosophy, self-generated, would suffice. But for reasons psychological as well as physical, that we cannot do. Sooner or later we must come down and mingle more or less intimately with populations more or less dense. Men we must meet, and when we meet them we meet Problems. The wisdom found on the mountaintop is not a sufficient guide in the populous lowlands. We must reckon with something which, up there, existed only in the mind or the memory.

But if wisdom, complete and adequate, cannot be brought down, there is something which can and that something is to be found no-where else. Only from such distance can man be seen either in perspec-tive or in his real context, and it is the absence of that context which in-validates all the solutions to human problems formulated — as today all such solutions are — in no context except that of men's own mak-ing. Without this perspective and this context, philosophy and religion degenerate into sociology; and sociology is merely a modern substitute for wisdom. What it lacks is not merely the context of nature, indi-spensible as that is. It lacks also the context of human nature itself, for which it tries foolishly to substitute some mere observations of human behavior. It calls itself the science of Man, but it has forgotten to ask what Man is really like. The sociologist leaves himself out (he calls this "objectivity") and therefore he leaves out the only thing which would give him a clue to the rest.

Not to have known — as most men have not — either the moun-tain or the desert is not to have known one's self. Not to have known one's self is to have known no one, and to have known no one makes it relatively easy to suppose, as sociology commonly does, that the cen-tral problems are the problems of technology and politics. It makes it possible to believe that if the world has gone wrong — and seems like-ly to go wronger — that is only because production and distribution are out of balance or the proper exercise of the franchise has not yet been developed; that a different tax structure or even, God save the mark, the abolition of the poll tax in Alabama, point the way to Utopia. It is to forget too easily that the question of the Good Life — both the ques-tion what it is and the question how it can be found — has to do, first of all, not with human institutions but with the human being himself; that what one needs to ask first is not "What is a just social order?" or, "In what does true democracy consist?" but "What is Man?"

That question neither the usual politician, nor the usual econom-ist, nor the usual scientist has ever asked, because he has never been alone. No man in the middle of a desert or on top of a mountain ever fell victim to the delusion that he himself was nothing except the pro-duct of social forces, that all he needed was a proper orientation in his economic group, or that production per man hour was a true index of happiness. No such man, if he permitted himself to think at all, ever thought anything except that consciousness was the grandest of all facts and that no good life for either the individual or a group was possible on any other assumption. No man in such a position ever doubted that he himself was a primary particle, an ultimate reality.

Respectable universities, before they confer the degree which certifies that the recipient is now wise in philosophy, in science, or in sociology, commonly require a minimum period of "residence." They might well require also a supplementary period of "non-residence," to be passed neither at the university nor in any other populous place but alone. They might consider the fact that a knowledge of one's self is as important as a knowledge of Latin and two modern languages. Already having an athletic field, they might even persuade some wealthy alumnus to make the gift of a Thebaid to which candidates could retire for six months. I can think of nothing more likely to change the direction of our thinking, and many who agree on nothing else agree that it ought to be changed.

JOSEPH WOOD KRUTCH (1898 - 1970) was an author, editor, naturalist, and conservationist. A teacher and scientist, he feared the effect science and modern technology might have on the future of land and wildlife. A respiratory ailment encouraged him to move to the arid southwest, where he lived out his final years in the Sonoran Desert near Tucson, where he came to thoroughly enjoy the beauty of the desert and its wildlife. This selection brings us to the awareness the wilderness has played in history to philosophers, religious figures, and finally, to ourselves.

Loren Eiseley

The Immense Journey
"The Flow of the River"

If there is magic on this planet, it is contained in water. Its least stir even, as now in a rain pond on a flat roof opposite my office, is enough to bring me searching to the window. A wind ripple may be translating itself into life. I have a constant feeling that some time I may witness that momentous miracle on a city roof, see life veritably and suddenly boiling out of a heap of rusted pipes and old television aerials. I marvel at how suddenly a water beetle has come and is submarining there in a spatter of green algae. Thin vapors, rust, wet tar and sun are an alembic remarkably like the mind; they throw off odorous shadows that threaten to take real shape when no one is looking.

Once in a lifetime, perhaps, one escapes the actual confines of the flesh. Once in a lifetime, if one is lucky, one so merges with sunlight and air and running water that whole eons, the eons that mountains and deserts know, might pass in a single afternoon without discomfort.

The mind has sunk away into its beginnings among old roots and the obscure tricklings and movings that stir inanimate things. Like the charmed fairy circle into which a man once stepped, and upon emergence learned that a whole century had passed in a single night, one can never quite define this secret; but it has something to do, I am sure, with common water. Its substance reaches everywhere; it touches the past and prepares the future; it moves under the poles and wanders thinly in the heights of air. It can assume forms of exquisite perfection in a snowflake, or strip the living to a single shining bone cast up by the sea.

Many years ago, in the course of some scientific investigations in a remote western county, I experienced, by chance, precisely the sort of curious absorption by water — the extension of shape by osmosis — at which I have been hinting. You have probably never experienced in yourself the meandering roots of a whole watershed or felt your outstretched fingers touching, by some kind of clairvoyant extension, the brooks of snow-line glaciers at the same time that you were flowing toward the Gulf over the eroded debris of worn-down mountains. A poet, MacKnight Black, has spoken of being "limbed . . . with waters gripping pole and pole." He had the idea, all right, and it is obvious that these sensations are not unique, but they are hard to come by; and the sort of extension of the senses that people will accept when they put their ear against a sea shell, they will smile at in the confessions of a bookish professor. What makes it worse is the fact that because of a traumatic experience in childhood, I am not a swimmer, and am inclined to be timid before any large body of water. Perhaps it was just this, in away, that contributed to my experience.

As it leaves the Rockies and moves downward over the high plains towards the Missouri, the Platte River is a curious stream. In the spring floods, on occasion, it can be a mile-wide roaring torrent of destruction, gulping farms and bridges. Normally, however, it is a rambling, dispersed series of streamlets flowing erratically over great sand and gravel fans that are, in part, the remnants of a mightier Ice Age stream bed. Quicksands and shifting islands haunt its waters. Over it the prairie suns beat mercilessly throughout the summer. The Platte, "a mile wide and an inch deep," is a refuge for any heat-weary pilgrim along its shores. This is particularly true on the high plains before its long march by the cities begins.

The reason that I came upon it when I did, breaking through a willow thicket and stumbling out through ankle-deep water to a dune in the shade, is of no concern to this narrative. On various purposes of science I have ranged over a good bit of that country on foot, and I know the kinds of bones that come gurgling up through the gravel pumps, and the arrowheads of shining chalcedony that occasionally spill out of water-loosened sand. On that day, however, the sight of sky and willows and the weaving net of water murmuring a little in the shallows on its way to the Gulf stirred me, parched as I was with miles of walking, with a new idea: I was going to float. I was going to undergo a tremendous adventure.

The notion came to me, I suppose, by degrees. I had shed my clothes and was floundering pleasantly in a hole among some reeds when a great desire to stretch out and go with this gently insistent water began to pluck at me. Now to this bronzed, bold, modern generation, the struggle I waged with timidity while standing there in knee-deep water can only seem farcical; yet actually for me it was not so. A near-drowning accident in childhood had scarred my reactions; in addition to the fact that I was a nonswimmer, this "inch-deep river" was treacherous with holes and quicksands. Death was not precisely infrequent along its wandering and illusory channels. Like all broad wastes of this kind, where neither water nor land quite prevails, its thickets were lonely and untraversed. A man in trouble would cry out in vain.

I thought of all this, standing quietly in the water, feeling the sand shifting away under my toes. Then I lay back in the floating position that left my face to the sky, and shoved off. The sky wheeled over me. For an instant, as I bobbed into the main channel, I had the sensation of sliding down the vast tilted face of the continent. It was then that I felt the cold needles of the alpine springs at my fingertips, and the warmth of the Gulf pulling me southward. Moving with me, leaving its taste upon my mouth and spouting under me in dancing springs of sand, was the immense body of the continent itself, flowing like the river was flowing, grain by grain, mountain by mountain, down to the sea. I was streaming over ancient sea beds thrust aloft where giant reptiles had once sported; I was wearing down the face of time and trundling cloud-wreathed ranges into oblivion. I touched my margins with the delicacy of a crayfish's antennae, and felt great fishes glide about their work.

I drifted by stranded timber cut by beaver in mountain fastnesses; I slid over shallows that had buried the broken axles of prairie schooners and the mired bones of mammoth. I was streaming alive through the hot and working ferment of the sun, or oozing secretively through shady thickets. I *was* water and the unspeakable alchemies that gestate and take shape in water, the slimy jellies that under the enormous magnification of the sun writhe and whip upward as great barbeled fish mouths, or sink indistinctly back into the murk out of which they arose. Turtle and fish and the pinpoint chirpings of individual frogs are all watery projections, concentrations — as man himself is a concentration — of that indescribable and liquid brew which is compounded in varying proportions of salt and sun and time. It has appearances, but at its heart lies water, and as I was finally edged gently against a sand bar and dropped like any log, I tottered as I rose. I knew once more the body's revolt against emergence into the harsh and unsupporting air, its reluctance to break contact with that mother element which still, at this late point in time, shelters and brings into being nine tenths of everything alive.

As for men, those myriad little detached ponds with their own swarming corpuscular life, what were they but a way that water has of going about beyond the reach of rivers? I, too, was a microcosm of pouring rivulets and floating driftwood gnawed by the mysterious animalcules of my own creation. I was three fourths water, rising and subsiding according to the hollow knocking in my veins: a minute pulse like the eternal pulse that lifts Himalayas and which, in the following systole, will carry them away.

LOREN EISELEY (1907-1977) was born in Lincoln, Nebraska. He had a Ph.D. in Anthropology and was called by some a "scientist who could write." His provocative writing was filled with discovery of man's place in this world. This selection was taken from *The Immense Journey,* one of Eiseley's best known works on discovery of life and sense of place on the plains near his home.

Barry Holstun Lopez

River Notes:
The Dance of Herons
"The Shallows"

The overall impression here, as one surveys the river spread out over the gravel bars, is of a suspension of light, as though light were reverberating on a membrane. And a loss of depth. The slope of the riverbed here is nearly level, so the movement of water slows; shallowness heightens the impression of transparency and a feeling for the texture of the highly polished stones just underwater. If you bring your eye to within a few inches of the surface, each stone appears to be submerged in glycerin yet still sharply etched, as if held closely under a strong magnifying glass in summer light. An illusion — that insight into the stone is possible, that all distraction can be peeled away or masked off, as in preparation for surgery, while sunlight penetrates and highlights — is encouraged.

Beyond the light, a loss of depth, as the subsurface nears the surface as though the river were exposing itself to examination. Kneel with your ear to the water; beyond the *plorp* of it in a hollow and the slooshing gurgle through labyrinthine gravels, are the more distant sound of its fugue. A musical notebook lies open — alto and soprano clefs, notes tied and trills, turned notes, indications of arpeggio and glissando. Plunge your ear in suddenly — how it vanishes. Take the surface of the river between your thumb and forefinger. These textures are exquisite, unexpected.

Step back. The light falling on the dry rocks beneath our feet seems leathery by comparison. And this is another difference: the light on the dry rock is direct, shaftlike, almost brutal, so rigid one can imagine a sound like crystal lightly stung with a fingernail if it were touched; while the cooler light on the rocks in the water is indirect, caressing. This is why if you pluck a stone from the water and allow it to dry it seems to shrivel. It is the same as that phenomenon where at dusk you are able to see more clearly at the periphery of your vision. An indirect approach, the sidelong glance of the sun through the water, coaxes out the full character of the naturally reticent stone.

Fish are most exposed in the shallows, and so move through quickly. One afternoon I saw an osprey here, reminiscent of a grizzly at the water's edge anticipating salmon. A fish came by: he took off lightly and snatched it from the water.

Here, step across; you'll be able to examine things better out on the gravel bars. (We are fortunate for the day — temperatures in the eighties I understand.) Look, now at the variety of stones. Viewed from the bank these gravel bars seem uniformly gray, but bend close and you see this is not true. It's as though at first glance nothing were given away. You could regard this as the stone's effort to guard against intrusion by the insincere. Here, look at these: the red, chert, a kind of quartz; this streaked gray, basalt; the greenish one, a sedimentary rock, shale, stained with copper; the blue — this is uncommon: chrysocolla, a silicate. The white, quartzite. Obsidian. Black glass. This brown, andesite. It's reassuring to hear the names, but it's not so important to remember them. It's more important to see that these are pieces of the earth, reduced, ground down to an essential statement, that in our lifetime they are irreducible. This is one of the differences between, say, stones and flowers.

I used to throw a few stones out into the river — underhand with a flick of the wrist, like this.

It is relatively simple, in a place where the river slows like this, fans out over the gravel, to examine aspects of its life, to come to some understanding of its history. See, for example, where this detritus has caught in the rocks? Raccoon whisker. Hemlock twig. Dead bumblebee. Deer-head orchid. Maidenhair fern. These are dry willow leaves of some sort. There are so many willows, all of which can interbreed. Trying to hold each one to a name is like trying to give a name to each rill trickling over the bar here, and making it stick. Who is going to draw the lines? And yet it is done. Somewhere this leaf has a name, *Salix hookeriana*, *Salix lasiandra*.

Piece of robin's egg, perhaps after a raid by a long-tailed weasel. Chip of yew tree bark. Fireweed. Snail shell — made out of the same thing as your fingernail. Here, tap it — Or a rattlesnake's rattles. Roll it around in your hand. Imagine the clues in just this. Counting the rings would tell you something, but no one is sure what. Perhaps all that is recorded is the anguish of snails. Oh, this is rare: fox hairs. You can tell by the coloring. Some say it is the degree of taper, the shape. Up above someplace a fox crossed over. Or was killed by someone.

Behind the larger stones — let's walk up this way — hung up in their crevices is another kind of detritus entirely, a layer of understanding that becomes visible only under certain circumstances, often after a thunderstorm, for example, when the air has a sudden three-dimensional quality and it appears it might be slit open neatly and examined from the inside. What you see then, tethered to the rocks as though floating on the silken threads of spider webs adrift in the balmy air, are the sighs of sparrows passing overhead. The jubilation of wind-touched aspens. The persistence of crayfish, the tentative sipping of deer, who have stepped clear of the cover of trees, the circumspection of lone fish.

And there are still other revelations beyond these. You can imagine what might be learned in a place like this if one took the time. Think only of the odors, some single strand of which might be nipped between rocks, of wildflowers (lupine, avalanche lily, the white blossoms of bunchberry, yellow balsamroot, crimson currant), of musk (needle-toothed weasel, sleek-furred mink, bright-eyed fisher, grizzly bear on his rump, eating the seed pods of dogtooth violet), of sun-cracked earth, the odor of granite. Just so, by these invisible extensions is the character of the river revealed, is there some clue to what goes unexamined.

If you lie out flat on the stones — it seems odd to try, I know — you will feel — here, that's it — the warmth of the sunlight emanating from the stones. Turn your head to the side, ear to rock, and you will hear the earth revolving on its axis and an adjustment of stones in the riverbed. The heartbeats of salmon roe. One day I heard the footsteps of someone miles away, following someone else.

If you look up into the sky, straight up, eight or ten miles, it is possible to imagine the atmospheric tides, oceans of air moving against the edge of space in an ebb and flow as dependent on the phases of the moon. I believe lying here on the gravel bars cannot be too different from lying on your back on the bottom of the ocean. You can choose to take this view or not, with no fear of consequence. The tides go on, regardless.

Let's walk along the edge.

The fish this garter snake has just snatched is called a dace, a relative of the creek chub, a life more obscure than most. The snake is *Thamnophis couchi hydrophila*, a western species. You can take the naming as far as you want. Some of the most enjoyable things — the way the water folds itself around that rock and drops away — have no names.

You are beginning to shiver, but it's nothing to be alarmed over. The stones warmed you; you sensed you were nestled in the earth. When you stood up fear pooled in an exposed feeling around your back. This is what to leave the earth means. To stand up, which you see bears do on occasion. At the very heart of this act is the meaning of personal terror.

Along the very edge of these gravel bars are some of the earth's seams. A person with great courage and balance could slip between the water and the rock, the wet and the dry, and perhaps never come back. But I think it must take as much courage to stay.

I have stood for hours on these gravel bars. I have seen the constellations reflected in chips of obsidian glass. My hands have gone out to solitary willows in the darkness. Once I lay without moving for days

§ 137 §

until, mistaking me for driftwood, birds landed nearby and began speaking in murmurs of Pythagoras and winds that blew in the Himalayas.

I regretted throwing stones into the river.

BARRY HOLSTUN LOPEZ (born 1945) is a writer with a fascination for the natural world. He is a contributing editor to *Harper's* and *North American Review* and the author of a number of books including *Of Wolves and Men*, *Winter Count*, and *Arctic Dreams*. He has been called a writer who can write on that narrow line where fact and fiction meet. This selection is taken from *River Notes: The Dance of Herons*, a book of fictional observations about man's interplay with the forces of nature. It is an experience of the factual magic one can discover in the land.

Rosalind Richards

"A Northern Countryside"
from *White Pine and Blue
Water: A State of Maine Reader*

Our county lies in a northern State, in the midst of one of those districts known geographically as "regions of innumerable lakes." It is in good part wooded – hilly, irregular country, not mountainous, but often bold and marked in outline. Save for its lakes, strangers might pass through it without especial notice; but its broken hills have a peculiar intimacy and loveableness, and to us it is so beautiful that new wonder falls on us year after year as we dwell in it.

There is a marked trend of the land. I suppose the first landmark a bird would distinguish in its flight would be our long, round-shouldered ridges, running north and south. Driving across country, either eastward or westward, you go up and up in leisurely rises, with plenty of fairly level resting places between, up long calm shoulder after shoulder, to the Height of Land. And there you take breath of wonder, for lo, before you and below you, behold a whole new countryside framed by new hills.

Sometimes the lower country thus revealed is in its turn broken into lesser hills, or moulded into noble rounding valleys. Sometimes there are stretches of intervale or old lake bottom of real flat-land, a rare beauty with us, on which the eyes rest with delight. More often than not there is shining water, lake or pond or stream. Sometimes this lower valley extends for miles before the next range rises, so that your glance travels restfully out over the wide spaces. Sometimes it is little, like a cup.

As you get up towards the Height of Land you come to what makes the returning New Englander draw breath quickly, the pleasure is so poignant: upland pastures dotted with juniper and boulders, and broken by clumps of balsam fir and spruce. Most fragrant, most beloved places. Dicksonia fern grows thick about the boulders. The pasturage is thin June-grass, the color of beach sand, as it ripens, and in August this is transformed to a queen's garden by the blossoming of blue asters and the little nemoralis golden-rod, which grew unnoticed all the earlier summer. Often whole stretches of the slope are carpeted with mayflowers and checkerberries, and as you climb higher, and meet the wind from the other side of the ridge, your foot crunches on gray reindeer-moss.

Last week, before climbing a small bare-peaked mountain, I turned aside to explore a path which led through a field of scattered balsam firs, with lady-fern growing thick about their feet. A little further on, the firs were assembled in groups and clumps, and then group was joined to group. The valley grew deeper and darker, and still the same small path led on, till I found myself in the tallest and most solemn wood of firs that I have ever seen. They were sixty feet high, needle-pointed, black, and they filled the long hollow between the hills, like a dark river.

The woods alternate with fields to clothe the hills and intervales and valleys, and make a constant and lovely variety over the landscape. Sometimes they seem a shore instead of a river. They jut out into the meadow-land, in capes and promontories, and stand in little islands, clustered around an outcropping ledge or a boulder too big to be removed. You are confronted everywhere with this meeting of the natural and indented shore of the woods, close, feathery, impenetrable, with the bays and inlets of field and pasture and meadow. The jutting portions are apt to be made more sharp and marked by the most striking part of our growth, the evergreens. There they grow, white pine and red pine, black spruce, hemlock, and balsam fir, in lovely sisterhood. Their needles shine in the sun. They taper perfectly, finished at every point, clean, dry, and resinous; and the fragrance distilled from them by our crystal air is as surely the very breath of New England as that of the Spice Islands is the breath of the East.

Our soil is often spoken of as barren, but this is only where it has been neglected. Hay and apples give us abundant crops; indeed our apples have made a name at home and abroad. Potatoes also give us a very fine yield, and a great part of the State is rich in lumber. When it is left to itself, the land reverts to wave after wave of luxuriant pine forest. Forty miles east of us they are cutting out masts again where the Constitution's masts were cut.

The apple orchards are scattered over the slopes. In the more upland places, sheep are kept, and the sheep-pastures are often hillside orchards of tall sugar maples. We have neat fields of oats and barley, more or less scattered, and once in a while a buckwheat patch, while every farm has a good cornfield, beans, pumpkins, and potatoes, besides "the woman's" little patch of "garden truck." A good many bees are kept, in colonies of gray hives under the apple trees.

The people who live on the farms are, I suppose, much like farm people everywhere. "Folks are folks"; yet, after being much with them, certain qualities impress themselves upon one's notice as characteristic; they have a dry sense of humor, and quaint and whimsical ways of expressing it, and with this, a refinement of thought and speech that is almost fastidious; a fine reticence about the physical aspects of life such as is only found, I believe, in a strong race, a people drawing their vigor from deep and untainted springs. I often wonder whether there is another place in the world where women are sheltered from any possible coarseness of expression with such considerate delicacy as they find among the rough men on a New England farm.

The life is so hard, the hours so necessarily long, in our harsh climate, that small-natured persons too often become little more than machines. They get through their work, and they save every penny they can; and that is all. The Granges, however, are increasing a pleasant and wholesome social element which is beyond price, and all winter you meet sleighs full of rosy-cheeked families, driving to the Hall for Grange Meeting or Sunday Meeting, or for the weekly dance.

Many of the farm people are large-minded enough to do their work well, and still keep above and on top of it; and some of these stand up in a sort of splendor. Their fibres have been seasoned in a life that calls for all a man's powers. Their grave kind faces show that, living all their lives in one place, they have taken the longest of all journeys, and traveled deep into the un-map-able country of Life. I do not know how to write fittingly of some of these older farm people; wise enough to be simple, and deep-rooted as the trees that grow round them; so strong and attuned to their work that the burdens of others grow light in their presence, and life takes on its right and happier proportions when one is with them.

If the first impression of our countryside is its uniformity, the second and amazing one is its surprises, its secret places. The long ridges accentuate themselves suddenly into sharp slopes and steep cup-shaped valleys, covered with sweet-fern and juniper. The wooded hills are often full of hidden cliffs (rich gardens in themselves, they are so deep in ferns and moss), and quick brooks run through them, so that you are never long without the talk of one to keep you company. There are rocky glens, where you meet cold, sweet air, the ceaseless comforting of a waterfall, and moss on moss, to velvet depths of green.

The ridges rise and slope and rise again with general likeness, but two of them open amazingly to disclose the wide blue surface of our great River. We are rich in rivers, and never have to journey far to reach one, but I never can get quite used to the surprise of coming among the hills on this broad strong full-running stream, with gulls circling over it.

One thing sets us apart from other regions: our wonderful lakes. They lie all around us, so that from every hill-top you see their shining and gleaming. It is as if the worn mirror of the glacier had been splintered into a thousand shining fragments, and the common saying is that our State is more than half water. They are so many that we call them ponds, not lakes, whether they are two miles long, or ten, or twenty.[3] I have counted over nine hundred on the State map, and then given up counting. No one person could ever know them all; there still would be new "Lost Ponds" and "New Found Lakes."

The greater part of them lie in the unbroken woods, but countless numbers are in open farming country. They run from great sunlit sheets with many islands to the most perfect tiny hidden forest jewels, places utterly lonely and apart, mirroring only the depths of the green woods.

Each "pond," large or little, is a world in itself. You can almost believe that the moon looks down on each with different radiance, that the south wind has a special fragrance as it blows across each; and each one has some peculiar, intimate beauty; deep bays, lovely and secluded channels between wooded islands, or small curved beaches which shine between dark headlands, lit up now and then by a camp fire.

Hill after hill, round-shouldered ridge after ridge; low nearer the salt water, increasing very gradually in height till they form the wild amphitheatre of blue peaks in the northern part of the State; partly farming country, and greater part wooded; this is our countryside, and across it and in and out of the forests its countless lovely lakes shine and its great rivers thread their tranquil way to the sea.

ROSALIND RICHARDS was born in 1874 in Boston and spent most of her life in Maine. She wrote several books and articles including *Two Children in the Woods*. This selection speaks of the huge world that surrounds our little worlds of understanding. It is reminiscent of the kind of discovery we realize for the first time that our world is as small and yet as infinite as our own backyards.

Henry David Thoreau

The Variorum Walden
In the Woods and
*   Fields of Concord*
A Writer's Journal
The Heart of Thoreau's Journals

Walden

When first I took up my abode in the woods, that is, began to spend my nights as well as days there, which, by accident, was on Independence day, or the fourth of July, 1845, my house was not finished for winter, but was merely a defence against the rain, without plastering or chimney, the walls being of rough weather-stained boards, with wide chinks, which made it cool at night. The upright white hewn studs and freshly planed door and window casings gave it a clean and airy look, especially in the morning, when its timbers were saturated with dew, so that I fancied that by noon some sweet gum would exude from them. To my imagination it retained throughout the day more or less of this auroral character, reminding me of a certain house on a mountain which I had visited the year before. This was an airy and unplastered cabin, fit to entertain a travelling god, and where a goddess might trail her garments. The winds which passed over my dwelling were such as sweep over the ridges of mountains, bearing the broken strains, or celestial parts only, of terrestrial music. The morning wind forever blows, the poem of creation is uninterrupted; but few are the ears that hear it. Olympus is but the outside of the earth everywhere.

I went to the woods because I wished to live deliberately, to front only the essential facts of life, and see if I could not learn what it had to teach, and not, when I came to die, discover that I had not lived. I did not wish to live what was not life, living is so dear; nor did I wish to practice resignation, unless it was quite necessary. I wanted to live deep and suck out all the marrow of life, to live so sturdily and Spartanlike as to put to rout all that was not life, to cut a broad swath and shave close, to drive life into a corner, and reduce it to its lowest terms, and if it proved to be mean, why then to get the whole and genuine meanness of it, and publish its meanness to the world; or if it were sublime, to know it by experience, and be able to give a true account of it in my next excursion. For most men, it appears to me, are in a strange uncertainty about it, whether it is of the devil or of God, an have *somewhat hastily* concluded that it is the chief end of man here to "glorify God and enjoy him forever."

Our village life would stagnate if it were not for the unexplored forests and meadows which surround it. We need the tonic of wildness, — to wade sometimes in marshes where the bittern and the meadow-hen lurk, and hear the booming of the snipe; to smell the whispering sedge where only some wilder more solitary fowl builds her nest, and the mink crawls with its belly close to the ground. At the same time that we are earnest to explore and learn all things, we require that all things be mysterious and unexplorable, that land and sea be infinitely wild, unsurveyed and unfathomed by us because unfathomable. We can never have enough of Nature. We must be refreshed by the sight of inexhaustible vigor, vast and Titanic features, the sea-coast with its wrecks, the wilderness with its living and its decaying trees, the thunder cloud, and the rain which lasts three weeks and produces freshets. We need to witness our own limits transgressed, and some life pasturing freely where we never wander. We are cheered when we observe the vulture feeding on the carrion which disgusts and disheartens us and deriving health and strength from the repast. There was a dead horse in the hollow by the path to my house, which compelled me sometimes to go out of my way, especially in the night when the air was heavy, but the assurance it gave me of the strong appetite an inviolable health of Nature was my compensation for this. I love to see that Nature is so rife with life that myriads can be afforded to be sacrificed and suffered to prey on one another; that tender organizations can be so serenely squashed out of existence like pulp, — tadpoles which herons gobble up, and tortoises and toads run over in the road; and that sometimes it has rained flesh and blood! With the liability to accident, we must see how little account is to be made of it. The impression made on a wise man is that of universal innocence. Poison is not poisonous after all, nor are any wounds fatal. Compassion is a very untenable ground. It must be expeditious. Its pleadings will not bear to be stereotyped.

Early in May, the oaks, hickories, maples, and other trees, just putting out amidst the pine woods around the pond, imparted a brightness like sunshine to the landscape, especially in cloudy days, as if the sun were breaking through mists and shining faintly on the hill-sides here and there. On the third or fourth of May I saw a loon in the pond, and during the first week of the month I heard the whippoorwill, the brown-thrasher, the veery, the wood-pewee, the chewink, and other birds. I had heard the wood-thrush long before. The phoebe had already come once more and looked in at my door and window, to see if my house was cavern-like enough for her, sustaining herself on humming wings with clinched talons, as if she held by the air, while she surveyed the premises. The sulphur-like pollen of the pitch-pine soon covered the pond and the stones and rotten wood along the shore, so that you could have collected a barrel-ful. This is the "sulphur showers" we hear of. Even in Calidas' drama of Sacontala, we read of "rills dyed yellow with the golden dust of the lotus." And so the seasons went rolling on into summer, as one rambles into higher and higher grass.

Thus was my first year's life in the woods completed; and the second year was similar to it. I finally left Walden September 6th, 1847.

I left the woods for as good a reason as I went there. Perhaps it seemed to me that I had several more lives to live, and could not spare any more time for that one. It is remarkable how easily and insensibly we fall into a particular route, and make a beaten track for ourselves. I had not lived there a week before my feet wore a path from my door to the pondside; and though it is five or six years since I trod it, it is still quite distinct. It is true, I fear that others may have fallen into it, and so helped to keep it open. The surface of the earth is soft and impressible by the feet of men; and so with the paths which the mind travels. How worn and dusty, then, must be the highways of the world, how deep the ruts of tradition and conformity! I did not wish to take a cabin passage, but rather to go before the mast and on the deck of the world, for there I could best see the moonlight amid the mountains. I do not wish to go below now.

I learned this, at least, by my experiment; that if one advances confidently in the direction of his dreams, and endeavors to live the life he has imagined, he will meet with a success unexpected in common hours. He will put some things behind, will pass an invisible boundary; new, universal, and more liberal laws will begin to establish themselves around and within him; or the old laws be expanded, and interpreted in his favor in a more liberal sense, and he will live with the license of a higher order of beings. In proportion as he simplifies his life, the laws of the universe will appear less complex, and solitude will not be solitude, nor poverty poverty, nor weakness weakness. If you have built castles in the air, your work need not be lost; that is where they should be. Now put the foundations under them.

Journals

September 17, 1839
Nature never makes haste; her systems revolve at an even pace. The bud swells imperceptibly, without hurry or confusion, as though the short spring days were an eternity. All her operations seem separately, for the time, the single object for which all things tarry. Why, then, should man hasten as if anything less than eternity were allotted for the least deed? Let him consume never so many aeons, so that he go about the meanest task well, though it be but the paring of his nails.

If the setting sun seems to hurry him to improve the day while it lasts, the chant of the crickets fails not to reassure him, even-measured as of old, teaching him to take his own time henceforth forever. The wise man is restful, never restless or impatient. He each moment abides there where he is, as some walkers actually rest the whole body at each step, while others never relax the muscles of the leg till the accumulated fatigue obliges them to stop short.

October 8, 1852

P.M. Walden. As I was paddling along the north shore, after having looked in vain over the pond for a loon, suddenly a loon, sailing toward the middle, a few rods in front, set up his wild laugh and betrayed himself. I pursued with a paddle and he dived, but when he came up I was nearer than before. He dived again, but I miscalculated the direction he would take, and we were fifty rods apart when he came up, and again he laughed long and loud. He managed very cunningly, and I could not get within half a dozen rods of him. Sometimes he would come up unexpectedly on the opposite side of me, as if he had passed directly under the boat. So long-winded was he, so unweariable, that he would immediately plunge again, and then no wit could divine where in the deep pond, beneath the smooth surface, he might be speeding his way like a fish, perchance passing under the boat. He had time and ability to visit the bottom of the pond in its deepest part. A newspaper authority says a fisherman — giving his name — has caught loon in Seneca Lake, N.Y., eighty feet beneath the surface, with hooks set for trout. Miss [Susan F.] Cooper [author of *Rural Hours* (1850)] has said the same. Yet he appeared to know his course as surely under water as on the surface, and swam much faster there than he sailed on the surface. It was surprising how serenely he sailed off with unruffled bosom when he came to the surface. It was as well for me to rest on my oars and await his reappearing as to endeavor to calculate where he would come up. When I was straining my eyes over the surface, I would suddenly be startled by his unearthly laugh behind me. But why, after displaying so much cunning, did he betray himself the moment he came to the surface with that loud laugh? His white breast enough betrayed him. He was indeed a silly loon, I thought. Though he took all this pains to avoid me, he never failed to give notice of his whereabouts the moment he came to the surface. After an hour he seemed as fresh as ever, dived as willingly, and swam yet farther than at first. Once or twice I saw a ripple where he approached the surface, just put his head out to reconnoitre, and instantly dived again. I could commonly hear the splash of the water when he came up, and so also detected him. It was commonly a demoniac laughter, yet somewhat like a water-bird, but occasionally, when he had balked me most successfully and come up a long way off, he uttered a long-drawn unearthly howl, probably more like a wolf than any other bird. This was his looning. As when a beast puts his muzzle to the ground and deliberately howls; perhaps the wildest sound I ever heard, making the woods ring; and I concluded that he laughed in derision of my efforts, confident of his own resources. Though the sky was overcast, the pond was so smooth that I could see where he broke the surface if I did not hear him. His white breast, the stillness of the air, the smoothness of the water, were all against [him]. At length, having come up fifty rods off, he uttered one of those prolonged unearthly howls, as if calling on the god of loons to aid him, and immediately there came a wind from the east and rippled the surface, and filled the whole air with misty rain. I was impressed as if it were the prayer of the loon and his god was angry with me. How surprised must be the fishes to see this ungainly visitant from another sphere speeding his way amid their schools!

I have never seen more than one at a time in our pond, and I believe that that is always a male.

January 3, 1853

I love Nature partly *because* she is not man, but a retreat from him. None of his institutions control or pervade her. There a different kind of right prevails. In her midst I can be glad with an entire gladness. If this world were all man, I could not stretch myself, I should lose all hope. He is constraint, she is freedom to me. He makes me wish for another world. She makes me content with this.

March 23, 1856

I spend a considerable portion of my time observing the habits of the wild animals, my brute neighbors. By their various movements and migrations they fetch the year about to me. Very significant are the flight of geese and the migration of suckers, etc., etc. But when I consider that the nobler animals have been exterminated here — the cougar, panther, lynx, wolverene, wolf, bear, moose, deer, the beaver, the turkey, etc., etc. — I cannot but feel as if I lived in a tamed, and, as it were, emasculated country. Would not the motions of those larger and wilder animals have been more significant still? Is it not a maimed and imperfect nature that I am conversant with? As if I were to study a tribe of Indians that had lost all its warriors. Do not the forest and the meadow now lack expression, now that I never see nor think of the moose with a lesser forest on his head in the one, nor of the beaver in the other? When I think what were the various sounds and notes, the migrations and works, and changes of fur and plumage which ushered in the spring and marked the other seasons of the year, I am reminded that this my life in nature, this particular round of natural phenomena which I call a year, is lamentably incomplete. I listen to [a] concert in which so many parts are wanting. The whole civilized country is to some extent turned into a city, and I am that citizen whom I pity. Many of those animal migrations and other phenomena of the spring, for instance, thinking that I have here the entire poem, and then, to my chagrin, I hear that it is but an imperfect copy that I possess and have read, that my ancestors have torn out many of the first leaves and grandest passages, and mutilated it in many places. I should not like to think that some demigod had come before me and picked out some of the best of the stars. I wish to know an entire heaven and an entire earth. All the great trees and beasts, fishes and fowl are gone. The streams, perchance, are somewhat shrunk.

January 4, 1857

After spending four or five days surveying and drawing a plan incessantly, I especially feel the necessity of putting myself in communication with nature again, to recover my tone, to withdraw out of the wearying and unprofitable world of affairs. The things I have been doing have but a fleeting and accidental importance, however much men are immersed in them, and yield very little valuable fruit. I would fain have been wading through the woods and fields and conversing with the sane snow. Having waded in the very shallowest stream of time, I would now bathe my temples in eternity. I wish again to participate in the serenity of nature, to share the happiness of the river and the woods. I thus from time to time break off my connection with eternal truths and go with the shallow stream of human affairs, grinding at the mill of the Philistines; but when my task is done, with never-failing confidence I devote myself to the infinite again. It would be sweet to deal with men more, I can imagine, but where dwell they? Not in the fields which I traverse.

January 16, 1860

I see a flock of tree sparrows busily picking something from the surface of the snow amid some bushes. I watch one attentively, and find that it is feeding on the very fine brown chaffy-looking seed of the panicled andromeda. It understands how to get its dinner, to make the plant give down, perfectly. It flies up and alights on one of the dense brown panicles of the hard berries, and gives it a vigorous shaking and beating with its claws and bill, sending down a shower of the fine chaffy-looking seed on to the snow beneath. It lies very distinct, though fine almost as dust, on the spotless snow. It then hops down and briskly picks up from the snow what it wants. How very clean and agreeable to the imagination, and withal abundant, is this kind of food! How delicately they fare! These dry persistant seed-vessels hold their crusts of bread until shaken. The snow is the white tablecloth on which they fall. No anchorite with his water and his crust fares more simply. It shakes down a hundred times as much as it wants at each shrub, and shakes the same or another cluster after each successive snow. How bountifully Nature feeds them! No wonder they come to spend the winter with us, and are at ease with regard to their food. These shrubs ripen an abundant crop of seeds to supply the wants of these immigrants from the far north which annually come to spend the winter with us. How neatly and simply it feeds!

This shrub grows unobserved by most, only known to botanists, and at length matures its hard dry seed-vessels, which, if noticed, are hardly supposed to contain seed. But there is no shrub nor weed which is not known to some bird. Though you may have never noticed it, the tree sparrow comes from the north in the winter straight to this shrub, and confidently shakes its panicle, then feasts on the fine shower of seeds that falls from it.

HENRY DAVID THOREAU was born in Concord, Massachusetts in 1817. Throughout his life he consistently supported integrity, independence, and personal freedom. Ralph Waldo Emerson was his friend and mentor, and he spent two years living with the Emerson family. His books include: *Walden, A Week on the Concord and Merrimac Rivers, Maine Woods, Cape Cod,* and *A Yankee in Canada.* For his entire life he kept journals, and several of the following selections are taken from his journals.

INTERLUDE 1

*Songs of the
American Spirit*

Songs, like poetry and prose, were also an expression of this newly-forming American character. Over every rise of the land, there seemed to be something to celebrate, and voices sang of the beauty and majesty of this American land.

In folk music, in hymns, in anthems, in marches, and ballads, Americans raised their voices in song. Samuel Francis Smith, Steven Foster, Daniel Decatur Emmett, John Phillips Sousa, Irving Berlin, Woody Guthrie, and countless others wrote music about the American Spirit. Other forms of music, ranging from jazz and Dixieland to Aaron Copland's symphonic works, also emerged, capturing both the sense of land and of the American character. Here are just three of the most famous folk tunes that are songs of the land.

Katherine Lee Bates

"America the Beautiful"

Oh, beautiful for spacious skies, for amber waves of grain
For purple mountain majesties above the fruited plain
America! America! God shed His grace on thee
And crown thy good with brotherhood from sea to shining sea

Oh beautiful for Pilgrim feet whose stern impassioned stress
A thoroughfare for freedom beat across the wilderness
America! America! God mend thine ev'ry flaw
Confirm thy soul in self-control, thy liberty in law

Oh beautiful for heroes proved in liberating strife
Who more than self their country loved, and mercy more than life
America! America! May God thy gold refine
Till all success be nobleness, And ev'ry gain divine

Oh beautiful for patriot dream that sees beyond the years
Thine alabaster cities gleam undimmed by human tears
America! America! God shed his grace on thee
And crown thy good with brotherhood from sea to shining sea

KATHERINE LEE BATES was a New Englander who taught at Wellesley College. She came to Colorado in 1893 to lecture at Colorado College, where she saw for the first time the Rocky Mountains rising from the Great Plains. She was moved to write these lyrics, first as a poem, which was later published in the *Boston Transcript* in 1904. The poem was set to music written by Samuel Ward in 1882, known originally as a hymn, entitled "Materna."

Brewster M. Higley

"Home on the Range"

Oh give me a home where the buffalo roam
Where the deer and the antelope play
Where seldom is heard a discouraging word
And the skies are not cloudy all day

Chorus

Home, home on the range
Where the deer and the antelope play
Where seldom is heard a discouraging word
And the skies are not cloudy all day

Where air is so pure and the zephyrs so free
And the breezes so balmy and light
I would not exchange my own home on the range
Not for all of the cities so bright

Chorus:

How often a night when the heavens are bright
With the light of the glittering stars
I stood there amazed and I asked as I gazed
If their glory exceeds that of ours

Chorus:

I love the wild flowers in this dear land of ours
And the curlew I love to hear scream
I love the white rocks and the antelope flocks
That are grazing on mountain tops green

Chorus:

BREWSTER M. HIGLEY (1823-1911) was a country medical doctor in Beaver Creek, Kansas, when he wrote the lyrics to "Home on the Range," which first appeared in the December, 1873, issue of *The Smith County Pioneer* (Kansas) magazine. Daniel E. Kelly composed the music later. Today, "Home on the Range" is the Kansas state song.

C. W. McCall

"Wilderness"

Come along and sing a song we knew before.
Come along and sing . . . once more.
Come along and live a life we knew before.
Come along and live . . . once more.

Wake with me and feel the misty blue dawn,
Come hear the wild bird sing her morning song,
See the sun that only wilderness sees.
Then walk with me and let your heart be free.

Come on along and chase the wind once more,
Come on along and try one more time.
Come on along and find the trail once more,
Come on along and live again.

Come with me and see the river run wild.
Come hear the canyon call her wandering child.
Breathe the air that only wilderness breathes
Then walk with me and let your heart run free.

Come on along and climb the mountain once more,
Come on along and try one more time.
Come on along and cross the river with me,
Come on along and live again.

Come with me and hear the night bird cry,
And see the starlight fill the wonderous sky.
Feel the joy that only wilderness feels,
Come on along, along and we'll be free.

Fly with me and find the end of time,
Run with me and feel the wilderness high.
Come on along and live forever with me,
Come on along, along and we'll be free.

WILLIAM D. FRIES, SR. is better known to America's legions of over-the-road truck drivers as C. W. McCall, the baritone whose lyrics and music keeps the "drivers" company through long nights and rainy days as they move cargo from coast to coast. His "Convoy," "Wolf Creek Pass," and dozens of others long have been tops in the country-western music field. But there's another side to C. W. McCall. William Fries is, at this writing, mayor of Ouray, a Colorado mining town and vacation paradise high on the north slope of his beloved San Juan Mountains.

SECTION TWO

Nature and Challenge

Challenge can come in many forms and be nurtured by many inspirations. Opportunity – perceived or real – can inspire humans to take on external challenges they did not before recognize. Desire or passion, often a result of special effort and dedication, can bolster the human character to surmount external as well as internal exigencies. As man set out across the ocean to the North American continent, and later as he set across the wild continent itself, he faced new and continual challenge. It was challenge not from the constraints of society or government, but from the land and from nature. Many of the elements of nature – the vast spaces, the absence of human communities and social contact, the deep forests, the high plains, and the abundance of wildlife on the American continent – were conditions which European man had neither anticipated nor had contended with before.

These external challenges – of learning to deal with the sheer immensity and untamed quality of this new land – inspired internal challenges for the psyche. They posed continual and undeniable reminders that nature is not a world separate

Courtesy of Museum of Western Art, Denver, Colorado

from man, but something of which he is a part, and from which he cannot live independently. Internally, in the human consciousness, this presented still another demand: the testing of fortitude, the strength of character to persevere, at times against and at other times in partnership with nature and the land. The experience of internal pertinacity, our unyielding persistence, brought about a fierce love for this American land – a love of the challenge itself.

This section offers a panoply of the experiences this challenge from nature presents. It begins with the enigma Yellowstone presented to early explorers: how can something so beautiful be so mortally dangerous? And yet, is not the danger wilderness presents part of its beauty? Other forms of challenge found in the American westering experience seem to retell the same story: it is a tale of quest and human development, search and perseverance, but witnessed from many different viewpoints, ranging from Cooper, to Cather's Bohemians, to Rölvaag's Norweigans, to the 20th century continuation of this persistence offered by sheep rancher and artist Bill Stockton.

As we see in the selections, once man committed to staying on the land, there emerged the challenge of making the decision work. "For the courtesies of ordinary life, he must substitute unselfishness, forbearance and tolerance . . . In short, he must substitute the deed for the word, the spirit for the letter," Jack London writes when describing the tools needed in dealing with life in the wilderness. The need for axe and gun are secondary to the need for a strong will.

Finally, some selections address the challenge we ourselves construct and place in way so that we may learn more about the land and, in the process, learn more about ourselves. As we put ourselves into a position of experiencing nature, such as the Jenkins or the Muries did, we recognize how fortunate we are to still have existing today such land, raw and beautiful. Barbara and Peter Jenkins walked west in order to taste, in the 20th century, the challenge that was faced daily by other Americans earlier in our history. As John McPhee writes, people moved to Alaska to put a 19th century challenge in front of them in a 20th century world. The American character has relied on challenge for its mortar; it will be a sad day when we can no longer seek out these experiences in nature that will fortify this vital piece of our character.

The significance of challenge presented by nature and the land is that it forces us to consider our real, internal need for this experience with it. Nature – and the primordial test it offers – is something we all need to touch at one time or another to put into perspective our own life and to help us recognize our place in this world. The continued existence of wild land, of nature unbound, rests upon our own willingness to exercise self-limitation. This is the real challenge facing us today: to allow nature to simply remain nature.

Bayard Taylor

Wonders of the Yellowstone
"The Peril of Mr. Everts"

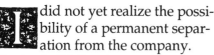did not yet realize the possibility of a permanent separation from the company. Instead of following up the pursuit of their camp, I engaged in an effort to recover my horse. Half a day's search convinced me of its impracticability. I wrote and posted in an open space several notices, which, if my friends should chance to see, would inform them of my condition and the route I had taken, and then struck out into the forest in the supposed direction of their camp. As the day wore on without any discovery, alarm took the place of anxiety at the prospect of another night alone in the wilderness, and this time without food or fire. But even this dismal foreboding was cheered by the hope that I should soon rejoin my companions, who would laugh at my adventure, and incorporate it as a thrilling episode into the journal of our trip. The bright side of a misfortune, as I found by experience, even under the worst possible circumstances, always presents some features of encouragement.

When I began to realize that my condition was one of actual peril, I banished from my mind all fear of an unfavorable result. Seating myself on a log, I recalled every foot of the way I had travelled since the separation from my friends, and the most probable opinion I could form of their whereabouts was, that they had, by a course but little different from mine, passed by the spot where I had posted the notices, learned of my disaster, and were waiting for me to rejoin them there, or searching for me in that vicinity. A night must be spent amid the prostrate trunks before my return could be accomplished. At no time during my period of exile did I experience so much mental suffering from the cravings of hunger as when, exhausted with this long day of fruitless search, I resigned myself to a couch of pine foliage in the pitchy darkness of a thicket of small trees. Naturally timid in the night, I fully realized the exposure of my condition. I peered upward through the darkness, but all was blackness and gloom. The wind sighed mournfully through the pines. The forest seemed alive with the screeching of night birds, the angry barking of coyotes, and the prolonged, dismal howl of the gray wolf. These sounds, familiar by their constant occurrence throughout the journey, were now full of terror, and drove slumber from my eye-lids, but above all this, however, was the hope that I should be restored to my comrades the next day.

Early the next morning I rose unrefreshed, and pursued my weary way over the prostrate trunks. It was noon when I reached the spot where my notices were posted. No one had been there. My disappointment was almost overwhelming. For the first time, I realized that I was lost. Then came a crushing sense of destitution. No food, no fire; no means to procure either; alone in an unexplored wilderness, one hundred and fifty miles from the nearest human abode, surrounded by wild beasts, and famishing with hunger. It was no time for despondency. A moment afterwards I felt how calamity can elevate the mind, in the formation of the resolution "not to perish in that wilderness."

The hope of finding the party still controlled my plans. I thought, by traversing the peninsula centrally, I would be enabled to strike the shore of the lake in advance of their camp, and near the point of departure for the Madison River. Acting upon this impression, I rose from a sleepless couch, and pursued my way through the timber-entangled forest. A feeling of weakness took the place of hunger. Conscious of the need of food, I felt no cravings. Occasionally, while scrambling over logs and through thickets, a sense of faintness and exhaustion would come over me, but I would suppress it with audible expression, "This won't do; I *must* find my company." Despondency would sometimes strive with resolution for the mastery of my thoughts. I would think of home – of my daughter – and of the possible chance of starvation, or death in some more terrible form; but as often as these gloomy forebodings came, I would strive to banish them with reflections better adapted to my immediate necessities. I recollect at this time discussing the question, whether there was not implanted by Providence in every man a principle of self-preservation equal to any emergency which did not destroy his reason. I decided this question affirmatively a thousand times afterwards in my wanderings, and I record this experience here, that any person who reads it, should he ever find himself in like circumstances, may not despair. There is life in the thought. It will revive hope, allay hunger, renew energy, encourage perseverance, and, as I have proved in my own case, bring a man out of difficulty, when nothing else can avail.

It was mid-day when I emerged from the forest into an open space at the foot of the peninsula. A broad lake of beautiful curvature, with magnificent surroundings, lay before me, glittering in the sunbeams. It was full twelve miles in circumference. A wide belt of sand formed the margin which I was approaching, directly opposite to which, rising seemingly from the very depths of the water, towered the loftiest peak of a range of mountains apparently interminable. The ascending vapor from innumerable hot springs, and the sparkling jet of a single geyser added the feature of novelty to one of the grandest landscapes I ever beheld. Nor was the life of the scene less noticeable than its other attractions. Large flocks of swans and other water-fowl were sporting on the quiet surface of the lake; otters in great numbers performed the most amusing aquatic evolutions; mink and beaver swam around unscared, in most grotesque confusion. Deer, elk, and mountain sheep stared at me, manifesting more surprise than fear at my presence among them. The adjacent forest was vocal with the songs of birds, chief of which were the chattering notes of a species of mocking-bird, whose imitative efforts afforded abundant merriment. Seen under favorable circumstances, this assemblage of grandeur, beauty, and novelty would have been transporting; but jaded with travel, famishing with hunger, and distressed with anxiety, I was in no humor for ecstasy. My tastes were subdued and chastened by the perils which environed me. I longed for food, friends, and protection. Associated with my thoughts, however, was the wish that some of my friends of peculiar tastes could enjoy this display of secluded magnificence, now, probably, for the first time beheld by mortal eyes.

The lake was at least one thousand feet lower than the highest point of the peninsula, and several hundred feet below the level of Yellowstone Lake. I recognized the mountain which overshadowed it as the landmark which, a few days before, had received from General Washburn the name of Mount Everts; and as it is associated with some of the most agreeable and terrible incidents of my exile, I feel that I have more than a mere discoverer's right to the perpetuity of that christening. The lake is fed by innumerable small streams from the mountains, and the countless hot springs surrounding it. A large river flows from it, through a canyon a thousand feet in height, in a southeasterly direction, to a distant range of mountains, which I conjectured to be Snake River; and with the belief that I had discovered the source of the great southern tributary of the Columbia, I gave it the name of Bessie Lake, after the "Sole daughter of my house and heart."

BAYARD TAYLOR (1825-1878) was the first of the Scribner journalists to write in a news magazine style – taking from the actual reports of discovery and science information collected by Major Doane and other United States Geological Surveyors sent to record the unknown wilderness that was the interior of the Rocky Mountain West. The primary purpose of Taylor's book was to popularize the notion of traveling to see the wonders of Yellowstone; in his last chapter, however, he both entices and thrills his readers with the tale of the near calamity one of the explorers met when he became separated from his party. True or not, it is a good example of the kind of challenge encountered by the early explorers of Yellowstone.

O. E. Rölvaag

Giants of the Earth
"Toward the Sunset"

There were giants in the earth
in those days; and also after that,
when the sons of God came in
    unto
the daughters of men, and they
bear children to them, the same
became mighty men which were
of old, men of renown."
GENESIS vi:4

Bright, clear sky over a plain so wide that the rim of the heavens cut down on it around the entire horizon. . . . Bright, clear sky today, tomorrow, and for all time to come.

    . . . And sun! And still more sun! It set the heavens afire every morning; it grew with the day to quivering golden light – then softened into all the shades or red and purple as evening fell . . . Pure colour everywhere. A gust of wind, sweeping across the plain, threw into life waves of yellow and blue and green. Now and then a dead black wave would race over the scene . . . a cloud's gliding shadow . . . now and then . . .

    It was late afternoon. A small caravan was pushing its

way through the tall grass. The track that it left behind was like the wake of a boat – except that instead of widening out astern it closed in again.

"Tish-ah!" said the grass. . . . "Tish-ah, tish-ah!" . . . Never had it said anything else – never would it say anything else. It bent resiliently under the trampling feet; it did not break, but it complained aloud every time – for nothing like this had ever happened to it before . . . "Tish-ah, tish-ah!" it cried, and rose up in surprise to look at this rough, hard thing that had crushed it to the ground so rudely, and then moved on.

A stocky, broad-shouldered man walked at the head of the caravan. He seemed shorter than he really was, because of the tall grass around him and the broad-brimmed hat of coarse straw which he wore. A few steps behind him followed a boy of about nine years of age. The boy's blond hair was clearly marked against his brown, sunburnt neck; but the man's hair and neck were of exactly the same shade of brown. From the looks of these two, and still more from their gait, it was easy to guess that here walked father and son.

Behind them a team of oxen jogged along; the oxen were drawing a vehicle which once upon a time might have been a wagon, but which now, on account of its many and grave infirmities, ought long since to have been consigned to the scrap heap – exactly the place in point of fact, where the man had picked it up. Over the wagon box long willow saplings had been bent, in the form of arches in a church chancel – six of them in all. On these arches, and tied down to the body on each side, were spread first of all two handwoven blankets, that might well have adorned the walls of some manor house in the olden times; on top of the blankets were thrown two sheepskin robes, with the wool side down, which were used for bed-coverings at night. The rear of the wagon was stowed full of numberless articles, all the way up to the top. A large immigrant chest at the bottom of the pile, very long and high, devoured a big share of the space; around and above it were piled household utensils, tools, implements, and all their clothing.

Hitched to this wagon and trailing behind was another vehicle, homemade and very curious-looking, so solidly and quaintly constructed that it might easily have won a place in any museum. Indeed, it appeared strong enough to stand all the jolting from the Atlantic to the Pacific . . . It, too, was a wagon, after a fashion; at least, it had been intended for such. The wheels were made from pieces of plank fitting roughly together; the box, considerably wider than that of the first wagon, was also loaded full of provisions and household gear, covered over with canvas and lashed down securely. Both wagons creaked and groaned loudly every time they bounced over a tussock or hove out of a hollow. . . . "Squeak, squeak!" said the one . . . "Squeak, squeak!" answered the other . . . The strident sound broke the silence of centuries.

A short distance behind the wagons followed a brindle cow. The caravan moved so slowly that she occasionally had time to stop and snatch a few mouthfuls, though there was never a chance for many at a time. But what little she got in this way she sorely needed. She had been jogging along all day, swinging and switching her tail, the rudder of the caravan. Soon it would be night, and then her part of the work would come – to furnish milk for the evening porridge, for all the company up ahead.

Across the front end of the box of the first wagon lay a rough piece of plank. On the right side of this plank sat a woman with a white kerchief over her head, driving the oxen. Against her thigh rested the blond head of a little girl, who was stretched out on the plank and sleeping sweetly. Now and then the hand of the mother moved across the child's face to chase away the mosquitoes, which had begun to gather as the sun lowered. On the left side of the plank, beyond the girl, sat a boy about seven years old – a well-grown lad, his skin deeply tanned, a certain clever, watchful gleam in his eyes. With hands folded over one knee, he looked straight ahead.

This was the caravan of Per Hansa, who with his family and all his earthly possessions was moving west from Fillmore County, Minnesota, to Dakota Territory. There he intended to take up land and build himself a home; he was going to do something remarkable out there, which should become known far and wide. No lack of opportunity in that country, he had been told! . . . Per Hansa himself strode ahead and laid out the course; the boy Ole, or *Olamand*, followed closely after, and explored it. Beret, the wife, drove the oxen and took care of little Anna Marie, pet-named *And-Ongen* (which means "The Duckling"), who was usually bubbling over with happiness. Hans Kristian, whose everyday name was *Store-Hans* (meaning "Big Hans," to distinguish him from his godfather, who was also named Hans, but who, of course, was three times his size), sat there on the wagon, and saw to it that everyone attended to business . . . The cow Rosie trailed behind, swinging and switching her tail, following the caravan farther and farther yet into the endless vista of the plain.

"Tish-ah, tish-ah!" cried the grass . . . "Tish-ah, tish-ah!" . . .

II

The caravan seemed a miserably frail and Lilliputian thing as it crept over the boundless prairie toward the sky line. Of road or trail there lay not a trace ahead; as soon as the grass had straightened up again behind, no one could have told the direction from which it had come or whither it was bound. The whole train – Per Hansa with his wife and children, the oxen, the wagons, the cow, and all – might just as well have dropped down out of the sky. Nor was it at all impossible to imagine that they were trying to get back there again; their course was always the same – straight toward the west, straight toward the sky line. . . .

Poverty-stricken, unspeakably forlorn, the caravan creaked along, advancing at a snail's pace, deeper and deeper into a bluish-green infinity – on and on, and always farther on . . . It steered for Sunset Land! . . .

For more than three weeks now, and well into the fourth, this caravan had been crawling across the plain . . . Early in the journey it had passed through Blue Earth; it had left Chain Lakes behind; and one fine day it had crept into Jackson, on the Des Moines River. But that seemed ages ago . . . From Jackson, after a short lay-up, it had pushed on westward – always westward – to Worthington, then to Rock River . . . A little west of Rock River, Per Hansa had lost the trail completely. Since then he had not been able to find it again; at this moment he literally did not know where he was, nor how to get to the place he had to reach. But Split Rock Creek must lie out there somewhere in the sun; if he could only find that landmark, he could pick his way still farther without much trouble . . . Strange that he hadn't reached Split Rock Creek before this time! According to his directions, he should have been there two or three days ago; but he hadn't seen anything that even looked like the place . . . Oh, my God! If something didn't turn up soon! . . . My God! . . .

The wagons creaked and groaned. Per Hansa's eyes wandered over the plain. His bearded face swung constantly from side to side as he examined every inch of ground from the northeast to the southwest. At times he gave his whole attention to that part of the plain lying between him and the western sky line; with head bent forward and eyes fixed and searching, he would sniff the air, like an animal trying to find the scent. Every now and then he glanced at an old silver watch which he carried in his left hand; but his gaze would quickly wander off again, to take up its fruitless search of the empty horizon.

It was now nearing six o'clock. Since three in the afternoon he had been certain of his course; at that time he had taken his bearings by means of his watch and the sun . . . Out here one had to get one's cross-bearings from the very day itself – then trust to luck . . .

For a long while the little company had been silent. Per Hansa turned halfway around, and without slackening his pace spoke to the boy walking behind.

"Go back and drive for a while now, Ola[4] . . . You must talk to mother, too, so that it won't be so lonesome for her. And be sure to keep as sharp a lookout as you can."

"I'm not tired yet!" said the boy, loath to leave the van.

"Go back, anyway! Maybe you're not, but I can feel it beginning to tell on me. We'll have to start cooking the porridge pretty soon. . . You go back, and hold her on the sun for a while longer."

"Do you think we'll catch up with them tonight, Dad?" The boy was still undecided.

"Good Lord, no! They've got too long a start on us . . . Look sharp, now! If you happen to see anything suspicious, sing out!" . . . Per Hansa glanced again at his watch, turned forward, and strode steadily onward.

Ole said no more; he stepped out of the track and stood there waiting till the train came up. Then Store-Hans jumped down nimbly, while the other climbed up and took his seat.

"Have you seen anything?" the mother asked in an anxious voice.

"Why, no . . . not yet," answered the boy, evasively.

"I wonder if we shall ever see them again," she said, as if speaking to herself, and looked down at the ground. "This seems to be taking us to the end of the world . . . beyond the end of the world!"

Store-Hans, who was still walking beside the wagon, heard what she said and looked up at her. The buoyancy of childhood shone in his brown face . . . Too bad that mother should be so scared! . . .

"Yes, Mother, but when we're both steering for the sun, we'll both land in the same place, won't we? . . . the sun is a sure guide, you know!"

These were the very words which he had heard his father use the night before; now he repeated them. To Store-Hans the truth of them seemed as clear as the sun itself; in the first place, because dad had said it, and then because it sounded so reasonable.

He hurried up alongside his father and laid his hand in his – he always felt safer thus.

The two walked on side by side. Now and then the boy stole a glance at the face beside him, which was as stern and fixed as the prairie on which they were walking. He was anxious to talk, but couldn't find anything to say that sounded grown-up enough; and so he kept quiet. At last, however, the silence grew too heavy for him to bear. He tried to say indifferently, just like his father:

"When I'm a man and have horses, I'm going to make a road over these plains, and . . . and put up some posts for people to follow. Don't you think that'll be a good idea?"

A slight chuckle came from the bearded face set toward the sun.

OLE EDVART RÖLVAAG was born in Norway in 1876 near the Arctic Circle. As a young man, he read the letters to home from emigrants new to the United States who wrote of the unlimited opportunity to be found in America, especially in the open land of the high plains of the Dakotas. Rölvaag followed these other emigrants to this new land and came to write seven books on the emigrant's experience. He wrote in his native Norwegian, but all his works are American in theme and flavor. He wrote of not just the New World/Old World experience immigrants encountered, but also of the other world which plagued them: the internal conscious where hopes were born and disappointment could paralyze the strongest of pioneers. His books were faithful accounts of the sometimes bitter challenge with which the land confronted the new American.

James Fenimore Cooper

The Prairie

Much was said and written at the time concerning the policy of adding the vast regions of Louisiana to the already immense and but half-tenanted territories of the United States. As the warmth of controversy, however, subsided and party considerations gave place to more liberal views, the wisdom of the measure began to be generally conceded. It soon become apparent to the meanest capacity that while nature had placed a barrier of desert to the extension of our population in the West, the measure had made us the masters of a belt of fertile country which, in the revolutions of the day, might have become the property of a rival nation. It gave us the sole command of the great thoroughfare of the interior and placed the countless tribes of savages who lay along our borders entirely within our control; it reconciled conflicting rights and quieted national distrusts; it opened a thousand avenues to the inland trade and to the waters of the Pacific; and if ever time or necessity shall require a peaceful division

of this vast empire, it assures us of a neighbor that will possess our language, our religion, our institutions, and it is also to be hoped, our sense of political justice.

Although the purchase was made in 1803, the spring of the succeeding year was permitted to open before the official prudence of the Spaniard, who held the province for his European master, admitted the authority or even the entrance of its new proprietors. But the forms of the transfer were no sooner completed and the new government acknowledged than swarms of that restless people which is ever found hovering on the skirts of American society plunged into the thickets that fringed the right bank of the Mississippi, with the same careless hardihood that had already sustained so many of them in their toilsome progress from the Atlantic states to the eastern shores of the "father of rivers."[5]

Time was necessary to blend the numerous and affluent colonists of the lower province with their new compatriots; but the thinner and more humble population above was almost immediately swallowed in the vortex which attended the tide of instant emigration. The inroad from the East was a new and sudden outbreaking of a people who had endured a momentary restraint after having been rendered nearly resistless by success. The toils and hazards of former undertakings were forgotten as these endless and unexplored regions, with all their fancied as well as real advantages, were laid open to their enterprise. The consequences were such as might easily have been anticipated from so tempting an offering, placed as it was before the eyes of a race long trained in adventure and nurtured in difficulties.

Thousands of the elders of what were then called the New States[6] broke up from the enjoyment of their hard-earned indulgences and were to be seen leading long files of descendants, born and reared in the forests of Ohio and Kentucky, deeper into the land in quest of that which might be termed, without the aid of poetry, their natural and more congenial atmosphere. The distinguished and resolute forester who first penetrated the wilds of the latter state was of the number. This adventurous and venerable patriarch was now seen making his last remove, placing the endless river between him and the multitude his own success had drawn around him and seeking for the renewal of enjoyments which were rendered worthless in his eyes when trammeled by the forms of human institutions.[7]

In the pursuit of adventures such as these, men are ordinarily governed by their habits or deluded by their wishes. A few, led by the phantoms of hope and ambitious of sudden affluence, sought the mines of the virgin territory; but by far the greater portion of the emigrants were satisfied to establish themselves along the margins of the larger watercourses, content with the rich returns that the generous alluvial bottoms of the rivers never fail to bestow on the most desultory industry. In this manner were communities formed with magical rapidity; and most of those who witnessed the purchase of the empty empire have lived to see already a populous and sovereign state parceled from its inhabitants and received into the bosom of the national Union on terms of political equality.

The incidents and scenes which are connected with this legend occurred in the earliest periods of the enterprises which have led to so great and so speedy a result.

The harvest of the first year of our possession had long been passed, and the fading foliage of a few scattered trees was already beginning to exhibit the hues and tints of autumn when a train of wagons issued from the bed of a dry rivulet to pursue its course across the undulating surface of what, in the language of the country of which we write, is called a "rolling prairie." The vehicles, loaded with household goods and implements of husbandry, the few straggling sheep and cattle that were herded in the rear, and the rugged appearance and careless mien of the sturdy men who loitered at the sides of the lingering teams united to announce a band of emigrants seeking for the Eldorado of the West. Contrary to the usual practice of the men of their caste, this party had left the fertile bottoms of the low country and had found its way, by means only known to such adventurers, across glen and torrent, over deep morasses and arid wastes, to a point far beyond the usual limits of civilized habitations. In their front were stretched those broad plains which extend with so little diversity of character to the bases of the Rocky Mountains, and many long and dreary miles in their rear foamed the swift and turbid waters of La Platte.

The appearance of such a train in that bleak and solitary place was rendered the more remarkable by the fact that the surrounding country offered so little that was tempting to the cupidity of speculation, and if possible, still less that was flattering to the hopes of an ordinary settler of new lands.

The meager herbage of the prairie promised nothing in favor of a hard and unyielding soil over which the wheels of the vehicles rattled as lightly as if they traveled on a beaten road, neither wagons nor beasts making any deeper impression than to mark that bruised and withered grass which the cattle plucked from time to time, and as often rejected as food too sour for even hunger to render palatable.

Whatever might be the final destination of these adventurers or the secret causes of their apparent security in so remote and unprotected a situation, there was no visible sign of uneasiness, uncertainty, or alarm among them. Including both sexes, and every age, the number of the party exceeded twenty.

At some little distance in front of the whole marched the individual who by his position and air appeared to be the leader of the band. He was a tall, sunburnt man, past the middle age, of a dull countenance and listless manner. His frame appeared loose and flexible, but it was vast and in reality of prodigious power. It was only at moments, however, as some slight impediment opposed itself to his loitering progress that his person, which, in its ordinary gait seemed so lounging and nerveless, displayed any of those energies which lay latent in his system, like the slumbering and unwieldy, but terrible, strength of the elephant. The inferior lineaments of his countenance were coarse, extended, and vacant, while the superior, or those nobler parts which are thought to affect the intellectual being, were low, receding, and mean.

The dress of this individual was a mixture of the coarsest vestments of a husbandman with the leathern garments that fashion as well as use had in some degree rendered necessary to one engaged in his present pursuits. There was, however, a singular and wild display of prodigal and ill-judged ornaments blended with his motley attire. In place of the usual deerskin belt, he wore around his body a tarnished silken sash of the most gaudy colors; the buckhorn haft of his knife was profusely decorated with plates of silver; the marten's fur of his cap was of a fineness and shadowing that a queen might covet; the buttons of his rude and soiled blanket-coat were of the glittering coinage of Mexico: the stock of his rifle was of beautiful mahogany riveted and banded with the same precious metal; and the trinkets of no less than three worthless watches dangled from different parts of his person. In addition to the pack and the rifle which were slung at his back, together with the well-filled and carefully guarded pouch and horn, he had carelessly cast a keen and bright wood-ax across his shoulder, sustaining the weight of the whole with as much apparent ease as if he moved unfettered in limb and free from encumbrance.

A short distance in the rear of this man came a group of youths very similarly attired and bearing sufficient resemblance to each other and to their leader to distinguish them as the children of one family. Though the youngest of their number could not much have passed the period that in the nicer judgment of the law is called the age of discretion, he had proved himself so far worthy of his progenitors as to have reared already his aspiring person to the standard height of his race. There were one or two others, of different mold, whose descriptions must, however, be referred to the regular course of the narrative.

Of the females, there were but two who had arrived at womanhood, though several white-headed, olive-skinned faces were peering out of the foremost wagon of the train with eyes of lively curiosity and characteristic animation. The elder of the two adults was the sallow and wrinkled mother of most of the party, and the younger was a sprightly, active girl of eighteen who in figure, dress, and mien seemed to belong to a station in society several gradations above that of any one of her visible associates. The second vehicle was covered with a top of cloth so tightly drawn as to conceal its contents with the nicest care. The remaining wagons were loaded with such rude furniture and other personal effects as might be supposed to belong to one ready at any moment to change his abode without reference to season or distance.

Perhaps there was little in this train or in the appearance of its proprietors that is not daily to be encountered on the highways of this changeable and moving country. But the solitary and peculiar scenery in which it was so unexpectedly exhibited gave to the party a marked character of wildness and adventure.

In the little valleys which, in the regular formation of the land, occurred at every mile of their progress, the view was bounded on two of the sides by the gradual and low elevations which give name to the description of prairie we have mentioned; while on the others, the meager prospect ran off in long, narrow, barren perspectives but slightly relieved by a pitiful show of coarse though somewhat luxuriant vegetation. From the summits of the swells, the eye became fatigued with the sameness and chilling dreariness of the landscape. The earth was not unlike the ocean when its restless waters are heaving heavily after the agitation and fury of the tempest have begun to lessen. There was the same waving and regular surface, the same absence of foreign objects, and the same boundless extent to the view. Indeed so very striking was the resemblance between the water and the land that however much the geologist might sneer at so simple a theory, it would have been difficult for a poet not to have felt that the formation of the one had been produced by the subsiding dominion of the other. Here and there a tall tree rose out of the bottoms, stretching its naked branches abound like some solitary vessel; and to strengthen the delusion, far in the distance appeared two or three rounded thickets looming in the misty horizon like islands resting on the waters. It is unnecessary to warn the practiced reader that the sameness of the surface and the low stands of the spectators exaggerated the distances, but as swell appeared after swell and island succeeded island, there was a disheartening assurance that long and seemingly interminable tracts of territory must be passed before the wishes of the humblest agriculturist could be realized.

Still, the leader of the emigrants steadily pursued his way, with no other guide than the sun, turning his back resolutely on the abodes of civilization and plunging at each step more deeply, if not irretrievably, into the haunts of the barbarous and savage occupants of the country. As the day drew nigher to a close, however, his mind, which was, perhaps, incapable of maturing any connected system of forethought beyond that which related to the interest of the present moment, became in some slight degree troubled with the care of providing for the wants of the hours of darkness.

On reaching the crest of a swell that was a little higher than the usual elevations, he lingered a minute and cast a half-curious eye on either hand in quest of those well-known signs which might indicate a place where the three grand requisites of water, fuel, and fodder were to be obtained in conjunction.

JAMES FENIMORE COOPER was one of the first important American writers. He was born in 1789, and attended Yale for three years until he was expelled for disciplinary reasons. After a time at sea and a few years spent as a farmer, he began to write. In his thirty years of writing, he produced over fifty publications including: *The Spy, The Pilot, The Deerslayer, The Last of the Mohicans, The Pathfinder,* and *The Prairie.*

Zane Grey

The Thundering Herd

Autumn winds had long waved the grass in the vast upland valley and the breath of the north had tinged the meandering lines of trees along the river bottoms. Gold and purple, and a flame of fire, shone brightly in the morning sunlight.

Birds and beasts of that wild open northland felt stir in them the instinct to move toward the south. The honk of wild geese floated down upon the solitudes and swift flocks of these heralds of winter sped by, sharply outlined against the blue sky.

High upon the western rampart of that valley perched an eagle, watching from his lonely crag. His telescopic eye ranged afar. Beneath him on the endless slope and boundless floor of the valley, moved a black mass, creeping with snail-like slowness toward the south. It seemed as long as the valley and as wide. It reached to the dim purple distances and disappeared there. The densest part covered the center of the valley, from which ran wide straggling arms, like rivers narrowing toward their sources in the hills. Patches of gray grass, dotted with gold, shone here and there against the black background. Always the dark moving streams and blots seemed encroaching upon these patches of grass. They spread over them and covered them. Then other open spaces appeared at different points. How slow the change! Yet there was a definite movement.

This black mass was alive. The eagle was gazing down upon leagues and leagues of buffalo. Acres of buffalo, miles of buffalo, millions of buffalo! The shaggy, irregular, ragged herd had no end. It dominated slopes, and bottomlands, and the hazy reaches beyond.

The vision of the eagle was an organ for self-preservation, not capable of appreciating the beauty and sublimity of the earth and its myriads of wild creatures. Yet with piercing eye the eagle watched from his lonely crag. Boundless void, with its moving coverlet of black, the wide space of sky keen with its cool wind – valley of leagues, with its living heritage of a million years! Wild, primitive, grand was the scene. It was eloquent of the past. The future stretched away like the dim, strange, unknown purple distances, with an intimation of tragedy. But the hour was one of natural fruition, wild life in the open, with the sun like an eye of the Creator, shining over the land. Peace, silence, solitude attended the eagle in his vigil.

Yet a brooding sadness, like an invisible mantle, lay over the valley. Was it the dreamy, drowsy spell of autumn? Was it the pervading spirit of a dying season, reluctant to face the rigor of snow and ice? The fact was that autumn lingered, and nature brooded over some mystery, some problem, some blunder. Life was sweet, strong – scented on the wind, but there was death lurking somewhere, perhaps in the purple shadow of distance to the southward. The morning was bright, golden, glorious, yet it did not wait, and night was coming. So there was more than the melancholy languor of autumn in the still air. A mighty Being seemed breathing there, invisible and infinite, all-encompassing. It kept its secret.

Suddenly the eagle plunged like a thunderbolt from his crag and shot down and down, at last to spread his closed wings, and sail slowly and majestically round and round, over an open grassy patch encircled by buffalo.

In this spot, well toward the center and front of the vast herd, appeared about to be enacted a battle between a monarch and his latest rival for supremacy.

The huge leader, shaggy, brown, ragged, was not a creature of beauty, but he was magnificent. He had twice the bulk of an ox, and stood as high as a horse. His massive head, with the long shaggy hair matted with burrs, was held low, muzzle almost to the ground, showing the big curved short horns widely separated. Eyes of dark fire blazed from beneath the shaggy locks. His great back slowly arched and his short tufted tail rose stiffly erect. A hoarse rumble issued from the cavern of his chest – a roar at the brazen effrontery of this young bull that dared to face him.

Many and many had been the battles of this old monarch. For years he had reigned, so many that he had forgotten the instinct of his youth, when he, like the rival before him, had bearded the king of the buffaloes. He had to fight again, in obedience to that law which respected only the survival of the fittest.

The bull that had challenged the king to battle was also magnificent. He too lowered his huge head, and with short prodigious strokes he pawed tufts of grass and heaps of earth up into the air. His color was a glossy seal brown and he did not have the ragged, worn appearance of the monarch. His shaggy hair hung thick and wooly from head and shoulders and knees. Great rippling muscles swelled on his flanks as he pawed and moved round his enemy. He meant to attack. He shone resplendent. He seemed the epitome of animal vigor and spirit. The bawl with which he answered the roar of the monarch rang clear and hard, like a blast. He possessed something that the old warrior had lost. He had beauty and youth.

The surrounding buffalo did not appear concerned over this impending battle. They were aware of it, for they would raise their shaggy heads from the grass and gaze a moment at the king and his jealous aspirant. Then they would return to their feeding. It was noticeable, however, that the circle did not narrow; if anything, it gradually widened.

The king did not wait for his foe to begin the struggle. He charged. His dash was incredibly fast for so heavy a beast and his momentum tremendous. Square against the lowered head of the young bull he struck. The shock sent forth a sodden crash. The bull staggered under the impact. His whole bulk shook. Then he was lifted, head up, fore-feet off the ground, higher, and with grinding clash of horns he was hurled heavily upon his back.

Under the great force of that charge the old monarch went to his knees, and the advantage which might have been his was lost. He heaved in his rage.

Nimbly the young bull rolled over and bounded to his feet, un-hurt. Nature had by this time developed him to a perfect resisting force. His front was all bone, covered by matted hair. Swifter than a horse, as quick as a cat, he launched his bulk at his antagonist, and hit him with a shock no less terrific than the one that had opened the bat-tle. But the old warrior received it as if he had been a great oak rooted in the earth.

Then with heads pounding and horns grinding, these beasts, re-lentless as nature itself, settled down to the wonderful and incredible battle of buffalo bulls. Bent and bowed, always head to head, they per-formed prodigious feats of ramming and butting, and endeavoring to give each other a fatal thrust with horn.

But under that heavy mat of wool was skin over an inch thick and tougher than hardened leather. These bulls were made to fight. They had extraordinary lung capacity and very large nostrils. Their endur-ance was as remarkable as their physical structure.

In a cloud of dust they plowed up the prairie, driving the grazing buffalo back and forth, and covering acres of ground in their struggle. The crash of heads and rattle of horns gradually diminished in vigor of sound, indicating that the speed and strength of the rivals were wearing down. Not so their ferocity and courage! It was a battle to death or complete vanquishment. In time the dust cloud blew away on the wind, and then the bulls could be seen in action less strenuous but still savage.

The old monarch was near the end of his last battle. His race was run. Torn and dirt-covered and bloody, he backed before the on-slaughts of his foe. His lungs, like great bellows, sent out gasps that were as well utterances of defeat. He could not withstand the relentless young bull. Age must go down. He was pushed to his knees and al-most bowled over. Recovering he wearily fronted that huge battering black head, and then was shoved to his haunches. Again, narrowly, he escaped the following lunge. That was the moment of defeat. He was beaten. The instinct for life took the place of the instinct for supremacy. Backward, step by step, he went, always facing the bellowing young conqueror. There came intervals when he was free of that lowered battering head; and during the last of these he sheered away among the stragglers of the herd, leaving the field to the visitor. The old monarch had retired to the ranks and there was a new leader of the herd.

The eagle soared back to his lonely perch, there to clutch the crag with his talons and sweep the valley with crystal eye.

Out to the front of the black mass of buffalo a whirlwind twisted up a column of dust. Funnel-shaped it rose, yellow and spreading, into the air, while it raced across the valley. That, or something as natural, stirred a movement in the foreranks of buffalo. All at once the leaders broke into a run, heading south. The movement, and the growing pound of their hoofs, ran through the herd as swiftly as a current. Then, magically and wondrously, the whole immense mass moved as if one spirit, one mind, dominated it. The throbbing pound of hoofs suddenly increased to a roar. Dust began to rise and blow back, like low clouds of yellow smoke, over the acres, and then the miles of bobbing black backs. The vast herd seemed to become a sea in swift and accelerating action.

Soon a rising pall of dust shrouded the thousands of buffalo, running under what seemed an obscure curtain. The volume of sound had swelled from rhythmic pound and beat to a mighty and appalling roar. Only the battlements of the upper air, assailed in storm by the ripping of lightning, could send back such thunder as now rose from the shaking earth. But this was one long continuous roll. The movement of buffalo in unison resembled a tidal wave and the sound was that of an avalanche. The ground trembled under the thundering herd.

The eagle perched motionless on his crag, indifferent to the rolling chaos beneath him. The valley-wide cloud of dust floated low down. Time passed. Halfway to the zenith rose the sun. Then gradually the tremor of the earth and the roar of hoofs diminished, rolled, and died away. The herd had passed. On his lofty perch the eagle slept, and the valley cleared of dust and movement. Solitude, loneliness, and silence reigned at the solemn noontide.

It was spring of an era many years after the lone eagle had watched the buffalo herd.

An upland prairie country rolled and waved down from snow-capped Rocky Mountains to spread out into the immense eastern void. Over the bleached white grass had come a faint tinge of green. The warm sun had begun its renewal of the covering of the earth. A flock of wild geese, late on their annual pilgrimage, winged swift flight toward the northland. On the ridges elk grazed, and down in the hollows, where murmuring streams rushed, clouded with the blue color of melted snow, deer nibbled at the new tender shoots of grass.

Below the uplands, where the plain began, herds of buffalo dotted the patches and streaked the monotony of the gray vastness. Leagues and leagues it spread, always darker for the increase of buffalo, until all was a dense black that merged into the haze of distance.

A river wended its curving way out across the plains, and in a wooded bend an Indian encampment showed its white tepees, and red blankets, and columns of blue smoke lazily rising.

Hidden in the brush along the river half-naked red men lay in wait for the buffalo to come down to drink. These hunters did not need to sally forth for their game. They had only to wait and choose the meat and the hide that best served them for their simple needs. They did not kill more than they could use.

Along the river bank, far as eye could see, the shaggy monsters trooped down to drink. Bulls and cows and calves came in endless procession. In some places, where the bank was steep, the thirsty buffalo behind pushed the row ahead into the water, whence rose a splashing *melee*. The tawny calves, still too young to shed their coats and turn the seal brown of their mothers, bawled lustily as they were shoved into the river.

Near the encampment of the Indians, where trees and brush lined the shore, the buffalo were more wary. They like the open. But stragglers came along, and the choicest of these fell prey to the deadly arrows of the red men. A shaggy young bull, sleek and brown, superb in his approaching maturity, passed within range of the chieftain of that hunting clan. He rose from his covert, a lean, dark Indian, tall and powerful of build, with intense face and piercing eyes turned toward his quarry. He bent a bow few Indians could have drawn. He bent it till the flint head of the arrow touched his left hand. Then he released the arrow. Like a glint of light it flashed and, striking the bull behind the shoulder, buried half its length there. The animal grunted. He made no violent movements. He walked back as he had come, only more and more slowly. The chief followed him out to the edge of the timber. There other buffalo coming in saw both Indian and wounded bull, but they only swerved aside. The bull halted, and heaving heavily, he plunged to his knees, and then rolled over on his side.

After the hunters came the squaws with their crude flint and bone implements, to skin the buffalo and cut up the meat and pack it to the encampment.

There the chief repaired to rest on his buffalo hide under a tree, and to think the thoughts and dream the dreams of the warrior. Beyond the white-peaked mountain range lived enemies of his, red men of a hated tribe. Other than remembrance of them he had no concern. His red gods could not tell him of the future. The paleface, who was to drive him and his people into the fastnesses of the arid hills, was unknown and undreamed of. Into his lofty serene mind no thought flashed of a vanishing of the buffalo while yet his descendants lived. The buffalo were as many as the sand of the river bottoms. They had always been; they would always be. The buffalo existed to furnish food, raiment, shelter for the red man.

So the chief rested in his camp, watching beaver at work on the river bank, as tame as were the buffalo. Like these animals, he and his tribe were happy and self-sufficient. Only infrequent battles with other tribes marred the serenity of their lives. Always the endless herds were to be found, to the south or the north. This chief worshiped the sun, loved his people and the wild, lonely land he believed was his; and if there was in his tribe a brave who was liar or coward or thief, or a squaw who broke the law, death was his or her portion.

A straggling band of white men wearily rode and tramped across the great plains centuries before that wonderful level prairie was to be divided into the Western states of America.

These white travelers were the Spanish explorers under the command of the intrepid Coronado. It was a large band. Many of them rode horses – Arabian horses of the purest breed, from which the Western mustang was descended. But most of them walked, wearing queer apparel and armor not suitable to such arduous travel. They carried strange weapons.

Hardy, indomitable, and enduring, this first band of white men to penetrate the great plains and the deserts of the South and West, recorded for history something of their marvelous adventures and terrible experiences and strange sights.

Many hundreds of leagues they traveled, according to their historian, Castaneda, over tremendous plains and reaches of sand, stark and level, and so barren of trees and stones that they erected heaps of the ox dung they found, so that they could be guided back by the way they had come. They lost horses and men.

All the way across these great plains of grass and sand the Spaniards encountered herds of crooked-back oxen, as many as there were sheep in Spain. But they saw no people with the crooked-back cattle. These weary and lost travelers, almost starved, found in the oxen succor they so grievously needed. Meat gave them strength and courage to go on through obstacles none save crusaders could have overcome. Sometimes in this strange country it rained great showers of hailstones as big as oranges; and these storms caused many tears and injuries.

Castaneda wrote:

These oxen are the bigness and color of our bulls. . . . They have a great bunch of hair on their fore shoulders, and more on their fore part than their hinder part, and it is like wool. They have a horsemane upon their backbone, and much hair, and very long from their knees downward. They have great tufts of hair hanging down their foreheads, and it seemeth they have beards because of the great store of hair hanging down at their chins and throats. The males have very large tails, and a great knob or flock at the end, so that in some respects they resemble the lion, and in some others the camel. They push with their horns; they run; they overtake and kill a horse when they are in their rage and anger. The horses fled from them, either because of their deformed shape, or else because they had never before seen them. Finally it is a foul and fierce beast of countenance and form of body.

Coronado and Castaneda, with their band of unquenchable spirits, were the first white people to see the American buffalo.

ZANE GREY (1872-1939) is looked upon as the writer of the quintessential western experience. From 1910 - 1925 many of his books appeared on the best seller list. Although he started out a dentist, he moved to Pennsylvania in 1905 to pursue his life-long dream of writing. It was not until he was introduced to the west a couple of years later that Grey found the subject of his novels. While visiting a ranch in Arizona, he came across the formula which guaranteed his place in history's literature: the growth of a neophyte, through innocence to experience and ultimately success in the wild west. This passage from *The Thundering Herd* tells of what earlier explorers must have witnessed – if not in reality then in their dreams, on the open plains of the unknown west.

John Wesley Powell

*History of the Exploration of the
Canyons of the Colorado*

August 14, 1869

At daybreak we walk down the bank of the river, on a little sandy beach, to take a view of a new feature in the canyon. Heretofore, hard rocks have given us bad river; soft rocks, smooth water; and a series of rocks harder than any we have experienced sets in. The river enters the granite!

We can see but a little way into the granite gorge, but it looks threatening.

After breakfast we enter on the waves. At the very introduction, it inspires awe. The canyon is narrower than we have ever before seen it; the water is swifter; there are but few broken rocks in the channel; but the walls are set, on either side, with pinnacles and crags; and sharp, angular buttresses, bristling with wind and wave polished spires, extend far out into the river.

Ledges of rocks jut into the stream, their tops sometimes just below the surface, sometimes rising few or many feet above; and island ledges, and island pinnacles, and island towers break the swift course of the stream into chutes, and eddies, and whirlpools. We soon reach a place where a creek comes in from the left, and just below, the channel is choked with boulders, which have washed down this lateral canyon and formed a dam, over which there is a fall of thirty or forty feet; but on the boulders we can get foothold, and we make a portage.

Three more such dams are found. Over one we make a portage; at the other two we find chutes, through which we can run.

As we proceed, the granite rises higher, until nearly a thousand feet of the lower part of the walls are composed of this rock.

About eleven o'clock we hear a great roar ahead, and approach it very cautiously. The sound grows louder and louder as we run, and at last we find ourselves above a long, broken fall, with ledges and pinnacles of rock obstructing the river. There is a descent of, perhaps, seventy-five or eighty feet in a third of a mile, and the rushing waters break into great waves on the rocks, and lash themselves into a mad, white foam. We can land just above, but there is no foothold on either side by which we can make a portage. It is nearly a thousand feet to the top of the granite, so it will be impossible to carry our boats around, though we can climb to the summit up a side gulch, and, passing along a mile or two, can descend to the river. This we find on examination; but such a portage would be impracticable for us, and we must run the rapid, or abandon the river. There is no hesitation. We step into our boats, push off and away we go, first on smooth but swift water, then we strike a glassy wave, and ride to its top, down again into the trough, up again on a higher wave, and down and up on waves higher and still higher, until we strike one just as it curls back, and a breaker rolls our little boat. Still, on we speed, shooting past projecting rocks, till the little boat is caught in a whirlpool, and spun around several times. At last we pull out again into the stream, and now the other boats have passed us. The open compartment of the *Emma Dean* is filled with water, and every breaker rolls over us. Hurled back from a rock, now on this side, now on that, we are carried into an eddy, in which we struggle for a few minutes, and are then out again, the breakers still rolling over us. Our boat is manageable, but she cannot sink, and we drift down another hundred yards, through breakers; how, we scarcely know. We find the other boats have turned into an eddy at the foot of the fall, and are waiting to catch us as we come, for the men have seen that our boat is swamped. They push out as we come near, and pull us in against the wall. We bail our boat, and on we go again.

The walls, now, are more than a mile in height – a vertical distance difficult to appreciate. Stand on the south steps of the Treasury building, in Washington, and look down Pennsylvania Avenue to the Capitol Park, and measure this distance overhead, and imagine cliffs to extend to that attitude, and you will understand what I mean; or, stand at Canal street, in New York and look up Broadway to Grace Church, and you have about the distance; or, stand at Lake Street bridge, in Chicago, and look down to the Central Depot, and you have it again.

A thousand feet of this is up through granite crags, then steep slopes and perpendicular cliffs rise, one above another, to the summit. The gorge is black and narrow below, red and gray and flaring above, with crags and angular projections on the walls, which cut in many places by side canyons, seem to be a vast wilderness of rocks. Down in these grand, gloomy depths we glide, ever listening, for the mad waters keep up their roar; ever watching, ever peering ahead, for the narrow canyon is winding, and the river is closed in so that we can see but a few hundred yards, and what there may be below we know not; but we listen for falls, and watch for rocks, or stop now and then, in the bay of a recess, to admire the gigantic scenery. And ever, as we go, there is some new pinnacle or tower, some crag or peak, some distant view of the upper plateau, some strange-shaped rock, or some deep, narrow side canyon. Then we come to another broken fall, which appears more difficult than the one we ran this morning.

A small creek comes in on the right, and the first fall of the water is over boulders, which have been carried down by this lateral stream. We land at its mouth, and stop for an hour or two to examine the fall. It seems possible to let down with lines, at least a part of the way, from point to point, along the right-hand wall. So we make a portage over the first rocks, and find footing on some boulders below. Then we let down one of the boats to the end of her line, when she reaches a corner of the projecting rock, to which one of the men clings, and steadies her, while I examine an eddy below. I think we can pass the other boats down by us, and catch them in the eddy. This is soon done and the men in the boats in the eddy pull us to their side. On the shore of this little eddy there is about two feet of gravel beach above the water. Standing on this beach, some of the men take the line of the little boat and let it drift down against another projecting angle. Here is a little shelf, on which a man from my boat climbs, and a shorter line is passed to him, and he fastens the boat to the side of the cliff. Then the second one is let down, bringing the line of the third. When the second boat is tied up, the two men standing on the beach above spring into the last boat, which is pulled up alongside of ours. Then we let down the boats, for twenty-five or thirty yards, by walking along the shelf, landing them again in the mouth of a side canyon. Just below this there is another pile of boulders, over which we make another portage. From the foot of these rocks we can climb to another shelf, forty or fifty feet above the water.

On this bench, we camp for the night. We find a few sticks, which have lodged in the rocks. It is raining hard, and we have no shelter, but kindle a fire and have our supper. We sit on the rocks all night, wrapped in our ponchos, getting what sleep we can.

August 15, 1869

This morning we find we can let down for three or four hundred yards, and it is managed in this way: We pass along the wall, by climbing from projecting point to point, sometimes near the water's edge, at other places, fifty or sixty feet above, and hold the boat with a line, while two men remain aboard, and prevent her from being dashed against the rocks, and keep the line from getting caught on the wall. In two hours we had brought them all down, as far as it is possible, in this way. A few yards below, the river strikes with great violence against a projecting rock, and our boats are pulled up in a little bay above. We must now manage to pull out of this, and clear the point below. The little boat is held by the bow obliquely up the stream. We jump in, and pull out only a few strokes, and sweep clear of the dangerous rock. The other boats follow in the same manner, and the rapid is passed.

It is not easy to describe the labor of such navigation. We must prevent the waves from dashing the boats against the cliffs. Sometimes, where the river is swift, we must put a bight of rope around a rock, to prevent her being snatched from us by a wave; but where the plunge is

too great, or the chute too swift, we must let her leap, and catch her be-
low, or the undertow will drag her under the falling water, and she
sinks. Where we wish to run her out a little way from shore, through
a channel between rocks, we first throw in little sticks of driftwood,
and watch their course, to see where we must steer, so that she will
pass the channel in safety. And so we hold, and let go, and pull, and
lift, and ward, among rocks, around rocks, and over rocks.

And now we go on through this solemn, mysterious way. The riv-
er is very deep, the canyon very narrow, and still obstructed, so that
there is no steady flow of the stream; but the waters wheel, and roll,
and boil, and we are scarcely able to determine where we can go. Now,
the boat is carried to the right, perhaps close to the wall; again, she is
shot into the stream, and perhaps is dragged over to the other side,
where, caught in a whirlpool, she spins about. We can neither land
nor run as we please. The boats are entirely unmanageable; no order in
their running can be preserved; now one, now another, is ahead, each
crew laboring for its own preservation. In such a place we come to an-
other rapid. Two of the boats run it perforce. One succeeds in landing,
but there is no foothold by which to make a portage, and she is pushed
out again into the stream. The next minute a great reflex wave fills the
open compartment; she is water logged, and drifts unmanageably.
Breaker after breaker rolls over her, and one capsizes her. The men are
thrown out; but they cling to the boat, and she drifts down some dis-
tance, alongside of us, and we are able to catch her. She is soon bailed
out, and the men are aboard once more; but the oars are lost, so a pair
from the *Emma Dean* is spared. Then for two miles we find smooth
water.

Clouds are playing in the canyon today. Sometimes they roll down
in great masses, filling the gorge with gloom; sometimes they hang
above, from wall to wall, and cover the canyon with a roof of impend-
ing storm; and we can peer long distances up and down this canyon
corridor, with its cloud roof overhead, its walls of black granite, and its
river bright with the sheen of broken waters. Then, a gust of wind
sweeps down a side gulch, and, making a rift in the clouds, reveals the
blue heavens, and a stream of sunlight pours in. Then, the clouds drift
away into the distance, and hang around crags, and peaks, and pin-
nacles, and towers, and walls, and cover them with a mantle, that lifts

from time to time, and sets them all in sharp relief. Then, baby clouds creep out of side canyons, glide around points, and creep back again, into more distant gorges. Then, clouds, set in strata, across the canyon, with intervening vista views, to cliffs and rocks beyond. The clouds are children of the heavens, and when they play among the rocks, they lift them to the region above.

It rains! Rapidly little rills are formed above, and these soon grow into brooks, and the brooks grow into creeks, and tumble over the walls in innumerable cascades, adding their wild music to the roar of the river. When the rain ceases, the rills, brooks, and creeks run dry. The waters that fall, during a rain, on these steep rocks, are gathered at once into the river; they could scarcely be poured in more suddenly, if some vast spout ran from the clouds to the stream itself. When a storm bursts over the canyon, a side gulch is dangerous, for a sudden flood may come, and the inpouring waters will raise the river, so as to hide the rocks before your eyes.

Early in the afternoon, we discover a stream, entering from the north, a clear, beautiful creek, coming down through a gorgeous red canyon. We land, and camp on a sand beach, above its mouth, under a great, overspreading tree, with willow-shaped leaves.

JOHN WESLEY POWELL was born in 1834 in New York. He served in the Civil War, rising from private to major through action he saw at the Battle of Shiloh and Vicksburg. He lost his right arm at the Battle of Shiloh. In 1867, he made a field trip to the Rocky Mountains, where he scaled Pikes Peak with his wife Emma and developed a life-long enchantment with the region. Encouraged by the Smithsonian Institution, he set out to float the Colorado River in 1869 on four boats he had especially made for the trip through the unknown. Powell notes he had been warned not to enter the Grand Canyon, and its unknown waters, by the Indians who thought it to be disobedience to the gods.

For 100 days, Powell and his crew ventured through the unknown canyon and into history, contending with treacherous rapids, and exploring a place never seen by European man, and filled with the incredible wonders of nature. At journey's end the explorer and self-taught naturalist began planning his next trip into the timelessness of the Grand Canyon. He went on to serve as director of the United States Geological Survey and founded the Bureau of Ethnology for the Smithsonian.

Willa Cather

O Pioneers!
"The Wild Land"

Although it was only four
o'clock, the winter day was
fading. The road led south-
west, toward the streak of pale,
watery light that glimmered in
the leaden sky. The light fell up-
on the two sad young faces that
were turned mutely toward it:
upon the eyes of the girl, who
seemed to be looking with such
anguished perplexity into the fu-
ture; upon the sombre eyes of
the boy, who seemed already to
be looking into the past. The lit-
tle town behind them had van-
ished as if it had never been, had
fallen behind the swell of the
prairie, and the stern frozen
country received them into its
bosom. The homesteads were
few and far apart; here and there
a windmill gaunt against the sky,
a sod house crouching in a hol-
low. But the great fact was the
land itself, which seemed to over-
whelm the little beginnings of
human society that struggled in
its sombre wastes. It was from
facing this vast hardness that the
boy's mouth had become so bit-
ter; because he felt that men
were too weak to make any mark

here, that the land wanted to be let alone, to preserve its own fierce strength, its peculiar, savage kind of beauty, its uninterrupted mournfulness.

The wagon jolted along over the frozen road. The two friends had less to say to each other than usual, as if the cold had somehow penetrated to their hearts.

"Did Lou and Oscar go to the Blue to cut wood to-day?" Carl asked.

"Yes. I'm almost sorry I let them go, it's turned so cold. But mother frets if the wood gets low." She stopped and put her hand to her forehead, brushing back her hair. "I don't know what is to become of us, Carl, if father has to die. I don't dare to think about it. I wish we could all go with him and let the grass grow back over everything."

Carl made no reply. Just ahead of them was the Norwegian graveyard, where the grass had, indeed, grown back over everything, shaggy and red, hiding even the wire fence. Carl realized that he was not a very helpful companion, but there was nothing he could say.

"Of course," Alexandra went on, steadying her voice a little, "the boys are strong and work hard, but we've always depended so on father that I don't see how we can go ahead. I almost feel as if there were nothing to go ahead for."

"Does your father know?"

"Yes, I think he does. He lies and counts on his fingers all day. I think he is trying to count up what he is leaving for us. It's a comfort to him that my chickens are laying right on through the cold weather and bringing in a little money. I wish we could keep his mind off such things, but I don't have much time to be with him now."

"I wonder if he'd like to have me bring my magic lantern over some evening?"

Alexandra turned her face toward him. "Oh, Carl! Have you got it?"

"Yes. It's back there in the straw. Didn't you notice the box I was carrying? I tried it all morning in the drug-store cellar, and it worked ever so well, makes fine big pictures."

"What are they about?"

"Oh, hunting pictures in Germany, and Robinson Crusoe and funny pictures about cannibals. I'm going to paint some slides for it on glass, out of the Hans Andersen book."

Alexandra seemed actually cheered. There is often a good deal of the child left in people who have had to grow up too soon. "Do bring it over, Carl. I can hardly wait to see it, and I'm sure it will please father. Are the pictures colored? Then I know he'll like them. He likes the calendars I get him in town. I wish I could get more. You must leave me here, mustn't you? It's been nice to have company."

Carl stopped the horses and looked dubiously up at the black sky. "It's pretty dark. Of course the horses will take you home, but I think I'd better light your lantern, in case you should need it."

He gave her the reins and climbed back into the wagon-box, where he crouched down and made a tent of his overcoat. After a dozen trials he succeeded in lighting the lantern, which he placed in front of Alexandra, half covering it with a blanket so that the light would not shine in her eyes. "Now, wait until I find my box. Yes, here it is. Good-night, Alexandra. Try not to worry." Carl sprang to the ground and ran off across the fields toward the Linstrum homestead. "Hoo, hoo-o-o-o!" he called back as he disappeared over a ridge and dropped into a sand gully. The wind answered him like an echo, "Hoo, hoo-o-o-o-o-o!" Alexandra drove off alone. The rattle of her wagon was lost in the howling of the wind, but her lantern, held firmly between her feet, made a moving point of light along the highway, going deeper and deeper into the dark country.

II

On one of the ridges of that wintry waste stood the low log house in which John Bergson was dying. The Bergson homestead was easier to find than many another, because it overlooked Norway Creek, a shallow, muddy stream that sometimes flowed, and sometimes stood still, at the bottom of a winding ravine with steep, shelving sides overgrown with brush and cottonwoods and dwarf ash. This creek gave a sort of identity to the farms that bordered upon it. Of all the bewildering things about a new country, the absence of human landmarks is one of the most depressing and disheartening. The houses on the Divide were small and were usually tucked away in low places, you did not see them until you came directly upon them. Most of them were built of the sod itself, and were only the unescapable ground in another form. The roads were but faint tracks in the grass, and the fields were scarcely noticeable. The record of the plow was insignificant, like the feeble scratches on stone left by prehistoric races, so indeterminate that they may, after all, be only the markings of glaciers, and not a record of human strivings.

In eleven long years John Bergson had made but little impression upon the wild land he had come to tame. It was still a wild thing that had its ugly moods; and no one knew when they were likely to come, or why. Mischance hung over it. Its Genius was unfriendly to man. The sick man was feeling this as he lay looking out of the window, after the doctor had left him, on the day following Alexandra's trip to town. There it lay outside his door, the same land, the same lead-colored miles. He knew every ridge and draw and gully between him and the horizon. To the south, his plowed fields; to the east, the sod stables, the cattle corral, the pond, – and then the grass.

Bergson went over in his mind the things that had held him back. One winter his cattle had perished in a blizzard. The next summer one of his plow horses broke its leg in a prairie-dog hole and had to be shot. Another summer he lost his hogs from cholera, and a valuable stallion died from a rattlesnake bite. Time and again his crops had failed. He had lost two children, boys, that came between Lou and Emil, and there had been the cost of sickness and death. Now, when he had at last struggled out of debt, he was going to die himself. He was only forty-six, and had, of course, counted upon more time.

Bergson had spent his first five years on the Divide getting into debt, and the last six getting out. He had paid off his mortgages and had ended pretty much where he began, with the land. He owned exactly six hundred and forty acres of what stretched outside his door; his own original homestead and timber claim, making three hundred and twenty acres, and the half-section adjoining, the homestead of a younger brother who had given up the fight, gone back to Chicago work in a fancy bakery and distinguish himself in a Swedish athletic club. So far John had not attempted to cultivate the second half-section, but used it for pasture land, and one of his sons rode herd there in open weather.

John Bergson had the Old-World belief that land, in itself, is desirable. But this land was an enigma. It was like a horse that no one knows how to break to harness, that runs wild and kicks things to pieces. He had an idea that no one understood how to farm it properly, and this he often discussed with Alexandra. Their neighbors, certainly, knew even less about farming than he did. Many of them had never worked on a farm until they took up their homesteads. They had been *hand-werkers* at home; tailors, locksmiths.

For weeks, John Bergson had been thinking about these things. His bed stood in the sitting-room, next to the kitchen. Through the day, while the baking and washing and ironing were going on, the father lay and looked up at the roof beams that he himself had hewn, or out at the cattle in the corral. He counted the cattle over and over. It diverted him to speculate as to how much weight each of the steers would probably put on by spring. He often called his daughter in to talk to her about this. Before Alexandra was twelve years old she had begun to be a help to him, and as she grew older he had come to depend more and more upon her resourcefulness and good judgment. His boys were willing enough to work, but when he talked with them they usually irritated him. It was Alexandra who read the papers and followed the markets, and who learned by the mistakes of their neighbors. It was Alexandra who could always tell about what it had cost to fatten each steer, and who could guess the weight of a hog before it went on the scales closer than John Bergson himself. Lou and Oscar were industrious, but he could never teach them to use their heads about their work.

WILLA CATHER (1873 - 1947) divided her childhood between her native Shenandoah Valley, Virginia and Red Cloud, Webster County-area, Nebraska. Her parents moved permanently to Red Cloud when she was nine. Within her new homeland on the High Plains, she found the topics of many of her books, as she wrote about "the effect of a new country . . . on people transplanted to it from the old traditions of a stable, complex civilization." She went on to win a Pulitzer Prize for *One of Ours* (1922). In *O' Pioneers* – the book she calls her first real novel– she captures the metaphor the challenge, yet nuturing, strength the westering experience presented to new Americans.

Jack London

The Call of the Wild
"In A Far Country"

When a man journeys into a far country, he must be prepared to forget many of the things he has learned, and to acquire such customs as are inherent with existence in the new land; he must abandon the old ideals and the old gods, and oftentimes he must reverse the very codes by which his conduct has hitherto been shaped. To those who have the protean faculty of adaptability, the novelty of such change may even be a source of pleasure; but to those who happen to be hardened to the ruts in which they were created, the pressure of the altered environment is unbearable, and they chafe in body and in spirit under the new restrictions which they do not understand. This chafing is bound to act and react, producing divers evils and leading to various misfortunes. It were better for the man who cannot fit himself to the new groove to return to his own country; if he delays too long, he will surely die.

The man who turns his back upon the comforts of an elder civilization, to face the savage youth, the primordial simplicity of the North, may estimate success at an inverse ratio to the quantity and quality of his hopelessly fixed habits. He will soon discover, if he be a fit candidate, that the material habits are the less important. The exchange of such things as a dainty menu for rough fare, of the stiff leather shoe for the soft, shapeless moccasin, of the feather bed for a couch in the snow, is after all a very easy matter. But his pinch will come in learning properly to shape his mind's attitude toward all things, and especially toward his fellow man. For the courtesies of ordinary life, he must substitute unselfishness, forbearance, and tolerance. Thus, and thus only, can he gain that pearl of great price – true comradeship. He must not say "Thank you"; he must mean it without opening his mouth, and prove it by responding in kind. In short, he must substitute the deed for the word, the spirit for the letter.

When the world rang with the tale of Arctic gold, and the lure of the North gripped the heartstrings of men, Carter Weatherbee threw up his snug clerkship, turned the half of his savings over to his wife, and with the remainder bought an outfit. There was no romance in his nature – the bondage of commerce had crushed all that; he was simply tired of the ceaseless grind, and wished to risk great hazards in view of corresponding returns. Like many another fool, disdaining the old trails used by the Northland pioneers for a score of years, he hurried to Edmonton in the spring of the year; and there, unluckily for his soul's welfare, he allied himself with a party of men.

There was nothing unusual about the party, except its plans. Even its goal, like that of all the other parties, was the Klondike. But the route it had mapped out to attain that goal took away the breath of the hardiest native, born and bred to the vicissitudes of the Northwest. Even Jacques Baptiste, born of a Chippewa woman and a renegade *voyageur* (having raised his first whimpers in a deerskin lodge north of the sixty-fifth parallel, and had the same hushed by blissful sucks of raw tallow), was surprised though he sold his services to them and agreed to travel even to the never-opening ice. He shook his head ominously whenever his advice was asked.

Percy Cuthfert's evil star must have been in the ascendant, for he, too, joined this company of argonauts. He was an ordinary man, with a bank account as deep as his culture, which is saying a good deal. He had no reason to embark on such a venture – no reason in the world, save that he suffered from an abnormal development of sentimentality. He mistook this for the true spirit of romance and adventure. Many another man has done the like, and made as fatal a mistake.

The first break-up of spring found the party following the ice-run of Elk River. It was an imposing fleet, for the outfit was large, and they were accompanied by a disreputable contingent of half-breed *voyageurs* with their women and children. Day in and day out, they labored with the bateaux and canoes, fought mosquitoes and other kindred pests, or sweated and swore at the portages. Severe toil like this lays a man naked to the very roots of his soul, and ere Lake Athabasca was lost in the south, each member of the party had hoisted his true colors.

The two shirks and chronic grumblers were Carter Weatherbee and Percy Cuthfert. The whole party complained less of its aches and pains than did either of them. Not once did they volunteer for the thousand and one petty duties of the camp. A bucket of water to be brought, an extra armful of wood to be chopped, the dishes to be washed and wiped, a search to be made through the outfit for some suddenly indispensable article – and these two effete scions of civilization discovered sprains or blisters requiring instant attention. They were the first to turn in at night, with score of tasks yet undone; the last to turn out in the morning, when the start should be in readiness before the breakfast was begun. They were the first to fall to at meal-time, the last to have a hand in the cooking; the first to dive for a slim delicacy, the last to discover they had added to their own another man's share. If they toiled at the oars, they slyly cut the water at each stroke and allowed the boat's momentum to float up the blade. They thought nobody noticed; but their comrades swore under their breaths and grew to hate them, while Jacques Baptiste sneered openly and damned them from morning till night. But Jacques Baptiste was no gentlemen.

At the Great Slave, Hudson Bay dogs were purchased, and the fleet sank to the guards with its added burden of dried fish and pemmican. Then canoe and bateau answered to the swift current of the Mackenzie, and they plunged into the Great Barren Ground. Every likely-looking "feeder" was prospected, but the elusive "pay-dirt" danced ever to the north. At the Great Bear, overcome by the common dread of the

Unknown Lands, their *voyageurs* began to desert, and Fort of Good Hope saw the last and bravest bending to the towlines as they bucked the current down which they had so treacherously glided. Jacques Baptiste alone remained. Had he not sworn to travel even to the never-opening ice?

The lying charts, compiled in main from hearsay, were now constantly consulted. And they felt the need of hurry, for the sun had already passed its northern solstice and was leading the winter south again. Skirting the shores of the bay, where the Mackenzie disembogues into the Arctic Ocean, they entered the mouth of the Little Peel River. Then began the arduous up-stream toil, and the two Incapables fared worse than ever. Towline and pole, paddle and tumpline, rapids and portages – such tortures served to give the one a deep disgust for great hazards, and printed for the other a fiery text on the true romance of adventure. One day they waxed mutinous, and being vilely cursed by Jacques Baptiste, turned, as worms sometimes will. But the half-breed thrashed the twain, and sent them, bruised and bleeding, about their work. It was the first time either had been manhandled.

Abandoning their river craft at the headwaters of the Little Peel, they consumed the rest of the summer in the great portage over the Mackenzie watershed to the West Rat. This little stream fed the Porcupine, which in turn joined the Yukon where that mighty highway of the North countermarchs on the Arctic Circle. But they had lost in the race with winter, and one day they tied their rafts to the thick eddy-ice and hurried their goods ashore. That night the river jammed and broke several times; the following morning it had fallen asleep for good.

JACK LONDON was born in 1876 in San Francisco. He became a seaman, a gold prospector in Alaska, a foreign correspondent, an adventurer and a writer of some of the best stories written by an American. His stories include: *Tales of the Far North, The Call of the Wild, The Sea-Wolf, White Fang, Martin Eden,* and *The Iron Heel.*

Sheila Burnford

*Highlights from 125 Years
of the Atlantic*
"Canadian Spring,"

Our heralds of spring in northwest Canada bear no resemblance to the traditional and seldom inspire the poet within us: no primroses, lambs, or forsythia here, no tender green over the earth and soft unfolding buds. Instead we have the ice-breaker battering a channel through the ice cap, smelt running in snow-swollen creeks, frost boils erupting on the roads, municipal drains backing up, and finally an inch-by-inch clearing of the snowdrifts in the garden until the exhausted daffodils push their way through the iron-bound earth at last – in June. One's whole soul cries out for spring hats and blossom, new-mown grass, the mayfly hatch, the first young tender morels; instead one pokes ineffectually with a stick at overflowng gutters, yearns over the etiolated narcissus brought up from the cellar, and plucks not primroses but long-lost overshoes and last year's oyster shells from the snow receding at the porch.

In the first week of May, Susan and I reach the peak of delayed-spring frustration, and on a morning when the returning geese fly low over the city in an exultant, baying, clamorous pack, we receive their message especially loud and clear, for we are on our way to Whitefish, to the little hunting cabin on the shore of a lonely, hill-ringed lake, peaceful and timeless: Susan to paint and I to putter; Raimie, my Labrador, to escort us and investigate possible strange noises in the night. We have discarded our families for the weekend.

The track down the hillside to the cabin turns into a fast-running creek at this time of year, carrying off the melting snow from the hills, but the ground is hard and frozen, and the car coasts down in a childishly satisfying welter of flying spray. We leave it in a clearing, load ourselves up like pack mules, then walk or stagger the last quarter of a mile. The trail winds through spruce and poplar, the branches interlaced overhead, and always I come upon the little cabin crouched by the water's edge long before I am prepared for it, so secretly does it seem to camouflage itself against the background of trees. Weather-beaten and gray, wearing its roof and chimney slightly askew, its one half-lidded eye bleary from the winter's gales, it huddles like some shabby, eccentric old woman on a park bench in spring, blinking in the sunshine; and around her skirts, instead of cheeping sparrows, the peaty brown snow creeks make little murmurous singing sounds.

We open the door, and then, as quickly as possible, the window, when the familiar stuffy, sunbaked smell of mouse nests, straw, waders, and mud-encrusted gunnysacks hits us. The boats are stored there, and we haul out the light punt, then the heavy freight canoe, and a tangled mass of decrepit reed blinds – all the paraphernalia of last fall's hunting; sweep out the first layer of powdered mud and little fluffy piles of duck and partridge feathers; then, lastly, after tossing for the victim, out go all the visible mouse corpses, hurled into the bush, from where they are conscientiously retrieved by the dog and returned to the steps. We leave the door and windows open to the cold sweet northern air; then, mutually unenthusiastic about housework at any time, we call it a day and sit on the wooden steps, at peace with the world, a bottle of beer apeice, so sheltered from the wind and warm in the noon sun that we take off our heavy sweaters and roll up our shirt sleeves.

Almost immediately the cabin's own particular chipmunk appears on the lower branches of an ash, rather leaner than usual after the winter, but recognizable at once by his unusually stubby tail and exuberant personality. He resumes the teasing of the dog from where he left off last November, chattering excitedly. Raime rises to his baiting like a trout to a fly and is soon reduced to hysterical, impotent rage, until at last the chipmunk becomes a little too bold and is chased up a flue pipe lying under the cabin. A brief but blessed silence follows, until Raimie's eyes close and the next round starts. This has gone on for years.

II

The ice is going out on the lake, and there is open water before us for about a hundred yards from the shoreline, edged by a new high bank of turf and reeds built up through the winter by ice pressure. The marsh water close in reflects a sky pierced with reed stalks and patterned with a faint constant movement of infinitesimal bubble rings, but out beyond the channel little rippling waves lap greedily against the ice stretching across the lake to the far shore – gray, sodden ice, heavy with age, the darkness of the imprisoned water lying shadowlike a few inches below the surface. There is no hint of green yet in the hills beyond – rather, a quickening of purple; and the three long plumes of the waterfall are vivid and white even at this distance.

The first frog chorus tunes up in the bulrushes a few feet from where we sit, and the mallards who were disturbed at our coming return in quacking pairs to the open water. Four whistlers pass like children's bath toys drawn on a string, line astern, three drakes and a demure little hen leading. One drake is courting extravagantly, head bobbing and turning from side to side to a slow beat of six, then a fantastic arching of neck to twist his head back down the length of his body; but the little hen is not impressed by these contortions and swims on unheeding. The other two watch admiringly, then suddenly rise in unison and fly off with faint despondent cries; and so relieved by their departure apparently is the hen that she turns and acknowledges at last her exhibitionist suitor. They glide and posture in an endless fascinating ritual, the handsome drake in shining black and white, the drab little hen.

A long raft of ice and twigs sails by in a sudden gust of wind, with six mallard passengers aboard; sober and serious as priests on a cruise ship, they stare solemnly as they glide by, all heads turning together. The dog, inquisitive about our laughter, picks his way on heaving planks down to the water's edge, but is taken off guard by the sudden splash of an equally surprised muskrat and slips on the precarious plank, so that his hindquarters slide into the water and he hangs on with scrabbling forepaws. I help him up, because he is nine years old and not so agile, but I laugh so much that he is offended; he shakes his coat, soaking us with moody satisfaction, then disappears into the bush. I know that he will not go far, but will return stealthily and take up position concealed by some bush or tree so that he can keep me within range; and I know that if I turn suddenly I will be able to catch him at it, to his embarrassment – but not this time, for I am feeling a little guilty.

I make amends with a piece of cheese when we settle down on the steps again to eat our lunch – satisfying hunks of homemade bread and cheese, dill pickles, and another bottle of beer to celebrate our weekend emancipation. Redwings chatter in the mountain ash above, chatter in a desultory way, rather as we do ourselves, with long silences savored peacefully between their observations. The frog activity is dying down, but the muskrats are suddenly busy, the V of their wake spreading in the still water close to shore, preoccupied, bewhiskered little faces forging through the reeds. More ducks fly in and settle on the larger ice floes, preening themselves, their cheerful garrulity suddenly silenced when an osprey appears overhead and hovers watchfully. They rise in a body and circle, rising and falling uneasily, until the hawk drifts off down the shoreline on an eddy of wind, effortless as a feather.

Now the wind rises and falls too, sighing through the topmost pine branches, and all around is a chorus of protesting creaks and groans of trees bearing the chafing weight of others uprooted in the winter gales and fallen against them. I am very content; lambs, primroses, and sprays of blossom are suddenly revealed as banal, hackneyed manifestations before this north land subtlety. I find myself filled with pity for the unfortunate masses who must wait another year before picking their next daffodil.

Susan settles down in a protected dip with easel and paint box and all the colorful clutter of a painter. She will be lost to the world for the next three hours. I whistle to Raimie, and we strike off from the trail into the bush, where the snow has receded, walking softly on a carpet of damp brown leaves; through the willow and alder clumps, whippy with new life, striking like a lash across the unwary face; over the mossy, rotting deadfalls; and around the impenetrable branches of new-fallen jack pine, the needles still dark green, the last desperate growth of cones in rubbery clusters like brown sea snails; between towering spruce and white pine; through enchanting sunlit clearings of terraced rock slabs, covered in pinky-gray lichen and long trailing tendrils of twinflower – the stems and leaves are brown now, but at the angle of each geometrically perfect pair is a minuscule of green. The surrounding moss is ankle deep, beautiful hummocky moss, and however soggy it may be within, I cannot resist it; I throw myself down and try to count the uncountable flowerets in a quarter inch. My eyes are on a level with the ledge of rock; caught below an overhang is a papery garter-snake skin, old, yet still clearly patterned and wonderfully supple, over two feet long. I tie it in a neat bow on Raimie's tail; he is not amused, but suffers it as a collar instead.

I meander along the banks of a trout-brown creek, sun-dappled until it winds through the dark gloom of a cedar swamp, the twisted, agonized roots and branches of the giant fallen trees forming a dark dramatic frieze against the new vivid green of the living spruce beyond. The cold strikes suddenly, for the sun cannot penetrate the intertwined vaulting, and even the creek contributes to the brooding eeriness with weird shapes and fantastic grottoes sculptured from the overhanging ledges of ice.

Suddenly Raimie hurtles past, nearly knocking me into the creek, tail streaming, nose to the ground like a hound. He disappears into the thick undergrowth, his golden coat flashing momentarily in a patch of sun, and as I walk on, his quarry erupts from the bush across my path, then pauses to look back, upright on his haunches, still as a plaster rabbit on a suburban lawn, save for his twitching nose. A mighty crashing heralds Raimie's reappearance, and the rabbit bounds off with a flash of full white winter trousers, contrasting absurdly with his neat tan summer coat. My idiot dog will now make the full round of the

rabbit's tracks before starting off on this new line, for he stubbornly re-
fuses to hunt on anything but scent, and I have often wondered what
would happen if a rabbit decided to run in ever-diminishing circles.

Of course, Raimie should not be hunting rabbits – or even his dear-
est enemy, the groundhog, for that matter – for he is a gundog, trained,
with nine years' wisdom and experience. *He* knows that, and I know
that, but after several argumentative years together, we long ago ar-
rived at a mature and satisfactory compromise: in return for should-
ering a few extra duties (watchdog, child-sitter, sled dog, juvenile cir-
cus performer, lost-hamster retriever, plus the full-time summer job
of bear-scare on mushrooming expeditions), he may hunt for his own
amusement, without let or hindrance, throughout the year until Sep-
tember 15, or such time as the upland game and wildfowl season
opens, when he must immediately put aside all temptation and revert
forthwith to his professional capacity of model gundog. It was his ter-
rible misfortune to be born a scion of the great Shedd of Arden, to
spring from a long illustrious line of field-trial champions and inherit
the nose of an inspired cross between radar and a divining rod – and
yet be subject for his lifetime to the whim of a woman-wielded gun.
Any other dog would have a nervous breakdown, and because of his
most generous acceptance of the inequalities of fate, I feel I must make
allowances.

He never betrays our agreement, and would not acknowledge a
rabbit if he fell over one during the shooting season; and even my
hunting companions, critical field-trial purists though they are, admit
that it would be difficult to find his equal as a retriever of lost and giv-
en-up birds, or a heart more eager and willing for work, whatever the
conditions. Their only accusation, in fact, is that he smells faintly – but
deliciously, I contend – of Schiaparelli's "Shocking," just behind the
ears. He is the only dog I know who has been confronted with eleven
mallards down in a treacherous, ice-fringed Manitoba slough and has
set to work, systematically and entirely under his own directive, to
bring them in (his mistress watching admiringly but uselessly, as her
boots were leaking), then disappeared into the surrounding country-
side, to reappear at ten-minute intervals with four more crippled birds.
And only a woman owner could appreciate the gallantry of his compli-
ment in bringing all fifteen birds to me, even though I had not fired a

shot – a dogless companion being responsible for the massacre. And I know of no sight more fascinating than to watch him paddle painstakingly back and forth across a suspect area of water, submerging his head at intervals, until he finally dives straight down and comes up with a live but suicidally minded duck.

If I have digressed, it could be suspected that I dote on him.

III

I leave the creek to come out from the darkness of the bush at the edge of a field, part of a long-abandoned fox farm, and there, less than a hundred yards away, in a dip before the sagging barn, is a black bear. We stare at one another in mutual horror for a long second; then he turns and bolts across the field, galloping so fast that his back legs cross over his front ones, and disappears into the far trees. But that is the direction I want to go in as well, back to the lake, and I don't feel entirely happy about bears, and however antisocial this one may be, perhaps he has a mother or a cousin or a sister (with cubs) who isn't. I call my moral support away from his rabbit hunting and hear the reassuring sounds of his coming almost immediately. He arrives, panting, with beaming eyes and half a yard of pink tongue lolling out of a grinning mouth; I gather he has had a wonderful time. I am delighted, even more than usual, to see him. I am interested to see him sniff the wind as we cross the fields, and the ridge of hair rise along his back, but he trots along beside me unconcerned; and so, of course, am I – now.

Susan has had a satisfying afternoon as well; two canvases are propped against the backs of chairs, she has found the glove she lost last fall in the bush, and has seen two deer, one mink, and a flock of geese. We sit on the steps again before dinner, loath to come in until the last possible moment, and watch a spectacular sunset flaming in wild, windblown ragged clouds. The air below is still and soft and full of evening sounds: wings whistling overhead, throbbing frog chorus from the reeds, chickadees, and the solitary falling cadence of a white-throated sparrow far back in the bush; little whispers of wind rustling the dead brown bulrush spikes; and always the soft melodious tinkling of shifting ice in the background; coy bridling giggles of mallard hens in the next bay, protesting their virtue to the hoarse excited quacks of their swains; the occasional caustic comment of a raven. We sit there until the loons cry in the gathering darkness and the cold drives us into the snug, stuffy warmth of the cabin.

We have partridge for dinner, succulent gamy partridge shot in a Saskatchewan bluff last fall, marinated and cooked in homemade wine from a local Italian producer; Burgundy jelly from the Trappists in Quebec; and wild rice that grew along these shores only last year, dark and fragrant with woodsmoke from the Indian's fires across the lake. We drink the remainder of the wine – a muscatel, says the sticking-plaster label on the gin bottle, with a surprisingly pleasant though elusive bouquet (a quality enhanced perhaps by the fact that our wine-glasses once contained anchovy paste).

We play featherheaded chess until our eyes will no longer stay open and we realize that we are dozing between moves. Raimie is already asleep on a sagging cot, muzzle resting on a headless decoy, his nostrils twitching – dreaming of rabbits, probably. I lie awake in the darkness for a while, zipped into the cocoon of my sleeping bag, listening to the sighs and creaks of the wooden framework; there is a soft, intermittent scratching on the roof, which I finally identify as a scraping branch; outside there are faint little plops in the water, and a closer, intensified tinkling of the ice, which must mean that the wind is shifting.

In the middle of the night I waken with a sudden wide-awake alertness, almost as though someone had called me by name, but I hear nothing – only the sound of Raimie's tail thumping on the cot when he hears me sit up. I get out of bed and stand by the open door, looking out across the lake; a star is hanging low over the hills, and when the moon appears from a bank of clouds the lake is bright before me, half a mile or more of shining water triumphing over the sinking ice. And as I stand there I realize that the wind is warm and soft and full of promise – the promise of the northland spring, fulfilled at last in the silent, vanquished ice.

SHEILA BURNFORD was born in 1918 in Scotland. She was a Canadian writer, best known for her book, *The Incredible Journey*, which later became a Walt Disney movie. Her other books include: *One Woman's Arctic* , *Without Reserve*, and *Fields of Noon*. In this selection, Burnford shows another side of herself.

Theodore Roosevelt

*Ranch Life and
the Hunting Trail*
"The Home Ranch"

My home ranch lies on both sides of the Little Missouri, the nearest ranchman above me being about twelve, and the nearest below me about ten, miles distant. The general course of the stream here is northerly, but, while flowing through my ranch, it takes a great westerly reach of some three miles, walled in, as always, between chains of steep, high bluffs half a mile or more apart. The stream twists down through the valley in long sweeps, leaving oval wooded bottoms, first on one side and then on the other; and in an open glade among the thick-growing timber stands the long, low house of hewn logs.

Just in front of the ranch veranda is a line of old cottonwoods that shade it during the fierce heats of summer, rendering it always cool and pleasant. But a few feet beyond these trees comes the cut-off bank of the river, through whose broad, sandy bed the shallow stream winds as if lost, except when a freshet fills it from

brim to brim with foaming yellow water. The bluffs that wall in the river-valley curve back in semicircles, rising from its alluvial bottom generally as abrupt cliffs, but often as steep, grassy slopes that lead up to great level plateaus; and the line is broken every mile or two by the entrance of a coulee, or dry creek, whose head branches may be twenty miles back. Above us, where the river comes round the bend, the valley is very narrow, and the high buttes bounding it rise, sheer and barren, into scalped hill-peaks and naked knife-blade ridges.

The other buildings stand in the same open glade with the ranch house, the dense growth of cottonwoods and matted, thorny underbrush making a wall all about, through which we have chopped our wagon roads and trodden out our own bridle-paths. The cattle have now trampled down this brush a little, but deer still lie in it, only a couple of hundred yards from the house; and from the door sometimes in the evening one can see them peer out into the open, or make their way down, timidly and cautiously, to drink at the river. The stable, sheds, and other out-buildings, with the hayricks and the pens for such cattle as we bring in during winter, are near the house; the patch of fenced garden land is on the edge of the woods; and near the middle of the glade stands the high, circular horse-corral, with snubbing-post in the center, and a wing built out from one side of the gate entrance, so that the saddle-band can be driven in without trouble. As it is very hard to work cattle where there is much brush, the larger cow-corral is some four miles off on an open bottom.

A ranchman's life is certainly a very pleasant one, albeit generally varied with plenty of hardship and anxiety. Although occasionally he passes days of severe toil, – for example, if he goes on the round-up he works as hard as any of his men, – yet he no longer has to undergo the monotonous drudgery attendant upon the tasks of the cowboy or of the apprentice in the business. His fare is simple; but, if he chooses, it is good enough. Many ranches are provided with nothing at all but salt pork, canned goods, and bread; indeed, it is a curious fact that in travelling through the cow country it is often impossible to get any milk or butter; but this is only because the owners or managers are too lazy to take enough trouble to insure their own comfort. We ourselves always keep up two or three cows, choosing such as are naturally tame, and so we invariably have plenty of milk and, when there is time for churning, a good deal of butter. We also keep hens, which, in spite of the damaging inroads of hawks, bob-cats, and foxes, supply us with eggs, and in time of need, when our rifles have failed to keep us in game, with stewed, roast, or fried chicken also. From our garden we get potatoes, and unless drought, frost, or grasshoppers interfere (which they do about every second year), other vegetables as well. For fresh meat we depend chiefly upon our prowess as hunters.

During much of the time we are away on the different round-ups, that "wheeled house," the great four-horse wagon, being then our home; but when at the ranch our routine of life is always much the same, save during the excessively bitter weather of midwinter, when there is little to do except to hunt, if the days are fine enough. We breakfast early – before dawn when the nights have grown long, and rarely later than sunrise, even in midsummer. Perhaps before this meal, certainly the instant it is over, the man whose duty it is rides off to hunt up and drive in the saddle-band. Each of us has his own string of horses, eight or ten in number, and the whole band usually split up into two or three companies. In addition to the scattered groups of the saddle-band, our six or eight mares, with their colts, keep by them-selves, and are rarely bothered by us, as no cowboy ever rides anything but horses, because mares give great trouble where all the animals have to be herded together. Once every two or three days somebody rides round and finds out where each of these smaller bands is, but the man who goes out in the morning merely gathers one bunch. He drives these into the corral, the other men (who have been lolling idly about the house or stable, fixing their saddles or doing any odd job) coming out with their ropes as soon as they hear the patter of the un-shod hoofs and the shouts of the cowboy driver. Going into the corral, and standing near the center, each of us picks out some one of his own string from among the animals that are trotting and running in a com-pact mass round the circle; and after one or more trials, according to his skill, ropes it and leads it out. When all have caught their horses the rest are again turned loose, together with those that have been kept up overnight. Some horses soon get tame and do not need to be roped; my pet cutting pony, little Muley, and good old Manitou, my compan-ion in so many hunting trips, will neither of them stay with the rest of their fellows that are jamming and jostling each other as they rush round in the dust of the corral, but they very sensibly walk up and stand quietly with the men in the middle, by the snubbing-post. Both are great pets, Manitou in particular; the wise old fellow being very fond of bread and sometimes coming up of his own accord to the ranch house and even putting his head into the door to beg for it.

Once saddled, the men ride off on their different tasks; for almost everything is done in the saddle, except that in winter we cut our firewood and quarry our coal, – both on the ranch, – and in summer attend to the garden and put up what wild hay we need.

THEODORE ROOSEVELT (1858-1919) was one of America's great presidents. Born in New York City of a prosperous and influential family, he graduated from Harvard and then entered politics, serving in the New York legislature. Saddened by the deaths of his wife and his mother, he retired to his ranch in the Dakota Territory. This selection is taken from his book about those days. He returned two years later to New York where he became a member of the Civil Service Commission, Head of the New York City Police Board, Assistant Secretary of the Navy, leader of the Rough Riders in the Spanish American War, Governor of New York, Vice President of the United States, and upon the assassination of McKinley, President of the United States. No American president had more influence on this country's public lands policy. (See Lands of Brighter Destiny by one of the editors of this anthology.)

Edward Hoagland

Walking the
Dead Diamond River

came to Augusta in April 1971 to find out how much was left of New England's wilderness and what was in store for it. The people I'd corresponded with had made it plain that there was very little left, if any, and since that little ought not to be publicized they weren't eager to help me find it – the mountains I climbed ought at least to be unnamed mountains. I defined wilderness as a place where one should carry a compass and wouldn't meet other people; where one would be alone willy-nilly and couldn't beg off from the experience by hailing a ride from a passing log truck if supper was spoiled or the weather soured. I was surprised and disappointed to learn that there was no such thing any more, though from a personal standpoint I did find enough pockets of wild country to be less discouraged – I'd know where to go in the woods, if nobody else did. With seventy million people living within driving distance of the north woods for a long weekend, no place is inaccessible. Sixty

§ 217 §

thousand people a year climb Mount Monadnock in New Hampshire. Two hundred and fifty thousand climb or ride to the top of Mount Washington.

Of course the worst slopes of the Presidentials are always there for those who think wind and cold and the danger of falling and killing oneself are wilderness – wilderness to them being nine feet of slick-rock,"the ecstasy of insignificance," as a climber at the Appalachian Mountain Club put it. Yet by September the paths had been so over-hiked that the Trail Crew were talking about how much the mountains must like the hard, cleansing fall rains and wondering why the land didn't just get up and walk away. Huge loads of sewage and trash from the huts up on top were being helicoptered out; the trails had been worn into root-studded ruts; rare timber-line vegetation had been trampled to death; and the campgrounds down in the woods were almost disaster areas, not because people selfishly litter but because there are so many of them. All the manuals of the past taught a whimsical pioneer lore that was more appropriate to the frontier solitudes – like camping at random where the heart pleases, cutting a fresh, fragrant bed of balsam boughs, digging a drainage ditch around one's tent, digging a firepit and cutting wood for it. Now people should pack in Coleman stoves and fuel instead – "Carry in, carry out," "Leave nothing but footprints" – and apply for what in the West is called a Wilderness Permit.

At the Maine Department of Fish and Game I talked with the man in charge of planning in the windowless office he shares with Civil Defense. Though his excitement about his computer was dizzying, it seemed unsecured. He told me a box and a half of shotgun shells is shot off for every duck killed, but seemed to know very little about ducks themselves. The publications of the department are sumptuous, but the warren of green cubicles reminded me of a Gogol novel – all these government clerks modestly shuffling papers, overlooked by enlarged photographs of the lagomorphs and the mustelids on whose lives their work had little bearing. At their meetings a faculty-club pettiness was apparent, and they regularly change the names of their Refuges to honor retiring colleagues. Most Fish and Game offices are satrapies, and Maine's is no exception – self-funded by license fees so that the legislature has no handle on it. Salaries are low, nonetheless.

The pay scale for biologists in New Hampshire, for instance, goes from seven thousand dollars to a top of eleven thousand dollars for the chief himself.

One hopes that at least the departments won't do any harm. At the time of my visit Maine's was campaigning to open a limited season on moose, which not long ago were nearly gone from the state and had not been hunted extensively since 1921. The herd had finally grown to fifteen thousand, but this rush to hunt them struck many people as foolishness, since it publicly declared them surplus when, as it was, five hundred a year were being poached. (Wildlife managers tend to regard as "waste" any animal that lives to a ripe old age without being part of a "harvest.") The state legislature voted the proposal down, whereupon Fish and Game, in its pique, canceled the one study of moose life and habitat it had going, inadequate though that was (budgeted for four thousand dollars, out of the department's annual three million dollars). The explanation was that this marvelous great wilderness animal, descended from a beached whale, as the Indians say, wasn't "game."

I talked to Howard Spencer, the Chief of Game, a smooth, politic man, who was wearing a tie dappled with flying ducks. Back in 1954 he was gutting bears to look at their stomach contents, but in middle age he has taken to writing about waterfowl. He told me that teal, wood ducks, goldeneye and mergansers are doing all right, and Canada geese even better, but that black ducks, the most important species from a hunting standpoint, are on a downtrend, both in Maine and throughout the East, with a 55-65 percent annual mortality. Eagle and osprey reproduction has virtually stopped – no more than twenty grown eagles remain in the state. As for beavers, the season is juggled according to local conditions, the landowners sometimes objecting to them because they drown trees, while the fisherman and hunters root for them because they build ponds. Flying in and out, a pilot in Patten had trapped four hundred beavers that winter. Spencer said that two hundred thousand deer licenses are sold every year, that the deer kill is thirty-five thousand, and the bear kill from nine to twelve hundred. In 1957 a $25 bounty on bear was revoked, and since then they have been given a five-month closed season, a one-bear limit per hunter, and the cubs are protected.

The Chief of Inland Fisheries, Lyndon Bond, whom I spoke to next, is a sallow, reflective man – good company – who says that since most lakes in northern Maine are as infertile as battery water, phosphate or sewage pollution isn't yet much of a problem; indeed, its first effect would be to increase the fish food. His staff, he said, stocks 600,000 brook trout fingerlings annually, 400,000 landlocked salmon, 300,000 Atlantic salmon, 230,000 lake trout, 100,000 brown trout and 50,000 rainbow trout. These are all cold-water fish, requiring clean flowing water and more oxygen than such warm-water fish as pickerel, bass, horned pout and perch, which may be transplanted between weedy ponds but needn't be raised in a hatchery. Both brown trout, originally a European fish, and rainbows, which are Western, are hardier than brook trout, able to survive in marginal water. The browns, which grow to four or five pounds, are especially tough, but are unpopular with the go-go, impatient modern angler because, being such good survivors, they are cautious and difficult to catch.

With the standard fish there's no question of extinction – Maine alone has thirteen hatcheries – but only the problem of reclaiming the rivers and lakes. For a couple of centuries logs by the million have been tearing the spawning beds out of the streams, covering the beds that they missed with silt, while the bark turned the water acid. Then there's factory pollution, and the dams are the greatest impediment. Even at present, only one of three hundred sea salmon smolts put in the water will live enough of its life to make a real spawning run. But fishing is like motherhood in New England as an issue; what's more, these problems are rather easily solved. Little by little the log drives have been brought to an end, and sophisticated fish elevators and ladders, with "attraction water," are being installed at the big dams. Salmon, alewives and shad can withstand more pollution than people have thought. In the Connecticut River sea-running fish already can reach Turners Falls, Mass., and in another decade will be spawning in Vermont on the White River.

On the other hand, what's good for the fish may not be so good for the game. As the loggers have switched to hauling by road instead of letting the rivers do that chore for them, they've crosshatched the puckerbrush with roads; cumulatively up to 10 percent of the woods is becoming road.

I went to the University of Maine to talk to the state's deer-research leader, Fred Gilbet. He's first-rate, a Canadian three years out of graduate school. He has a heavy face, a massive broken nose, a level look, a muscular straightforward bulkiness, and is graying prematurely. Like most game men, he's thoroughly a predator and has to restrain a certain irritation in speaking of the camera-hunters and birdwatchers who get a free ride as things stand, having access to thousands of acres of wildlife lands purchased with hunters fees. He says that the main tug of war in the outdoors is not between hunters and Audubon types, however, but between the vacationers and the natives. He doesn't look forward to the time when every well-paid electrician in the city wakes up to the fact that for about the price of a new car he can buy himself a woods cottage in Maine. Summer people hollow out a rural community to a shell of itself – empty four-fifths of the year – and to an ecologist they are much more destructive of habitat than the most reckless logging practices because they simply take the land out of circulation altogether. Like everyone else I was to talk to who was concerned with the subjects I was investigating, Gilbert believes the best solution is large-scale zoning designed to keep open land in the hands of the public, so that instead of thousands of cottagers, each hoarding his tiny parcel in a summer-suburb arrangement, everybody will have access on an equal basis to recreational land, land of a size to provide a real contrast to life nearer the city.

In theory, Maine's unique system of private ownership of enormous chunks of the state might make this easier to achieve. Great Northern has 2.4 million acres; International Paper 1.1 million; the Seven Islands Land Company manages 1.7 million acres; Scott Paper Company owns perhaps 750,000; St. Regis and Georgia Pacific each have in excess of 500,000 acres; and the Dunn Heirs, the Huber Company and Brown Company own another 300,000 apiece. Public zoning might be made to stick more effectively when applied to these voteless corporations than to a multitude of private citizens – except that if citizens do well in the legislature, corporations do well behind the scenes. For example, a Nader group recently discovered that for forty years tax assessments on all these timberlands had been determined by the landowners' own surveying firm, the James W. Sewall Company of Oldtown, Maine. This caused quite a stir in the state. Another Nader group, in

California, has proposed the radical notion that so basic a commodity as land should be subjected to the anti-trust laws if holdings exceed, say, fifteen thousand acres. Paradoxically, however, such anti-trust action and tougher taxation could hasten the end of what wilderness is left.

EDWARD HOAGLAND was born in New York in 1932. A novelist and an essayist, he has a number of books to his credit including *The Circle Home*, *Notes from the Century Before*, *The Courage of Turtles*, and *Red Wolves and Black Bears*. This selection is from his book of essays, *Walking the Dead Diamond River*. Although more journalistic in tone, it describes the discovery of man's effect upon a place that once was wild and is now more under man's influence than even man suspects.

John Muir

Stickeen

On our way back to camp after these first observations I planned a far-and-wide excursion for the morrow. I awoke early, called not only by the glacier, which had been on my mind all night, but by a grand floodstorm. The wind was blowing a gale from the north and the rain was flying with the clouds in a wide passionate horizontal flood, as if it were all passing over the country instead of falling on it. The main perennial streams were booming high above their banks, and hundreds of new ones, roaring like the sea, almost covered the lofty gray walls of the inlet with white cascades and falls. I had intended making a cup of coffee and getting something like a breakfast before starting, but when I heard the storm and looked out I made haste to join it; for many of Nature's finest lessons are to be found in her storms, and if careful to keep in right relations with them, we may go safely abroad with them, rejoicing in the grandeur and beauty of their works and ways, and chanting with the old Norsemen, "The blast of the tempest aids our oars,

the hurricane is our servant and drives us whither we wish to go." So, omitting breakfast, I put a piece of bread in my pocket and hurried away.

Mr. Young and the Indians were asleep, and so, I hoped, was Stickeen; but I had not gone a dozen rods before he left his bed in the tent and came boring through the blast after me. That a man should welcome storms for their exhilarating music and motion, and go forth to see God making landscapes, is reasonable enough; but what fascination could there be in such tremendous weather for a dog? Surely nothing akin to human enthusiasm for scenery or geology. Anyhow, on he came, breakfastless, through the choking blast. I stopped and did my best to turn him back. "Now don't," I said, shouting to make myself heard in the storm, "now don't, Stickeen. What has got into your queer noddle now? You must be daft. This wild day has nothing for you. There is no game abroad, nothing but weather. Go back to camp and keep warm, get a good breakfast with your master, and be sensible for once. I can't carry you all day or feed you, and this storm will kill you."

But Nature, it seems, was at the bottom of the affair, and she gains her ends with dogs as well as with men, making us do as she likes, shoving and pulling us along her ways, however rough, all but killing us at times in getting her lessons driven hard home. After I had stopped again and again, shouting good warning advice, I saw that he was not to be shaken off; as well might the earth try to shake off the moon. I had once led his master into trouble, when he fell on one of the topmost jags of a mountain and dislocated his arm; now the turn of his humble companion was coming. The pitiful little wanderer just stood there in the wind, drenched and blinking, saying doggedly, "Where thou goest I will go." So at last I told him to come on if he must, and gave him a piece of the bread I had in my pocket; then we struggled on together, and thus began the most memorable of all my wild days.

JOHN MUIR was born in Scotland and moved to Wisconsin as a young boy. He traveled widely, walking through much of the country, settling in California, and also visited Alaska, Russia, and Australia. He wrote extensively about his travels and his observations. His books include: *The Mountains of California, The Story of My Boyhood and Youth, Steep Trails,* and *John of the Mountains.* His journals about California and Alaska have been widely read. This selection is from *Stickeen,* the true story of Muir's experience on an Alaskan glacier, alone with the dog he called Stickeen.

Mari Sandoz

Old Jules
"Rain Makers and a Hunt
to the Big Horns"

The early nineties were so dry even the old-timers wondered if it would ever rain again in the Panhandle. They had learned not to expect too much moisture in June or July, but when the young August moon, horned as an antelope, settled into the black wool bed of the horizon, and the hay was down, there should be rain.

All summer the homesteaders cultivated deep, under the spur of hunger, cracking the clodding earth, trying to maintain the mulch Old Jules believed would hold the moisture. But there was none to hold. They watched the skies until their eyes were like old wounds, and still it did not rain. A man on Box Butte Creek fortunate enough to get a shower from a June thunderhead won first prize for winter wheat at the state fair. But on the Flats the wheat never headed; oats sat white and curled as grass, the root soil baked and cracked.

About the time the clouds of blackbirds from the painted

wood of the river darkened the fields in search of nubbins, the settlers began to leave. The Iowa colony went first, leaving only Elmer Sturgeon and Johnny Burrows. Several of them had shipped in carloads of goods and stock. They let their claims go to Eastern loan companies for the money they once needed for cattle, horses, implements, seed, wire, lumber. They drove out with nothing except a crowbait team and wagon. Scarcely were they over the horizon before their homes were torn down and hauled away by those who needed the lumber to hang on a little longer. First the stores, then the banks of the Panhandle, went bankrupt. Of the four banks in Rushville only one weathered these years.

"Now is the time to buy land cheap," Jules pointed out, but there was no money – and his father with five thousand dollars out at 2 per cent in the Old Country. Jules did not go to Mirage much any more. To him a hundred sixty acres of wild Susans was not a field of gold but a field going back to sod, a dead venture.

Rain makers arose. In eastern Nebraska a Pawnee Indian promised a shower for ten dollars, a soaking rain for twenty. Someone gave him a jug of whiskey and the hail pounded the grass into the ground. It was a good story, told not without envy.

At Goodland, Kansas, Melbourne and his assistants produced half an inch of rain within forty-eight hours for a thousand dollars. They were given the same offer at Sidney, south of the Platte. Jules, mounted on a sturdy pinto he got from the Indians for two eagles, rode down with several of the Flatters. From their horses they watched the three men carry a long black box into an old barn, well guarded. Three times a day baskets were taken in full of food and came out empty. Once, the second day, the sky clouded over and awe swept the watching crowd like wind in a young field of wheat. Thunder rumbled, a few heavy drops splattered like shot in the dust, the wind blew, and the sun was out with a double rainbow.

"I'll keep catching skunks for a living," Jules told his neighbors.

Rushville tried powder and the Flats, both the Lutherans and the Catholics, prayer. Some said that the church steeples split the clouds. Jules laughed – only empty houses with the dead smell of religion in them.

When the settlers got clear down in the mouth a walking sky pilot appeared and called a revival at Alkali Lake, on the Flats, not far from Hay Springs.

"Wouldn't you jest know them critters'd have to come to pester us! Ain't we got troubles enough as 'tis?" Ma Green told Jules as she stopped her team for a rest at the river. The boys were haying and the freighting had to be done, so she had climbed the heavy wagon.

"Guess I kin handle them eight broncs's well as anybody!"

She was timing her loading at Hay Springs so she would make Alkali in time for the revival.

Two days later she stopped while her horses blew before they took the long climb out of the river valley. It had been a fine spectacle, with folks thick as flies around a puddle of syrup, and that sky pilot, with his red beard cut like Christ's in the Sunday-school pictures, preaching hell and damnation from the back of a grasshopper buggy, and women crying and men ripping their only shirts. Then they all moved into the lake and the preacher stuck them under like so many old rag dolls until the Flats smelled of stale water and dead salamanders. "It done me more good to see that dirty parson get wet to his middle. I'll bet he ain't ever had a bath all the way up."

Mrs. Schmidt, with eight children at home and a husband laid out behind a saloon somewhere, sang all the way home from the revival. The next week they sent her to the insane asylum and scattered the children. The youngest Frahm girl took pneumonia and died, and a lone Bohemian from the Breaks hung himself. Henriette came away sad. Only Ma Green seemed to have enjoyed it.

Still there was no rain.

The Mirage Flatters talked irrigation day and night, held meetings. Jules sent for government bulletins showing corn man-high with a little water. But when Pine Creek settlers sold out and bought land on the Flats, hoping to reap the irrigation profits, Jules protested. "Better stick to what you got."

Mirage Flats had the choice of drilling for artesian water or depending on the flow of the Niobrara, one to two hundred feet below the level of the hard-land table. If they got the water up at Dunlap, south of Chadron, it meant ditching through twelve miles of waste land and building long flumes across Pepper Creek and Sand Canyon before they could apply a drop of water to the parched land. That would take money, much money. Those most able to help finance the project set their bearded faces against it. It was taking too great a chance with their last few dollars. Surely the Lord would provide, some said piously.

That was too much for Big Andrew, who had never spoken ten consecutive words at a meeting and who always hunched over his heels along the back wall of the schoolhouse, his head against the blackboard. He rose awkwardly to his feet, opened his mouth, and talked steadily for twenty minutes.

This was no time for caution or waiting on the Lord, he cried to them. They had waited and prayed; they had been cautious, and what did it give? Look across the Flats, so level and fine a farming land as God ever made smooth with trowel – and not grass enough this year on all of it to keep a sheep's ribs from wearing the wool off his sides. It gives crops when it rains. He pointed out half a dozen there who raised two and three thousand bushels of corn alone in good years. Water was all they needed. For three years it had not come; maybe it would never come. Now it was not the time for caution, but for courage; not for prayer and waiting, but for work. If they sank their last dollar in irrigation and lost, was that worse than if they did not try? A year or two longer, – at the best, – with more of them hanging from the ridgepoles by ropes and more getting free rides to Norfolk to the crazy house. In the end it was all gone anyway.

"Money I have nothing. But a good team I have – and a strong back for the scraper and two hard hands for the spade. Take them!"

When Big Andrew was through he saw for the first time that every face was turned back toward him. Gulping, he pulled his head into the protection of his shoulders and sat down upon his heels, his ears standing out stiff and red in embarrassment while hobnails and burlap-wrapped feet gave their approval.

Mirage Flats would have irrigation.

While the hard-land settlers talked of artesian well and surface irrigation, those along the Niobrara and Pine Creek got along somehow. The wet years would come, Jules preached, pointing to the rain graphs of the state. Nebraska rainfall came in cycles. There must be wet years just ahead.

Hans looked at him dully. He had taken to drinking lately and the last shreds of the boy his Anna kissed good-bye were going. "It will be dry all the time," he said. He would plant no more.

When the Flats no longer had socials and dances, no longer saw anything amusing in the drouth parodies of church hymns, the Pine Creek settlers and the small cattlemen took them up, singing lustily:

> I've reached the land of drouth and heat,
> Where nothing grows for man to eat,
> The wind that blows with burning heat,
> O'er all our land is hard to beat.
>
> O! Nebraska land, sweet Nebraska land!
> As on your burning soil I stand,
> I look away across the plains,
> And wonder why it never rains,
> Till Gabriel calls, with trumpet sound,
> And says the rain has gone around.

MARI SANDOZ was born in 1896 in Nebraska near the northwest corner– the Niobrara region – to which her Swiss parents emigrated and homestead-ed. She quit school in the eighth grade and taught, before talking her way into the University of Nebraska. By the time she entered college, she claimed to have received 1000 rejection slips for her short stories; it is a testament to her perseverance as well as to her prolific writing. *Old Jules* is the biography of Sandoz's father, Jules Ami Sandoz, for which she won the Atlantic prize for non-fiction. *Old Jules* is also the biography of an entire generation of frontiersmen who came west to take the lands of Nebraska, in which few wanted to try to build their futures. *Old Jules* is also the biography of a land – the high arid plains of the western Nebraska panhandle. Underlying all of Sandoz' work is an awareness of the power and beauty of the natural world.

Margaret E. Murie

Two in the Far North
"By Main Strength"

On June 28 we camped at Black Fox Creek, three tumble-down cabins atop a high grassy bank in a thick stand of spruces. No one was there of course. If another human being had appeared anywhere on this river we would have thought we were seeing things, for we were to be the only people in the Old Crow Basin that summer. ("Even the natives stay out of there.") But sometime long ago someone had had a winter camp here. We knew we were getting close to the end of timber.

Next morning, hot and fair, we were purring along as usual, the folding canvas canoe set up now and being towed behind us, every eye looking out for geese. "There's a slough coming in up ahead. Might be geese on that beach." Olaus reached for his glasses.

Suddenly we heard a "clank, clank" – not a loud noise, but ominous; then silence. The engine had stopped. "What the Sam Hill!" Jess exclaimed, and began jigging this and that and muttering to himself. Finally he said: "Well, guess we'll have to pole over to shore till I see what it is. It might . . . but I'm afraid it's the crankshaft."

The moment the motor died the mosquitoes attacked. It was a great relief to get into the tent which Olaus quickly set up in the thick moss on top of the cut bank. I lay there playing with the baby. He was the one perfectly serene member of the party. I heard metallic sounds from below, but no explosions from Jess; this was a bad sign. Pretty soon I heard him say in a strangely quiet voice: "Well, we might as well go up and tell Mardy."

They both came crawling through the netting. Olaus was smiling at me. "Well, Mardy, our days of mechanized travel are over. Do you mind?"

The crankshaft. I'd never known there were such things. Now I found out how important they were. Jess had brought along practically a whole second engine. In the bottom of the boat lay a spare propeller shaft; stored away in the lockers were dozens of spark plugs, three extra wheels, all kinds of repair parts. But none of these things broke. Only the one most expensive, vital part that breaks only once in a million times!

We were just reaching the waterfowl grounds; the work for which we had come had just begun. They had banded twelve geese so far.

Quite a long time they sat there, discussing what had happened. My mind was leaping on to "What next?" but Olaus had not said any-thing about that yet and I suddenly remembered the government con-tract signed in Fairbanks. Jess and his motorboat had been hired toge-ther. He was under no obligation to go any farther. Twelve geese band-ed so far.

Jess was sitting cross-legged, tossing a bolt or nut and catching it as he talked. Suddenly the piece of iron went sailing against the tent wall and Jess said: "Well, by Jesus, we don't need to be stuck! We came up here to band geese and by Criminy we're *going* to band geese. I'm ready to go on if you are."

Olaus heaved a big sigh, and a big smile appeared on his face. "By golly, Jess, do you really mean that? Of course I want to; I've never been stuck on an assignment yet; only, I hate to ask you . . ."

Jess went right on. "Hell, of course we can. We'll take that boat back down to Black Fox Creek and tie her up; there's a good bank there.

We'll put all the stuff we need in the scow and pull her and pole her on up – they said it was sluggish water all the way to the head of the river. Must be about two hundred and fifty miles, I guess. But if there's geese anywhere in the country we'll find 'em, even without an engine!"

Three hours later the motorboat, with the canvas canoe trailing behind, was disappearing round the bend downstream, two paddles dipping in rhythm, both raised in a reassuring salute as they slid from view. I climbed the ten-foot bank above the wet sand beach and knelt at the tent door, holding the netting close to my face so I could see inside. Martin was sound asleep on our bed, clad only in a diaper, arms flung out wide. It was a hot day and the tent was warm. How safe, how defenseless! I rose and went back down to the beach. Except for the incessant din of the mosquitoes, the world was quiet and still. Across the brown stream a white-crowned sparrow sang a lazy midday song; there was no other sound in this green world under the warm blue sky. The river was empty, the other shore just a thick green wall. At my back, beyond the little tent, stretched the limitless tundra, mile upon mile, clear to the Arctic Ocean. Somehow that day I was very conscious of that infinite quiet space.

But it was better to get busy. They had left me a pile of firewood. In a flour sack lay two geese, skinned the day before for specimens. I built up a fire. I would make rice stuffing for the geese. Where was the rice? Ah, that was a question! Here along the beach, in a heap measuring about ten by twenty feet, were piled all our possessions, everything but the cases of gas and oil and the tools for the engine. These were on their way downstream to Black Fox Creek. I began poking and peering and climbing about over the pile of boxes and waterproofed bags. It took quite a while to find and assemble the food needed for the next day's cooking, but eventually the two geese were simmering in the Dutch oven, and the baby cereal and dried fruit were on the grate. By the time those three thick chunks of wood burned down, they would be cooked. I drew the tarp back over the pile of goods, looked again at the line running from the precious scow to be sure it was securely tied, took a bowl of cooked mixed vegetables for the baby, and climbed up to the tent.

Before going in, I looked out over the tundra once more.

Wavering, hummocky, softly green, it stretched to the sky, here and there a stunted spruce, a small feathery birch, tussocks of white Labrador tea in bloom. A white-crowned sparrow flipped into a nearby birch, and on the tip of a small spruce a tree sparrow was singing blithely. There was no other visible life. I crawled into the tent, pulled off my hat and veil and gloves, and unlaced my high leather boots.

There the baby and I stayed, all that day and the following night – night in which the sunlight was only slightly less intense. I played with the baby when he was awake, tossing the red rubber lamb back and forth for a long time, playing peek-a-boo behind his box – all the little games I could think of.

When he lay quiet with his bottle, or slept, it was still again. Almost afraid to look, I gave the river a quick glance – empty; then out over the tundra – nothing moving, every little tree in its place – good. And nothing moved across the river on the green grass either. Just the wilderness itself, friendly, and normal. My eyes were looking, not for any life, but for a reassuring lack of it. If I had spied a human form coming across the tundra, I would have been terrified; a bear or a wolf would have seemed excitingly normal.

So every little while, all that day and night, I had to go out and be reassured by looking all about, reassured that the baby and I were still safely alone. At two in the morning I banked some coals around the Dutch oven and lay down fully dressed beside the sleeping baby.

Someone was in the tent! Then the nicest voice in the world. "Hello, darlin', it's four in the morning and pretty cold, and the skeeters are gone for a while, and Jess and I are awfully hungry!"

MARGARET "MARDY" MURIE (born 1902) grew up in Fairbanks, Alaska, half a century before the territory gained statehood. Throughout the years, Mardy has returned again and again to Alaska, exploring it with her eminent biologist- and illustrator-husband, Olaus Murie. For Mardy, returning to the wilderness of Alaska was always "going home" to the land without people. This selection tells of one of the Murie's trips into the Arctic, by boat up the Porcupine and Old Crow rivers to band geese. The trip took them through what is still today wilderness. Their eight month old son, Martin, and guide, Jess, accompanied them.

Ivan Doig

This House of Sky

Little by little, and across more time than I want to count, I have come to see where our lives fit then into the valley. If Dad ever traced it at any length for himself, he never said so in more than one of his half-musings, half-jokes: *As the fellow says, a fool and his money are soon parted, but ye can't even get introduced around here.* Yet I believe he too came to know, and to the bone, exactly where it was we had stepped when we went from Clifford's sheltering. On the blustery near-winter day when we left the highway and drove onto the gray clay road of our new ranch, the pair of us began to live out the close of an unforgiving annal of settlement which had started itself some eighty years earlier.

It is not known just when in the l860's the first white pioneers trickled into our area of south-central Montana, into what would come to be called the Smith River Valley. But if the earliest of them wagoned in on a day when the warm sage smell met the nose and the clear air lensed close the details of peaks

two days' ride from there, what a glimpse into glory it must have seemed. Mountains stood up blue-and-white into the vigorous air. Closer slopes of timber offered the logs to hew homestead cabins from. Sage grouse nearly as large as hen turkeys whirred from their hiding places. And the expanse of it all: across a dozen miles and for almost forty along its bowed length, this home valley of the Smith River country lay open and still as a gray inland sea, held by buttes and long ridges at its northern and southern ends, and east and west by mountain ranges.

A new county had been declared here, bigger than some entire states in the East and vacant for the taking. More than vacant, evacuated: the Piegan Blackfeet tribes who had hunted across the land by then were pulling north, in a last ragged retreat to the long-grass prairies beyond the Missouri River. And promise of yet another sort: across on the opposite slopes of the Big Belt Mountains, placer camps around Helena were flushing gold out of every gravel gulch. With the Indians vanished and bonanza gold drawing in the town builders, how could this neighboring valley miss out on prosperity? No, unbridle imagination just for a moment, and it could not help but foretell all these seamless new miles into pasture and field, roads and a rail route, towns and homes.

Yet if they had had eyes for anything but the empty acres, those firstcomers might have picked clues that this was a somewhat peculiar run of country, and maybe treacherous. Hints begin along the eastern skyline. There the Castle Mountains poke great turrets of stone out of black-green forest. From below in the valley, the spires look as if they had been engineered prettily up from the forest floor whenever someone took the notion, an entire mountain range of castle-builders' whims — until the fancy stone thrusts wore too thin in the wind and began to chink away, fissure by slow fissure. Here, if the valley comers could have gauged it in some speedup of time, stood a measure of how wind and storm liked to work on that country, gladly nubbing down boulder if it stood in the way.

While the Castle Mountains, seen so in the long light of time, make a goblin horizon for the sun to rise over, the range to the west, the Big Belts, can cast some unease of its own on the valley. The highest peak of the range — penned into grandness on maps as Mount

Edith, but always simply Old Baldy to those of us who lived with mountain upon mountain — thrusts up a bare summit with a giant crater gouged in its side. Even in hottest summer, snow lies in the great pock of crater like a patch on a gape of wound. Always, then, there is this reminder that before the time of men, unthinkable forces broke apart the face of the biggest landform the eye can find from any inch of the valley.

Nature's crankiness to the Big Belts did not quit there. The next summit to the south, Grass Mountain, grows its trees and grass in a pattern tipped upside down from every other mountain in sight. Instead of rising leisurely out of bunchgrass slopes which give way to timber reaching down from the crest, Grassy is darkly cowled with timber at the bottom and opens into a wide generous pasture — a brow of prairie some few thousand feet higher than any prairie ought to be, all the length of its gentle summit.

Along the valley floor, omens still go on. The South Fork of the Smith River turns out to be little more than a creek named by an optimist. Or, rather, by some frontier diplomat, for as an early newspaperman explained in exactly the poetry the pawky little flow deserved, the naming took notice of a politician in the era of the Lewis and Clark expedition — *Secretary Smith of the Navy Department/The most progressive member of Jefferson's cabinet/ . . . thus a great statesman, the expedition giver/is honored for all time in the name of "Smith River."* The overnamed subject of all that merely worms its way across the valley, generally kinking up three times the distance for every mile it flows and delivering all along the way more willow thickets and mud-browed banks than actual water. On the other hand, the water that is missing from the official streambed may arrive in some surprise gush somewhere else. A hot mineral pool erupting at an unnotable point of the valley gave the name to the county seat which built up around the steaming boil, White Sulphur Springs.

But whatever the quirks to be discovered in a careful look around, the valley and its walls of high country did fit that one firm notion the settlers held: empty country to fill up. Nor, in justice, could the eye alone furnish all that was vital to know. Probably it could not even be seen, at first, in the tides of livestock which the settlers soon were sending in seasonal flow between the valley and those curious mountains.

What it took was experience of the climate, to remind you that those grazing herds of cattle and bands of sheep were not simply on the move into the mountains or back to the valley lowland. They were traveling between high country and higher, and in that unsparing landscape, the weather is rapidly uglier and more dangerous the farther up you go.

The country's arithmetic tells it. The very floor of the Smith River Valley rests one full mile above sea level. Many of the homesteads were set into the foothills hundreds of feet above that. The cold, storm-making mountains climb thousands of feet more into the clouds bellying over the Continental Divide to the west. Whatever the prospects might seem in a dreamy look around, the settlers were trying a slab of lofty country which often would be too cold and dry for their crops, too open to a killing winter for their cattle and sheep.

It might take a bad winter or a late and rainless spring to bring out this fact, and the valley people did their best to live with calamity whenever it descended. But over time, the altitude and climate added up pitilessly, and even after a generation or so of trying the valley, a settling family might take account and find that the most plentiful things around them still were sagebrush and wind.

By the time I was a boy and Dad was trying in his own right to put together a life again, the doubt and defeat in the valley's history had tamped down into a single word. Anyone of Dad's generation always talked of a piece of land where some worn-out family eventually had lost to weather or market prices not as a farm or a ranch or even a homestead, but as a *place.* All those empty little clearings which ghosted that sage countryside — just the McLoughlin place there by that butte, the Vinton place over this ridge, the Kuhnes place, the Catlin place, the Winters place, the McReynolds place, all the tens of dozens of sites where families lit in the valley or its rimming foothills, couldn't hold on, and drifted off. All of them epitaphed with that barest of words, *place.*

One such place was where our own lives were compassed from. Southwest out of the valley into the most distant foothills of the Big Belts, both the sage and the wind begin to grow lustier. Far off there, beyond the landmark rise called Black Butte and past even the long green pasture hump of Grassy Mountain, a set of ruts can be found snaking away from the county road. The track, worn bald by iron wagonwheels and later by the hard tires of Model T's, scuffs along red shale bluffs and up sagebrush gulches and past trickling willow-choked creeks until at last it sidles across the bowed shoulder of a summit ridge. Off there in the abrupt openness, two miles and more to a broad pitch of sage-soft slope, my father was born and grew up.

This sudden remote bowl of pasture is called the Tierney Basin — or would be, if any human voice were there to say its name. Here, as far back into the tumbled beginnings of the Big Belts as their wagons could go, a double handful of Scots families homesteaded in the years just before this century. Two deep Caledonian notions seem to have pulled them so far into the hills: to raise sheep, and to graze them on mountain grass which cost nothing.

A moment, cup your hands together and look down into them, and there is a ready map of what these homesteading families had in mind. The contours and life lines in your palms make the small gulches and creeks angling into the center of the Basin. The main flow of water, Spring Creek, drops down to squirt out there where the bases of your palms meet, the pass called Spring Gulch. Toward these middle crinkles, the settlers clustered in for sites close to water and, they hoped, under the wind. The braid of lines, now, which runs square across between palms and wrists can be Sixteenmile Creek, the canyoned flow which gives the entire rumpled region its name — *the Sixteen country*. Thumbs and the upward curl of your fingers represent the mountains and steep ridges all around. Cock the right thumb a bit outward and it reigns as Wall Mountain does, prowing its rimrock out and over the hollowed land below. And on all that cupping rim of unclaimed high country, the Scots families surely instructed one another time and again, countless bands of sheep could find summer grass.

IVAN DOIG was born in 1939 in White Sulphur Springs, Montana, near the ranch his father and mother and their flocks of sheep came to call home earlier in the century. This selection from *This House of Sky* describes how intimately man and nature are connected while attempting to earn a living in partnership with a land that, at least in the Rockies, can be wild or beautiful or dangerous, or all of the above at any moment.

Bill Stockton

Today I Baled Some Hay to
Feed the Sheep the Coyotes Eat

The four foremost enemies of any agricultural enterprise are the weather, insects, predators, and markets. A rancher can usually devise some means to combat the latter three, but the weather is such a formidable force that we are at its mercy most of the time.

We can build shelters and listen to weather forecasts, of course. This we do. But there seems to be, almost every year, that one storm which has escaped the attention of the meteorologists or the availability of our shelters – especially in Montana.

In this northern, Rocky Mountain region, the weather is a paradox, and one must have lived there most of his life to understand it – which we don't try to do, incidentally – or to appreciate it. I can't imagine myself living, for instance, under the constant sun of Southern California. My God, what a bore.

Our climate, east of the Rocky Mountains in Montana – a climate affected from the west by the warm Chinook winds of the Pacific, from the north by the arctic fronts, from the southeast by the humid, upslope conditions coming out of the Gulf of Mexico and the highs from the desert southwest – is dramatic, severe, and to say the least, diversified. We can have summer in winter and winter in summer.

I have seen the weather change in a twelve-hour period from 40 below zero to 40 above zero. I have seen the earth baked for weeks on end beneath a desert sun of 110 degrees, so not even a grasshopper could find a bite to eat, and drenched under a downpour of sixteen inches of rain in the month of May. I have battled three feet of snow and temperatures that never rose above 20 below zero for the entire month of February, and I have fixed fence in my shirt sleeves and walked among the blooming crocuses on Lincoln's birthday. When I was a kid, I once went swimming in the creek on the first day of March.

I have also walked knee-deep on the 20th of April among the frozen bodies of hundreds of dead sheep, piled in fence corners in their efforts to escape a drop of four feet of snow.

The Chinook winds which invade Montana's winter weather are more responsible than any other factor in making our weather unique. The word "Chinook" is used to describe these winds, since in the early days of the West, they were thought to originate in the Chinook Indian villages on the West Coast. All I can really explain about the Chinooks is that they are the cool Pacific fronts which are compressed against the west side of the Rockies. The compression causes the air to heat, and it then spills over the mountains as warm, dry winds. They usually come in quite shallow and sometimes their air mass is only a few hundred feet thick. Most of the time the currents blow in about 30 miles per hour, hugging the valleys and pushing the cold air masses to higher altitudes. But I have watched the Chinooks melt snow high on the mountain tops, while the valleys remained frigid.

It is interesting to observe the Chinook's skirmishes with the massive arctic fronts. Although they have never won the "Climatic War," the Chinook currents have won many battles against "General Cold" and have so often given ourselves and our animals a touch of spring in the middle of January and dreams of another season.

It is cold,
And the hold
That winter has
Will not pass
Till spring is old.

I wrote this little observation many years ago and, if I remember correctly, a Chinook came in and made me out a liar two days after I had written it.

Although the Chinooks are periodically chased back over the mountains or completely absorbed by the massive cold, their influence does remain, sometimes for only a few hours but usually for a couple of days. Often, however, their patrols against the cold of the north are sufficient to invite the enormous warm highs from the desert southwest – and then we have summer in winter.

This is our weather – unpredictable, to say the least. And, regardless of all the severe conditions we have endured and of all the memories of lost livestock, it takes only two lovely days of Indian Summer in late September – days I cannot describe – to make Montana's climate the most enjoyable one I have ever lived in.

What is nature without contrast? What are days that never change? What is life without anticipation? Urban life, perhaps. May God deliver me from that particular air-conditioned monotony.

BILL STOCKTON was "dropped in Minnesota but born in Montana," the sheep rancher-artist says of himself. He studied art in Paris and raises sheep with his family at their place in Grass Range, Montana. His book is a landscape of "the commonness of death, birth and the uncommonness of life," he writes, a raw example of man's challenge of life and living with the variations of nature.

John McPhee

Coming into the Country

Brad Snow and Lilly Allen came into the country in 1974. They were twenty-six and twenty-one. Their route had begun in New Hampshire and had included Anchorage, where they took jobs to collect enough money to venture into the bush. Like many other young couples who wished to get past the turnstiles of urban Alaska, they studied the map and guessed at the merits of this or that possible destination. Many people they encountered seemed to be headed for McGrath and Bethel and points between on the Kuskokwim River. Allen and Snow therefore looked the other way. "None of those people even knew where Eagle *was* . We figured it was the place to go."

They arrived in a pickup – with their axes and hammers, drill bits and drawknife, whipsaw; their new, lovely, seventeen-foot Chestnut Prospector canoe. They were exploring in more ways than the geographical. They were looking for a milieu – and a manner of developing their lives. For necessary money, they could work from

time to time in Fairbanks – and, possibly, in Eagle. But they hoped to live much of the year apart from any community. "I reject suburbia," Snow was not shy to explain. "I reject crowds. I do not want a new car, a fancy house. They are not worth working for. In the Lower Forty-eight, economic pressure made it impossible for me to have the land and space I would like to have without spending twenty years to get it and then being surrounded by box houses. In order to get anything like what I wanted, in New Hampshire, I would have had to deal in large figures. I was unwilling to complicate my life to get those figures."

What he and Lilly sought was terrain where the individual spirit might be confined only by the metes and bounds and rules of nature. They meant to go down the Yukon, whose banks were just the beginnings of millions of acres of wilderness. They asked around – of others, like Dick Cook, who had pursued the same idea – and they discovered the country's code of seniority right. Tributary rivers were prime locations. There was someone already living on each incoming stream for a considerable distance below Eagle. The first vacancy was the Nation River, forty-six miles away – a little far, but it would do. Snow had brought with him a sense of impending catastrophe, in large part because he had staked his plans on the character of the Yukon without even knowing if it was safely navigable or a boiling flume of rapids. When he had become assured that for all its great power the big river ran smooth, his confidence improved. He felt expansive as he loaded the canoe with seven hundred pounds of grain.

He was an electrician by trade – a fact of no value on the Nation. He was good at carpentry, though, and he was a sharpshooter – skills enough for a beginning. Seven miles up the Nation, he and Lilly built a ten-by-fourteen-foot cabin of unpeeled, saddle-notched logs. It had two windows, paned with soft clear plastic. It was chinked with moss. Its roof consisted of layers of sod, moss, and plastic. It was a tight, well-made, neatly made cabin. Its door, for some months, was nothing more than a hanging blanket, but even on nights at thirty-five below zero the cabin was so warm that the blanket was kept to one side. They had an airtight heat stove ("a poor man's Ashley"), and their cook-stove was a sheepherder's unit, its firebox scarcely a cubic foot. With the whipsaw, Snow made boards for a bench and table. From dry spruce he made dowels, which he tapped into holes drilled in the wall logs, and on these he set shelves for their pinto beans and bulgur, their whole-wheat-soy ribbon noodles, their cherry butter and corn-germ oil, rolled oats, popcorn, brown rice, and wheat berries. He killed a moose, and they hung strips of the meat from the ridgepole to dry. They preserved blueberries, cranberries, rose hips. In the clear Nation, they fished for grayling and northern pike.

They had only two dogs with them, and one night Miki, a Siberian husky, was off scenting the neighborhood when Snow and Allen heard the nearby howl of a wolf. Snow took a shotgun and walked in the direction of the sound. He came back with Miki on a stick. The wolf had ripped the dog's throat. The winter was otherwise safely un-eventful, with the exception that Snow one day decided he had appen-dicitis and took off for Fairbanks, leaving Lilly Allen behind. For five weeks, she was there alone, more than fifty miles from Eagle, with no idea if he was dead or alive. In the end, it was Snow's woman, and not his appendix, that was inflamed.

Not many months before, they had made a trip to Basking Ridge, New Jersey, to be married. The bride's father wore lillies of the valley. He is an Exxon executive. Lilly went to Ridge High School and for one semester to the University of Arizona. She was working as a waitress on Route 16 outside Conway, New Hampshire, when Snow came into her life. She wanted someday to own fields of sheep, she told him, be-cause she was "into spinning and weaving." He wanted to go where even fleece would freeze. He was from Reading, Massachusetts, had studied some at the Universities of Massachusetts and Hawaii, and had been to trade school, but he had found a deeper interest working in New Hampshire forests for the Appalachian Mountain Club. A lithe man of middle height, he has a big brown beard, a tumble of shin-ing brown hair, a serious turn of mind. Lilly Allen – handsome, un-adornedly feminine – is facially Puritan, sober, with a touch of ana-chronism about her, as if on Sundays somehow she occupies a front pew, listening to Cotton Mather.

"We came here to get away from lots of people, lots of machines, and into a simpler way of life, " she will say. "Everybody in Eagle says they came here 'to get away from it all.' We found 'it all' in Eagle. We came here to do without unnecessary things, to live out, to deal with the land in a more natural way."

In the vernacular of the river people, hunting moose, caribou, porcupine, duck, bear, rabbit is known as "getting your meat," and for Snow the task was complicated from the beginning by more than the problems of stalking and marksmanship. He had trouble, sometimes, pulling the trigger on a wild creature. "I hunt for meat, but I don't really enjoy hunting," he confesses. "It comes down to having or not having a spirit of predatorship. If Dick Cook or Charlie Edwards sees a goose, he doesn't hesitate. Bang. But I stop and admire the goose, and then I think of the gun. When I shoot a moose, I walk up to it with profound reverence – this beautiful beast that I, a scrawny little thing, am destroying. The last time I shot my moose, I cried. I really sympathized with him. I don't know how to put it. Having shot the animal – and seeing it lying there, dying – shakes me up."

In their search for ways to make a living in the country, Snow and Allen avoided trapping altogether. "I would do that if I had no other way to get money," he explains. "But I don't want to kill animals up here to clothe fat whores in New York. I don't mind wearing furs, but I prefer not to sell them." Meanwhile, there was money to be made fighting fires – in a smoking forest with a water bag on his back – and from two such experiences he earned a thousand dollars, or more than half of what they needed for a year.

They were still tasting their new and more natural life when Lilly's parents arrived for a visit in Eagle. In two canoes, the four went down the Yukon for a few days, just to have a look at the cabin on the Nation. The journey was more than Lilly's mother could complete, but Snow and his father-in-law left the women camped behind and tracked the Chestnut up the stream. It was a laborious effort, and they had been at it several hours when a helicopter suddenly came over the trees and passed them. Just the sight of it angered Snow, because – fifty miles from civilization – it ruined the wild scene. The two men tracked on, forgot the chopper, and finally arrived at the cabin. It had a door now, and an ingenious Oriental-puzzle sort of lock, which Snow had devised. Scarcely had he brought out some gear to air when the helicopter returned. It circled, landed on a gravel bar. "Let me do the talking," said Snow.

The pilot got out, and so did a man with a federal patch on his shirt. He was a short, slight, briefcase of a man. "Hello," he said. "I'm

Dave Williams, of the Bureau of Land Management. You're on a ca-
noe trip. I'm very sorry to disturb your wilderness experience. We're
just checking here. Do you mind if we look around? This isn't your
place, is it?"

Snow was noncommittal, but he became increasingly irritated as
Williams went into the cabin and rummaged among its goods. The
pilot said, "Really nice place here – nice, well-built cabin. This your
place?"

Brad and Lilly own a framed copy of a celebrated photograph made
by Dorothea Lange in Kern County, California, in the nineteen-thir-
ties, which shows a compressed-air pump at a rundown rural filling
station and two prominent signs – one saying "AIR," the other saying
"This is your country. Don't let the big men take it away from you."

"Yes, it's *my* place," Snow blurted.

Williams reappeared like a genie. "Did you say *your* place?" he
asked.

"Those are my things in the cabin," Snow said. "I'd rather you
didn't go through my things."

"I said, 'Is this your place?'"

"You seem to think it's yours."

As he left, Williams said,"The cabin is in trespass. Very likely
you'll be hearing from me in a short while. This is now the twentieth
century. You can't just do what you want to do. You cannot play with
the wilderness."

Snow was shortly given written notice that the cabin was on feder-
al ground, that its presence conflicted with "the necessary and appropri-
ate use of said land," and that if he left his personal property there it
would be removed and stored at his expense. Lilly Allen was men-
tioned only as "any and all other persons." Alaska had attracted them.
The United States had rebuffed them. Sarge Waller got a notice, too,
about his cabin at the Kandik. Other notices went down the river. In
the hundred and sixty miles between Eagle and Circle, the exact small
number of people living on or near the Yukon had always been inde-
terminate, and as the scrutiny of the Bureau of Land Management
drew closer the number became even less determinate than before.
Under blue wisps of smoke separated by pieces of land the size of

Eastern counties, people did what they could to remain invisible, knowing they were in trespass on federal land.

From time immemorial until the nineteen-seventies, anyone who had the drive and spirit to build a cabin in this northern wilderness was not restrained from doing so. For a long time, gold was the almost exclusive draw, and, as Lieutenant Frederick Schwatka had observed when he was sent to scout the region in 1883, "the discovery of gold in paying quantities is probably the only incentive for men to enter the country, and were it not that indications are seen all along the river, white men would probably never venture in." In more recent times, though, as the pressure of population in the Lower Forty-eight increased toward critical levels, a quite different incentive presented itself as well. Some of the hardiest people in the society were drawn to bush Alaska in search of a sense of release – of a life that remembered the past. The Alaskan wild was, as advertised, the last frontier – where people willing to combat its cold and run its risks could live an existence free from supererogatory rules as long as they did no harm to one another. The government did not interfere, and through the Homestead Act and other legislative provisions it even assisted this dream; but, with the discovery of oil at Prudhoe Bay on the edge of the Arctic Ocean, events began to occur that would change, apparently forever, the use and demarcation of Alaskan land. Meanwhile, certain long-established forms of freedom would disappear – the sort of freedom that drew a family like the Gelvins a generation earlier into the country, the sort of freedom envisioned by young people who set off to live in the wild of the upper Yukon. If the oil had never been discovered, there would not have been an eviction notice prepared for Brad Snow.

The discovery of the oil was in 1968, and after it became clear that there would be no pipeline until the land claims of the natives were satisfactorily extinguished, the United States Congress (attempting to satisfy not only the natives but at the same time the conflicting ambitions of conservationists and developers; attempting to promote the economy, protect the ecology, and respond multifariously to the sudden demand for this long-ignored but now prime segment of American national real estate) got together in a single bill the mighty ziggurat of legislation within which the catalytic pipeline would seem, while important, almost minor. Long after the publicity had receded and the pipeline had become as little discussed as the Big Inch, the social and political effects of its progenitive congressional bill would still be poignantly felt. Everyone of any race in all Alaska would be affected by the Alaska Native Claims Settlement Act. In elemental respects, the character of Alaska would change.

The natives would be afforded some variety in the choosing of their forty million acres of land, but much of it would be close to established villages. Included, meanwhile, among the epic consolations given the conservationists – the big pieces of land that were to be set aside for consideration as national parks, forests, rivers, wildlife refuges – were more than two million acres along the Yukon between Eagle and Circle. Many millions of additional acres – including the valley where the Gelvins legally staked gold claims – were to be closed to all but those in pursuit of "metalliferous minerals." Meanwhile, the State of Alaska was still choosing the hundred and three million acres awarded to it in the Statehood Act. It had until 1984 to complete the selection, and for the time being the land under scrutiny would remain – to the individual – beyond reach. When one adds in the existing parks, government forest, and wildlife refuges and a vast federal petroleum reserve in the north, not much remains, so it is one of the ironies of Alaska that in the midst of this tremendous wilderness people consider themselves fortunate to have (anywhere at all) a fifty-by-a-hundred-foot lot they can call their own.

JOHN McPHEE was born in 1931 and attended Princeton University. He has written a number of books including *A Sense of Where You Are, Levels of the Game, The Crofter and Laird, Encounters with the Archdruid,* and *The Curve of Binding Energy.* This selection is taken from one of his most popular works, *Coming into the Country,* a story of a search in Alaska for a new challenge from nature, and thus from life, in the 20th century.

Richard M. Ketchum

*Second Cutting: Letters
from the Country*

ach April finds us pondering once more the arcane tongue spoken at Internal Revenue Service headquarters. The opening line of Instructions for Schedule F (Form 1040), Farm Income and Expense, suggests what all those who farm are up against. It reads:

> **Note:** You may be entitled to claim the new jobs credit if you hired additional employees this year. However, you may not take a deduction for that portion of the wages or salaries paid or incurred which is equal to the amount of the new jobs credit allowable before application of the tax liability limitation. Please see **Form 5884, New Jobs Credit,** for additional information.

We read on. Past Cash Receipts and Disbursements Method of Reporting, through discussions of the accrual method, cooperative allocations, commodities futures, deductions for farming syndicates (with a long pause over a mysterious note that states: *To determine whether you participated materially in the farm management or production, do not consider the activities of any agent who acted for you*), and finally to Retirement Plans. On Line 48, it was explained, you should "enter the amount you claim as a deduction for contributions to a pension, profit-sharing or annuity plan . . . for the benefit of your employees." It was the only instruction that seemed to fit Charley's situation. We entered $2.10 on Line 48.

As a rooster, Charley is not actually an employee. But we don't know how to describe his present state unless it is retirement, and it's difficult to see where we should enter the $2.10 – what we paid for twenty-five pounds of laying mash – unless it's as part of Charley's retirement program.

We have never known what type of rooster he is – only that when he first came to the farm he was a splendid specimen, a real cock o' the walk, in his prime and proud of it, constantly preening his black and yellow-white feathers, the fiery red comb, and the dark-green plumes that arched like a fountain when he strutted around the corner of the barn. Every now and then he would cross the road to survey the scene from Edith's big pine, but most of the time he stayed around our barn, content to be with the cows, which he seemed to regard as large brown-and-white chickens.

After he lost his comb, Charley's personality underwent a change. Before then, he was a popinjay, vain, concerned only with appearances; now he was transformed into an old reprobate, a roue with a rolling gait and a wandering eye, and we heard later that he had made several forays to neighboring henhouses, only to be driven off by younger, bigger roosters.

Time passed, and Charley looked tackier than ever – no comb, tail feathers all askew, a rake gone to seed. Meantime, the cattle were sold, except for two young bulls that roamed the small pasture at the east end of the barn, and Charley moved over to roam with them. Then the bulls were sold and Charley was alone, still crowing before break of day, wandering in and out of the empty bullpens, occasionally strutting around to the other side of the barn to visit the goats (which ranked far below cows in Charley's caste system).

One day Charley vanished, and for a week there was neither sight nor sound of him. Maybe, we thought, he's moved to the Butlers' hen-house, beyond the swamp, and has found companionship at last. But no, he was not at the Butlers; we heard him crowing in the middle of the swamp, on the far side of the pond, where he must have been liv-ing off what seeds he could scrounge. Then silence. No Charley. Per-haps a hawk or a fox had surprised the old boy, we worried.

In December we had an early snow, an unusually big one – snow that kept falling softly day after day until the woods were full and even the pond vanished beneath the blanket of white. It turned cold – down to minus fifteen degrees one night – and still no news from Charley. The next morning we went in search of him, expecting to find nothing but a bundle of feathers on the snow, but as we emerged from the kit-chen door we heard his *cock-a-doodle-doo* for the first time in a week – he was somewhere in the vicinity of the biggest pine tree in the swamp and we headed through knee-deep snow for it, carrying a little can of seed to see if we might tempt him. We caught sight of him roosting on a limb halfway up the pine tree, but try as we might there was no lur-ing Charley down. He gave us a baleful stare, crowed once or twice, and then looked the other way. We left the seed on a small hummock, thinking he might come down to eat if we went away. Not until later did it dawn on us why Charley hadn't left his perch. He'd be helpless in the deep snow. Charley was marooned.

Next afternoon the two of us set out for the swamp. It was bitter cold, and when we looked up into the pine's branches we saw that Charley was gone. Back and forth through the swamp we tramped, peering into every tree and bush, finally spotting him huddled on a low branch at the edge of the back pasture, where he could catch the last rays of a dying sun. He looked like a goner. We walked up, making comforting noises, but just as we reached out to grab him he squawked raucously and flapped off, landing in a pile of snow by the spring-house, where he flailed about. Back to the house we went for a bushel basket, back once more through the drifting snow to the springhouse, and after a couple of tries we managed to get the basket over Charley. He began to scream – the piercing, unearthly shrieks of a nightmare – and all the way back to the barn we wondered what the neighbors thought we had tucked beneath our arm.

We brought Charley into the bullpen, emptied him out of the

basket, and he lay on the hay too exhausted to move. Only when we gave him a bit of grain and some warm water did we begin to think he might make it. For a few days he remained in a catatonic state and then began to perk up noticeably, as though he had made a decision to live. Several mornings later when we walked into the milkhouse and heard him crowing, we knew he was going to be all right.

That was when we bought the laying mash – $2.10 worth, knowing we would have to provide for the old boy's retirement. Through the winter Charley roosted on a metal stanchion, looking like a disreputable remittance man, disdaining the nest we created for him. Each time we fed him he fixed us with a malevolent eye, as if to say that life wasn't a patch on those days when he had the company of the cows. And when the wind was out of the east you had the feeling Charley was getting the wanderlust again and might strike out to seek his fortune if only the snow would melt.

Soon it will be spring and we'll have to get Charley some hens – a couple of maiden ladies that will cluck solicitously over him and look after the old vagabond in his declining years.

RICHARD M. KETCHUM was an editor of *American Heritage* and the co-founder of *The Country Journal*, one of the outstanding magazines of the last two decades. He is the author of several volumes of American history including *The Battle of Bunker Hill, The World of George Washington, The Winter Soldiers, Faces From the Past* and the editor of *The American Heritage Picture History of the Civil War* and *The American Heritage Book of the Revolution.*

Peter and Barbara Jenkins

The Walk West
"One Step Below Heaven"

To our east was almost half the state. There were no mountains out there, only land that could make a Comanche look for company. To the west, mountains often rose to over 14,000 feet. Lake City was 150 miles away.

In the silent, drowsy town of Blanca a thin Spanish man walked up to us, looking very serious. He had an old, but clean, white T-shirt on and a turquoise cross that hung from his long tan neck.

"Why are you walking in this wind? Winter will soon be with us," he said.

"We're headed for the mountains."

"Those packs look so heavy. Don't they hurt your backs?"

"No, they feel good," I said. They felt like friends.

"Are you and the *senora* doing penance?" the Spanish man asked.

"What's that?"

"Are you repenting by walking and carrying those heavy burdens?" He looked so sorry for us. "Are you being punished?"

"No, we are not being punished," I said. "We are being blessed."

The snowstorms didn't come that first week, but there was a snow shower when we were almost into Del Norte (el. 7,882). The fall sun warmed our faces from the bluest skies I'd ever seen. It sent shafts of light through the falling snow in the foothills to the south. People in Del Norte had heard of Lake City but warned against trying to make it. About 1,500 people lived here in Del Norte through the winter. Stores, even a cafe, were open year-round. "I ain't even sure twenty-five people spend the winter in Lake City. You get caught in a blizzard between South Fork, west a here, and Lake City, and they might never find ya. Coyotes'll eat you before the spring thaw."

Now the mountains showed themselves to us. They had intense powers of attraction. A kind of suction pulled us deeper into their hidden forests, their unnamed river gorges and their thinning air that made a person feel invincible, light-headed, high.

They drew us on as the nights dropped below freezing and the cottonwoods shed their yellow leaves into a shallow blue Rio Grande. The leaves that stayed on the cottonwoods reflected in the river and turned whole stretches of it gold. Water-rounded white rocks stuck out of the blue and gold water. We were very close to the headwaters of the Rio Grande, born from the melting snows and rocky springs of the mountains.

The Rio Grande rushed by some big trout and carried fallen aspen leaves till it drained this part of the Rockies. It picked up speed and eventually wove south through New Mexico till it formed the curved border of South Texas and Mexico. Mexicans swam across it, and it didn't stop till it mingled with the Gulf of Mexico. I'd never seen the headwaters of a river before.

I couldn't get my mind off Lake City. We both felt drawn to this supposed ghost town. Heading for Lake City, Colorado, reminded me of heading for Homer Davenport's cabin on top of his mountain in Appalachia.

My map said it was fifty-four miles of no towns but ghost towns. If we could make it over Spring Creek Pass, we would cross the Continental Divide. We were going to spend the winter on the western side of the continent.

Two elk broke and ran from some willow thickets by the Rio Grande. Because the river narrowed here and rushed loudly over a smooth rock bottom, I at first did not hear them. When they ran across the river and clattered over the loose rocks, I looked up just in time to see them run toward a mountainside of deep green pine.

Then I saw it. First my eye caught some white. The sun shone through it. It was a fanned-out white tail. I saw a white head. Because of the dark background of the trees, the eagle's dark brown body was not visible. All I could see was a flying white head and a white tail. It was a bald eagle diving toward the river, splashing in a deep round pool. It flew out with wet, empty claws.

The eagle flew over the river, landing in a bone-white aspen tree. A few remaining aspen leaves shook in the down mountain breeze and circled the eagle in yellow. When we walked closer, the eagle lifted from its perch and flapped slowly up the Rio Grande. We were close enough that I could see its beautiful white head bobbing, tilting, concentrating on another deep blue pool. Where was that trout? I couldn't see its strong, X-ray-vision eyes, but I knew they were a fierce, freeing yellow. It dove again. Its yellow feet held a squirming rainbow trout.

The eagle flew farther up the river with its catch, settled in a tree and began to eat. We sat on a bare warm rock and watched. This was the bald eagle of the U.S.A. We ate some Cheddar cheese and a couple of apples and the bald eagle ate its trout. It flew south, down the river toward Goose Creek. We walked north toward Spring Creek Pass (el. 10,901) and the Continental Divide.

It was 4:20 P.M. when we crossed that invisible barrier, the divide, October 27, 1977. Four years and twelve days ago I'd taken my first step toward this. One more step and I was on the western side of our huge continent.

A mile before crossing the divide, we came upon a porcupine. It plodded along in some dried grass headed for a stand of yellowish, wind-deformed aspens. At first it seemed so goofy, too slow, as if it were wandering aimlessly. But it was in no hurry. Above, in the almost navy blue skies of late fall, a jet left tracks of white lines, headed somewhere.

In a jet we could be to the Pacific in not much more than an hour

. . . We thought of the jet . . . We thought of the porcupine. We had chosen the pace of the porcupine.

Being in the midst of these mountains was different from anything we'd ever known. Inside the Rockies even the colors of things were different. Instead of the orange and red skies that seemed to cover the earth on the plains and in West Texas, the sky was so blue you had to wear sunglasses to look into it.

The scraggly gray sagebrush of Texas and the red clays, brown prairie grass, and windmills of New Mexico were replaced by building-sized boulders of faded grays. Slashes of white rock cut upward into the blue sky that dared you to try to look to the end of it. The sky seemed to be so deep and clear here in Colorado it had to stretch till it blended to black in the outer galaxy.

When we walked over Slumgullion Pass (el. 11,361), one of the highest in the Rockies, we were higher than we'd ever been before. Since we'd left Dallas, early in the summer, we'd been climbing, sometimes slightly, lately dramatically, always higher. Our backs, our legs, our lungs and our hearts had adjusted slowly to less oxygen. These mountain roads seemed to go up for days. They climbed enough that they ate up car transmissions and burned up brakes. These mountains also killed people who lacked respect for them. Some came and thought they could run up a Rocky Mountain the way they could a base path in a softball game. Too often their hearts burst.

We began an equally dramatic climb down. We rounded a sharp, dangerous curve in the road, and before us was a string of mountain peaks. They made everything that we'd seen before practically forgettable. Strung along a line were five Rocky Mountains. They looked as jagged and sharp as shark's teeth, stuck up from the mammoth rock below. They were gleaming white and all of them were over 14,000 feet tall.

In all of Colorado there were fifty-three mountains taller than 14,000 feet. These five formed the castle walls for Lake City. Uncompahgre Peak, the most dramatically shaped of them, was the sixth tallest in the state at 14,309 feet. Adjoining it were Wetterhorn, Red Cloud, Handies and Sunshine peaks. I'd heard the word "breathtaking" before, but this was the first time in *my* life that I ever had my breath taken away by a turn in the road. Our hearts beat harder; we actually had to gasp deeper for air to keep up with the overwhelming mountains before us. Lake City must be at the bottom of them somewhere.

We came to the sharpest curve, as hard to the right as any road could turn. Many thousand feet below us was a river. It was so far down in the steep-sided valley that it looked like a thin silver trickle. To its left were some miniature-looking green fields, a couple of buildings, just specks. A couple of dirt roads, as thin as a pencil line, went across the river. It was the Lake Fork of the Gunnison River.

PETER JENKINS (born 1951) is the son of an industrialist and a nurse. He said in a recent biography that he never wanted to be a writer, "I just wanted to walk across America to see if America was as bad as I really thought it was. After walking 4,751 miles and living and working with the real people of this country, I had to write about them. They inspired me and changed my outlook totally." In this selection the authors take you on a journey through southwestern Colorado near Lake City, a small town nestled in the San Juan Mountains. He met his wife, Barbara, while on his walk, and they completed the walk together.

John Steinbeck

The Grapes of Wrath

Once California belonged to Mexico and its land to Mexicans; and a horde of tattered feverish Americans poured in. And such was their hunger for land that they took the land – stole Sutter's land, Guerrero's land, took the grants and broke them up and growled and quarreled over them, those frantic hungry men; and they guarded with guns the land they had stolen. They put up houses and barns, they turned the earth and planted crops. And these things were possession, and possession was ownership.

The Mexicans were weak and fled. They could not resist, because they wanted nothing in the world as frantically as the Americans wanted land.

Then, with time, the squatters were no longer squatters, but owners; and their children grew up and had children on the land. And the hunger was gone from them, the feral hunger, the gnawing, tearing hunger for land, the water and earth and the good sky over it, for the green thrusting grass, for the swelling roots. They had these things so

completely that they did not know about them any more. They had no more the stomach-tearing lust for a rich acre and a shining blade to plow it, for seed and a windmill beating its wings in the air. They arose in the dark no more to hear the sleepy birds' first chittering, and the morning wind around the house while they waited for the first light to go out to the dear acres. These things were lost, and crops were reckoned in dollars, and land was valued by principal plus interest, and crops were bought and sold before they were planted. Then crop failure, drought, and flood were no longer little deaths within life, but simple losses of money. And all their love was thinned with money, and all their fierceness dribbled away in interest until they were no longer farmers at all, but little shopkeepers of crops, little manufacturers who must sell before they can make. Then those farmers who were not good shopkeepers lost their land to good shopkeepers. No matter how clever, how loving a man might be with earth and growing things, he could not survive if he were not also a good shopkeeper. And as time went on, the business men had the farms, and the farms grew larger, but there were fewer of them.

Now farming became industry, and the owners followed Rome, although they did not know it. They imported slaves, although they did not call them slaves: Chinese, Japanese, Mexicans, Filipinos. They live on rice and beans, the business men said. They don't need much. They wouldn't know what to do with good wages. Why, look how they live. Why, look what they eat. And if they get funny – deport them.

And all the time the farms grew larger and the owners fewer. And there were pitifully few farmers on the land any more. And the imported serfs were beaten and frightened and starved until some went home again, and some grew fierce and were killed or driven from the country. And the farms grew larger and the owners fewer.

And the crops changed. Fruit trees took the place of grain fields, and vegetables to feed the world spread out on the bottoms: lettuce, cauliflower, artichokes, potatoes – stoop crops. A man may stand to use a scythe, a plow, pitchfork; but he must crawl like a bug between the rows of lettuce, he must bend his back and pull his long bag between the cotton rows, he must go on his knees like a penitent across a cauliflower patch.

And it came about that owners no longer worked on their farms. They farmed on paper; and they forgot the land, the smell, the feel of it, and remembered only that they owned it, remembered only what they gained and lost by it. And some of the farms grew so large that one man could not even conceive of them any more, so large that it took batteries of bookkeepers to keep track of interest and gain and loss; chemists to test the soil, to replenish; straw bosses to see that the stooping men were moving along the rows as swiftly as the material of their bodies could stand. Then such a farmer really became a storekeeper, and kept a store. He paid the men, and sold them food, and took the money back. And after a while he did not pay the men at all, and saved bookkeeping. These farms gave food on credit. A man might work and feed himself and when the work was done, might find that he owed money to the company. And the owners not only did not work the farms any more, many of them had never seen the farms they owned.

And then the dispossessed were drawn west – from Kansas, Oklahoma, Texas, New Mexico; from Nevada and Arkansas families, tribes, dusted out, tractored out. Carloads, caravans, homeless and hungry; twenty thousand and fifty thousand and a hundred thousand and two hundred thousand. They streamed over the mountains, hungry and restless – restless as ants, scurrying to find work to do – to lift, to push, to pull, to pick, to cut – anything, any burden to bear, for food. The kids were hungry. We got no place to live. Like ants scurrying for work, for food, and most of all for land.

We ain't foreign. Seven generations back Americans, and beyond that Irish, Scotch, English, German. One of our folks in the Revolution, an' they was lots of our folks in the Civil War – both sides. Americans.

They were hungry, and they were fierce. And they had hoped to find a home, and they found only hatred. Okies – the owners hated them because the owners knew they were soft and the Okies strong, that they were fed and the Okies hungry; and perhaps the owners had heard from their grandfathers how easy it is to steal land from a soft man if you are fierce and hungry and armed. The owners hated them. And in the towns, the storekeepers hated them because they had no money to spend. There is no shorter path to a storekeeper's contempt, and all his admirations are exactly opposite. The town men, little bankers, hated Okies because there was nothing to gain from them. They had nothing. And the laboring people hated Okies because a hungry man must work, and if he must work, if he has to work, the wage payer automatically gives him less for his work; and then no one can get more.

And the dispossessed, the migrants, flowed into California, two hundred and fifty thousand, and three hundred thousand. Behind them new tractors were going on the land and the tenants were being forced off. And new waves were on the way, new waves of the dispossessed and the homeless, hardened, intent, and dangerous.

And while the Californians wanted many things, accumulation, social success, amusement, luxury, and a curious banking security, the new barbarians wanted only two things – land and food; and to them the two were one. And whereas the wants of the Californians were nebulous and undefined, the wants of the Okies were beside the roads, lying there to be seen and coveted: the good fields with water to be dug for, the good green fields, earth to crumble experimentally in the hand, grass to smell, oaten stalks to chew until the sharp sweetness was in the throat. A man might look at a fallow field and know, and see in his mind that his own bending back and his own straining arms would bring the cabbages into the light, and the golden eating corn, the turnips and carrots.

And a homeless hungry man, driving the roads with his wife beside him and his thin children in the back seat, could look at the fallow fields which might produce food but not profit, and that man could know how a fallow field is a sin and the unused land a crime against the thin children. And such a man drove along the roads and knew temptation at every field, and knew the lust to take these fields and make them grow strength for his children and a little comfort for his wife. The temptation was before him always. The fields goaded him and the company ditches with good water flowing were a goad to him.

And in the south he saw the golden oranges hanging on the trees, the little golden oranges in the dark green trees; and guards with shotguns patrolling the lines so a man might not pick an orange for a thin child, oranges to be dumped if the price was low.

He drove his old car into a town. He scoured the farms for work. Where can we sleep the night?

Well, there's Hooverville on the edge of the river. There's a whole raft of Okies there.

He drove his old car to Hooverville. He never asked again, for there was a Hooverville on the edge of every town.

The rag town lay close to water; and the houses were tents, and weed-thatched enclosures, paper houses, a great junk pile. The man drove his family in and became a citizen of Hooverville – always they were called Hooverville. The man put up his own tent as near to water as he could get; or if he had no tent, he went to the city dump and brought back cartons and built a house of corrugated paper. And when the rains came the house melted and washed away. He settled in Hooverville and he scoured the countryside for work, and the little money he had went for gasoline to look for work. In the evening the men gathered and talked together. Squatting on their hams they talked of the land they had seen.

There's thirty thousan' acres, out west of here. Layin' there. Jesus, what I could do with that, with five acres of that! Why, hell, I'd have everything to eat.

Notice one thing? They ain't no vegetables nor chickens nor pigs at the farms. They raise one thing – cotton, say, or peaches, or lettuce. 'Nother place'll be all chickens. They buy the stuff they could raise in the dooryard.

Jesus, what I could do with a couple pigs!

Well, it ain't yourn, an' it ain't gonna be yourn.

What we gonna do? The kids can't grow up this way.

In the camps the word would come whispering, There's work at Shafter. And the cars would be loaded in the night, the highways crowded – a gold rush for work. At Shafter the people would pile up, five times too many to do the work. A gold rush for work. They stole away in the night, frantic for work. And along the roads lay the temptations, the fields that could bear food.

That's owned. That ain't our'n.

Well, maybe we could get a little piece of her. Maybe – a little piece. Right down there – a patch. Jimson weed now. Christ, I could git enough potatoes off'n that little patch to feed my whole family!

It ain't our'n. It got to have Jimson weeds.

Now and then a man tried; crept on the land and cleared a piece, trying like a thief to steal a little richness from the earth. Secret gardens hidden in the weeds. A package of carrot seeds and a few turnips. Planted potato skins, crept out in the evening secretly to hoe in the stolen earth.

Leave the weeds around the edge – then nobody can see what we're a-doin'. Leave some weeds, big tall ones, in the middle.

Secret gardening in the evenings, and water carried in a rusty can.

And then one day a deputy sheriff: Well, what you think you're doin'?

I ain't doin' no harm.

I had my eye on you. This ain't your land. You're trespassing.

The land ain't plowed, an' I ain't hurtin it none.

You goddamned squatters. Pretty soon you'd think you owned it. You'd be sore as hell. Think you owned it. Get off now.

And the little green carrot tops were kicked off and the turnip greens trampled. And then the Jimson weed moved back in. But the cop was right. A crop raised – why, that makes ownership. Land hoed and the carrots eaten – a man might fight for land he's taken food from. Get him off quick! He'll think he owns it. He might even die fighting for the little plot among the Jimson weeds.

Did ya see his face when we kicked them turnips out? Why, he'd kill a fella soon's he'd look at him. We got to keep these here people down or they'll take country. They'll take the country.

Outlanders, foreigners.

Sure, they talk the same language, but they ain't the same. Look how they live. Think any of us folks'd live like that? Hell, no!

In the evening, squatting and talking. And an excited man: Whyn't twenty of us take a piece of lan'? We got guns. Take it an' say, "Put us off if you can." Whyn't we do that?

They'd just' shoot us like rats.

Well, which'd you ruther be, dead or here? Under groun' or in a house all made of gunny sacks? Which'd you ruther for your kids, dead now or dead in two years with what they call malnutrition? Know what we et all week? Biled nettles an' fried dough! Know where we got the flour for the dough? Swep' the floor of a boxcar.

Talking in the camps, and the deputies, fat-assed men with guns slung on fat hips, swaggering through the camps: Give 'em somepin to think about. Got to keep 'em in line or Christ only knows what they'll do. Why, Jesus, they're as dangerous as niggers in the South! If they ever get together there ain't nothin' that'll stop 'em.

Quote: In Lawrenceville a deputy sheriff evicted a squatter, and the squatter resisted, making it necessary for the officer to use force. The eleven-year-old son of the squatter shot and killed the deputy with a .22 rifle.

Rattlesnakes! Don't take chances with 'em, an' if they argue, shoot first. If a kid'll kill a cop, what'll they men do? Thing is, get tougher'n they are. Treat 'em rough. Scare 'em.

What if they won't scare? What if they stand up and take it and shoot back? These men were armed when they were children. A gun is an extension of themselves. What if they won't scare? What if some time an army of them marches on the land as the Lombards did in Italy, as the Germans did on Gaul and the Turks did on Byzantium? They were land-hungry, ill-armed hordes too, and the legions could not stop them. Slaughter and terror did not stop them. How can you frighten a man whose hunger is not only in his own cramped stomach but in the wretched bellies of his children? You can't scare him – he has known a fear beyond every other.

In Hooverville the men talking: Grampa took his lan' from the Injuns.

Now, this ain't right. We're a-talkin' here. This here you're talkin' about is stealin. I ain't no thief.

No? You stole a bottle of milk from a porch night before last. An' you stole some copper wire and sold it for a piece of meat.

Yeah, but the kids was hungry.

It's stealin', though.

Know how the Fairfiel' ranch was got? I'll tell ya. It was all gov'ment lan', an' could be took up. Ol' Fairfiel', he went into San Francisco to the bars, an' he got him three hundred stew bums. Them bums took up the lan'. Fairfiel' kep em in food an' whisky, an' then when they'd proved the lan', ol' Fairfiel' took it from 'em. He used to say the lan' cost him a pint of rot gut an acre. Would you say that was stealin'?

Well, it wasn't right, but he never went to jail for it.

No, he never went to jail for it. An' the fella that put a boat in a wagon an' made his report like it was all under water 'cause he went in a boat – he never went to jail neither. An' the fellas that bribed congressmen and the legislatures never went to jail neither.

All over the State, jabbering in the Hoovervilles.

And then the raids – the swoop of armed deputies on the squatter's camps. Get out. Department of Health orders. This camp is a menace to health.

Where we gonna go?

That's none of our business. We got orders to get you out of here. In half an hour we set fire to the camp.

They's typhoid down the line. You want ta spread it all over?

We got orders to get you out of here. Now get! In half an hour we burn the camp.

In half an hour the smoke of paper houses, of weed-thatched huts, rising to the sky, and the people in their cars over the highways, looking for another Hooverville.

And in Kansas and Arkansas, in Oklahoma and Texas and New Mexico, the tractors moved in and pushed the tenants out.

Three hundred thousand in California and more coming. And in California the roads full of frantic people running like ants to pull, to push, to lift, to work. For every manload to lift, five pairs of arms, extended to lift it; for every stomachful of food available, five mouths open.

And the great owners, who must lose their land in an upheaval, the great owners with access to history, with eyes to read history and to know the great fact: when property accumulates in too few hands it is taken away. And that companion fact: when a majority of the people are hungry and cold they will take by force what they need. And the little screaming fact that sounds through all history: repression works only to strengthen and knit the repressed. The great owners ignored the three cries of history. The land fell into fewer hands, the number of the dispossessed increased, and every effort of the great owners was directed at repression. The money was spent for arms, for gas to protect the great holdings, and spies were sent to catch the murmuring of revolt so that it might be stamped out. The changing economy was ignored, plans for the change ignored: and only means to destroy revolt were considered, while the causes of revolt went on.

The tractors which throw men out of work, the belt lines which carry loads, the machines which produce, all were increased; and more and more families scampered on the highways, looking for crumbs from the great holdings, lusting after the land beside the roads. The great owners formed associations for protection and they met to discuss ways to intimidate, to kill, to gas. And always they were in fear of a principal – three hundred thousand – if they ever move under a leader – the end. Three hundred thousand, hungry, and miserable; if they ever know themselves, the land will be theirs and all the gas, all the rifles in the world won't stop them. And the great owners, who had become through their holdings both more and less than men, ran to their destruction, and used every means that in the long run would destroy them. Every little means, every violence, every raid on a Hooverville, every deputy swaggering through a ragged camp put off the day a little and cemented the inevitability of the day.

The men squatted on their hams, sharp-faced men, lean from hunger and hard from resisting it, sullen eyes and hard jaws. And the rich land was around them.

D'ja hear about the kid in the fourth tent down?

No, I jus' come in.

Well, that kid's been a-cryin' in his sleep an' a rollin' in his sleep. Them folks thought he got worms. So they give him a blaster, an' he died. It was what they call black-tongue the kid had. Comes from not gettin' good things to eat.

Poor little fella.

Yeah, but them folks can't bury him. Got to go to the county stone orchard.

Well, hell.

And hands went into pockets and little coins came out. In front of the tent a little heap of silver grew. And the family found it there.

Our people are good people; our people are kind people. Pray God some day kind people won't all be poor. Pray God some day a kid can eat.

And the association of owners knew that some day the praying would stop.

And there's the end.

———————————————

JOHN STEINBECK (1902-1968) was born in Salinas, California, the son of a country treasurer and a school teacher. He was alternately employed as a hod-carrier, fruit-picker, apprentice painter, laboratory assistant, caretaker, and a reporter and writer. He was a foreign correspondent in North Africa and Italy for the *New York Herald Tribune* in 1943 and reported for *Newsday* in Viet Nam in 1966-1967. His writing is uniquely American in its distrust and anger at American society, offset by the faith in the land and people he writes about. In 1962, he was awarded a Nobel prize.

David Brower

from *Wildlands*
in Our Civilization
"Wilderness –
Conflict and Conscience"

You like Wilderness, let's suppose, and you want to see some of it saved. Not just a thin strip of roadside with a sign saying "Don't pick the flowers." Not just a wild garden behind the hotel or a pleasant woods within shouting distance of the highway. But *real* wilderness – country big enough to have a beyond to it and an inside. With space enough to separate you from the buzz, bang, screech, ring, yammer, and roar of the 24-hour commercial you wish hard your life wouldn't be. Wilderness that is a beautiful piece of world. Where as you start up a trail and your nine-year-old Bob asks, "Is there civilization behind that ridge?" you can say no and share his "That's good!" feeling.

Yes, a place where you can rescue your *self* from what Ortega calls the *other* – all the extraneities that pile on you too deep. So deep, to quote my wife Anne's *bon mot*, that "the life you lead is not your own."

So you want a place where you can be serene, that will let you contemplate and connect two consecutive thoughts, or that if need be can stir you up as you were made to be stirred up, until you blend with the wind and water and earth you almost forgot you came from.

You like wilderness, then, and need it. And suddenly you encounter a practical man who never learned that he needs it too, or doesn't remember. It doesn't take you long to encounter him, because there are a lot of him, many of him in places of influence, all adding up to a political force that can jeopardize wilderness if it chooses to, and choose it seems to.

You can malign him, and insure that the conflict will continue over the need for wilderness. But let's assume you'd rather align him, get straight to his conscience, end the conflict, and save the wilderness. Then what?

I have tried to develop one approach. Let's call it a starting point, and let us hope that it will suggest to you a different and better approach to a goal that happily still remains and should persist.

Let's address ourselves to a very important question. How much right does one generation have to another generation's freedom? Can we of this generation, in conscience, pay for our freedom by mortgaging the freedom of our children? Is it our ethic that we are privileged to write the rules to which all the subsequent generations of our civilization must be committed, and by which they must abide, irrespective of their own wishes?

Thomas Jefferson, long ago, said that one generation could not bind another; each had the right to set its own course. Go out across this land and try to find someone to argue that he was wrong. You don't find a taker. It is the national consensus that we don't have this right.

But deeds are not matching words. This generation is speedily using up, beyond recall a very important right that belongs to future generations – the right to have wilderness in their civilization, even as we have it in ours; the right to find solitude somewhere; the right to see, and enjoy, and be inspired and renewed, somewhere, by those places where the hand of God has not been obscured by the industry of man.

Our decisions today will determine the fate of that right, so far as people of our time can pass opportunity along to our sons. Apathy here can mean that we pass them a dead torch. Or we can keep it aflame, knowing that this is a very special torch that man cannot light again.

Belatedly we are becoming generally concerned about our scenic resources and about resolving conflicts that must be resolved if we are to retain islands of open space in the sea of tomorrow's civilization. The early history of civilization dealt with the problem of finding enough enclosed spaces – caves in the beginning, then crude shelters, then walled cities, followed by the early beginnings of suburbia when there was no longer room enough within the walls for all the people of the cities. Only recently have we begun to change our concern. The problem seems no longer to be one of enclosing space, but of leaving enough of it open to meet our needs for greenery and for every man's "slice of sky" Wallace Stegner speaks of. We know we need some of this in our own garden for the edges of our daily existence – something to look out upon at breakfast, or before dinner. We need more space near by for our weekends, where on a March day a boy may fly a kite, or a family may picnic and stroll. For our holidays we need accessible open space within range of our faster transportation and better roads, bearing in mind that we shall soon have more three-day weekends than we have now. For our lengthening vacations we'll need the big spaces of national parks and wilderness.

These outdoor spaces – daylight-saving *plots,* weekend and holiday *areas,* and vacation *regions* – won't set themselves aside. We have to plan for them as the population avalanche flows over the land, and plan generously if civilization is not only to improve living standards, but also to sustain man's standards for life.

The Sierra Club has been concerned with man's use of wildlife, wilderness, and national parks ever since John Muir founded the club in 1892 with the general purpose of exploring, enjoying, and protecting our scenic resources. In none of its 65 years has the club been free of the controversy that results when one seeks to protect what another would exploit. That has meant 65 years' experience in trying to resolve a crescendo of conflicts – experience that we can draw upon as we consider today's major controversies and the still more critical contests that tomorrow will inevitably bring.

These conflicts will underline the need for conservation education; more than that, they will require the education of conservationists. There's quite a difference.

On the one hand, *conservation* alludes to management of the commodity resources, to using them wisely that they may last longer. We all approve of conservation, even as we approve of motherhood – even while we go on expending our nonrenewable resources at a constantly accelerating rate (more in this century than in all previous history). We intend to do better. In the end, however, we know that no matter how well we manage our commodity resources and our raw materials, time will catch up with us. Conservation means spreading a given resource over a given period of time. Time finally runs out and the resource is gone, or at best, is a rarity.

On the other hand, the *conservationist,* and I stress the *-ist,* has come to be known as the man who is concerned with preserving for all our time certain important scenic resources – our resources of wilderness, parks, wildlife, and the recreation and inspiration man may always derive from them. Always, that is, if each generation, including ours, takes care of the few places we have left where those resources still survive.

To use a figure, there are two sides to conservation just as there are two sides to a coin. On one side, tangible quantities; on the other, intangible qualities. Each side is presently oriented to look in opposite directions. Yet each must live with the other. We may need a coin of transparent material, so that each side can look in both directions.

The conservationist, then, is the man more concerned about what certain natural resources do for his soul than for his bank balance. Every man is a conservationist part of the time in his thinking, if not in his action.

There are a great number of people who are conservationists in their action also – more than 11,000 [now 25,000] in the Sierra Club, and about two million who are loosely organized in the Natural Resources Council of America. The numbers are growing more rapidly than is our population. Every time a scenic hill is bulldozed for a new tract of houses, or a new freeway blots out more acres of green quietude, or a new dam inundates a trout stream, or there's a vacant space where a great tree was, or another whooping crane turns up missing – every time one of these things happens, the conservationist force grows stronger as more people realize the need to protect a rarity from extinction. Theirs is not a force of blind opposition to progress, but of opposition to blind progress. Theirs is a force determined to see that progress does not take away important things from mankind, forever, in order to benefit a few men now.

The conservationist force, I submit, is not a pressure group. It merely demonstrates the pressure of man's conscience, of his innate knowledge that there are certain things he may not ethically do to the only world he will ever have, and to the strictly rationed resource of natural beauty which still exists in that world. The conservationist force does not need to be pressed into action. It need only be made to realize what is happening, and its voice of conscience speaks.

That sounds simple. It isn't. I need not go into any detail to convince you of the difficulty of making people realize something – of their making it real to themselves, not imaginary, but actual. You know how hard it is to be heard in the clamor around us. And we all know how hard it is to get the voice of conscience to speak audibly enough to have effect. For example, how many times a week do you feel something needs to be done for the public good – and how many of those times can you find the few minutes to do something about it yourself?

So the conservationist force, for all its conscience, still needs to realize more, and to speak more. Conservation controversies, like prefabricated telephone booths, are ubiquitous. All of them are conflicts for space. The resolution of these conflicts should depend upon the answer to the question – Who needs the space most? Unfortunately, the decisions are being made now, and irrevocably, not on the basis of who needs the space most, but on who got there first with the most dramatic plan of development and the biggest earth-moving equipment.

DAVID BROWER (born 1912) is an outdoorsman as well as a leading figure in the movement to preserve some of the wilder lands left on the American continent. He has been executive director of the Sierra Club and the founder of Friends of the Earth. This message written in l96l for *Wildlands in Our Civilization* is one of challenge in itself: once recognizing the importance of the land to us, how can we stand by and let it be tamed or destroyed?

Wendell Berry

The Gift of Good Land
"Home of the Free"

was writing not long ago about a team of Purdue engineers who foresaw that by 2001 practically everything would be done by remote control. The question I asked – because such a "projection" *forces* one to ask it – was, *Where does satisfaction come from?* I concluded that there probably wouldn't be much satisfaction in such a world. There would be a lot of what passes for "efficiency," a lot of "production" and "consumption," but little satisfaction.

What I failed to acknowledge was that this "world of the future" is already established among us, and is growing. Two advertisements that I have lately received from correspondents make this clear, and raise the question about the sources of satisfaction more immediately and urgently than any abstract "projection" can do.

The first is the legend from a John Deere display at Waterloo Municipal Airport:

INTRODUCING SOUND-GARD BODY . . .
A DOWN TO EARTH SPACE CAPSULE.

New Sound-Gard body from John Deere, an "earth space capsule"
to protect and encourage the American farmer at his job of being
"Breadwinner to a world of families."

Outside: dust, noise, heat, storm, fumes.
Inside: all's quiet, comfortable, safe.

Features include a 4 post Roll Gard, space-age metals, plastics,
and fibers to isolate driver from noise, vibration, and jolts. He
dials 'inside weather', to his liking . . . he push buttons radio or
stereo tape entertainment. He breathes filtered, conditioned air
in his pressurized compartment. He has remote control over
multi-ton and multi-hookups, with control tower visibility . . .
from his scientifically padded seat.

The second is an ad for a condominium housing development:

HOME OF THE FREE.

We do the things you hate. You do the things you like. We mow
the lawn, shovel the walks, paint and repair and do all exterior
maintenance.

You cross-country ski, play tennis, hike, swim, work out,
read or nap. Or advise our permanent maintenance staff as
they do the things you hate.

Different as they may seem at first, these two ads make the same
appeal, and they represent two aspects of the same problem: the wide-
spread, and still spreading, assumption that we somehow have the
right to be set free from anything whatsoever that we "hate" or don't
want to do. According to this view, what we want to be set free from
are the natural conditions of the world and the necessary work of
human life; we do not want to experience temperatures that are the
least bit too hot or too cold, or to work in the sun, or be exposed to

§ 275 §

wind or rain, or come in personal contact with anything describable as dirt, or provide for any of our own needs, or clean up after ourselves. Implicit in all this is the desire to be free of the "hassles" of mortality, to be "safe" from the life cycle. Such freedom and safety are always for sale. It is proposed that if we put all earthly obligations and the rites of passage into the charge of experts and machines, then life will become a permanent holiday.

What these people are really selling is insulation – cushions of technology, "space age" materials, and the menial work of other people – to keep fantasy in and reality out. The condominium ad says flat out that it is addressed to people who "hate" the handwork of household maintenance, and who will enjoy "advising" the people who do it for them; it is addressed in other words, to those who think themselves too good to do work that other people are not too good to do. But it is a little surprising to realize that the John Deere ad is addressed to farmers who not only hate farming (that is, any physical contact with the ground or the weather or the crops), but also hate tractors, from the "dust," "fumes," "noise, vibration, and jolts" of which they wish to be protected by an "earth space capsule" and a "scientifically padded seat."

Of course, the only real way to get this sort of freedom and safety – to escape the hassles of earthly life –is to die. And what I think we see in these advertisements is an appeal to a desire to be dead that is evidently felt by many people. These ads are addressed to the perfect consumers – the self-consumers, who have found nothing of interest here on earth, nothing to do, and are impatient to be shed of earthly concerns. And so I am at a loss to explain the delay. Why hasn't some super salesman sold every one of these people a coffin – an "earth space capsule" in which they would experience no discomfort or inconvenience whatsoever, would have to do no work that they hate, would be spared all extremes of weather and all noises, fumes, vibrations, and jolts?

I wish it were possible for us to let these living dead bury themselves in the earth space capsules of their choice and think no more about them. The problem is that with their insatiable desire for comfort, convenience, remote control, and the rest of it, they cause an unconscionable amount of trouble for the rest of us, who would like a fair crack at living the rest of our lives within the terms and conditions of the real world. Speaking for myself, I acknowledge that the world, the weather, and the life cycle have caused me no end of trouble, and yet I look forward to putting in another forty or so years with them because they have also given me no end of pleasure and instruction. They interest me. I want to see them thrive on their own terms. I hate to see them abused and interfered with for the comfort and convenience of a lot of spoiled people who presume to "hate" the more necessary kinds of work and all the natural consequences of working outdoors.

When people begin to "hate" the life cycle and to try to live outside it and to escape its responsibilities, then the corpses begin to pile up and to get into the wrong places. One of the laws the world imposes on us is that everything must be returned to its source to be used again. But one of the first principles of the haters is to violate this law in the name of convenience or efficiency. Because it is "inconvenient" to return bottles to the beverage manufacturers, "dead soldiers" pile up in the road ditches and in the waterways. Because it is "inconvenient" to be responsible for wastes, the rivers are polluted with everything from human excrement to various carcinogens and poisons. Because it is "efficient" (by what standard?) to mass-produce meat and milk in food "factories," the animal manures that once would have fertilized the fields have instead become wastes and pollutants. And so to be "free" of "inconvenience" and "inefficiency" we are paying a high price – which the haters among us are happy to charge to posterity.

And what a putrid (and profitable) use they have made of the idea of freedom! What a tragic evolution has taken place when the inheritors of the Bill of Rights are told, and when some of them believe, that "the home of the free" is where somebody else will do your work!

Let me set beside those advertisements a sentence that I consider a responsible statement about freedom: "To be free is precisely the same thing as to be pious, wise, just and temperate, careful of one's own, abstinent from what is another's, and thence, in fine, magnanimous and brave." That is John Milton. He is speaking out of the mainstream of our culture. Reading his sentence after those advertisements is coming home. His words have an atmosphere around them that a living human can breathe in.

How do you get free in Milton's sense of the word? I don't think you can do it in an earth space capsule or a space space capsule or a capsule of any kind. What Milton is saying is that you can do it only by living in this world as you find it, and by taking responsibility for the consequences of our life in it. And that means doing some chores that, highly objectionable in anybody's capsule, may not be at all unpleasant in the world.

Just a few days ago I finished up one of the heaviest of my spring jobs: hauling manure. On a feed lot I think this must be real drudgery even with modern labor-saving equipment – all that "waste" and no fields to put it on! But instead of a feed lot I have a small farm – what would probably be called a subsistence farm. My labor-saving equipment consists of a team of horses and a forty-year-old manure spreader. We forked the manure on by hand – forty-five loads. I made my back tired and my hands sore, but I got a considerable amount of pleasure out of it. Everywhere I spread that manure I knew it was needed. What would have been a nuisance in a feed lot was an opportunity and a benefit here. I enjoyed seeing it go out onto the ground. I was working some two-year-olds in the spreader for the first time, and I enjoyed that – mostly. And, since there were no noises, fumes, or vibrations the loading times were socially pleasant. I had some help from neighbors, from my son, and, toward the end, from my daughter who arrived home well rested from college. She helped me load, and then read *The Portrait of a Lady* while I drove up the hill to empty the spreader. I don't think many young women have read Henry James while forking manure. I enjoyed working with my daughter, and I enjoyed wondering what Henry James would have thought of her.

WENDELL BERRY was born in 1934. His name is synonymous with a sense of agricultural America. His work has been rooted in the land, much as his daily subsistence has been from his farm in his native Kentucky. He once wrote, "in surroundings to which man is closest, which he lives and understands best, he makes his greatest contribution to his fellow men . . ."

Norman Maclean

A River Runs Through It

Paul and I fished a good many big rivers, but when one of us referred to "the big river" the other knew it was the Big Blackfoot. It isn't the biggest river we fished, but it is the most powerful, and per pound, so are its fish. It runs straight and hard – on a map or from an airplane it is almost a straight line running due west from its headwaters at Rogers Pass on the Continental Divide to Bonner, Montana, where it empties into the South Fork of the Clark Fork of the Columbia. It runs hard all the way.

Near its headwaters on the Continental Divide there is a mine with a thermometer that topped at 69.7 degrees below zero, the lowest temperature ever officially recorded in the United States (Alaska omitted). From its headwaters to its mouth it was manufactured by glaciers. The first sixty-five miles of it are smashed against the southern wall of its valley by glaciers that moved in from the north, scarifying the earth; its lower twenty-five miles were made overnight when the great

glacial lake covering northwestern Montana and northern Idaho broke its ice dam and spread the remains of Montana and Idaho mountains over hundreds of miles of the plains of eastern Washington. It was the biggest flood in the world for which there is geological evidence; it was so vast a geological event that the mind of man could only conceive of it but could not prove it until photographs could be taken from earth satellites.

The straight line on the map also suggests its glacial origins; it has no meandering valley, and its few farms are mostly on its southern tributaries which were not ripped up by glaciers; instead of opening into a wide flood plain near its mouth, the valley, which was cut overnight by a disappearing lake when the great ice dam melted, gets narrower and narrower until the only way a river, an old logging railroad, and an automobile road can fit into it is for two of them to take to the mountainsides.

It is a tough place for a trout to live – the river roars and the water is too fast to let algae grow on the rocks for feed, so there is no fat on the fish, which must hold most trout records for high jumping.

Besides, it is the river we knew best. My brother and I had fished the Big Blackfoot since nearly the beginning of the century – my father before then. We regarded it as a family river, as a part of us, and I surrender it now only with great reluctance to dude ranches, the unselected inhabitants of Great Falls, and the Moorish invaders from California.

Early next morning Paul picked me up in Wolf Creek, and we drove across Rogers Pass where the thermometer is stuck at three tenths of a degree short of seventy below. As usual, especially if it were early in the morning, we sat silently respectful until we passed the big Divide, but started talking the moment we thought we were draining into another ocean. Paul nearly always had a story to tell in which he was the leading character but not the hero.

He told his Continental Divide stories in a seemingly light-hearted, slightly poetical mood such as reporters often use in writing "human-interest" stories, but, if the mood were removed, his stories would appear as something about him that would not meet the approval of his family and that I would probably find out about in time anyway. He also must have felt honor-bound to tell me that he lived other lives, even if he presented them to me as puzzles in the form of funny stories. Often I did not know what I had been told about him as we crossed the divide between our two worlds.

"You know," he began, "it's been a couple of weeks since I fished the Blackfoot." At the beginning, his stories sounded like factual reporting. He had fished alone and the fishing had not been much good, so he had to fish until evening to get his limit. Since he was returning directly to Helena he was driving up Nevada Creek along an old dirt road that followed section lines and turned at right angles at section corners. It was moonlight, he was tired and feeling in need of a friend to keep him awake, when suddenly a jackrabbit jumped on to the road and started running with the headlights. "I didn't push him too hard," he said, "because I didn't want to lose a friend." He drove, he said, with his head outside the window so he could feel close to the rabbit. With his head in the moonlight, his account took on poetic touches. The vague world of moonlight was pierced by the intense white triangle from the headlights. In the center of the penetrating isosceles was the jackrabbit, which, except for the length of his jumps, had become a snowshoe rabbit. The phosphorescent jackrabbit was doing his best to keep in the center of the isosceles but was afraid he was losing ground and, when he looked back to check, his eyes shone with whites and blues gathered up from the universe. My brother said, "I don't know how to explain what happened next, but there was a right-angle turn in this section-line road, and the rabbit saw it, and I didn't."

Later, he happened to mention that it cost him $175.00 to have his car fixed, and in 1937 you could almost get a car rebuilt for $175.00. Of course, he never mentioned that, although he did not drink when he fished, he always started drinking when he finished.

I rode part of the way down the Blackfoot wondering whether I had been told a little human-interest story with hard luck turned into humor or whether I had been told he had taken too many drinks and smashed hell out of the front end of his car.

Since it was no great thing either way, I finally decided to forget it, and, as you see, I didn't. I did, though, start thinking about the canyon where we were going to fish.

The canyon above the old Clearwater bridge is where the Blackfoot roars loudest. The backbone of a mountain would not break, so the mountain compresses the already powerful river into sound and spray before letting it pass. Here, of course, the road leaves the river; there was no place in the canyon for an Indian trail; even in 1806 when Lewis left Clark to come up the Blackfoot, he skirted the canyon by a safe margin. It is no place for small fish or small fishermen. Even the roar adds power to the fish or at least intimidates the fisherman.

When we fished the canyon we fished on the same side of it for the simple reason that there is no place in the canyon to wade across. I could hear Paul start to pass me to get to the hole above, and, when I realized I didn't hear him anymore, I knew he had stopped to watch me. Although I have never pretended to be a great fisherman, it was always important to me that I was a fisherman and looked like one, especially when fishing with my brother. Even before the silence continued, I knew that I wasn't looking like much of anything.

Although I have a warm personal feeling for the canyon, it is not an ideal place for me to fish. It puts a premium upon being able to cast for distance, and yet most of the time there are cliffs or trees right behind the fisherman so he has to keep all his line in front of him. It's like a baseball pitcher being deprived of his windup, and it forces the fly fisherman into what is called a "roll cast," a hard cast that I have never mastered. The fisherman has to work enough line into his cast to get distance without throwing any line behind him, and then he has to develop enough power from a short arc to shoot it out across the water.

He starts accumulating the extra amount of line for the long cast by retrieving his last cast so slowly that an unusual amount of line stays in the water and what is out of it forms a slack semiloop. The loop is enlarged by raising the casting arm straight up and cocking the wrist until it points to 1:30. There, then, is a lot of line in front of the fisherman, but it takes about everything he has to get it high in the air and out over the water so that the fly and leader settle ahead of the line – the arm is a piston, the wrist is a revolver that uncocks, and even the body gets behind the punch. Important, too, is the fact that the extra amount of line remaining in the water is a little like a rattlesnake striking, with a good piece of his tail on the ground as something to strike from. All this is easy for a rattlesnake, but has always been hard for me.

Paul knew how I felt about my fishing and was careful not to seem superior by offering advice, but he had watched so long that he couldn't leave now without saying something. Finally he said, "The fish are out farther." Probably fearing he had put a strain on family relations, he quickly added, "Just a little farther."

I reeled in my line slowly, not looking behind so as not to see him. Maybe he was sorry he had spoken, but, having said what he said, he had to say something more. "Instead of retrieving the line straight toward you, bring it in on a diagonal from the downstream side. The diagonal will give you a more resistant base to your loop so you can put more power into your forward cast and get a little more distance."

Then he acted as if he hadn't said anything and I acted as if I hadn't heard it, but as soon as he left, which was immediately, I started retrieving my line on a diagonal, and it helped. The moment I felt I was getting a little more distance I ran for a fresh hole to make a fresh start in life.

It was a beautiful stretch of water, either to a fisherman or a photographer, although each would have focused his equipment on a different point. It was a barely submerged waterfall. The reef of rock was about two feet under the water, so the whole river rose into one wave, shook itself into spray, then fell back on itself and turned blue. After it recovered from the shock, it came back to see how it had fallen.

No fish could live out there where the river exploded into the colors and curves that would attract photographers. The fish were in that slow backwash, right in the dirty foam, with the dirt being one of the chief attractions. Part of the speckles would be pollen from pine trees, but most of the dirt was edible insect life that had not survived the waterfall.

I studied the situation. Although maybe I had just added three feet to my roll cast, I still had to do a lot of thinking before casting to compensate for some of my other shortcomings. But I felt I had already made the right beginning – I had already figured out where the big fish would be and why.

Then an odd thing happened. I saw him. A black back rose and sank in the foam. In fact, I imagined I saw spines on his dorsal fin until I said, to myself, "God, he couldn't be so big you could see his fins." I even added, "You wouldn't' even have seen the fish in all that

foam if you hadn't first thought he would be there." But I couldn't'
shake the conviction that I had seen the black back of a big fish, because
as someone often forced to think, I know that often I would not see a
thing unless I thought of it first.

Seeing the fish that I first thought would be there led me to won-
dering which way he would be pointing in the river. "Remember,
when you make the first cast," I thought, "that you saw him on the -
wash where the water is circling upstream, so he will be looking down-
stream, not upstream, as he would be if he were in the main current."

I was led by association to the question of what fly I would cast,
and to the conclusion that it had better be a large fly, a number four or
six, if I was going after the big hump in the foam.

From the fly, I went to the other end of the cast, and asked myself
where the hell I was going to cast from. There were only gigantic rocks
at this waterfall, so I picked one of the biggest, saw how I could crawl
up it, and knew from that added height I would get added distance, but
then I had to ask myself, "how the hell am I going to land the fish if I
hook him while I'm standing up there?" So I had to pick a smaller
rock, which would shorten my distance but would let me slide down it
with a rod in my hand and a big fish on.

I was gradually approaching the question all river fishermen
should ask before they make the first cast, "If I hook a big one, where
the hell can I land him?"

One great thing about fly fishing is that after a while nothing exists
of the world but thoughts about fly fishing. It is also interesting that
thoughts about fishing are often carried on in dialogue form where
Hope and Fear – or, many times, two Fears – try to outweigh each
other.

One Fear looked down the shoreline and said to me (a third per-
son distinct from the two fears), "There is nothing but rocks for thirty
yards, but don't get scared and try to land him before you get all the
way down to the first sandbar."

The Second Fear said, "It's forty, not thirty, yards to the first sand-
bar and the weather has been warm and the fish's mouth will be soft
and he will work off the hook if you try to fight him forty yards down-
river. It's not good but it will be best to try to land him on a rock that is
closer."

The First Fear said, "There is a big rock in the river that you will have to take him past before you land him, but, if you hold the line tight enough on him to keep him this side of the rock, you will probably lose him."

The Second Fear said, "But if you let him get on the far side of the rock, the line will get caught under it, and you will be sure to lose him."

That's how you know when you have thought too much – when you become a dialogue between *You'll probably lose* and *You're sure to lose*. But I didn't entirely quit thinking, although I did switch subjects. It is not in the book, yet it is human enough to spend a moment before casting in trying to imagine what the fish is thinking, even if one of its eggs is as big as its brain and even if, when you swim underwater, it is hard to imagine that a fish has anything to think about. Still, I could never be talked into believing that all a fish knows is hunger and fear. I have tried to feel nothing but hunger and fear and don't see how a fish could ever grow to six inches if that were all he ever felt. In fact, I go so far sometimes as to imagine that a fish thinks pretty thoughts. Before I made the cast, I imagined the fish with the black back lying cool in the carbonated water full of bubbles from the waterfalls. He was looking downriver and watching the foam with food in it backing upstream like a floating cafeteria coming to wait on its customers. And he probably was imagining that the speckled foam was eggnog with nutmeg sprinkled on it, and, when the whites of eggs separated and he saw what was on shore, he probably said to himself, "What a lucky son of a bitch I am that this guy and not his brother is about to fish this hole."

I thought all these thoughts and some besides that proved of no value, and then I cast and I caught him.

I kept cool until I tried to take the hook out of his mouth. He was lying covered with sand on the little bar where I had landed him. His gills opened with his penultimate sighs. Then suddenly he stood up on his head in the sand and hit me with his tail and the sand flew. Slowly at first my hands began to shake, and, although I thought they made a miserable sight, I couldn't stop them. Finally, I managed to open the large blade to my knife which several times slid off his skull before it went through his brain.

Even when I bent him he was way too long for my basket, so his tail stuck out.

There were black spots on him that looked like crustaceans. He seemed oceanic, including barnacles. When I passed my brother at the next hole, I saw him study the tail and slowly remove his hat, and not out of respect to my prowess as a fisherman.

I had a fish, so I sat down to watch a fisherman.

He took his cigarettes and matches from his shirt pocket and put them in his hat and pulled his hat down tight so it wouldn't leak. Then he unstrapped his fish basket and hung it on the edge of his shoulder where he could get rid of it quick should the water get too big for him. If he studied the situation he didn't take any separate time to do it. He jumped off a rock into the swirl and swam for a chunk of cliff that had dropped into the river and parted it. He swam in his clothes with only his left arm – in his right hand, he held his rod high and sometimes all I could see was the basket and rod, and when the basket filled with water sometimes all I could see was the rod.

The current smashed him into the chunk of cliff and it must have hurt, but he had enough strength remaining in his left fingers to hang to a crevice or he would have been swept into the blue below. Then he still had to climb to the top of the rock with his left fingers and his right elbow which he used like a prospector's pick. When he finally stood on top, his clothes looked hydraulic, as if they were running off him.

Once he quit wobbling, he shook himself duck-dog fashion, with his feet spread apart, his body lowered and his head flopping. Then he steadied himself and began to cast and the whole world turned to water.

Below him was the multitudinous river, and, where the rock had parted it around him, big-grained vapor rose. The mini-molecules of water left in the wake of his line made momentary loops of gossamer, disappearing so rapidly in the rising big-grained vapor that they had to be retained in memory to be visualized as loops. The spray emanating from him was finer-grained still and enclosed him in a halo of himself. The halo of himself was always there and always disappearing, as if he were candlelight flickering about three inches from himself. The images of himself and his line kept disappearing into the rising vapors of the river, which continually circled to the tops of the cliffs where, after becoming a wreath in the wind, they became rays of the sun.

The river above and below his rock was all big Rainbow water, and he would cast hard and low upstream, skimming the water with his fly but never letting it touch. Then he would pivot, reverse his line in a great oval above his head, and drive his line low and hard down-stream, again skimming the water with his fly. He would complete this grand circle four or five times, creating an immensity of motion which culminated in nothing if you did not know, even if you could not see, that now somewhere out there a small fly was washing itself on a wave. Shockingly, immensity would return as the Big Blackfoot and the air above it became iridescent with the arched sides of a great Rainbow.

He called this "shadow casting," and frankly I don't know whether to believe the theory behind it – that the fish are alerted by the sha-dows of flies passing over the water by the first casts, so hit the fly the moment it touches the water. It is more or less the "working up an ap-petite" theory, almost too fancy to be true, but then every fine fisher-man has a few fancy stunts that work for him and for almost no one else. Shadow casting never worked for me, but maybe I never had the strength of arm and wrist to keep line circling over the water until fish imagined a hatch of flies was out.

My brother's wet clothes made it easy to see his strength. Most great casters I have known were big men over six feet, the added height certainly making it easier to get more line in the air in a bigger arc. My brother was only five feet ten, but he had fished so many years his body had become partly shaped by his casting. He was thirty-two now, at the height of his power, and he could put all his body and soul into a four-and-a-half-ounce magic totem pole. Long ago, he had gone far beyond my father's wrist casting, although his right wrist was al-ways so important that it had become larger than his left. His right arm, which our father had kept tied to the side to emphasize the wrist, shot out of his shirt as if it were engineered, and it too, was larger than his left arm. His wet shirt bulged and came unbuttoned with his pivot-ing shoulders and hips. It was also not hard to see why he was a street fighter, especially since he was committed to getting in the first punch with his right hand.

Rhythm was just as important as color and just as complicated. It was one rhythm superimposed upon another, our father's four-count rhythm of the line and wrist being still the base rhythm. But superimposed upon it was the piston two count of his arm and the long overriding four count of the completed figure eight of his reversed loop.

The canyon was glorified by rhythms and colors.

I heard voices behind me, and a man and his wife came down the trail, each carrying a rod, but probably they weren't going to do much fishing. Probably they intended nothing much more than to enjoy being out of doors with each other and, on the side, to pick enough huckleberries for a pie. In those days there was little in the way of rugged sports clothes for women, and she was a big, rugged woman and wore regular men's bib overalls, and her motherly breasts bulged out of the bib. She was the first to see my brother pivoting on the top of the cliff. To her, he must have looked something like a trick rope artist at a rodeo, doing everything except jumping in and out of his loops.

She kept watching while groping behind her to smooth out some pine needles to sit on. "My, my!" she said.

Her husband stopped and stood and said, "Jesus." Every now and then he said, "Jesus." Each time his wife nodded. She was one of America's mothers who never dream of using profanity themselves but enjoy their husbands', and later come to need it, like cigar smoke.

I started to make for the next hole. "Oh, no," she said, "you're going to wait, aren't you, until he comes to shore so you can see his big fish?"

"No," I answered, "I'd rather remember the molecules."

She obviously though I was crazy, so I added, "I'll see his fish later." And to make any sense for her I had to add, "He's my brother."

As I kept going, the middle of my back told me that I was being viewed from the rear both as quite a guy, because I was his brother, and also as a little bit nutty, because I was molecular.

NORMAN MACLEAN (born 1902) is an English instructor who didn't start writing until his 70s. As a youth he worked in logging camps and with the U.S. Forest Service in Montana and Idaho, which left him with experiences he would always remember. This selection was taken from one of his two stories of his youth in Montana and describes the unique challenge men still seek to put in front of themselves while casting fishing line into a river. It is a story of communion with nature, self-definition, and of the necessity of challenge of a different kind – the search for a sense of place in nature.

INTERLUDE 2

450 Years of Writing
about the Land

hroughout the history of this country, the land has had special meaning to its people. The land and its riches, its size, and its character has made America what it is today. In novels, plays, songs, prose, poetry, cries of consternation or calls to battle, Americans have included the land in the expression of their thoughts in one way or another. The nature of the land has undergone a transformation in our eyes – as well as in physical appearance – over the years of our inhabiting this vast continent.

The following is a kind of journal of different American's attitudes about the land, expressed in chronological one-liners. Taken altogether, it is a short American history of our views about the land, about America and about ourselves.

*Those new regions [America]
which we found and explored
with the fleet . . . we may rightly
call a New World . . . a continent
more densely peopled and
abounding in animals than our
Europe or Asia or Africa; and, in
addition, a climate milder than in
any other region known to us."*
Amerigo Vespucci (1454 - 1512)
Letter to Lornezo de 'Medici

*"Our fathers were Englishmen
which came over this great ocean,
and were ready to perish in this
wilderness."*
William Bradford (1590-1657)
Of Plymouth Plantation

*"I write the wonders of the Christ-
ian religion, flying from the de-
pravations of Europe, to the
American strand: and, assisted by
the Holy Author of that religion,
I do, with all conscience of truth,
required therein by Him, who is
goodness, and faithfulness, where-
with his Divine Providence hath
irradiated an Indian wilderness."*
Cotton Mather (1663-1728)
Magnalia Christi Americana

*"Oh for a lodge in some
          vast wilderness,
Some boundless contiguity
          of shade,
Where rumor of oppression
          and deceit,
Of unsuccessful or successful war,
Might never reach me more."*
William Cowper (1731-1800)
The Timepiece

*"But though an old man, I am
but a young gardener."*
Thomas Jefferson (1743-1826)
Letter to Charles Wilson Peale

*"My reason teaches me that land
cannot be sold. The Great Spirit
gave it to his children to live
upon, and cultivate, as far as is
necessary for their subsistence;
and so long as they occupy and
cultivate it, they have the right to
the soil — but if they voluntarily
leave it, then any other people
have a right to settle upon it.
Nothing can be sold, but such
things as can be carried away."*
Black Hawk of the Sauk (1767-1838)
Speech

*"These lands are ours. No one
has a right to remove us, because
we were the first owners. The
Great Spirit above has appointed
this place for us, on which to
light our fires, and here we will
remain. As to boundaries, the
Great Spirit knows no bound-
aries, nor will his red children
acknowledge any."*
Tecumseh of the Shawnees
(1768-1813)
To Joseph Barron

*"Over all rocks, wood, and water,
brooded the spirit of repose, and
the silent energy of nature stirred
the soul to its inmost depths."*
Thomas Cole (1801-1848)
Essay on American Scenery

*"Nature is a mutable cloud,
which is always and never the
same."*
Ralph Waldo Emerson (1803-1882)
Essay

*My country, 'tis of thee,
Sweet land of liberty,
Of thee I sing:
Land where my fathers died,
Land of the pilgrims' pride,*

*From every mountainside,
Let freedom ring.*
Samuel Francis Smith (1808-1895)
America

*"A nation may be said to consist
of its territory, its people, and its
laws. The territory is the only part
which is of certain durability."*
Abraham Lincoln (1809-1865)
Second Annual Message to Congress

*"We need the tonic of wildness
. . . We can never have enough of
nature . . . In wildness is the
preservation of the world."*
Henry David Thoreau (1817-1862)
Journals

*"It is my land, my home, my
father's land, to which I now ask
to be allowed to return. I want to
spend my last days there, and be
buried among the mountains. If
this could be I might die in peace,
feeling that my people, placed in
their native homes, would in-
crease in numbers, rather than
diminish as at present, and that
our names would not become
extinct."*
Geronimo of the Apaches (1829-1909)
  Letter to President Grant

"What treaty that the white man ever made with us have they kept? Not one. When I was a boy the Sioux owned the world; the sun rose and set on their land; they sent ten thousand men to battle. Where are the warriors today? Who slew them? Where are our lands? Who owns them?"
Sitting Bull of the Sioux (1831-1890)

"The clearest way into the Universe is through a forest wilderness."
John Muir (1838-1914)
John of the Mountains

"To waste, to destroy, our natural resources, to waste and exhaust the land instead of using it so as to increase its usefulness, will result in undermining in the days of our children the very prosperity which we ought by right to hand down to them amplified and developed."
Theodore Roosevelt (1858-1919)
Message to Congress

"The promised land always lies on the other side of the wilderness."
Havelock Ellis (1859-1939)
The Dance of Life

"Only to the white man was nature a "wilderness" and only to him was the land "invested" with "wild" animals and "savage" people. To us it was tame. Earth was bountiful and we were surrounded by the blessings of the Great Mystery. Not until the hairy man from the east came and with brutal frenzy heaped injustices upon us and the families that we loved was it "wild" for us. When the very animals of the forest began fleeing from his approach, then it was that for us the "Wild West" began.
Luther Standing Bear of the Sioux (1868-1939)
Land of the Spotted Eagle

"America is my country and Paris is my home town and it is as it has come to be. After all anybody is as their land and air is. Anybody is as the sky is low or high, the air heavy or clear and anybody is as there is wind or no

wind there. It is that which
makes them and the arts they
make and the work they do and
the way they eat and the way they
drink and the way they learn and
everything."
Gertrude Stein (1874-1946)
An American and France

"We abuse land because we
regard it as a commodity belong-
ing to us. When we see land as a
community to which we belong,
we may begin to use it with love
and respect."
Aldo Leopold (1886-1948)
A Sand County Almanac

"From the mountains
        to the prairies,
To the oceans white with foam,
God bless America,
My home sweet home!
Irving Berlin (born 1888)
God Bless America

". . . the sixlane highway
that arched the reedy rivers and
skirted the fields of red clover,
now in whine of windfriction,
hiss of tires, valve-chatter,

grumble of diesels, drone of
        exhausts,
plunges under a
        rampaging bridge,
sixlane under sixlane."
John Dos Passos (1896-1970)

"Discovery is adventure. There is
an eagerness, touched at times
with tenderness as one moves
into the unknown. Walking the
wilderness is indeed like living.
The horizon drops away, bringing
new sights, sounds, and smells
from the earth."
William O. Douglas (1898-1980)
Of Men and Mountains

"Land is the only thing in the
world that amounts to anything,"
he shouted, his thick, short arms
making wide gestures of
indignation, "for 'tis the only
thing in this world that lasts, and
don't you be forgetting it! 'Tis the
only thing worth working for,
worth fighting for – worth dying
for."
Margaret Mitchell (1900-1949)
Gone With the Wind

"When the first white men came to America, they found a land of trees. Old records show that the Hudson Valley when Henry Hudson first saw it was one vast stand of towering pines. Most of the early settlements of New England were hemmed in close to the shore by the forests, dark and forbidding, the people said. By that time much of England was an old land with few virgin forests, but the legends persisted. Deep woods were full of terror and danger."
Hal Borland (1900-1978)
Book of Days

"On Admiralty Island nature's cycle is as yet unbroken. But the chain saws are very close, ready to move in the moment legal road-blocks are removed. By chance or intent, the first areas to go will be the most scenic, the most valu-able for conservation. The bears and the eagles, whose home this has been for thousands of years, have no direct voice in the matter. But they are powerful symbols of something priceless that we now realize we have all

but lost: what Henry Thoreau called "The tonic of wildness." If enough voices are raised in their behalf, they may yet save this greatest of wilderness islands."
Paul Brooks (born 1909)

This land is your land,
        this land is my land,
From California to the
        New York island,
From the redwood forest
        to the Gulf Stream waters.
This land was made for you
        and me.
Woody Guthrie (1912-1967)
This Land is Your Land

"A strange possessiveness seemed to surge through me. I had no right to call this big country mine, yet I felt it was".
Sam Keith from the
Journals of Richard Proenneke

"The most common trait of all primitive peoples is a reference for the lifegiving earth, and the native people shared this ele-mentary ethic: the land was alive to his loving touch, and he, its son, was brother to all creatures. His feelings were made visible in medicine bundles and dance rhythms for rain, and all of his religious rites and land attitudes savored the inseparable world of nature and God, the master of life. During the long Indian tenure the land remained undefiled save for the scars no deeper than the scratches of cornfield clearings or the farming canals of the Hohokams on the Arizona desert."

Stewart Lee Udall (born 1920)
The Quiet Crisis

"The only piece of scientific truth about which I feel totally confident is that we are profoundly ignorant about nature."

Lewis Thomas (born 1913)
The Medusa and the Snail

Nature, Peace and Self-Definition

 Da zi ran.

In the Chinese language, the concept of nature is built from characters meaning "the big place from which the self emerges." Although the indiginous peoples of the North American continent understood this concept of self-definition in nature, translated through their own cultures, it has taken a few thousand years for Western man to accept the same sense of self-definition from nature. One of European-American man's strongest expressions of awareness of the spiritual or self-defining connection with nature was written in 1841 by Ralph Waldo Emerson, and this tenet later became the creation of a religion based on nature's peace.

When the American land was no longer perceived as a continual source of danger and a perpetual, life-threatening wild land with which to be reckoned, more people began to revel in all that the land had brought Americans: plenty, wealth, strength, opportunity, and a vibrant

Courtesy of Museum of Western Art, Denver, Colorado

sense of limitlessness. Through first discovery, and later, meeting the challenges the land presented, Americans felt a sense of undaunted power. If we came to own this vast land of ours, we could do almost anything, or so it seemed. Almost unwittingly, we had already defined ourselves, our lives, our achievements and our potential by the land. We had but to enjoy the fruits of our work and strive to continue the search and discovery.

With the land settled, the passionate energy we had devoted to the art of discovery was turned inward, into the self, and the quest became one of man's place in nature. In 1864, the English scientist, George Perkins Marsh, pondered whether man was in fact a child of God or a child of nature. His conclusion was that we were children of both. Thus began a new cycle of looking to the land as a foundation for the process of discovery and challenge, only this time, we consciously searched for ourselves.

Many of the authors in this section found the source of their own expression in the land: Thomas Jefferson, Ralph Waldo Emerson, and Mary Austin wrote eloquently of the importance of self-discovery in nature. Poets, such as Emily Dickinson, James Kavanaugh, and rancher Wallace McRae have expressed their self-definition and self-affirmation in terms of nature. They illuminate the inner peace found by understanding their place in nature and, so by extension, wrote of their place in this world.

The last selection of Nature, Peace and Self-Definition, and of this anthology, is by William O. Douglas. We felt it best expresses the experience of discovery – of self and of the land – of challenge, imposed by self and by the forces of nature, and of the peace and self-definition that one can find in nature. It is the kind of affirming experience we all seek. It is the caliber of experience each of us hopes to enjoy. As Americans, we are all the more fortunate, as the opportunity for this kind of experience still exists outside of our doors and among our daily choices. It describes best the foundation – and the realization – of a distinct, American character.

The American character was forged by the experience of centuries of achievement, of battle in discovery and challenge, mandated by the necessity of dealing with the land and imposed by the physical demands of nature. In the end, we all return to nature in order to draw together the pieces of a life, a search, and the meaning of living itself.

Ralph Waldo Emerson

The Portable Emerson
"Nature"

To go into solitude, a man needs to retire as much from his chamber as from society. I am not solitary whilst I read and write, though nobody is with me. But if a man would be alone, let him look at the stars. The rays that come from those heavenly worlds will separate between him and what he touches. One might think the atmosphere was made transparent with this design, to give man, in the heavenly bodies, the perpetual presence of the sublime. Seen in the streets of cities, how great they are! If the stars should appear one night in a thousand years, how would men believe and adore; and preserve for many generations the remembrance of the city of God which had been shown! But every night come out these envoys of beauty, and light the universe with their admonishing smile.

The stars awaken a certain reverence, because though always present, they are inaccessible; but all natural objects make a kindred impression, when the mind is open to their influence.

Nature never wears a mean appearance. Neither does the wisest man extort her secret, and lose his curiosity by finding out all her perfection. Nature never became a toy to a wise spirit. The flowers, the animals, the mountains, reflected the wisdom of his best hour, as much as they had delighted the simplicity of his childhood.

When we speak of nature in this manner, we have a distinct but most poetical sense in the mind. We mean the integrity of impression made by manifold natural objects. It is this which distinguishes the stick of timber of the wood-cutter from the tree of the poet. The charming landscape which I saw this morning is indubitably made up of some twenty or thirty farms. Miller owns this field, Locke that, and Manning the woodland beyond. But none of them owns the landscape. There is a property in the horizon which no man has but he whose eye can integrate all the parts, that is, the poet. This is the best part of these men's farms, yet to this their warranty-deeds give no title.

To speak truly, few adult persons can see nature. Most persons do not see the sun. At least they have a very superficial seeing. The sun illuminates only the eye of the man, but shines into the eye and the heart of the child. The lover of nature is he whose inward and outward senses are still truly adjusted to each other; who has retained the spirit of infancy even into the era of manhood. His intercourse with heaven and earth becomes part of his daily food. In the presence of nature a wild delight runs through the man, in spite of real sorrows. Nature says, – he is my creature, and maugre all his impertinent griefs, he shall be glad with me. Not the sun or the summer alone, but every hour and season yields its tribute of delight; for every hour and change corresponds to and authorizes a different state of the mind, from breathless noon to grimmest midnight. Nature is a setting that fits equally well a comic or a mourning piece. In good health, the air is a cordial of incredible virtue. Crossing a bare common, in snow puddles, at twilight, under a clouded sky, without having in my thoughts any occurrence of special good fortune, I have enjoyed a perfect exhilaration. I am glad to the brink of fear. In the woods, too, a man casts off his years, as the snake his slough, and at what period soever of life is always a child. In the woods is perpetual youth. Within these plantations of God, a decorum and sanctity reign, a perennial festival is dressed, and the guest sees not how he should tire of them in a thousand years. In the woods, we return to reason and faith. There I feel that nothing can befall me in life, – no disgrace, no calamity (leaving me my eyes), which nature cannot repair. Standing on the bare ground, – my head bathed by the blithe air and uplifted into infinite space, – all mean egotism vanishes. I become a transparent eyeball; I am nothing; I see all; the currents of the Universal Being circulate through me; I am part or parcel of God. The name of the nearest friend sounds then foreign and accidental: to be brothers, to be acquaintances, master or servant, is then a trifle and a disturbance. I am the lover of uncontained and immortal beauty. In the wilderness, I find something more dear and connate than in streets or villages. In the tranquil landscape, and especially in the distant line of the horizon, man beholds somewhat as beautiful as his own nature.

The greatest delight which the fields and woods minister is the suggestion of an occult relation between man and the vegetable. I am not alone and unacknowledged. They nod to me, and I to them. The waving of the boughs in the storm is new to me and old. It takes me by surprise, and yet is not unknown. Its effect is like that of a higher thought or a better emotion coming over me, when I deemed I was thinking justly or doing right.

Yet it is certain that the power to produce this delight does not reside in nature, but in man, or in a harmony of both. It is necessary to use these pleasures with great temperance. For nature is not always tricked in holiday attire, but the same scene which yesterday breathed perfume and glittered as for the frolic of the nymphs is overspread with melancholy today. Nature always wears the colors of the spirit. To a man laboring under calamity, the heat of his own fire hath sadness in it. Then there is a kind of contempt of the landscape felt by him who has just lost by death a dear friend. The sky is less grand as it shuts down over less worth in the population.

RALPH WALDO EMERSON (1803-1882), one of the most influential figures in American literary history, was among the first of the American writers to speak of the spiritual connection between man and nature. It was during his lifetime that the American continent began to be perceived as a place of transcendent beauty as well as of wealth and opportunity. Through his writing, nature was for the first time enjoyed and celebrated rather than just the object of fear and conquering.

Nature was written in 1836 just after Emerson's marriage to his second wife. It was a time of intense emotional turmoil for him internally. With *Nature* he preached a primary tenet of the religion he founded: that nature was fully half of life and not to be relegated to something that doesn't affect us. His faith in nature developed into a religious philosophy known as Transcendentalism; the tenets of this religion were foreshadowed throughout *Nature* and in his 1841 book, *Essays.*

Thomas Jefferson

Jefferson's *Letters*
"To Whom the Earth Belongs"
To James Madison,
        Paris, September 6, 1789.

The question, whether one generation of men has a right to bind another, seems never to have been started either on this or our side of the water. Yet it is a question of such consequences as not only to merit decision, but place also among the fundamental principles of every government. The course of reflection in which we are immersed here, on the elementary principles of society, has presented this question to my mind; and that no such obligation can be transmitted, I think very capable of proof. I set out on this ground, which I suppose to be self-evident, that the *earth belongs in usufruct to the living*; that the dead have neither powers nor rights over it. The portion occupied by any individual ceases to be his when himself ceases to be, and reverts to the society. If the society has formed no rules for the appropriation of its lands in severality, it will be taken by the first occupants, and these will generally be the wife and

children of the decedent. If they have formed rules of appropriation, those rules may give it to the wife and children, or to some one of them, or to the legatee of the deceased. So they may give it to its creditor. But the child, the legatee or creditor, takes it, not by natural right, but by a law of the society of which he is member, and to which he is subject. Then, no man can, by *natural right,* oblige the lands he occupied, or the persons who succeed him in that occupation, to the payment of debts contracted by him. For if he could, he might during his own life, eat up the usufruct of the lands for several generations to come; and then the lands would belong to the dead, and not to the living, which is the reverse of our principle.

What is true of every member of the society, individually, is true of them all collectively; since the rights of the whole can be no more than the sum of the rights of the individuals. To keep our ideas clear when applying them to a multitude, let us suppose a whole generation of men to be born on the same day, to attain mature age on the same day, and to die on the same day, leaving a succeeding generation in the moment of attaining their mature age, all together. Let the ripe age be supposed of twenty-one years, and their period of life thirty-four years more, that being the average term given by the bills of mortality to persons of twenty-one years of age. Each successive generation would, in this way, come and go off the stage at a fixed moment, as individuals do now. Then I say, the earth belongs to each of these generations during its course, fully and in its own right. The second generation receives it clear of the debts and incumbrances of the first, the third of the second, and so on. For if the first could charge it with a debt, then the earth would belong to the dead and not to the living . . . .

To render this conclusion palpable, suppose that Louis the XIV. and XV. had contracted debts in the name of the French nation, to the amount of ten thousand milliards, and that the whole had been contracted in Holland. The interest of this sum would be five hundred milliards, which is the whole rent-roll or net proceeds of the territory of France. Must the present generation of men have retired from the territory in which nature produces them, and ceded it to the Dutch creditors? No; they have the same rights over soil on which they were produced, as the preceding generations had. They derive these rights not from them, but from nature. They, then, and their soil are, by nature, clear of the debts of their predecessors. To present this in another point of view, suppose Louis XV. and his contemporary generation, had said to the money lenders of Holland, give us money, that we may eat, drink, and be merry in our day; and on condition you will demand no interest till the end of thirty-four years, you shall then, forever after, receive an annual interest of fifteen per cent. The money is lent on these conditions, is divided among the people, eaten, drunk, and squandered. Would the present generation be obliged to apply the produce of the earth and of their labor to replace their dissipations? Not at all.

I suppose that the received opinion, that the public debts of one generation devolve on the next, has been suggested by our seeing, habitually, in private life, that he who succeeds to lands is required to pay the debts of his predecessor; without considering that this requisition is municipal only, not moral, flowing from the will of the society, which has found it convenient to appropriate the lands of a decedent on the condition of a payment of his debts; but that between society and society, or generation and generation, there is no municipal obligation, no umpire but the law of nature.

On similar ground it may be proved, that no society can make a perpetual constitution, or even a perpetual law. The earth belongs always to the living generation: they may manage it, then, and what proceeds from it, as they please, during their usufruct. They are masters, too, of their own person, and consequently may govern them as they please. But persons and property make the sum of the objects of government. The constitution and the laws of their predecessors are extinguished then, in their natural course, with those whose will gave them being. This could preserve that being, till it ceased to be itself, and no longer. Every constitution, then, and every law, naturally expires at the end of thirty-four years. If it be enforced longer, it is an act of force, and not of right. It may be said, that the succeeding generation exercising, in fact, the power of repeal, this leaves them as free as if the constitution or law had been expressly limited to thirty-four years only. In the first place, this objection admits the right, in proposing an equivalent. But the power of repeal is not an equivalent. It might be, indeed, if every form of government were so perfectly contrived, that the will of the majority could always be obtained, fairly and without impediment. But this is true of no form. The people cannot assemble themselves; their representation is unequal and vicious. Various checks are opposed to every legislative proposition. Factions get possession of the public councils, bribery corrupts them, personal interest lead them astray from the general interests of their constituents; and other impediments arise, so as to prove to every practical man, that a law of limited duration is much more manageable than one which needs a repeal.

This principle, that the earth belongs to the living and not to the dead, is of very extensive application and consequences in every country, and most especially in France. It enters into the resolution of the questions whether the nation may change the descent of lands holden in tail; whether they may change the appropriation of lands given anciently to the church, to hospitals, colleges, orders of chivalry, and otherwise in perpetuity; whether they may abolish the charges and privileges attached on lands, including the whole catalogue, ecclesiastical and feudal; it goes to hereditary offices authorities and jurisdictions, to hereditary orders, distinctions and appellations, to perpetual monopolies in commerce, the arts or sciences, with a long train of *et ceteras*. . . .

THOMAS JEFFERSON (1743-1826) was a farmer and writer as well as a patriot, Governor of Virginia, and eventually President of the United States. He kept copious journals of the passing of the seasons and the changes upon the land as well as a detailed garden book which speaks still more of his love for the details of the land. Through his vision, the Louisiana Purchase was made, which won, for the United States, a place to grow and, for Americans, the material out of which our characters have been formed. Think for a moment what it would have been like had America ended at the Appalachians and how this would have affected the character of the American people as we are today?

This letter was written to James Madison on Sept. 6, 1789, while Jefferson was in Paris. It resonates with the passion the man felt about ownership of land and the necessity of land to the future of man. Although the language reflects the formal stiffness of the day, a bit of the gardener shines through as Jefferson talks of self-definition of the American people in the land. [In 1987, Fulcrum will publish Thomas Jefferson's Garden and Farm Journals.]

Mary Austin

The Land of Journeys' Ending
"Hasta Manana"

Man is not himself only, not solely a variation on his racial type in the pattern of his immediate experience. He is all that he sees; all that flows to him from a thousand sources, half noted, or noted not at all except by some sense that lies too deep for naming. He is the land, the lift of its mountain lines, the reach of its valleys; his is the rhythm of its seasonal processions, the involution and variation of its vegetal patterns. If there is in the country of his abiding, no more than a single refluent color, such as the veiled green of sage-brush or the splendid wine of sunset spilled along the Sangre de Cristo, he takes it in and gives it forth again in directions and occasions least suspected by himself, as a manner, as music, as a prevailing tone of thought, as the line of his roof-tree, the pattern of his personal adornment.

Whatever this sense, always at work in man as the wheel is at work in the mill-race, taking up and turning into power the stuff of his sensory contacts, it works

so deeply in him that often the only notice of its perpetual activity is a profound content in the presence of the thing it most works upon. He is aware of a steady purr in the midriff of his being, which, if he is an American, comes to the surface in such half articulate exhalations as "Gosh, but this a great country!"

To feel thus about your home-land is a sign that the mysterious quality of race is at work in you. For new races are not made new out of the dust as the first man was. They are made out of old races by reactions to new environment. Race is the pattern of established adjustments between the within and the without of man. Where two or three racial strains are run together, as cooperative adventurers in the new scene, or as conqueror grafting himself upon an earlier arrival, the land is the determining factor in the new design. By land, I mean all those things common to a given region, such as have been lightly or deeply touched upon in this book: the flow of prevailing winds, the succession of vegetal cover, the legend of ancient life; and the scene, above everything the magnificently shaped and colored scene. Operating subtly below all other types of adjustive experience, these are the things most quickly and surely passed from generation to generation, marked, in the face of all the daunting or neglectful things a land can do to its human inhabitants, by that purr of inward content, the index of race beginning.

Here between the Rio Colorado and the Rio Grande, between the Colorado plateau and the deserts of Sonora and Chihuahua, it begins under such conditions as have always patterned the great cultures of the past, great, I mean, in their capacity to affect world culture and human history. In Greece, in Rome, in England, world power began with aboriginal cultures of sufficient rootage to have already given rise to adequate symbols, in art and social forms, of their assimilation to the land, upon which were engrafted later, invasive types, superior at least in their capacity to interrupt with determining force, the indigenous patterns. So, in our Southwest, we began with an aboriginal top-soil culture, rich in the florescence of assimilation, to which was added the overflow from the golden century of Spain, melting and mixing with the native strain to the point of producing a distinctive if not final pattern before it received its second contribution from the American East.

If I say that this American contribution is prevailingly Nordic, it is not because I commit myself to the swelling myth about a Nordic race, but because the term, for the moment, stands as the index of an accepted type. It is a type that, when its early representatives reached the land of its journey's ending across the incredible adventure of The Santa Fe Trail, was already established in a sense of race, a sense, at least, of reliance upon some deeply fleshed sinew of a common adaptive experience. It knew what it wanted, and moved instinctively by the shortest cuts to a generically Western accomplishment.

Your true man of race is always instinctive. It is only hybrids and the half-assimilated who rationalize and codify and suffer under the necessity of explaining themselves. For the first hundred years, not many Americans reached the Southwest who were not already partly assimilated to it, by their natures. It is, in fact, hardly three quarters of a century since the flag of American federation was raised in the plaza of Santa Fe. And already the land bites sharply into the deep self of the people who live upon it.

The first evidence of cultural evolution is the voiceless rhythm of acceptance . . . land . . . my land! . . . between which and the beginning of cultural expression lies a period, sometimes prolonged for generations, depending on the realization and general adoption of native symbols for experiences intimate and peculiar to that land. The profoundest implications of human experience are never stated rationally, never with explicitness, but indirectly in what we agree to call art forms, rhythms, festivals, designs, melodies, objective symbolic substitutions.

The business of assembling such a set of symbols for the expression of its deeper reactions is, to a people newly come to a country, likely to be a long one, complicated as it is by the absorbing preoccupation of getting a living. There are many provinces in the United States in which there is as yet scarcely more than the first letter of the alphabet of such expression. These are places where there was never sufficient aboriginal life to interpret the land's primary reactions, or such aboriginals as were found, were too quickly and completely exterminated. Along our eastern coast often the invasive culture is edged with a complex which bolsters itself against implications of inferiority by a stubborn insensibility to the aboriginal contribution. As if a tree should prove itself more a tree by declining to be nourished by the humus laid down on the bare sand by the grass and the brier! Yet, oddly, it is from just the generation that has declined the ten-thousand-year-old alphabet ready to his hand, that the fiercest diatribes against our American lack of adequate spiritual exchange proceeds.

Before there can be any nationally releasing expression, there must be a widely accepted set of releasing symbols. Such symbols must be generic, image and superscription of the land's true regnancy. We can no more produce, in any section of the United States, a quick and characteristic culture with the worn currency of classicism and Christianity, than we can do business with the coinage of imperial Rome.

Here in the Southwest, and up along the western coast, where our blood-stream reaches its New-World journey's ending, it finds itself possessed with no effort, along with beauty and food-and power-producing natural resources, of a competent alphabet of cultural expression. Thus it gains so enormously over all other sections, where such notation is still to be produced, that one confidently predicts the rise there, within appreciable time, of the *next* great and fructifying world culture.

It draws, this land of prophecy, from more than the region herein described, from all up the California coast to San Francisco, between the sea and the Sierras, from districts east of the Rio Grande toward Texas, from Chihuahua and Sonora of the South. But by virtue of its acceptance and use of aboriginal material as a medium of spiritual expression, it takes its dominant note from the place of the Sacred Mountains, from the place of our Ancients, the home of the Guardian of the Water Sources. Takes it, in point of time just so much in advance of other American provinces as goes to the development in them, of similar indigenous mediums of cultural expression.

Three strains of comparative purity lie here in absorbing contact, the Indian the Spanish, and the so-called Nordic-American, for by distance, by terror of vastness and raw surfaces, the more timorous, least adaptive elements of our population are strained out. Of these three the Spanish serves chiefly to mollify temperamentally the aboriginal strain, so that in New Mexico and Arizona we approach nearest, in the New World, to the cultural beginnings which produced the glory that was Greece, the energetic blond engrafture on a dark, earth-nurtured race, in a land whose beauty takes the breath like pain.

MARY HUNTER AUSTIN (1868-1934) authored more than thirty books and innumerable essays and articles on topics ranging from anthropology to metaphysics and fine arts. She was a naturist, a mystic, a folklorist, and a crusader for feminism, Indian rights, and the contribution of the Hispanic culture to the southwest. She recognized nature as being important to the experience of life itself, being "the pattern of life wherre it is lived in close relationship with the environment."

The Land of Journey's Ending was published in 1924; it was the result of Austin's 2500 mile journey between the Rio Colorado and the course of the Rio Grande. For her, it was a return to a land in which she felt spiritual nurturing and found resolution in her search for man's place in this world.

Ten Bears

Indian Oratory,
"Do Not Ask Us to Give up the
Buffalo for the Sheep"

I was born upon the prairie,
where the wind blew free,
and there was nothing to
break the light of the sun. I was
born where there were no enclos-
ures, and where everything drew
a free breath. I want to die there,
and not within walls. I know
every stream and every wood be-
tween the Rio Grande and the
Arkansas. I have hunted and
lived over that country. I lived
like my fathers before me, and
like them, I lived happily.

When I was at Washington,
the Great Father told me that all
the Comanche land was ours,
and that no one should hinder
us in living upon it. So why do
you ask us to leave the rivers,
and the sun, and the wind, and
live in houses? Do not ask us to
give up the buffalo for the sheep.
The young men have heard talk
of this, and it has made them sad
and angry. Do not speak of it
more. I love to carry out the talk
I get from the Great Father.
When I get goods and presents, I
and my people feel glad since it
shows that he holds us in his

eye. If the Texans had kept out of my country, there might have been peace. But that which you now say we must live on is too small.

The Texans have taken away the places where the grass grew the thickest and the timber was the best. Had we kept that, we might have done the thing you ask. But it is too late. The white man has the country which we loved and we only wish to wander on the prairie until we die. Any good thing you say to me shall not be forgotten. I shall carry it as near to my heart as my children, and it shall be as often on my tongue as the name of the Great Spirit. I want no blood upon my land to stain the grass. I want it all clear and pure, and I wish it so, that all who go through among my people may find peace when they come in, and leave it when they go out.

TEN BEARS led the majority of the Comanche after the Civil War. As Head Chief of the Yamperethka Comanches, he went to Washington D. C. for talks with the President in 1872. He returned to encourage his people to accept the white mans' ways and live in peace with them. His people spurned his advice. This speech was given at the Medicine Lodge Council on October 20, 1867, at a major gathering of warriors and chiefs.

Sara Brooks

You May Plow Here

The Dogwood would be bloomin everywhere when springtime come, and also the honeysuckle would be shootin out their blooms. They smell so good – you could smell the honeysuckle from the woods. And there was a bush called sweet shrub – they grew in the woods and they be smellin real good. Also the jonquils would bloom in the yard, and the bumblebees would be out. That's the time my father and them would start breakin up the land for planting.

My father would start breakin up the land in March. He would be plowing by himself – he'd plow from sunup to sundown – and the only company that he really had was listenin to the birds. Whatever it sound like the birds say, he would put it into words. He was plowing one day at a low place that had been wet and had done growed up with a whole lotta weeds, and a bird was singing when he was plowing, and he made a song from what the bird sung:

You may plow here
Just as much as you please.
You may plow here
Just as deep as your knees.
But I will tell you
Right before your face,
You ain't goin make nothin here
But burrs and weeds,
But burrs and weeds.

That'd mean cockleburs and jimson weeds. What he was plowin, I guess he had a feelin that the bird was tellin him he wasn't gonna make nothin there, so he made that song himself. But it was a great crowd of us, and as the kids grew my father took in more land – he would be extendin the crop by takin in some land which had been laid out so we could make enough to feed all of us.

So when farmin time came, my father would break up the land first. Then when time come to plant the crops, we'd have to stay home some days in order to help get things in line. See, it was four of us – my brother and Molly, Rhoda and me – plus Sally and them, too. They was small but they worked. My father would keep us out of school a half day – maybe two of us today or three today, and maybe two or three the next day. We'd work in the mornin and then go to school at noontime. Or sometime two'd work all day or three'd work all day and then go to school the next day. He wouldn't keep us out day after day – we'd rotate. Then we'd go to school until we finished school, and that was in May.

So we started stayin home from school when time come to make rows in the field and plant. My father got two plows goin then – course he would plow, and Rhoda would help. Davey used to help my daddy plow when he went to school, but he didn't finish high school – he went to workin out. He was workin at a place called Springfield. He was sawin logs and he wasn't makin nothin much, but when he'd make his money he'd bring it home and give it to my father. And when he went to workin out he was stayin over – he was comin home once a week – so that's why Rhoda was plowin.

I couldn't plow. I couldn't plow because I couldn't get along with the mule. An hour or so about all the mule and me could do because, you know, I always was the type that was quick. It had to be *now* or either we didn't get along. See, when I would plow the mule, if I tell the mule to gee or haw, if that mule didn't, I'd hit that mule, and then that mule gonna jump, and when he jump, well, I'll probably take up half of what would be there.

And then, too, we had this horse what my daddy had me plowin. Her name was Daisy – Old Daisy's the one I tried to plow. I fussed so and beat on that horse so till when I get to the end of the row and tried to turn that horse around, that horse would run at me and kick me. I'd turn that plow loose and I'd just leave there screamin cause I was afraid of her. I couldn't get along with no horse and no mule. Uhn, uhn! I'd fuss too much. Everybody'd know I was behind the plowstock cause I'd be "Whoa!" "Gee!" "Haw!" I couldn't do it. I didn't mind goin to field cause that was our livin. And I would *like* to ride the horse – we went to field on the horse cause the field was so far from the house. We'd tie the horse on a rope and let the horse graze around, and then when we come home, all three of us be on that horse. So I remember one day we done come all the way from the field, and when we got nearby the house, all of em sittin on the porch, and here we came ridin in. I wanted to show off – decided I'd make the horse trot. So I took and, unbenounced to the others, I kicked the horse and the horse jumped and we just went right off. We didn't have no saddle – my father would use the saddle whenever he'd go to mill or what not, but just us goin to field, we didn't have no saddle. We'd ride bareback if we didn't throw a sack up there, but most of the time we barebacked it. So we all slid right off that horse, right off her. Oh, boy! That's the truth! So I like to ride the horses and the mules – we mostly rode the mules to field because they were tamer – but I never could plow. Rhoda plowed. She's the easy type – never know she's there.

Rhoda or my daddy be openin the row, and I'd be puttin out fertilizer. It was something called guano – that was the fertilizer. It would be used in the cotton field and the cornfield. It would make them yield more. My father used manure in the garden and in the potato patch – when he clean up the cow pen and the lot, he'd always pull all the manure in one corner, and that's what he'd do with that manure. But you buy the guano in a sack. My father would get if from the store in town. He'd buy sacks of guano – he'd have wagonloads. He'd bring some home one day and then he'd go back another day until he brought it all home, and the corn would be out of the crib almost, and he put some in there cause it couldn't get wet.

But the way we was puttin this fertilizer out, you carried it in a sack on your back. And at that time they had something that was called a guano horn that you drop this fertilizer down through. The top of it was like a funnel, and it had a long tube to it that the fertilizer run down through into the row. It was about as long as a broom handle. You hold the guano horn in one hand, and you use your other hand to reach into the bag and get a hand fulla fertilizer and drop it down this horn – it was aimed down in the row. So you holdin it in your hand, and you'd be walkin fast – you gotta continue to walk in order that it didn't pile up in one place. You had to walk fast, and when that fertilizer give out, you put another handful in and just keep walkin. When you get to the end of the row, you turn right around and do another row. Reaching in the sack and dropping it down this horn – just reachin and goin. Go down one row and come up another and go down another. And then my father or Rhoda would come along behind you and cover it up with the plow. One would be openin the row with the scooter plow, and the other would bed up the row with a turnplow. That's the way we get the fertilizer in. Now, you know we did a lotta fertilizin – puttin out – didn't we!

Next thing would come the planting. My father would open up the rows in the field and if it's gonna be cotton, you plant cotton, and if it's gonna be corn you drop corn. The corn went in first – in April we would always plant the corn. My father always kept some of the healthy-looking ears of corn for seed, so we'd get these ears of corn from the crib and shell up enough to last all day – sometime we'd shell up enough to last two days – and we put it in a burlap sack. We would carry that sack on the shoulder, or either if you didn't want to take a sack, you could take a pail, but the sacks held more. You had to have enough corn to drop four or five rows. You drop the corn every step – you drop three or four grains in each hill so that if some didn't come up, some would come up.

We'd have to drop the corn, but now when it come to cotton, my daddy had a cotton planter. You put the seeds in this planter – it was pulled by a mule – and it would open the row and sow the seeds. Click, click, click, click – it would be dropping the seeds. Then somebody would cover it up behind, and that would stay there then until the seeds come up.

So everything would be planted accordin to schedule. But when it was real dry at planting time, my father used to wet the cotton seeds and roll them in the dirt before he planted them. That would cause them to sprout quicker. He never wet all of them, but would do that in order to help them germinate. But mostly it rains a lot in the spring, and if it had been raining and had everywhere wet for so long, then my father couldn't plow and that would put you behind, so then you would hurry to catch up, and to do that you would just go in and plant the seeds right on top of that fertilizer. You see, after you lay the fertilizer in the row, if it's not ready to plant, somebody covers over the rows, and then when it's ready, it's got to be opened up again and planted and covered over again. But when you're behind, you drop the seed on top of the fertilizer and that would be less work and less time.

When it rained my father'd make us cut the bushes what be done grew up in the fields – they would mostly be sassafras and gum bushes. We'd do that when it's too wet to do anything else – we'd get all those bushes cut down and outa the way and tied up on the edge of the field. Oh, we used to work! We didn't play – we worked! I'm glad to be from it – I've had enough of that. But when spring come, I still have to plant somethin. I'm used to it. Somethin that is really woven into me is that spring planting!

When school was out in May, we'd know we'd have to go to field every day then because it's nice and warm and everything begin to be big enough to get to work at. We'd hill cotton first. The cotton come up so thick, so when it gets about a hand high, my father and Rhoda would bar off the cotton with a turn plow, which mean they would narrow the row. They'd turn the dirt *from* the cotton row on each side so we could chop the cotton – thin it out and get rid of the grass. We'd go in with the hoe and you chop this, you leave that, you chop out that, and you leave this. That's what was leavin the hills of cotton. And Molly always was nearsighted and she'd just as soon leave a weed for a stalk of cotton. My father always would get after her about that, so what happened then, my father let her be the nurse and my mother would come out awhile in the mornings. But you thin the cotton out two or three stalks to a hill, no more. The healthiest ones you leave. So that's the way we do it till we got it all chopped out. And then they'd come back and they would dirt up the cotton with a sweep plow – that is, throw the dirt back up on both sides of the row, hilling up the row and leaving a furrow between the rows. And then it would stay like that until, if it got real grassy, Rhoda and my father would run the middles out with a larger sweep plow, which is run down the furrow left between the rows by the smaller sweep plow, and that'd throw more dirt back to the cotton. This removes the grass. Then one more time we'd probably hoe that cotton. When you thinnin it out, that's choppin the cotton. But the next time you go, you hoein the cotton – that mean you gettin the grass out of it so it can grow. And that's all then until around July it start bloomin, and oh, they were pretty blooms! It looked pretty when the cotton was all bloomed out. But when it start bloomin, well, you don't mess with it then because you'd be knockin the squares off.

So we'd chop cotton until we'd get it all chopped out, and then we'd thin corn – we'd go in the cornfield and thin corn and replant corn. You thin the corn when it get about a half a leg high – not quite to your knees. We'd have to thin it out cause it would be too thick. If you had it too thick the ears wouldn't be as large, so we'd have to dig it out with a hoe. Whether you pull it up or dig it up, it's got to come out by the roots cause if it didn't, it would come up again.

But sometime the corn didn't come up well. If you planted corn and it rained afterwards, the corn would rot in the ground and it didn't come up good – it was missin places. So if it's wet when you thinnin the corn, you can reset it by diggin it up and planting it in the next space that didn't have enough. Or either we'd take two or three ears of corn in a sack, and we always had pockets in our dresses, so we'd shell the corn and we'd put the corn in our pocket, and then where corn was missin and didn't come, we'd go along and dig a hole and drop corn and cover it up and go find another spot that needs corn planted. That's what you call replanting corn. We had to do that on rainy days because it would take root quicker if it was planted when it was wet. But we did that until we got the whole crop finished.

And we'd plant peas between some hills of early corn. Usually we had a pea patch, but we'd have peas growin in the early corn, and then we'd go there and pick peas and get roastin ears all the same time. Then too, we had peas planted in the cotton field around the house – sunflowers and peas in the missing places where the cotton didn't come up too well. And we'd put corn in there, too – we'd plant crib corn in the spaces in the cotton. So one field didn't produce just no one somethin – we'd put lotta different things in the fields.

From the corn and the cotton and the peas, we had to plant the sugar cane and sweet potatoes and peanuts. In the wintertime the cane that wasn't going to be made for syrup was put in a cane bank and you put dirt over that. You "bank the cane," as you call it, for the winter. And then when it get warm in the spring it start comin up through the dirt, and then you rakes the dirt back off the cane and you open the rows in the field and you lay the cane down with the eyes up, and it'll come up from those eyes. So that's the way we keep cane from the one end of the year to the other.

And then we'd set out potatoes – when it rained we'd set them out. When springtime comes it always was some little potatoes left in the potato bank. You dig a hole and you lay em down and then you cover em over – this bed is called a potato bed. You make the bed usually in a corner of the garden that's already fenced in so the hogs can't get there to eat it up. When it gets warm, the warm rain brings shoots up outa the potatoes, and when they get a little better than past your wrist you can just pull em off. And you have your rows already made up and you've got a stick – you take that stick and dig a hole and set your potato sprout and pat the dirt up to it. When they start growing, you can cut the vines off and set them out – reset them. They grow. We'd keep on settin em until we'd made rows and rows of potatoes!

And we grew our peanuts. We'd eat peanuts all winter until we'd eat down to so many my mother figured we had to save peanuts to plant, so we'd shell these peanuts and she would put em in a sack and put em away. She kept the sack in the little room closet, and I made me a hole in the sack about as big as my finger, and I would get me a few peanuts every so often. I'd eat them – I was *takin em*. But the peanuts would be shelled and we'd carry them in a bucket and we didn't have nothin to do but drop them in the row when they open up the row, and you slip a peanut in your mouth every once in awhile, when you be droppin them. They'd be so good! Now that's the way the peanuts started off for the next year.

So we had plenty to do in the springtime – there was always somethin to do. We'd plant the crops and then we'd chop cotton. When we'd get through choppin cotton there was corn to be thinned out, and by the time we'd get around doin corn and peanuts and potatoes and everything, it's time to go back and do that cotton over again. So it was from one field to the other one. We worked hard! We did! But I just loved it! I did! We had fresh air, sunshine, and wide-open spaces. Only time I was ready to leave home when Rhoda got married. Davey married first, then Rhoda's sister got married. After Rhoda's sister got married, it was Rhoda next got married. And I just said I wan't goin to stay home then because I was the oldest one and I knew all the *big work* was gonna be on me. And I knew that I wasn't gonna get a chance to go anyplace unless I gotta whole tag followin behind me, which woulda been the small kids. I didn't want that because you know how you do when you feel you've growed up – you don't wanta be foolin with the little ones all the time. And so I thought I was lovin this guy, but I didn't love him. And he couldn't never loved me to treat me like he did. So neither one of us did love each other, but I hurried up and I got married after the others did.

SARA BROOKS' story of plowing the land represents another kind of challenge. Imbedded within the description of the long hours and hard work reverberates an overwhelming sense of joy. Born in 1911 on her **parents'** subsistence farm in Alabama, her story is one of love and hardship, strength and perseverance. She lets her voice sing throughout her book. *You May Plow Here* was edited and encouraged by writer Thordis Simonsen.

Frederick Jackson Turner

*The Frontier in
American History*

The separation of the West-ern man from the sea-board, and his environ-ment, made him in a large de-gree free from European preced-ents and forces. He looked at things independently and with small regard or appreciation for the best Old World experience. He had no ideal of a philosophi-cal, eclectic nation, that should advance civilization by "inter-course with foreigners and fam-iliarity with their point of view, and readiness to adopt whatever is best and most suitable in their ideas, manners, and customs." His was rather the ideal of con-serving and developing what was original and valuable in this new country. The entrance of old society upon free lands meant to him opportunity for a new type of democracy and new popular ideals. The West was not conser-vative: buoyant self-confidence and self-assertion were distin-guishing traits in its composi-tion. It saw in its growth nothing less than a new order of society and state. In this conception were elements of evil and ele-ments of good.

But the fundamental fact in regard to this new society was its relation to land. Professor Boutmy has said of the United States, "Their one primary and predominant object is to cultivate and settle these prairies, forests, and vast waste lands. The striking and peculiar characteristic of American society is that it is not so much a democracy as a huge commercial company for the discovery, cultivation, and capitalization of its enormous territory. The United States are primarily a commercial society, and only secondarily a nation." Of course, this involves a serious misapprehension. By the very fact of the task here set forth, far-reaching ideals of the state and of society have been evolved in the West, accompanied by loyalty to the nation representative of these ideals. But M. Boutmy's description hits the substantial fact, that the fundamental traits of the man of the interior were due to the free lands of the West. These turned his attention to the great task of subduing them to the purposes of civilization, and to the task of advancing his economic and social status in the new democracy which he was helping to create. Art, literature, refinement, scientific administration, all had to give way to this Titanic labor. Energy, incessant activity, became the lot of this new American. Says a traveler of the time of Andrew Jackson, "America is like a vast workshop, over the door of which is printed in blazing characters, 'No admittance here, except on business.'" The West of our own day reminds Mr. Bryce "of the crowd which Vathek found in the hall of Eblis, each darting hither and thither with swift steps and unquiet mien, driven to and fro by a fire in the heart. Time seems too short for what they have to do, and the result always to come short of their desire."

But free lands and the consciousness of working out their social destiny did more than turn the Westerner to material interests and devote him to a restless existence. They promoted equality among the Western settlers, and reacted as a check on the aristocratic influences of the East. Where everybody could have a farm, almost for taking it, economic equality easily resulted, and this involved political equality. Not without a struggle would the Western man abandon this ideal, and it goes far to explain the unrest in the remote West today.

Western democracy included individual liberty, as well as equality. The frontiersman was impatient of restraints. He knew how to preserve order, even in the absence of legal authority. If there were cattle thieves, lynch law was sudden and effective: the regulators of the Carolinas were the predecessors of the claims associations of Iowa and the vigilance committees of California. But the individual was not ready to submit to complex regulations. Population was sparse, there was no multitude of jostling interests, as in older settlements, demanding an elaborate system of personal restraints. Society became atomic. There was a reproduction of the primitive idea of the personality of the law, a crime was more an offense against the victim than a violation of the law of the land. Substantial justice, secured in the most direct way, was the ideal of the backwoodsman. He had little patience with finely drawn distinctions or scruples of method. If the thing was one proper to be done, then the most immediate, rough and ready, effective way was the best way.

It followed from the lack of organized political life, from the atomic conditions of the backwoods society, that the individual was exalted and given free play. The West was another name for opportunity. Here were mines to be seized, fertile valleys to be preempted, all the natural resources open to the shrewdest and the boldest. The United States is unique in the extent to which the individual has been given an open field, unchecked by restraints of an old social order, or of scientific administration of government. The self-made man was the Western man's ideal, was the kind of man that all men might become. Out of his wilderness experience, out of the freedom of his opportunities, he fashioned a formula for social regeneration, – the freedom of the individual to seek his own. He did not consider that his conditions were exceptional and temporary.

Under such conditions, leadership easily develops, – a leadership based on the possession of the qualities most serviceable to the young society. In the history of Western settlement, we see each forted village following its local hero. Clay, Jackson, Harrison, Lincoln, were illustrations of this tendency in periods when the Western hero rose to the dignity of national hero.

The Western man believed in the manifest destiny of his country. On his border, and checking his advance, were the Indian, the Spaniard, and the Englishman. He was indignant at Eastern indifference and lack of sympathy with his view of his relations to these peoples; at the short-sightedness of Eastern policy. The closure of the Mississippi by Spain, and the proposal to exchange our claim of freedom of navigating the river, in return for commercial advantages to New England, nearly led to the withdrawal of the West from the Union. It was the Western demands that brought about the purchase of Louisiana, and turned the scale in favor of declaring the War of 1812. Militant qualities were favored by the annual expansion of the settled area in the face of hostile Indians and the stubborn wilderness. The West caught the vision of the nation's continental destiny. Henry Adams, in his *History of the United States*, makes the American of 1800 exclaim to the foreign visitor, "Look at my wealth! See these solid mountains of salt and iron, of lead, copper, silver, and gold. See these magnificent cities scattered broadcast to the Pacific! See my cornfields rustling and waving in the summer breeze from ocean to ocean, so far that the sun itself is not high enough to mark where the distant mountains bound my golden seas. Look at this continent of mine, fairest of created worlds, as she lies turning up to the sun's never failing caress her broad and exuberant breasts, overflowing with milk for her hundred million children." And the foreigner saw only dreary deserts, tenanted by sparse, ague-stricken pioneers and savages. The cities were log huts and gambling dens. But the frontiersman's dream was prophetic. In spite of his rude, gross nature, this early Western man was an idealist withal. He dreamed dreams and beheld visions. He had faith in man, hope for democracy, belief in America's destiny, unbounded confidence in his ability to make his dreams come true. Said Harriet Martineau in 1834, "I regard the American people as a great embryo poet, now moody, now wild, but bringing out results of absolute good sense: restless and wayward in action, but with deep peace at his heart; exulting that he has caught the true aspect of things past, and the depth of futurity which lies before him, wherein to create something so magnificent as the world has scarcely begun to dream of. There is the strongest hope of a nation that is capable of being possessed with an idea."

It is important to bear this idealism of the West in mind. The very materialism that has been urged against the West was accompanied by ideals of equality, of the exaltation of the common man, of national expansion, that makes it a profound mistake to write of the West as though it were engrossed in mere material ends. It has been, and is, preeminently a region of ideals, mistaken or not.

FREDERICK JACKSON TURNER, born in Wisconsin in 1861, studied history at the University of Wisconsin and received his Ph.D. at Johns Hopkins University. A professor of history, he taught at the University of Wisconsin, Harvard University, and finally helped build a major historical and literary research center at the Huntington Library in Pasadena, California. He was one of American's leading historians, and his paper, "The Significance of the Frontier in American History," presented in Chicago in 1893, is one of the more important American historical papers. This selection is taken from his most celebrated book of essays.

Roderick Nash

*Wilderness and
the American Mind*
"The Irony of Victory"

he woods are overrun and
sons of bitches like me are
half the problem.
                    Colin Fletcher, 1971

Irony, literary critics tell us,
occurs when a result is opposite
that which was intended or ex-
pected. Success turns out to be
failure. It is a case of too much of
a good thing becoming a bad
thing. Wilderness appreciation
offers a classic instance of irony
in our own time. For more than
a century the Thoreaus, Muirs,
Leopolds and Browers labored to
attract American attention to
wild country as a recreational
resource. Preserving wilderness
seemed dependent on building a
clientele for it. Hetch Hetchy
Valley was lost, Muir felt, be-
cause so few knew its glories first-
hand. Glen Canyon disappeared
under a reservoir in Brower's
time because it was the place no
one knew. And then, in the late
1960s and 1970s, victory! Wilder-
ness was suddenly "in." An in-
creasingly urban population
turned to the nation's remaining

empty places in unprecedented numbers. Although hard to document precisely, visits to wilderness areas grew 12 percent annually, doubling in a decade. Projections, which may be conservative, looked for a ten-fold increase by the year 2000.[8] In highly publicized wildernesses such as the Grand Canyon of Arizona the rate of visitor growth was almost exponential until stopped by the National Park Service . Popularity like this contributed to saving wilderness areas from development. In publicizing wilderness Muir and his colleagues had succeeded spectacu-larly. But even as preservationists were celebrating their apparent vic-tory, the more perceptive among them saw a disturbing new threat to wilderness in their own enthusiasm. Ironically, the very increase in ap-preciation of wilderness threatened to prove its undoing. Having made extraordinary gains in the public's estimation in the last century, wilderness could well be loved to death in the next.

The problem, of course, was people. Dams, mines, and roads are not the basic threat to the wilderness quality of an environment. Civil-ized people are, and whether they come with economic or recreational motives is, in a sense, beside the point. Wilderness values are such that even appropriate kinds of recreational use can, in sufficient quan-tity, destroy the wildness of a place. As ecologist Stanly A. Cain puts it, "innumerable people cannot enjoy solitude together." [9]

In retrospect it appears that four revolutions contributed to what Colin Fletcher called the overrunning of the woods. The *intellectual revolution* is, essentially, the subject of this book. As Chapter 13 sug-gests, a fully developed philosophy of the value of wilderness emerged by 1970. More importantly, from the standpoint of popularity, the rea-sons for wilderness appreciation filtered down from intellectuals to a broader base of acceptance in American society. The success of the Sierra Club's and David R. Brower's "Exhibit Format Series" of coffee-table books extolling wilderness is an instance. So, on a less expensive level, is Time-Life's series of books entitled *The American Wilderness*. In the 1970s wilderness oriented magazines such as *Backpacker, Wilder-ness Camping,* and *Outside* spread the message to still wider circles. From another perspective, Henry David Thoreau and Aldo Leopold, who were known to only a small circle of associates during their life-times, became celebrated savants of the wilderness movement. A revolutionary change in attitude explains the difference.

But ideas by themselves could not cause the woods to be overrun. A *revolution in equipment* has facilitated the implementation of love for wilderness. It is not easy today to examine, or even imagine, the kind of gear earlier generations of outdoorspeople used when they went into the wilderness.[10] Tents in the 1920s were made of white canvas and weighed fifty pounds. People slept in bulky woolen bedrolls fastened at the end with giant safety pins. Food came wet-packaged in cans. Understandably, horses and mules transported camping outfits.[11] Wilderness travelers who carried their equipment on their backs were so rare as to be considered eccentric. As recently as 1934, David Brower could complete a ten-week backpack in the Sierra Nevada and fill two pages of a journal with a list of the places he had seen that no one had previously visited.[12] But the technological breakthroughs at the time of the Second World War began to change all that. Plastic, nylon, aluminum, and foam rubber appeared along with the freeze-dried process for preserving food. By the 1950s it was possible for the average person to contemplate a backpacking trip of more than a few days.[13] Improvements in insulated clothing and cross-country skis opened the woods to winter visitors. Fiberglass and synthetic rubber revolutionized whitewater boating. The pace of the improvement is astonishing. In 1972, an early issue of *Backpacker* reviewed the nineteen backpacks then on the market. Five years later the magazine found 129 to evaluate. The figures are comparable for tents, sleeping bags, and hiking boots. Such rapid proliferation is both a response to and a cause of the popularity of wilderness.

Before the era of modern paved highways getting to the wilderness was almost as difficult as traveling in it. In 1916 it took three days of tough driving on dirt roads to go from the San Francisco area to Sierra Nevada trailheads such as Donner Summit. For easterners of that era who rode the rails it was virtually impossible to fit a vacation in a western national park into two weeks. As late as the 1950s the edges of Utah's canyonlands were several days' travel from transportation centers such as Denver, Salt Lake City, and Las Vegas. Today, by way of contrast, air travel and fast roads make wilderness a realistic objective for millions even for a long weekend.[14] The impact of the *transportation revolution* on wilderness use patterns is indisputable.

It can be argued that the piece of technology with the most devastating effect on the American wilderness was the family automobile.

The fourth and final factor in bringing wilderness to the point of being loved to death is the *information revolution*. A half century ago wilderness was indeed unknown country. Once in the wilderness, one learned by trial and error. John McPhee reports that by the end of the 1930s David Brower could have been left off at night anywhere in the Sierra Nevada, and in the morning he would have known where he was.[15] But that kind of intimacy with a piece of wild country resulted from ten years of almost constant travel in it. Brower carried maps and guidebooks in his head. Today aids to wilderness travel are published in pack-size paperback editions. The ancestor of western hiking guidebooks is *Starr's Guide to the John Muir Trail*, originally published by the Sierra Club in 1934. Newer ones take the beginning wilderness traveler by the hand, providing equipment lists and suggestions for routes that are "leisurely," "moderate," or "strenuous."[16] What took Muir, Brower, and John Wesley Powell, a lifetime to acquire is available today for $2.95. Along with the detailed 7.5 minute United States Geological Survey topographic maps, the guidebooks allow thousands of first-time wilderness explorers to plan wilderness trips in their living rooms. Those desiring more assistance can turn to the dozens of commercial guiding and outfitting operations that have sprung up in the last decade. According to the *Adventure Trip Guide*, over fifteen companies include wilderness in their titles.[17] The Sierra Club offers more than 300 outings each year. Confirming Muir's prediction, "thousands of tired, nerve-shaken, over-civilized people" *had* come to the wilderness and discovered that "wildness is a necessity."[18] Some also discovered that in the process the wildness had vanished.

This is most dramatically illustrated in the Grand Canyon, but there are surprising statistics all around the nation. Consider the East with little wilderness and lots of wilderness lovers. A 1940 study divided the number of users into trail miles to show that in the White Mountains of New Hampshire a backpacker could expect to encounter one other person every four and one-half miles. In the early 1970s that figure had shrunk to seventy-three yards![19] It was not much better in highly publicized parts of the once-wild West. One hiker described a trip to California's Mount Whitney with his father on August 6, 1949.

Proudly they signed the register on the summit of the highest peak in the forty-eight states, the sixth and seventh persons to do so that year. Twenty-three years later to the day, the hiker took *his* son to Mount Whitney. When they signed in they noted they were the 259th and 260th persons to do so that *day!*[20] Fortunately, they avoided the Labor Day weekend when an estimated two thousand enthusiasts jammed the mountain. "You literally can't find a square yard of ground without human feces on it," a Forest Service officer declared after an inspection of Mirror Lake midway through the climb. "The smell is just horrible."[21] In 1974 the Forest Service limited the number of climbers permitted on Mount Whitney on a given day to seventy-five. In the case of Mount San Jacinto, California, however, the number was not restricted and in the late 1970s Round Valley recorded five thousand visitors in a single day. A ranger let them up to the peak two-by-two every few seconds. Across the valley in the San Gorgonio Wilderness (also too near Los Angeles for its own good) a thousand people tried to camp in one small mountain meadow at once. Meanwhile, forty miles to the east on the Mojave Desert, several thousand off-road vehicles, lined up for hundred-mile races across some of the best remaining desert wilderness in California.[22] Clearly, it is not wilderness but people who need management.

Wilderness management rests on the assumption that uncontrolled wilderness recreation is just as much a threat to wilderness qualities as economic development. The history of this idea is not long, but then neither is the problem. For the first three decades of this century no one believed that wilderness preservation meant more than simple designation. You drew a circle on a map and concentrated on keeping things like roads and buildings out. What happened inside the wilderness boundary did not seem important by comparison. It was not a matter of oversight. In fairness to federal land mangers of the 1920s and 1930s, there was really little to manage. Relatively few Americans ventured into the backcountry. Most park visitors in this era wanted some degree of civilization: a room with a scenic view and entertainments such as scheduled bear feedings and Yosemite's famous firefall.[23]

The attitude toward management of Chief Forester, William B. Greeley, is representative. In 1926 he asked an assistant, L. F. Kneipp, to inventory the wilderness remaining in the national forests. Three years later some of the seventy-four areas Kneipp identified were placed in protective categories by the "L-20" regulations. Greeley stopped at this point. He made no attempt to determine what a wilderness experience should be and then manage in a positive way to attain this goal for visitors. In fact, Greeley explicitly disavowed any intent to regulate the numbers or behavior of recreational users of national forest wilderness. "I have no sympathy," he wrote in a directive to his field staff, "for the viewpoint that people should be kept out of wilderness areas because the presence of human beings destroys the wilderness aspect." According to Greeley the only factor limiting public use should be "the natural one set up by the modes of travel possible" in the area. Greeley concluded that "public use and enjoyment were the only justification for having wilderness reserves at all."[24]

RODERICK NASH is a professor of History and Environmental Studies at University of California at Santa Barbara. As a history graduate student, he began his continued study of wilderness and its place and importance to man. He suggested that wilderness was a state of mind as much as an external place to which we go for meaning and self-definition, and from this embarked on a provocative and amazing journey through history to explore the importance of land to man. *Wilderness and the American Mind* is the pre-eminent journal on this topic and makes fascinating reading for all who are interested in land, man, the American mind, and the interaction of all the elements that have created the American character.

Aldo Leopold

A Sand County Almanac
"The Land Ethic"

It is inconceivable to me that an ethical relation to land can exist without love, respect, and admiration for land, and a high regard for its value. By value, I of course mean something far broader than mere economic value; I mean value in the philosophical sense.

Perhaps the most serious obstacle impeding the evolution of a land ethic is the fact that our educational and economic system is headed away from, rather than toward, an intense consciousness of land. Your true modern is separated from the land by many middlemen, and by innumerable physical gadgets. He has no vital relation to it; to him it is the space between cities on which crops grow. Turn him loose for a day on the land, and if the spot does not happen to be a golf links or a 'scenic' area, he is bored stiff. If crops could be raised by hydroponics instead of farming, it would suit him very well. Synthetic substitutes for wood, leather, wool, and other natural land products suit him

better than the originals. In short, land is something he has 'outgrown.'

Almost equally serious as an obstacle to a land ethic is the attitude of the farmer for whom the land is still an adversary, or a taskmaster that keeps him in slavery. Theoretically, the mechanization of farming ought to cut the farmer's chains, but whether it really does is debatable.

One of the requisites for an ecological comprehension of land is an understanding of ecology, and this is by no means co-extensive with 'education'; in fact, much higher education seems deliberately to avoid ecological concepts. An understanding of ecology does not necessarily originate in courses bearing ecological labels; it is quite as likely to be labeled geography, botany, agronomy, history, or economics. This is as it should be, but whatever the label, ecological training is scarce.

The case for a land ethic would appear hopeless but for the minority which is in obvious revolt against these 'modern' trends.

The 'key-log' which must be moved to release the evolutionary process for an ethic is simply this: quit thinking about decent land-use as solely an economic problem. Examine each question in terms of what is ethically and esthetically right, as well as what is economically expedient. A thing is right when it tends to preserve the integrity, stability, and beauty of the biotic community. It is wrong when it tends otherwise.

It of course goes without saying that economic feasibility limits the tether of what can or cannot be done for land. It always has and it always will. The fallacy the economic determinists have tied around our collective neck, and which we now need to cast off, is the belief that economics determines *all* land-use. This is simply not true. An innumerable host of actions and attitudes, comprising perhaps the bulk of all land relations, is determined by the land-users' tastes and predilections, rather than by his purse. The bulk of all land relations hinges on investments of time, forethought, skill, and faith rather than on investments of cash. As a land-user thinketh, so is he.

I have purposely presented the land ethic as a product of social evolution because nothing so important as an ethic is ever 'written.' Only the most superficial student of history supposes that Moses 'wrote' the Decalogue; it evolved in the minds of a thinking community, and Moses wrote a tentative summary of it for a 'seminar.' I say tentative because evolution never stops.

The evolution of a land ethic is an intellectual as well as emotional process. Conservation is paved with good intentions which prove to be futile, or even dangerous, because they are devoid of critical understanding either of the land, or of economic land-use. I think it is a truism that as the ethical frontier advances from the individual to the community, its intellectual content increases.

The mechanism of operation is the same for any ethic: social approbation for right actions: social disapproval for wrong actions.

By and large, our present problem is one of attitudes and implements. We are remodeling the Alhambra with a steamshovel, and we are proud of our yardage. We shall hardly relinquish the shovel, which after all has many good points, but we are in need of gentler and more objective criteria for its successful use.

ALDO LEOPOLD (1887-1948) began his professional career in 1909 with the U.S. Forest Service. He became among the first of professional foresters to talk of conserving the commodities they were harvesting, breaking ranks with the use-it-now foresters that typified the era. He died in 1948 while fighting a grass fire on a neighbor's farm. Leopold's voice is bold, asking and demanding consideration for the earth which supports us.

This selection is his closing chapter of his essay *The Land Ethic.* "We abuse land because we regard it as a commodity belonging to us. Where we see land as a community to which we belong, we may begin to use it with love and respect," he wrote elsewhere in *The Land Ethic.* His words are a challenge to each of us to redefine our own attitudes toward the land and our own place in nature.

John Hay

In Defense of Nature

hrough the inescapable meetings with what we are, or what we may not be, there is all human experience for any man to know, and a way, I think, to meet the rest of life on earth. There is no discrepancy between what makes me go through the same inescapable problems as my fathers, and the vast energies that are put into the readiness of the seed, or the sending of a mouse or bird through a short hard life for the sake of its race. These necessities come out of those down-under continents where indivisible existence was generated. If nature is inside me, with its grace and inevitable demands, I can hardly deny it without excluding myself from most of earth's intentions.

This season in its flowing power is a measure of the whole earth. This putting forth of the gentle and implacable together in the realms of nature, the violet and the shark, of innocence to the ends of maturity, of rising up to send abroad, is part of world weather. And all the sacrifices made along the way are an immolation at one with all identity.

Nature is life's creation, life's spending. No amount of intellectual despair, nihilism or sense of worthlessness in men can alter their basic dependence on regeneration, that which sends every beauty, each excellence, in each detail, into everlasting fire. We will not survive without the seeds of grass, and the mass of minute animals twitching in the waters of the sea. We belong to these multitudes; all that is lacking is our commitment and our praise.

It may be that nothing is predictable but the precarious nature of human history; and this may be what the universe provides for us. From these endless conflicts, that tear us apart and throw us together, future standards of cooperation may be born, even out of a need that seems pitiless. We change after all, out of deeper, universal changes, unseen fruitions, the coalescing of elements out of disparate parts; our acts materialize out of an ageless adventuring. But our place in this universal equilibrium needs realistic allegiance, and the exercise of sight, in all humility. In the face of perverse human will, armed with superhuman powers of destruction, we have little time to wait.

How can we be optimistic about a technology that merely speeds us beyond our inherited capacity, in terms of genetics and physical attributes, to survive on earth? We cannot change the environment past the degree to which we are able to change ourselves. We cannot adapt to continual alterations of our own making that destroy our sources in natural energy and diversity. It is already obvious that technological changes are at variance with our ability to keep up with them, that we are falling into violence, mistrust and confusion. We are in no position to boast about a manipulated future. The pride we need is in something else.

A viable future needs its champions, those who will defend not only their own self-interest but function and belonging in nature. The future can be an entirety or a fragment. Divisions can breed divisions, as enemies breed enemies, until at last the universe will restore unity in what might be a catastrophic way.

Man against the natural world is man against himself. In spite of our rational endowments, we are now acting toward our earth environment with the random ferocity of bluefish attacking a school of herring. The equivalent greed in nature at least acts on behalf of fecundity. What is eaten up is a measure of reproduction, but we, with our limited and short-term means, are unable, all by ourselves, to make up what we consume.

Somewhere along the line, the demand exceeds the supply. Starvation and violence occur. This happens in human society. It is happening with respect to man's relationship with nature, now; and so long as we treat nature as a commodity instead of a life-and-death companion, the worse things will be.

As an old countryman in Vermont once said to me: "Ain't any of us know too much." That seems to be the soundest philosophical position a man could take, but, as he was talking about himself and a college professor at the time, I think he was really saying that each man has his validity. Each man has his democratic validity on behalf of his world, and how much he can speak, live and act in terms of its potentiality, but that world in isolation from nature is a world devalued. We cannot live in the full use of earth and earth's complex, expectant, vast experience and deny it at the same time. Worth is defined by participation.

The problem of man's undertaking his own evolution, the risks involved in human achievement and assumption, are not the whole point. The whole point is that we depend ultimately on an everlasting drive for unity whose wellsprings we did not create but can only draw upon or try to re-create. The whole point is the human commitment of human experience to universal nature and all its lives. We cannot divide one from the other, or neither will be sustained. When I look out on the rippling landscape and breathe the lasting air, walking in the right of earth and sun, I am a central part of the globe, humanly claimed, and I also depend on a reservoir of knowing and being forever incomplete. Buried deeper than our microscopes can see, there is a well of flux and motion, incomparable elaboration, a consuming joined with a proliferation, out of which all things are born, are required to be born.

So I go down to the shore again, not only as the old clammers did, day after day, with their own company, but in sight of our crowded world. There is no escaping from our fierce ventures, win, lose or draw, no escaping from resurrections, not only of the seed but human trouble, risk and brutality. These sands not only bear lone walkers and the tide, but all mankind. At the same time, we are also what we choose, by cultivation and association. The natural horizon has in it something that is rarer than sight. It is the source not only of taking and fear but of an unlimited potential beyond the survival of man or fish. We have to keep up with that potential not only in terms of our assumptions about it but in terms of how much we can cooperate, discriminate and cherish.

The earth insists on its intentions, however men may interpret them. Unity and use is what it asks. And use is what may be missing. To the degree that we become disassociated by our power to exploit from what it is we exploit, so our senses will become atrophied, our skills diminished, our earth-related vision hopelessly dimmed. Without a new equation in which natural and human need are together in eternal process and identity, we may be lost to one another, and starved of our inheritance.

JOHN HAY is a poet and author. A graduate of Harvard, he has written *The Great Beach* (winner of the John Burroughs medal), *The Run, The Atlantic Shore,* and *Nature's Year*. This selection is from his book *In Defense of Nature,* first published in 1973. It speaks eloquently of the importance nature plays in our self-definition.

Mark Twain

Roughing It

If there is any life that is happier than the life we led on our timber ranch for the next two or three weeks, it must be a sort of life which I have not read of in books or experienced in person. We did not see a human being but ourselves during the time, or hear any sounds but those that were made by the wind and the waves, the sighing of the pines, and now and then the far-off thunder of an avalanche. The forest about us was dense and cool, the sky above us was cloudless and brilliant with sunshine, the broad lake before us was glassy and clear, or rippled and breezy, or black and storm-tossed, according to Nature's mood; and its circling border of mountain domes, clothed with forests, scarred with landslides, cloven by canyons and valleys, and helmeted with glittering snow, fitly framed and finished the noble picture. The view was always fascinating, bewitching, entrancing. The eye was never tired of gazing, night or day, in calm or storm; it suffered but one grief, and that was that it could not look always, but must close sometimes in sleep.

We slept in the sand close to the water's edge, between two protecting boulders, which took care of the stormy night winds for us. We never took any paregoric to make us sleep. At the first break of dawn we were always up and running foot races to tone down excess of physical vigor and exuberance of spirits. That is, Johnny was — but I held his hat. While smoking the pipe of peace after breakfast we watched the sentinel peaks put on the glory of the sun, and followed the conquering light as it swept down among the shadows and set the captive crags and forests free. We watched the tinted pictures grow and brighten upon the water till every little detail of forest, precipice, and pinnacle was wrought in and finished, and the miracle of the enchanter complete. Then to "business."

That is, drifting around in the boat. We were on the north shore. There, the rocks on the bottom are sometimes gray, sometimes white. This gives the marvelous transparency of the water a fuller advantage than it has elsewhere on the lake. We usually pushed out a hundred yards or so from shore, and then lay down on the thwarts, in the sun, and let the boat drift by the hour whither it would. We seldom talked. It interrupted the Sabbath stillness, and marred the dreams the luxurious rest and indolence brought. The shore all along was indented with deep, curved bays and coves, bordered by narrow sand beaches; and where the sand ended, the steep mountainsides rose right up aloft into space — rose up like a vast wall a little out of the perpendicular, and thickly wooded with tall pines.

So singularly clear was the water that when it was only twenty or thirty feet deep the bottom was so perfectly distinct that the boat seemed floating in the air! Yes, where it was even *eighty* feet deep. Every little pebble was distinct, every speckled trout, every hand's-breadth of sand. Often, as we lay on our faces, a granite boulder, as large as a village church, would start out of the bottom apparently, and seem climbing up rapidly to the surface, till presently it threatened to touch our faces, and we could not resist the impulse to seize an oar and avert the danger. But the boat would float on, and the boulder descend again, and then we could see that when we had been exactly above it, it must still have been twenty or thirty feet below the surface. Down through the transparency of these great depths, the water was not merely transparent, but dazzlingly, brilliantly so. All objects seen through it had a bright, strong vividness, not only of outline, but of every minute detail, which they would not have had when seen simply through the same depth of atmosphere. So empty and airy did all spaces seem below us, and so strong was the sense of floating high aloft in mid-nothingness, that we called these boat excursions "balloon voyages."

We fished a good deal, but we did not average one fish a week. We could see trout by the thousand winging about in the emptiness under us, or sleeping in shoals on the bottom, but they would not bite — they could see the line too plainly, perhaps. We frequently selected the trout we wanted, and rested the bait patiently and persistently on the end of his nose at a depth of eighty feet, but he would only shake it off with an annoyed manner, and shift his position.

We bathed occasionally, but the water was rather chilly, for all it looked so sunny. Sometimes we rowed out to the "blue water," a mile or two from shore. It was as dead blue as indigo there, because of the immense depth. By official measurement the lake in its center is one thousand five hundred and twenty-five feet deep!

Sometimes, on lazy afternoons, we lolled on the sand in camp, and smoked pipes, and read some old well-worn novels. At night, by the campfire, we played euchre and seven-up to strengthen the mind — and played them with cards so greasy and defaced that only a whole summer's acquaintance with them could enable the student to tell the ace of clubs from the jack of diamonds.

We never slept in our "house." It never recurred to us, for one thing; and besides, it was built to hold the ground, and that was enough. We did not wish to strain it.

By and by our provisions began to run short, and we went back to the old camp and laid in a new supply. We were gone all day, and reached home again about nightfall, pretty tired and hungry. While Johnny was carrying the main bulk of the provisions up to our "house" for future use, I took the loaf of bread, some slices of bacon, and the coffeepot ashore, set them down by a tree, lit a fire, and went back to the boat to get the frying pan. While I was at this, I heard a shout from Johnny, and looking up I saw that my fire was galloping all over the premises!

Johnny was on the other side of it. He had to run through the flames to get to the lake shore, and then we stood helpless and watched the devastation.

The ground was deeply carpeted with dry pine needles, and the fire touched them off as if they were gunpowder. It was wonderful to see with what fierce speed the tall sheet of flame traveled! My coffee-pot was gone, and everything with it. In a minute and a half the fire seized upon a dense growth of dry manzanita chaparral six or eight feet high, and then the roaring and popping and crackling was some-thing terrific. We were driven to the boat by the intense heat, and there we remained, spellbound.

Within half an hour all before us was a tossing, blinding tempest of flame! It went surging up adjacent ridges — surmounted them and disappeared in the canyons beyond — burst into view upon higher and farther ridges, presently — shed a grander illumination abroad, and dove again — flamed out again, directly, higher and still higher up the mountainside — threw out skirmishing parties of fire here and there, and sent them trailing their crimson spirals away among remote ramparts and ribs and gorges, till as far as the eye could reach the lofty mountain fronts were webbed as it were with a tangled network of red lava streams. Away across the water the crags and domes were lit with a ruddy glare, and the firmament above was a reflected hell!

Every feature of the spectacle was repeated in the glowing mirror of the lake! Both pictures were sublime, both were beautiful; but that in the lake had a bewildering richness about it that enchanted the eye and held it with the stronger fascination.

We sat absorbed and motionless through four long hours. We ne-ver thought of supper, and never felt fatigue. But at eleven o'clock the conflagration had traveled beyond our range vision, and then dark-ness stole down upon the landscape again.

Hunger asserted itself now, but there was nothing to eat. The pro-visions were all cooked, no doubt, but we did not go to see. We were homeless wanderers again, without any property. Our fence was gone, our house burned down; no insurance. Our pine forest was well scorched, the dead trees all burned up, and our broad acres of manzani-ta swept away. Our blankets were on our usual sand bed, however, and so we lay down and went to sleep. The next morning we started back to the old camp, but while out a long way from shore, so great a storm came up that we dared not try to land. So I baled out the seas we shipped, and Johnny pulled heavily through the billows till we had reached a point three or four miles beyond the camp. The storm was increasing, and it became evident that it was better to take the hazard of beaching the boat than go down in a hundred fathoms of water; so we ran in, with tall whitecaps following, and I sat down in the stern sheets and pointed her head-on to the shore. The instant the bow struck, a wave came over the stern that washed crew and cargo ashore, and saved a deal of trouble. We shivered in the lee of a boulder all the rest of the day, and froze all the night through. In the morning the tempest had gone down, and we paddled down to the camp without any unnecessary delay. We were so starved that we ate up the rest of the brigade's provisions, and then set out to Carson to tell them about it and ask their forgiveness. It was accorded, upon payment of damages.

We made many trips to the lake after that, and had many a hair-breadth escape and bloodcurdling adventure which will never be recorded in any history.

MARK TWAIN (Samuel Langhorne Clemens) was born in Florida, Missouri in 1835 and raised in Missouri. In 1857, he went to New Orleans on his way to seek his fortune in South America but instead became a Mississippi River pilot. When the Civil War put an end to river traffic, Twain went to Nevada with his brother and became a miner and then a reporter. His books include *The Innocents Abroad*, the *Adventures of Tom Sawyer*, *Life on the Mississippi* and *Huckleberry Finn*, one of the greatest American novels. This selection is taken from one of his earliest books, *Roughing It*.

Wallace McRae

It's Just Grass and Water
"Our Communion"

He said, "this bread's my body."
He said, "My blood's the wine."
"Remember when you take it,
The blood and body's mine."

Our bodies are this fertile land.
This water is our blood.
Our plains form our communion.
Our god's organic mud.

Your blasting rends our very flesh.
Your mining cuts our veins.
Our fly-blown, bloating bodies
Lie piled upon the plains.

You'd load our bones on somber
Black, unit funeral trains.
Or burn them in cremation
Pyres. Dachaus of the plains.

By callous men, and greedy,
Our deaths are unsanctified.
A region, and its people,
Both being crucified.

Proffer up the other cheek?
Our cries should we subdue?
Say, "Forgive them Father, for
They know not what they do"?

Should we ignore the spectre
Of this base incubus?
As they debauch our country
Do they e're think of us?

The water is our life-blood.
Our bodies are the land.
Why can't they comprehend
            this?
Why don't they understand?

WALLACE McRAE is a rancher from Forsyth, Montana. He is known throughout the West as an eloquent voice for environmental stewardship and conservation. This is but one of the many poems Wally has written in his other career as a writer, which speaks about the importance of the land to men who rely upon it for their livelihood. In a way, that is all of us, whether we recognize the connection or not.

Abraham Lincoln

The Living Lincoln

My childhood's home I see again,
　　And sadden with the view;
And still, as memory crowds my brain,
　　There's pleasure in it too.

O Memory! thou midway world
　　'Twixt earth and paradise,
Where things decayed and loved ones lost
　　In dreamy shadows rise,

And, freed from all that's earthly vile,
　　Seem hallowed, pure, and bright,
Like scenes in some enchanted isle
　　All bathed in liquid light.

As dusky mountains please the eye
　　When twilight chases day;
As bugle notes that, passing by,
　　In distance die away;

As leaving some grand waterfall,
　　We, lingering, list its roar –
So memory will hallow all
　　We've known, but know no more.

Near twenty years have passed away
　　Since here I bid farewell
To woods and fields, and scenes of play,
　　And playmates loved so well.

Where many were, but few remain
    Of old familiar things;
But seeing them, to mind again
    The lost and absent brings.

The friends I left that parting day,
    How changed, as time has sped!
Young childhood grown, strong manhood gray,
    And half of all are dead.

I hear the loved survivors tell
    How nought from death could save,
Till every sound appears a knell,
    And every spot a grave.

I range the fields with pensive tread,
    And pace the hollow rooms,
And feel (companion of the dead)
    I'm living in the tombs.

ABRAHAM LINCOLN, (1809-1865) the 16th president, was one of the greatest Americans. While all of us have much knowledge about this man, much of our information is about his later life during the Civil War. It is very worthwhile to read about his early life, his humor, his caring, and his humanity. There are several interesting biographies about Lincoln including Sandburg's books. This selection is taken from one of Lincoln's letters to a friend.

Nancy Wood

Many Winters

Now this is what we believe.
The Mother of us all is Earth.
The Father is the Sun.
The Grandfather is the Creator
Who bathed us with his mind
And gave life to all things.
The Brother is the beasts and trees.
The Sister is that with wings.
We are the Children of Earth
And do it no harm in any way.
Nor do we offend the sun
By not greeting it at dawn.
We praise our Grandfather for his creation.
We share the same breath together –
The beast, the trees, the birds, the man.

My people are a multitude of one.
Many voices are within them.
Many lives they have lived as various Beings.
They could have been a bear, a lion, an eagle or even
A rock, a river or a tree.
Who knows?
All of these Beings are within them.
They can use them any time they want.
On some days it is good to be a tree
Looking out in all directions at once.
On some days it is better to be a rock
Saying nothing and blind to everything.

On some days the only thing to do is
To fight fiercely like a lion.
Then, too, there are reasons for being an eagle.
When life becomes too hard here
My people can fly away and see
How small the earth really is.
Then they can laugh and come back home again.

NANCY WOOD was born in 1936 in New Jersey. She is a writer and photographer who has included her interpretation of the Native American voice throughout her later works.

Emily Dickinson

Final Harvest
#273, 322, 572

[273]

"Nature" is what we see
The Hill – the Afternoon –
Squirrel – Eclipse –
    the Bumble bee –
Nay – Nature is Heaven –
Nature is what we hear –
The Bobolink – the Sea –
Thunder – the Cricket –
Nay – Nature is Harmony –
Nature is what we know –
Yet have no art to say –
So impotent Our Wisdom is
To her Simplicity.

[322]

Nature – the Gentlest Mother is,
Impatient of no Child –
The feeblest – or the waywardest –
Her Admonition mild –

In Forest – and the Hill –
By Traveller – be heard –
Restraining Rampant Squirrel –
Or too impetuous Bird –

How fair Her Conversation –
A Summer Afternoon –
Her Household – Her Assembly –
And when the Sun go down –

Her Voice among the Aisles
Incite the timed prayer
Of the minutest Cricket –
The most unworthy Flower –

When all the Children sleep –
She turns as long away
As will suffice to light
    Her lamps –
Then bending from the Sky –

With infinite Affection –
And infiniter Care –
Her Golden finger on Her lip –
Wills Silence – Everywhere –

[572]

To make a prairie it takes
    a clover and one bee,
One clover, and a bee,
And revery.
The revery alone will do,
If bees are few.

EMILY DICKINSON was born in 1830 in Amherst, Massachusetts and spent almost her entire life there. After finishing her schooling, she wrote poetry extensively, although only seven of her poems were published during her lifetime. Her subjects include nature, love, belief, and religious uncertainty. Shortly after her death in 1886, two volumes of her poetry were published, and she is now considered one of America's great poets.

Robert Frost

Poetry and Prose
"A Prayer in Spring"
"Reluctance"

A Prayer in Spring

Oh, give us pleasure in the flowers today;
And give us not to think so far away
As the uncertain harvest; keep us here
All simply in the springing of the year.

Oh, give us pleasure in the orchard white,
Like nothing else by day, like ghosts by night;
And make us happy in the happy bees,
The swarm dilating round the perfect trees.

And make us happy in the darting bird
That suddenly above the bees is heard,
The meteor that thrusts in with needle bill,
And off a blossom in mid-air stands still.

For this is love and nothing else is love,
The which it is reserved for God above
To sanctify to what far ends He will,
But which it only needs that we fulfill.

Reluctance

Out through the fields and the woods
And over the walls I have wended;
I have climbed the hills of view
And looked at the world, and descended;
I have come by the highway home,
And lo, it is ended.

The leaves are all dead on the ground,
Save those that the oak is keeping
To ravel them one by one
And let them go scraping and creeping
Out over the crusted snow,
When others are sleeping.

And the dead leaves lie huddled and still,
No longer blown hither and thither;
The last lone aster is gone;
The flowers of the witch hazel wither;
The heart is still aching to seek,
But the feet question "Whither?"

Ah, when to the heart of man
Was it ever less than a treason
To go with the drift of things,
To yield with a grace to reason,
And bow and accept the end
Of love or a season?

ROBERT FROST was born in 1874 in San Francisco but spent most of his life in New England. In 1912, he went to England where he received his first recognition as a poet. He was America's most popular 20th century poet. His books include : *A Boy's Will, North of Boston, New Hampshire, Collected Poems*, and *In The Clearing*. He recited one of his poems at the inauguration of President John Kennedy. Frost was awarded the Pulitzer Prize for poetry four times.

Carl Sandburg

Harvest Poems
"Wilderness"

There is a wolf in me . . .
fangs pointed for tearing gashes. . . a red tongue for raw meat . . .
and the hot lappingof blood –
I keep this wolf because the wilderness gave it to me
and the wilderness will not let it go.

There is a fox in me . . .
a silver-gray fox . . .
I sniff and guess . . . I pick things out of the wind and air . . .
I nose in the dark night
and take sleepers and eat them and hide the feathers . . .
I circle and loop and double-cross.

There is a hog in me . . .
a snout and a belly . . .
a machinery for eating and grunting . . .
a machinery for sleeping satisfied in the sun –
I got this too from the wilderness
and the wilderness will not let it go.

There is a fish in me . . .
I know I came from salt-blue watergates . . .
I scurried with shoals of herring . . .
I blew waterspouts with porpoises . . .
before land was . . .
before the water went down . . .
before Noah . . .
before the first chapter of Genesis.

There is a baboon in me . . .
clambering-clawed . . .
dog-faced . . .
yawping a galoot's hunger . . .
hairy under the armpits . . .
here are the hawk-eyed hankering men. . .
here are the blonde and blue-eyed women . . .
here they hide curled asleep waiting . . .
ready to snarl and kill . . .
ready to sing and give milk . . . waiting –
I keep the baboon because the wilderness says so.

There is an eagle in me and a mockingbird . . .
and the eagle flies among the Rocky Mountains of my dreams
and fights among the Sierra crags of what I want . . .
and the mockingbird warbles in the early forenoon
before the dew is gone,
warbles in the underbrush of my Chattanoogas of hope,
gushes over the blue Ozark foothills of my wishes –
And I got the eagle and the mockingbird from the wilderness.

O, I got a zoo,
I got a menagerie, inside my ribs,
under my bony head, under my red-valve heart –
and I got something else:
it is a man-child heart, a woman-child heart:
it is a father and mother and lover:
it came from God-Knows-Where:
it is going to God-Knows-Where – For I am the keeper of the zoo:
I say yes and no:
I sing and kill and work:
I am a pal of the world:
I came from the wilderness.

CARL SANDBURG was the poet and biographer of mid-America. Born in Illinois in 1878, he served in the Spanish America War and upon return, put himself through college. Married to Elizabeth Steichen, the sister of the great photographer Edward Steichen, he worked as a journalist. His books of poetry include *Chicago Poems*, *Smoke and Steel*, *The People Yes*, and *Harvest Poems*. He won the Pulitzer Prize for his six volume biography of Abraham Lincoln.

Stephen Vincent Benét

The Ballad of William Sycamore

My father, he was a mountaineer,
His fist was a knotty hammer;
He was quick on his feet as a running deer,
And he spoke with a Yankee stammer.

My mother, she was merry and brave,
And so she came to her labor,
With a tall green fir for her doctor grave
And a stream for her comforting neighbor.

And some are wrapped in the linen fine,
And some like a godling's scion;
But I was cradled on twigs of pine
And the skin of a mountain lion.

And some remember a white, starched lap
And a ewer with silver handles;
But I remember a coonskin cap
And the smell of bayberry candles.

The cabin logs, with the bark still rough,
And my mother who laughed at trifles,
And the tall, lank visitors, brown as snuff,
With their long, straight squirrel-rifles.

I can hear them dance, like a foggy song,
Through the deepest one of my slumbers,
The fiddle squeaking the boots along
And my father calling the numbers.

The quick feet shaking the puncheon-floor
And the fiddle squealing and squealing,
Till the dried herbs rattled above the door
And the dust went up to the ceiling.

There are children lucky from dawn till dusk,
But never a child so lucky!
For I cut my teeth on "Money Musk"
In the Bloody Ground of Kentucky!

When I grew tall as the Indian corn,
My father had little to lend me,
But he gave me his great, old powder-horn
And his woodsman's skill to befriend me.

With a leather shirt to cover my back,
And a redskin nose to unravel
Each forest sign, I carried my pack
As far as a scout could travel.

Till I lost my boyhood and found my wife,
A girl like a Salem clipper!
A woman straight as a hunting-knife
With eyes as bright as the Dipper!

We cleared our camp where the buffalo feed,
Unheard-of streams were our flagons;
And I sowed my sons like the apple-seed
On the trail of the Western wagons.

They were right, tight boys, never sulky or slow,
A fruitful, a goodly muster.
The eldest died at the Alamo.
The youngest fell with Custer.

The letter that told it burned my hand.
Yet we smiled and said,"So be it!"
But I could not live when they fenced the land,
For it broke my heart to see it.

I saddled a red, unbroken colt
And rode him into the day there;
And he threw me down like a thunderbolt
And rolled on me as I lay there.

The hunter's whistle hummed in my ear
As the city-men tried to move me,
And I died in my boots like a pioneer
With the whole wide sky above me.

Now I lie in the heart of the fat, black soil,
Like the seed of a prairie-thistle;
It has washed my bones with honey and oil
And picked them clean as a whistle.

And my youth returns, like the rains of Spring,
And my sons, like the wild-geese flying;
And I lie and hear the meadow-lark sing
And have much content in my dying.

Go play with the towns you have built of blocks.
The towns where you would have bound me!
I sleep in my earth like a tired fox,
And my buffalo have found me.

STEPHEN VINCENT BENÉT (1898-1943) was a poet, novelist, dramatist, and historian. He is primarily known for his poetry having to do with American history. He came from a military family and read extensively in American military history as a boy. Although not as famous as the poem *John Brown's Body, The Ballad of William Sycamore* was considered to be one of his better efforts in joining American history and verse.

George Miksch Sutton

. . . Forever and Ever, Amen
Audubon, September 1985

A very little time shall pass –
A White-crowned sparrow's song or two, a rustle in the grass –
Ere I shall die: ere that which now is grief and sense of loss
And emptiness unbearable shall vanish
As curved reflections vanish with the shattering of a glass.

By the wind I shall be scattered
Up and down the land,
By strong waves strewn along the farthest shore;
No part of the dear world shall I not reach and, reaching, understand,
No thing that I have loved shall I not love the more.

No leaf of sedge nor cattail blade shall push
Up from the dark mud toward the open sky
But I shall be there, in the tender tip,
Experiencing the steady surge of growing.
No drip of water shall move upward, cell by cell,

No sunlight fall on any opening fern,
No breeze send waves across the yellowing grain,
But I shall be there, intimately learning
All that all things know and, knowing all, discerning
The full significance of suffering and pain.

No bird of passage shall fly north or south
Breasting the stiff wind or pushing through the fog
But I shall be there, feeling the deep urge
That drives it otherwhere at summer's ending,
And otherwhere once more with spring's return;
Ever so thoroughly I shall learn.
The signs a bird must travel by,
The many ways in which a bird can die.

Knowing the fierce drive of hunger,
Day after day, season after season, brown in summer, white in winter,
With the slender weasel I shall hunt, and with the rabbit die –
I at the place where the sharp white teeth
Pierce the skin and the tearing hurts,
I, too, shivering while the hot blood spurts.

No vainly croaking, vainly struggling frog shall feel
The water snake's inexorable jaws
Moving over and round it, slowly engulfing it
But I shall be there struggling too, and crying
An anguished, futile protest against dying.

With the snake too I shall die:
Clutched by sharp talons, borne swiftly upward from the shallow
        creek,
I shall look down bewildered and surprised
By this new aspect of a familiar place.
Writhing, twisting, striking at the claws which hold me fast
I shall feel the hooked beak closing on my neck at last.

With the hawk, too, I shall die:
I shall feel the hot sting of shot, the loss of power, the sudden collapse,
The falling downward through unsupporting space,
The last swift rush of air past my face.

No creature the world over shall experience love,
Drying its wings impatiently while clinging to the old cocoon,
Leaping the swollen waterfall, yapping to the desert moon,
Looping the loop above some quaking bog,
Pounding out drum-music from some rotting log,
But I shall be there in each sound and move –
Now with the victor, now with the vanquished,
Now in the parted mouth, now in the feet,
Now in the lifted nose, now in the bloodstream,
Now in the pounding heart's accelerated beat –
Experiencing the tender, quiet joy of mating,
And blinding ecstasy of procreating.

A thousand thousand times I shall suffer pain,
And that will be a mere beginning.
A thousand thousand times I shall die,
Yet never finally, never irrevocably,
Always with enough left of life to start again: to be born,
To grow, give battle, win, lose, laugh, cry, sing, and mourn,
To love, hate, admire, and despise,
Never quite losing the feeling of surprise
That it is good to live and die;
Learning to forget the word "finally,"
Learning to unlearn the word "ultimately,"
Learning, the long stretch of eternity having just begun,
That joy, gladness, grief, and suffering are one.

GEORGE MIKSCH SUTTON (1898-1982) ranked with Audubon as a field ornithologist, artist, and naturalist. He was also a prolific writer. "Don't blame me for this restlessness," he wrote of his life-long wanderlust around the North American continent, "blame the birds." Known as Doc Sutton, he noted in a 1981 *Audubon* article that he can't remember a time when he wasn't interested in birds, and his life of action in the field as an ornithologist served as proof of that perception. One of his students mused that Doc Sutton had been around birds so long that he was beginning to take on their behavior; the first thing Sutton would do after killing a bird for his study was to preen the bird better than the bird itself might have. This poem was written by Sutton the year before he died; it speaks eloquently of the way in which a naturalist contends with his own mortality.

James Kavanaugh

Walk Easy on the Earth
"I Asked the River"

I asked the river
          Where he was going
                    and how he would know
                    when he got there.
He only laughed at me
          Splashing across the rocks.

I asked the mountain
          When he was high enough
                    and how he would know
                    when he reached the heavens.
His echo only laughed
          Like thunder in the valleys.

I asked the trees
          How long they would live
                    and how they would know
                    when they were a forest.
Their leaves only shook with mirth
          In the joy of a sudden wind storm.

Finally I was silent,
          As if there were no one else to please,
And I spent my time laughing
          With the river, the mountain,
                    and trees.

JAMES J. KAVANAUGH was born in 1934. He was ordained as Father Stephen Nash, a priest of the Catholic Church in 1956 and resigned his priesthood in 1967. He is the author of several books of poetry. This poem is a voice of wonderment and the experience of soul-searching one can trust to nature.

Aaron Bagg

*Bulletin of the Massachusetts
Audubon Society*
Farewell, December 1947

I found joy in common things that had the quiet majesty of great events. I have seen each returning Spring lay her warm and loving hand on our beloved New England countryside, sending northward the heart-stirring wedges of wild geese, clamorous for their Canadian homes, and bringing the wood thrush back from far southern latitudes to greet the first May morning in your yard and in mine. I have heard the robins' joyous caroling roll westward across our land before the sunrise, dipping into friendly valleys and surging over the dearly familiar hills of home. I took delight in June's fine flowering in hilltown meadows, one June being forever precious above all others. With great expectations and with greater companions I have seen the twilight deepen over dark waters where the crimson-finned trout rise gloriously to the 'parachenee belle.'

Yes, and I have heard the loon's wild music ring out over northern lakes, saluting the

Great Bear's first glimmerings in a September evening sky later to be brought alive by the aurora borealis. I have found a homespun happiness in the chill stillness of those gray December afternoons when I paused to listen for the winter's first snow or sleet to rattle on the last oak-leaf remnants of a summer gone. I took delight in January's boisterous blizzards that filled the forest aisles with snow and veiled the forthright, friendly evergreens standing dark against the hillside.

But best of all, perhaps, were those February days when the sky held a brighter blue and a bluebird's warble, and the chickadee's spring song combined with that suddenly softer, more genial atmosphere (that Henry Thoreau knew) to tell once more the best of all great stories: the fact that winter cannot last forever.

These things, and other such, I loved and made a joyous part of me. They remain. And in the generous bounty of our seasons, they return, identical and ever-fresh with each new year. And, having been made an intimate part of me, each of them can truly bring me back to him who seeks me joyously. If he should be so mistaken as to take sorrow for a companion, he will never find me. But whoever, alone or in a goodly company, has a joyous regard and a boy's enthusiasm for the things I loved, he shall surely find me. And I shall be looking for him.

Therefore, my beloved friends, look for me joyously, perceptively, and triumphantly. Only in such manner will you ever find me. Only in such manner will the long, last farewell become this triumphant fact: that I shall be with you forever.

AARON CLARK BAGG was one of the leading field naturalists in New England's Connecticut River Valley during the 1930s and 1940s. An honorary vice-president of the Massachusetts Audubon Society and a director of one of the Society's sanctuaries from 1934 to 1943, Bagg helped many adults and young people gain a greater appreciation for the beauty and complexity of nature. From this tribute, written by son, Aaron Moore Bagg, we can see that Bagg had much to teach us about death as well as life. The tribute was read at Aaron C. Bagg's funeral, October 22, 1947.

John Burroughs

Highlights from
125 Years of the Atlantic
"The Summit of My Years"

The longer I live the more my mind dwells upon the beauty and the wonder of the world. I hardly know which feeling leads, wonderment or admiration. After a man has passed the psalmist's deadline of seventy years, as Dr. Homes called it, if he is of a certain temperament, he becomes more and more detached from the noise and turmoil of the times in which he lives. The passing hubbub in the street attracts him less and less; more and more he turns to the permanent, the fundamental, the everlasting. More and more is he impressed with life and nature in themselves, and the beauty and the grandeur of the voyage we are making on this planet. The burning questions and issues of the hour are for the new generations, in whom life burns intensely also.

My life has always been more or less detached from the life about me. I have not been a hermit, but my temperament and love of solitude, and a certain constitutional timidity and shrinking from all kinds of strife, have kept me in the by-paths rather than on the great highways of life. My talent, such as it is, is distinctly a by-path talent, or at most, a talent for green lanes and sequestered roadsides; but that which has most interested me in life, Nature, can be seen from lanes and by-paths better even than from the turnpike, where the dust and noise and the fast driving obscure the view or distract the attention. I have loved the feel of the grass under my feet, and the sound of the running streams by my side. The hum of the wind in the tree-tops has always been good music to me, and the face of the fields has often comforted me more than the faces of men.

In my tranquil seclusion I am often on the point of upbraiding myself because I keep so aloof from the struggles and contentions and acrimonious debates of the political, the social, and the industrial world about me. I do not join any of the noisy processions, I do not howl with the reformers, or cry Fire! with the alarmists. I say to myself, What is all this noisy civilization and all this rattling machinery of government for, but that men may all have just the sane and the contented life that I am living, and on the same terms that I do. They can find it in the next field, beyond the next hill, in the town or in the country – a land of peace and plenty, if one has peace in his heart and the spirit of fair play in his blood.

Business, politics, government, are but the scaffoldings of our house of life; they are there that I may have a good roof over my head, and a warm and safe outlook into the beauty and glory of the universe, and let them not absorb more time and energy than the home itself. They have absorbed very little of mine, and I fancy that my house of life would have just as staunch walls, and just as many windows and doors, had they not absorbed so much of other men's. Let those who love turmoil arm for turmoil: their very arming will bring it; and let those who love peace disarm for peace; the disarming will hasten it. Those also serve who mind their own business and let others mind theirs.

I know that all this clamor and competition, all this heat and friction and turmoil of the world, are only the result of the fury with which we play the game of our civilization. It is like our college football, which is brutal and killing, and more like war than like sport. Why should I be more than an amused or a pained spectator?

I was never a fighter; I fear that at times I may have been a shirker, but I have shirked one thing or one duty that I might the more heartily give myself to another. He also serves who sometimes runs away.

From the summit of the years I look back over my life, and see what I have escaped and what I have missed, as a traveler might look back over his course from a mountain-top, and see where he had escaped a jungle or a wilderness or a desert, and where he had missed a fair field or a fountain, or pleasant habitations. I have escaped the soul-killing and body-wrecking occupations that are the fate of so many men in my time. I have escaped the greed of wealth, the "mania of owning things," as Whitman called it. I have escaped the disappointment of political ambition, of business ambition, of social ambition; I have never been a cog in anybody's wheel, or an attachment to the tail of anybody's kite. I have never lost myself in the procession of parties, or trained with any sect or clique. I have been fortunate in being allowed to go my own way in the world.

It is a question whether in escaping a college education I made a hit or a miss. I am inclined to the opinion that a little systematic training, especially in science, would have been a gain, though the systematic grind in literature which the college puts its students through, I am glad to have escaped. I thank heaven that in literature I have never had to dissect Shakespeare or Milton, or any other great poet, in the class-room, and that I have never had to dissect any animal in the laboratory. I have had the poets in their beautiful and stimulating unity and wholeness, and I have had the animals in the fields and woods in the joy of their natural activities. In my literary career I have escaped trying to write for the public or for editors; I have written for myself. I have not asked, "What does the public want?" I have only asked, "What do I want to say? What have I lived or felt or thought that is my own, and has its root in my inmost being?"

I have few of the aptitudes of the scholar, and fewer yet of the methodical habits and industry of the man of business. I live in books a certain part of each day, but less as a student of books than as a student of life. I go to books and to nature as a bee goes to the flower, for a nectar that I can make into my own honey. My memory for the facts and the arguments of books is poor, but my absorptive power is great.

There is no one, I suppose, who does not miss some good fortune in his life. We all miss congenial people, people who are going our way, and whose companionship would make life sweeter for us. Often we are a day too early, or a day too late, at the point where our paths cross. How many such congenial souls we miss we know not, but for my part, considering the number I have met, I think it may be many.

I have missed certain domestic good fortunes, such as a family of many children (I have only one), which might have made the struggle of life harder, but which would surely have brought its compensations. Those lives are, indeed, narrow and confined which are not blessed with several children. Every branch the tree puts out lays it open more to the storms and tempests of life; it lays it open also to the light and the sunshine, and to the singing and the mating birds. A childless life is a tree without branches, a house without windows.

I missed being a soldier in the armies of the Union during the Civil War, which was probably the greatest miss of my life. I think I had in me many of the qualities that go to the making of a good soldier – love of adventure, keenness of eye and ear, love of camp-life, ability to shift for myself, skill with the gun, and a sound constitution. But the rigidity of the military system, the iron rules, the mechanical unity and precision, the loss of the one in the many – all would have galled me terribly, though better men than I willingly, joyously, made themselves a part of the great military machine.

I got near enough to the firing line during our Civil War, – when Early made his demonstration against the Capital in 1864, and I was a clerk in the Treasury Department, – to know that I much prefer the singing of the birds to the singing of hostile bullets.

War is terrible business.

II

From youth to age I have lived with nature more than with men. In youth I saw nature as a standing invitation to come forth and give play to myself; the streams were for fishing and swimming, the woods were for hunting and exploring, and for all kinds of sylvan adventure; the fields were for berries and birds' nests, and color, and the delight of the world of grasses; the mountains were for climbing and the prospects and the triumphs of their summits.

The world was good; it tasted good, it delighted all my senses. The seasons came and went, each with its own charms and enticements. I was ready for each and contented with each. The spring was for the delights of sugar-making, and the returning birds – the naked maple woods flooded with the warm creative sunshine, the brown fields slipping off their covering of snow, the loosened rills, the first robin, the first phoebe, the first song sparrow – how all these things thrilled one! The summer was for bare feet, light clothes, freedom from school, strawberries, trout, hay-making, and the Fourth of July. Autumn was for apples, nuts, wild pigeons, gray squirrels, and the great dreamy tranquil days, winter for the fireside, school, games, coasting, and the tonic of frost and snow. How the stars twinkled in winter! How the ice sang, and whooped on the ponds! How the snow sculpturing decked all the farm fences! How the sheeted winds stalked across the hills!

Oh, the eagerness and freshness of youth! How the boy enjoys his food, his sleep, his sports, his companions, his truant days! His life is an adventure, he is widening his outlook, he is extending his dominion, he is conquering his kingdom. How cheap are his pleasures, how ready his enthusiasms! In boyhood I have had more delight on a haymow with two companions and a big dog – delight that came nearer intoxication – than I have ever had in all the subsequent holidays of my life. When youth goes, much goes with it. When manhood comes, much comes with it. We exchange a world of delightful sensations and impressions for a world of duties and studies and meditations. The youth enjoys what the man tries to understand. Lucky is he who can get his grapes to market and keep the bloom upon them, who can carry some of the freshness and eagerness and simplicity of youth into his later years, who can have a boy's heart below a man's head.

The birds have always meant much to me; as a farm-boy they were like a golden thread that knit the seasons together. In early manhood I turned to them with the fondness of youth, reinforced with an impetus obtained from literature. Books, especially the poets, may do this for a man; they may consecrate a subject, give it the atmosphere of the ideal, and lift it up in the field of universal interest. They seem to have done something like that for me in relation to birds. I did not go to books for my knowledge of the birds, except for some technical knowledge, but I think literature helped to endow them with a human interest to me, and relate them to the deeper and purer currents of my life. What joy they have brought me! How they have given me wings to escape the tedious and the deadening! I have not studied them so much as I have played with them, camped with them, gone berrying with them, summered and wintered with them, and my knowledge of them has filtered into my mind almost unconsciously.

The bird as a piece of living nature is what interests me, having vital relations to all out-of-doors, and capable of linking my mind to itself and its surroundings with threads of delightful associations. The live bird is a fellow passenger; we are making the voyage together, and there is a sympathy between us that quickly leads to knowledge. If I looked upon it as something to be measured and weighed and tabulated, or as a subject for laboratory experimentation, my ornithology would turn to ashes in my hands.

The whole of nature, directly or indirectly, goes with him who gives his mind to objects in the open air. The observer of bird-life in the open has heaven and earth thrown in. Well, I need not harp on this string. All lovers of life in the open know what I would say. The book of living nature is unlike other books in this respect: one can read it over and over, and always find new passages and new meanings. It is a book that goes to press new every night, and comes forth fresh every morning.

III

I began by saying how much the beauty and wonder of the world occupies me these later years. How these things come home to me as life draws near the end. I am like a man who makes a voyage and falls so much in love with the ship and the sea that he thinks of little else and is not curious about the new lands before him. I suppose if my mind had dwelt much upon the other world toward which we are headed, and which is the main concern with so many passengers, I should have found less to absorb and instruct me in this. In fact, the hypothetical other world has scarcely occupied me at all, and when it has, I have thought of it as a projection from this, a kind of Brocken shadow cast by our love of life upon futurity. My whole being is so well, so exquisitely attuned to this world, that I have instinctively felt that it was for this world that I was made.

I have never been able to see how I could be adjusted to two worlds unless they were much alike. A better world I have never wanted. I could not begin to exhaust the knowledge and the delights of this one. I have found in it deep beneath deep, worlds within a world – an endless series of beautiful and wonderful forms forever flowing out of itself. From the highest heavens of the telescope, to the minutest organisms of the microscope, all is beautiful and wonderful, and passeth understanding.

JOHN BURROUGHS was born in 1837 in Roxbury, New York. Starting life as a farmer, he soon became a naturalist and a writer. He traveled often and became a writer of nature essays. His books include: *Wake Robin, Signs and Seasons, Time and Change, Accepting the Universe,* and the book from which this selection is taken: *The Summit of My Years.*

William Cullen Bryant

"To a Waterfowl"
from *One Hundred and One Famous Poems*

Whither, 'midst falling dew,
While glow the heavens with the last steps of day,
Far, through their rosy depths, dost thou pursue
Thy solitary way?

Vainly the fowler's eye
Might mark thy distant flight to do thee wrong,
As, darkly painted on the crimson sky,
Thy figure floats along.

Seek'st thou the plashy brink
Of weedy lake, or marge of river wide,
Or where the rocking billows rise and sink
On the chafed ocean's side?

There is a Power whose care
Teaches thy way along that pathless coast –
The desert and illimitable air –
Lone wandering, but not lost.

All day thy winds have fanned,
At that far height, the cold, thin atmosphere,
Yet stoop not weary, to the welcome land,
Though the dark night is near.

And soon that toil shall end;
Soon shalt thou find a summer home, and rest,
And scream among thy fellows; reeds shall bend,
Soon, o'er thy sheltered nest.

Thou'rt gone! the abyss of heaven
Hath swallowed up thy form; yet on my heart
Deeply hath sunk the lesson thou has given,
And shall not soon depart.

He who, from zone to zone,
Guides through the boundless sky thy certain flight,
In the long way that I must tread alone
Will lead my steps aright.

WILLIAM CULLEN BRYANT (1784-1887) attended Williams College and
practiced law in Massachusetts from 1816-1825. Although his poetry was
responsible for his fame (*Thanatopsis*, 1817; *To A Waterfowl*, 1818; *The Ages* ,
1821), he was active politically throughout his life. He published an attack on
President Jefferson called *The Embargo* in 1808. In 1826 he became assistant
editor of the *New York Evening Post* and assumed the position of editor in 1829.
He was politically powerful as the editor, backing free trade, and anti-slavery
ideas. During his tenure, *The New York Evening Post* was considered to be one of
the most powerful publications during the Civil War. Bryant is said to have
influenced President Abraham Lincoln to issue the Emancipation Proclamation.

Edward Abbey

Beyond the Wall
"Desert Images"

Life is gaunt and spare in the desert; that's what old time desert rats like best about it. They feel they cannot breathe properly without at least a cubic mile of unshared space about them. Let another man or woman appear on their horizon and they begin to feel the urge to decamp, move on, climb to the pass. I investigate that purple range of barren hills beyond the gleaming salt flats, find out what's going on up in there, among those shadowy valleys, those ragged battlements, of broken-down rock. Where, as they should know damn well, they'll find nothing but the same scatter of dried-out brittlebush, the same fireplugs of barrel cactus with spines like fishhooks, the same herd of feral burros gaping at them from the ridgeline, the same dun-colored rattler coiled beneath a limestone shelf, waiting its chance to strike. Don't tread on me.

Desert plant life is much the same – private. Even the commonest shrub, like the creosote bush, keeps its distance from the

next. Each sets alone inside an ample circle of open ground. Botanists say that the roots of the plant secrete a poison, a growth inhibitor, that prevents new, seedling creosote from getting a start within that charmed circle of solitariness.

So it is with the flowers of the desert, though not without some exceptions. In certain years, not frequent, when the winter drizzles have fallen at the right times in the correct amounts, and when the weather achieves exactly the proper balance in March and April between heat and cold, sunlight and cloud cover, you may be lucky enough to see whole desert valleys and hills covered, "carpeted" as they say, with a solid blaze of flowering Mexican poppy, or globe mallow, or mimulus or coreopsis. These are splendid and rare occasions, attracting flower freaks, photographers, and desert flora fanciers from half the cities of the nation, odd people who think nothing of grabbing a jet plane and flying two thousand miles to see the flare-up of sudden orange when the *Calochortus kennedyi* takes over some Mojave valley down in California's wastelands. That or the Mexican poppies. Or the brittlebush itself, an otherwise humble and obscure knee-high shrub, which can perform wonders: nothing is more striking than to see the grim black cinder cones in the Pinacate Lava Fields take on suddenly – almost overnight – a rash of yellow, when twenty thousand brittlebushes break out in simultaneous golden bloom. Ridiculous. And sublime.

But these are, as said, the exceptions. Generally the flowers of the desert reveal themselves in solitary splendor. A primrose lurking on a sand dune. A single paloverde flaring by an arid watercourse. One wooly clump of *Baileya multiradiata* gracing the edge of the asphalt, shivering in the breeze from forty-ton freight trucks. The great *Agave palmeri*, or century plant, blooms only once in its entire existence ("the garland briefer than a girl's"), but in that supreme assertion of love and continuity it more than justifies the sacrifice required. For a decade or so the century plant grows, emerging slowly from the rock; the heavy spine-tipped blades that function as leaves wax fat, with an interlocking bulge in the center resembling an artichoke. Here the food and energy are stored. One spring a signal is given – we don't know what or why. The bulge unfolds, like a slow-motion explosion, and a shaft rises from the center, growing rapidly, reaching a height of ten or twelve feet within a week. This is the flower stalk, efflorescing as it rises with a series of alternate flower-bearing stems from midpoint to the top. The yellowish, heavy blooms wait there, upright on the towering stalk, for a week, two weeks, are pollinated by bats and insects, then begin to fade. As they fade the plant dies slowly, by degrees, from stem to root, though the strong, rigid shaft, supported by the base, may stand erect for a year after death. The death does not matter; the seeds have been sown.

The desert offers a second outburst of flowering in September and October, after the customary summer rains. This is the time of the globe mallow, or pink-eye poppy as it's also known, and rabbit brush, a stinking shrub with a showy display of yellow bloom, and the sunflowers – acres and acres of waist-high mule-ear (so named for the shape of the leaves) *Helianthus annuus*, visible from miles away.

Down in dank and shady places grows a shady customer – moonflower, angel's-trumpet, the sacred *Datura meteloides*. A large gross ivory-colored thing, set amid dark and shiny green leaves, the whole plant, flowers, stem leaves, roots, is rich in scopolamine, a potent alkaloid much prized by witch doctors. The correct dosage is said to be spiritually rewarding, but the problem is that a microgram too much may lead to convulsions, paralysis and death – also rewarding, perhaps, but usually considered premature.

I try to think of a favorite among my arid-country flowers. But I love them all. How could we be true to one without being false to all the others? Just the same I think I'll praise a few more individuals here, single them out from among the crowd.

The cliffrose, for example. A flowering shrub, *Cowania mexicana*, a true member of the rose family, the cliffrose can be found in many parts of the mesa country and high desert from Colorado to California. The shrub may grow from four to twelve feet high. Twisted and gnarled like a juniper, it is relatively inconspicuous most of the year. But in April and May it blooms, putting out a thick, showy cluster of pale yellow or cream-colored flowers with the fragrance of orange blossoms. On a breezy day in spring you can smell the faint, delicate but heart-intoxicating sweetness for miles. The cliffrose is a bold plant, flourishing in the most improbable places, clinging to the cliff's edge, overhanging the rim of a plateau, gracing the pockets of sand far out among the slickrock domes. Deer, bighorn sheep, domestic sheep and cattle all browse on the leaves of this plant in the winter, when little else is available.

Or how about the wild morning glory, *Evolvulus arizonicus?* Another beauty. A hardy annual that blooms from April to October. The flowers are small, scarcely half an inch in diameter, but of so clear and striking an azure blue, especially in contrast to the tiny leaves and scraggly stems of the plant itself, that they assert themselves – against the sun-bleached background of sand and rock – with eye-catching vigor.

Several varieties of lupine grow in the desert. In Arizona the violet-purple. *Lupinus sparsiflorus,* in western Texas the blue-purple *L. havardii,* in southwest California the royal-purple *L. odoratus.* Busy members of the pea family, the lupines generally grow from two to three feet tall in clusters along roadways, trails, and the edges of valley bottoms, wherever the runoff from rains tends to be a little heavier. Sometimes they grow in pure stands, turning the burnt umber and dun brown of the desert into a wind-shimmering lake of blue-pink-purple radiance. The lupine is not good for anything bankable; hungry livestock eat them, get sick and die (alkaloids). All they have to offer us is their own rare beauty.

One more. A secret flower, a hidden special, little known, seldom publicized: the desert prince's plume, *Stanleya pinnata,* a man-high plant that blooms from May to July in some of the hottest, dreariest, most godforsaken and otherwise life-forsaken places in the Southwest. In dried-out mud flats along arid watercourses; on the shale and gravel talus slopes under a Moenkopiformation rock bluff; around the alkaline edges of some desperate mudhole way out in the clay hills, the badlands, the Painted Desert. The flowers stand up in golden spikes, racemes of bright yellow blazing against the red cliffs and blue sky.

In those secret canyon glens where the hanging gardens grow, nourished on water percolating through the sandstone, you'll find yellow columbine. Certainly as beautiful a flower as anything on earth, though not so large and spectacular as the blue columbine of the mountains. Many others live here too, delicate as angel's breath, and tough. They've got to be tough, surviving in those precarious perches on a perpendicular slickrock wall.

And then you walk out in the badlands and see a single Indian paintbrush lifting its cup of salmon-colored, petallike bracts toward the sky. The paintbrush too is beautiful, with the special and extraordinary beauty of wild and lonely things. Every desert flower shares that quality. Anything that lives where it would seem that nothing could live, enduring extremes of heat and cold, sunlight and storm, parching aridity and sudden cloudbursts, among burnt rock and shifting sands, any such creature – beast, bird or flower – testifies to the grandeur and heroism inherent in all forms of life. Including the human. Even in us.

EDWARD ABBEY, born in 1927 in Pennsylvania, is a self-described "Agrarian Anarchist." He moved west, spent a winter at Canyonlands National Park as park ranger and has been inseparable from the desert land since. He has written for the rest of the world his clever, witty, and peculiar kind of discovery of the southwestern deserts. Every time a reader embarks on another literary voyage with Abbey through the desert, it is sure to be a wild trip of endless discovery and passion.

William O. Douglas

Of Men and Mountains
"Kloochman"

It was in 1913 when Doug was 19 and I was not quite 15 that the two of us made this climb of Kloochman. Walter Kohagen, Doug, and I were camped in the Tieton Basin at a soda spring. The basin was then in large part a vast rich bottom-land. We were traveling light, one blanket each. The night, I recall, was so bitter cold that we took turns refueling the camp-fire so that we could keep our backs warm enough to sleep. We rose at the first show of dawn, and cooked frying-pan bread and trout for breakfast. We had not planned to climb Kloochman, but somehow the challenge came to us as the sun touched her crest.

After breakfast we started circling the rock. There are fairly easy routes up Kloochman, but we shunned them. When we came to the southeast face (the one that never has been con-quered, I believe) we chose it. Walter decided not to make the climb, but to wait at the base of the cliff for Doug and me. The July day was warm and cloudless. Doug led. The beginning was easy. For 100 feet or so we found ledges six to twelve inches wide we could follow to the left or right. Some ledges ran up the rock ten feet or more at a gentle grade. Others were merely steps to another ledge higher up. Thus by hugging the wall we could either ease ourselves upward or hoist ourselves from one ledge to another.

When we were about 100 feet up the wall, the ledges became narrower and footwork more precarious. Doug suggested we take off our shoes. This we did, tying them behind us on our belts. In stocking feet we wormed up the wall, clinging like flies to the dark rock. The pace was slow. We gingerly tested each toehold and fingerhold for loose rock before putting our weight on it. At times we had to inch along sidewise, our stomachs pressed tightly against the rock, in order to gain a point where we could reach the ledge above us. If we got on a ledge that turned out to be a cul-de-sac, the much more dangerous task of going down the rock wall would confront us. Hence we picked our route with care and weighed the advantages of several choices which frequently were given us. At times we could not climb easily from one ledge to another. The one above might be a foot or so high. Then we would have to reach it with one knee, slowly bring the other knee up, and then, delicately balancing on both knees on the upper ledge, come slowly to our feet by pressing close to the wall and getting such purchase with our fingers as the lava rock permitted.

In that tortuous way we made perhaps 600 feet in two hours. It was late forenoon when we stopped to appraise our situation. We were in serious trouble. We had reached the feared cul-de-sac. The two- or three-inch ledge on which we stood ended. There seemed none above us within Doug's reach. I was longer-legged than Doug; so perhaps I could have reached some ledge with my fingers if I were ahead. But it was impossible to change positions on the wall. Doug was ahead and there he must stay. The problem was to find a way to get him up.

Feeling along the wall, Doug discovered a tiny groove into which he could press the tips of the fingers of his left hand. It might help him maintain balance as his weight began to shift from the lower ledge to the upper one. But there was within reach not even a lip of rock for his right hand. Just out of reach, however, was a substantial crevice, one that would hold several men. How could Doug reach it? I could not boost him, for my own balance was insecure. Clearly, Doug would have to jump to reach it – and he would have but one jump. Since he was standing on a ledge only a few inches wide, he could not expect to jump for his handhold, miss it, and land safely. A slip meant he would go hurtling down some 600 feet onto the rocks. After much discussion and indecision, Doug decided to take the chance and go up.

He asked me to do him a favor: If he failed and fell, I might still make it, since I was longer-legged; would I give certain messages to his family in that event? I nodded.

"Then listen carefully. Try to remember my exact words," he told me. "Tell Mother that I love her dearly. Tell her I think she is the most wonderful person in the world. Tell her not to worry – that I did not suffer, that God willed it so. Tell Sister that I have been a mean little devil but I had no malice towards her. Tell her I love her too – that some day I wanted to marry a girl as wholesome and cheery and good as she.

"Tell Dad I was brave and died unafraid. Tell him about our climb in full detail. Tell Dad I have always been very proud of him, that some day I planned to be a doctor too. Tell him I lived a clean life, that I never did anything to make him ashamed . . . Tell Mother, Sister, and Dad I prayed for them."

Every word burned into me. My heart sick, my lips quivered. I pressed my face against the rock so Doug could not see. I wept.

All was silent. A pebble fell from the ledge on which I squeezed. I counted seconds before it hit 600 feet below with a faint, faraway tinkling sound. Would Doug drop through the same space? Would I follow? When you fall 600 feet do you die before you hit the bottom? Closing my eyes, I asked God to help Doug up the wall.

In a second Doug said, in a cheery voice, "Well, here goes."

A false bravado took hold of us. I said he could do it. He said he would. He wiped first one hand then the other on his trousers. He placed both palms against the wall, bent his knees slowly, paused a split second, and jumped straight up. It was not much of a jump – only six inches or so. But that jump by one pressed against a cliff 600 feet in the air had daredevil proportions. I held my breath; my heart pounded. The suspense was over.

Doug made the jump, and in a second was hanging by two hands from a strong, wide ledge. There was no toehold; he would have to hoist himself by his arms alone. He did just that. His body went slowly up as if pulled by some unseen winch. Soon he had the weight of his body above the ledge and was resting on the palms of his hands. He then put his left knee on the ledge, rolled over on his side, and chuckled as he said, "Nothing to it."

A greater disappointment followed. Doug's exploration of the ledge showed he was in a final cul-de-sac. There was no way up. There was not even a higher ledge he could reach by jumping. We were now faced with the nightmare of going down the sheer rock wall. We could not go down frontwards because the ledges were too narrow and the wall too steep. We needed our toes, not our heels, on the rock; and we needed to have our stomachs pressed tightly against it. Then we could perhaps feel our way. But as every rock expert knows, descent of a cliff without ropes is often much more difficult than ascent.

That difficulty was impressed on us by the first move. Doug had to leave the ledge he had reached by jumping. He dared not slide blindly to the skimpy ledge he had just left. I must help him. I must move up the wall and stand closer to him. Though I could not possibly hold his weight, I must exert sufficient pressure to slow up his descent and to direct his toe onto the narrow ledge from which he had just jumped.

I was hanging to the rock like a fly, twelve feet or more to Doug's left. I inched my way toward him, first dropping to a lower ledge and then climbing to a higher one, using such toeholds as the rock afforded and edging my way crabwise.

When I reached him I said, "Now I'll help."

Doug lowered himself and hung by his fingers full length. His feet were about six inches above the ledge from which he had jumped. He was now my responsibility. If he dropped without aid or direction he was gone. He could not catch and hold to the scanty ledge. I had little space for maneuvering. The surface on which I stood was not more than three inches wide. My left hand fortunately found an overhead crevice that gave a solid anchor in case my feet slipped.

I placed my right hand in the small of Doug's back and pressed upward with all my might. "Now you can come," I said.

He let go gently, and the full weight of his body came against my arm. My arm trembled under the tension. My left hand hung onto the crack in the rock like a grappling hook. My stomach pressed against the wall as if to find mucilage in its pores. My toes dug in as I threw in every ounce of strength.

Down Doug came – a full inch. I couldn't help glancing down and seeing the rocks 600 feet below.

Down Doug moved another inch, then a third. My left hand seemed paralyzed. The muscles of my toes were aching. My right arm shook. I could not hold much longer.

Down came Doug a fourth inch. I thought he was headed for destruction. His feet would miss the only toehold within reach. I could not possibly hold him. He would plunge to his death because my arm was not strong enough to hold him. The messages he had given me for his family raced through my mind. And I saw myself, sick and ashamed, standing before them, testifying to my own inadequacy, repeating his last words.

"Steady, Doug. The ledge is a foot to your right." He pawed the wall with the toes of his foot, searching.

"I can't find it. Don't let go."

The crisis was on us. Even if I had been safely anchored, my cramped position would have kept me from helping him much more. I felt helpless. In a few seconds I would reach the physical breaking point and Doug would go hurtling off the cliff. I did not see how I could keep him from slipping and yet maintain my own balance.

I will never know how I did it. But I tapped some reserve and directed his right foot onto the ledge from which he had earlier jumped. I did it by standing for a moment on my left foot alone and then using my right leg as a rod to guide his right foot to the ledge his swinging feet had missed.

His toes grabbed the ledge as if they were the talons of a bird. My right leg swung back to my perch.

"Are you OK?" I asked.

"Yes," said Doug. "Good work."

My right arm fell from him, numb and useless. I shook from exhaustion and for the first time noticed that my face was wet with perspiration. We stood against the rock in silence for several minutes, relaxing and regaining our composure

Doug said: "Let's throw our shoes down. It will be easier going." So we untied them from our belts and dropped them to Walter

Kohagen, who was waiting at the rock field below us.

Our descent was painfully slow but uneventful. We went down backwards, weaving a strange pattern across the face of the cliff as we moved from one side to the other. It was perhaps midafternoon when we reached the bottom, retrieved our shoes, and started around the other side of the rock. We left the southeast wall unconquered.

But, being young, we were determined to climb the rock. So once more we started to circle. When we came to the northwest wall, we selected it as our route.

Here, too, is a cliff rising 1000 feet like some unfinished pyramid. But close examination shows numerous toe- and fingerholds that make the start at the least fairly easy. So we set out with our shoes on.

Again it was fairly easy going for a hundred feet or so, when Doug, who was ahead, came to a ledge to which he could not step. On later occasions Doug himself has used a rope to traverse this spot. But this day success of the climb depended at this point on Doug's short legs alone. The ledge to which he must move was up to his hips. There were few fingerholds overhead, and none firm enough to carry his whole weight. Only a few tiny cracks were within reach to serve as purchase for him. But Doug would not give up.

He hitched up his trousers, and grasped a tiny groove of rock with the tips of the fingers of his left hand, pressing his right hand flat against the smooth rock wall as if it had magical sticking power. Slowly he lifted his left knee until it was slightly over the ledge above him. To do so he had to stand tiptoe on his right foot. Pulling with his left hand, he brought his right knee up. Doug was now on both knees on the upper ledge. If he could find good purchase overhead for his hands, he was safe. His hands explored the wall above him. He moved them slowly over most of it without finding a hold. Then he reached straight above his head and cried out, "This is our lucky day."

He had found strong rough edges of rock, and on this quickly pulled himself up. His hands were on a ledge a foot wide. He lay down on it on his stomach and grasped my outstretched hand. The pull of his strong arm against the drop of 100 feet or more was as comforting an experience as any I can recall. In a jiffy I was at his side. We pounded each other on the shoulders and laughed.

My own most serious trouble was yet to come. For a while Doug and I were separated. I worked laterally along a ledge to the south, found easier going, and in a short time was 200 feet or more up the rock wall. I was above Doug, 25 feet or so, and 50 feet to his right. We had been extremely careful to test each toe- and fingerhold before putting our trust in it. Kloochman is full of treacherous rock. We often discovered thin ledges that crumbled under pressure and showered handfuls of rock and dust down below. Perhaps I was careless; but whatever the cause, the thin ledge on which I was standing gave way.

As I felt it slip, I grabbed for a hold above me. The crevasse I seized was solid. But there I was, hanging by my hands 200 feet in the air, my feet pawing the rock. To make matters worse, my camera had swung between me and the cliff when I slipped. It was a crude and clumsy instrument, a box type that I carried on a leather strap across my shoulders. Its hulk was actually pushing me from the cliff. I twisted in an endeavor to get rid of it, but it was firmy lodged between me and the wall.

I yelled to Doug for help. He at once started edging toward me. It seemed hours, though it was probably not over a few minutes. He shouted, "Hang on, I'll be there."

Hang on I did. My fingers ached beyond description. They were frozen to the rock. My exertion in pawing with my feet had added to the fatigue. The ache of my fingers extended to my wrists and then along my arms. I stopped thrashing around and hung like a sack, motionless. Every second seemed a minute, every minute an hour. I did not see how I could possibly hold.

I would slip, I thought, slip to sure death. I could not look down because of my position. But in my mind's eye I saw in sharp outline the jagged rocks that seemed to pull me toward them. The camera kept pushing my fingers from the ledge. I felt them move. they began to give way before the pull of a force too great for flesh to resist.

Fright grew in me. The idea of hanging helpless 200 feet above the abyss brought panic. I cried out to Doug but the words caught in my dry throat. I was like one in a nightmare who struggles to shout – who is then seized with a fear that promises to destroy him.

Then there flashed through my mind a family scene. Mother was sitting in the living room talking to me, telling me what a wonderful man Father was. She told me of his last illness and his death. She told me of his departure from Cleveland, Washington to Portland, Oregon, for what proved to be a fatal operation. His last words to her were: "If I die it will be glory. If I live, it will be grace."

The panic passed. The memory of those words restored reason. Glory to die? I could not understand why it would be glory to die. It would be glory to live. But as Father said, it might take grace to live, grace from One more powerful than either Doug or I.

And so again that day I prayed. I asked God to save my life, to save me from destruction on this rock wall. I asked God to make my fingers strong, to give me strength to hang on. I asked God to give me courage, to make me unafraid. I asked God to give me guts, to give me power to do the impossible.

My fingers were as numb as flesh that is full of novocaine. They seemed detached from me, as if they belonged to someone else. My wrists, my shoulders, cried out for respite from the pain. It would be such welcome relief if they could be released from the weight that was on them.

Hang on? You can't hang on. You are a weakling. The weaklings die in the woods.

Weakling? I'll show you. How long must I hang on? All day? OK, all day then. I'll hang on, I'll hang on. O God, dear God, help me hang on!

I felt someone pushing my left foot upwards. It was Doug. As if through a dream his voice was saying, "Your feet are 18 inches below your toehold." Doug found those toeholds for my feet.

I felt my shoes resting in solid cracks. I pulled myself up and leaned on my elbows on the ledge to which my hands had been glued. I flexed my fingers and bent my wrists to bring life back.

Doug came up abreast of me an said, "We're even Stephen now."

"Even Stephen?"

"Today each of us has saved the other's life."

It was shortly above the point where Doug saved my life that we discovered a classic path up Kloochman. It is a three-sided chimney chute, a few feet wide, that leads almost to the top. There are several such chutes on Kloochman. In later years Cragg Gilbert and Louis Ulrich went up Devil's Chimney on the northeast face in a seven-hour nerve-wracking climb with ropes. Clarence Truitt and many others have gone up the chimney chute that Doug and I discovered.

Then as now this chute was filled with loose rock that had to be cleared away. To negotiate the chute we took off our shoes and tied them to our belts. We climbed the chute in stocking feet, pressing our hands and feet against the opposing walls as we kept our backs to the abyss below us. This day we went up the chute with ease, stopping every eight feet or so to measure our progress.

The sun was setting when we reached the top. We were gay and buoyant. We talked about the glories of the scene in front of us. We bragged a bit about our skill in rock work – how we must be part mountain goat to have reached the top. We shouted and hallooed to the empty meadows far below us.

On Kloochman Rock that July afternoon both Doug and I valued life more because death had passed so close. It was wonderful to be alive, breathing, using our muscles, shouting, seeing.

We stayed briefly at the top. We went down as we came up, in stocking feet. We raced against darkness, propelled by the thought of spending the night on Kloochman's treacherous wall.

It was deep dusk when we rejoined Walter on the rock fields at the base. We put on our shoes and hurried on. We entered the woods at double-quick time, seeking the trail that led toward the South Fork of the Tieton. We saw the trail from the edge of a clearing as a faint, light streak in a pitch-black night. We had two ways of keeping on it. We had no matches or torch or flashlight. But we could feel the edges with our feet. And we could search out the strip of night sky over the path.

We finally decided that it would take too long to follow the trail to camp in this groping way. We'd take a short cut to Westfall Rocks, whose formless shape we could see against the sky. We took to the brush on our right, and kept our hands out in front to ward off boughs and branches. We crossed a marshy bog where we went in up to our knees. We came to soft earth where we went in up to our hips.

There were animals in the brush. We could hear them in the thickets, disturbed by our approach, and going out ahead of us. Thinking they might be bear, we paused to listen. "Cattle," said Doug.

We reached the Tieton River, which we knew could not be forded in many places in that stretch. So we took off our pants, shoes, and shirts and rolled them in bundles which we held on our heads. We waded out into the dark, cold, swift river, Doug in the lead. We had by accident picked one of the few good fords in the Tieton. We were never in water over our waists.

Then we dressed and located the road leading back to camp. As we started along it Doug said: "You know, Bill, there is power in prayer."

That night I prayed again. I knelt on a bed of white fir boughs beside the embers of a campfire and thanked God for saving Doug's life and mine, for giving us the strength to save each other.

When I climbed Kloochman in 1948, my steps were more cautious and measured then they had been in 1913. There was less dash, less abandon in this adult ascent. I took my ease, feeling my way with care. But the memories of the earlier trip were still fresh in my mind as if it had happened only the previous week instead of thirty-five years ago.

As I climbed, I realized how conservative man became in his physical endeavors as he passed his thirties. I was not thinking of wind or stamina, for mine were both good. I was thinking of the subtle forces that control the reflexes. It struck home why only young men make good fighter pilots – how it is that age fast takes the daredevil out of man. There was a thrill in this adult climb, but the reckless, carefree attitude of the earlier day had gone.

Yet I relived the experience of 1913. Places, as well as smells and shapes and sounds, can be symbols of fear and terror. He who, after long years of absence, revisits a place associated with sadness or guilt or suffering is likely to relive for a moment the sensations he experienced there. The forces at work are subtle; and unless he is aware of their influences, he may be painfully disturbed or upset. Unless he recognizes the part these imponderables play in human emotions, he may indeed be seized with a new discomfiture greater than the one that seized him earlier at the selfsame place.

The day I climbed Kloochman as a man, all the sensations of the earlier trip returned to me. There was the the trembling excitement of the start. Doug's messages to his family raced once more through my mind, as if he had just uttered them. I saw Doug make his jump up the side of the cliff while he was 600 feet in the air. I saw him hanging on the ledge, doomed to die. I felt the weight of his body against my arm. I felt myself slipping slowly from the rock to destruction. It seemed once more that demons were pulling at my feet with a power too great for flesh and blood to resist. Once again little vestiges of the old fear passed through me.

Those, however, were fleeting sensations. When I came to the top a sense of calm came over me, a deep peace, the feeling a man has when he is with the woman he loves. And with the calm came pride.

Kloochman was in my very heart. Here we had accomplished the impossible. We had survived terrible ordeals on her sheer walls. We had faced death down; and because of our encounter with it, we had come to value life the more. On these dark walls in 1913 I had first communed with God. Here I had felt the presence of a Mighty Force, infinitely beyond man. Here I had known the strength of unseen hands helping me along ledges.

I sat on the top of the rock looking to the west. The sun was dipping. The milky waters of the Tieton Reservoir hid forever from the eyes of man the gorgeous McAllister Meadows where we used to camp. Beyond was the wild panorama of the Tieton – cliffs, snowy peaks, hillsides of evergreen as soft in the late sun as the folds of a velvet gown, jagged fingers of rocks, jumbled ridges. It is the country that Doug and I have long loved. It is where Doug once said he wanted his ashes scattered. There was not a breath of wind. There was a deep and profound quiet. The only life in sight was a hawk, the slow-flying mouser type. But he uttered no sound as he caught mysterious currents of air and glided away to some resting place on Short and Dirty Ridge to the southwest.

I wondered if Kloochman had been a testing ground for other lads. I wondered if others had met on her walls the challenge of life and death. I knew now what a boy could not know, that fear of death was the compound of all other fears. I knew that long years ago I had begun to shed on Kloochman's walls the great, overpowering fear.

Kloochman became that day a symbol of adversity and challenge – of the forces that have drawn from man his greatest spiritual and physical achievements.

Voltaire said that "History is the sound of heavy boots going upstairs and the rustle of satin slippers coming down." This country fortunately is still in the "heavy boots" stage of history. That is a stage of a nation's life that is often marked by the tramp of the boots of armies bent on conquest. It is usually evidenced by robust attitudes. But those attitudes can be expressed in ways less destructive than war. The growth of society, as Arnold Toynbee shows, is the successful response to challenge. The challenge may be the existence of some form of slavery, the poverty of a desert, the rigors of mountains, or a war. When the challenge is met and the goal achieved, there is a tremendous impetus for growth. A powerful energizing force is let loose that produces men and ideas that are dynamic.

This country is in that stage of growth. It is not bent on military conquest as were most of the countries which have sent armies across continents and oceans. In the realm of physical forces this nation has its true bent on the conquest of angry rivers, unproductive wastelands, erosion, the atom. In the realm of human relations it is bent on conquest of poverty and disease, high prices and scarcity, industrial injustice, racial prejudices, and the virus of political ideologies that would corrode and destroy the values of Western civilization.

These are powerful challenges. The fact that many of them are subtle and invisible makes them no less potent. A prejudice can be as ominous and threatening as a man with a bayonet. The issues that challenge this generation call for bold and daring action. They demand men who live dangerously – men who place adventure ahead of security, men who would trade the comfort of today for the chance of scaling a new peak of progress tomorrow. That activity demands men who fear neither men nor ideas. For it is only when fear is cast out that the full creative energies are unleashed. Then one is unhampered by hesitation and indecision. One's energies are not diverted to the making of some futile or hideous sacrifice at the altar of a sick ego.

When man knows how to live dangerously, he is not afraid to die. When he is not afraid to die, he is, strangely, free to live. When he is free to live, he can become bold, courageous, reliant. There are many ways to learn how to live dangerously. Men of the plains have had the experience in the trackless blizzards that sweep in from the north. Those who go out in boats from Gloucester have known it in another form. The mountains that traverse this country offer still a different way, and one that for many is the most exciting of all. The mountians can be reached in all seasons. They offer a fighting challenge to heart, soul, and mind, both in summer and winter. If throughout them the youth of the nation accept the challenge the mountains offer, they will help keep alive in our people the spirit of adventure. That spirit is a measure of the vitality of both nations and men. A people who climb the ridges and sleep under the stars in high mountain meadows, who enter the forest and scale the peaks, who explore glaciers and walk ridges buried deep in snow – these people will give their country some of the indomitable spirit of the mountains.

A light wind came up from the northwest. The sun slipped behind the jaggedness of Hogback Mountain far to the west. I started down Kloochman so as to have the treacherous ledges behind and above me before darkness. I had not gone far when the evening star appeared. By the time I cleared the brush below the rock fields, this would be my only sure guide to the road where I had left my car.

I stood in the silence of the gathering night, charting my course by it. Then the words my father had spoken came back: "If I die it will be glory. If I live, it will be grace."

That was his evening star – a faith in a power greater than man. That was the faith of our fathers – a belief in a God who controlled man and the universe. It manifested itself in different ways to different people. It was written by scholars and learned men into dozens of different creeds. There were sects and schisms and religious disputes. But riding high above all such secular controversies was the faith in One who was the Creator, the Giver of Life, the Omnipotent.

Man's age-long effort has been to be free. Throughout time he has struggled against some form of tyranny that would enslave his mind or his body. So far in this century three epidemics of it have been let loose in the world.

We can keep our freedom through the increasing crises of history only if we are self-reliant enough to be free. We cannot become self-reliant if our dominant desire is to be safe and secure; under that influence we could never face and overcome the adversities of this competitive age. We will be self-reliant only if we have a real appetite for independence.

Dollars, guns, and all the wondrous products of science and the machine will not be enough: "This night thy soul shall be required of thee."

We need a faith – the faith of our fathers. We need a faith that dedicates us to something bigger and more important than ourselves or our possessions. We need a faith to which we commit our lives. We need a faith for which it would be glory to die. Only if we have such a faith are we free to live.

I dropped off the cliff, cleared the rocks below, and entered the dark woods.

WILLIAM O. DOUGLAS was born in 1898 in Minnesota. He received a law degree from Columbia and was a professor of law at Yale. He entered public service when he was appointed Chairman of the Securities and Exchange Commission. He was appointed to the Supreme Court by President Franklin Delano Roosevelt and over the next three decades was one of the most consistent supporters of the rights of individuals. His books include: *A Living Bill of Rights, My Wilderness, Russian Touring,* and *Men and Mountains.*

End Notes

Bernard DeVoto

1   Not, it must be made clear, the sign language of the Plains Indians, the exceedingly effective means of communication that will be important in this narrative later on.

2   Here and in my statements about Cabeza de Vaca's route I follow Hallenbeck (1). From the northern border of Sonora on, Hallenbeck follows Sauer. Elsewhere I make a general statement about routes.

Rosalind Richards

3   The legal distinction in our State is not between ponds and "Great Ponds." All land-locked waters over ten acres in area are Great Ponds; in which the public have rights of fishing, ice-cutting, etc. R. R.

O. E. Rölvaag

4   In most dialects of Norway the name Ole becomes Ola when spoken.

James Fenimore Cooper

5   The Mississippi is thus termed in several of the Indian languages. The reader will gain a more just idea of the importance of this stream if he recalls to mind the fact that the Missouri and the Mississippi are properly the same river. Their united lengths cannot be greatly short of four thousand miles.

6   All the states admitted to the American Union since the revolution are called New States, with the exception of Vermont; that had claims before the war, which were not, however, admitted until a later day.

7   Colonel Boone, the patriarch of Kentucky. This venerable and hardy pioneer of civilization emigrated to an estate three hundred miles west of the Mississippi in his ninety-second year because he found a population of ten to the square mile inconveniently crowded!

Roderick Nash

8   Wildland Research Center, *Wilderness and Recreation*, pp. 213-54 and especially pp. 236-37; Ezra Bowen, *The High Sierra* (New York, 1972), p. 156.

9   As quoted in Ann and Myron Sutton, *The Wilderness World of the Grand Canyon* (Philadelphia, 1971), p. 204.

10 For help look at the early editions of the book regarded as the campers "bible" in the early twentieth century: Horace Kephart, *The Book of Camping and Woodcraft: A Guide For Those Who Travel in the Wilderness* (New York, 1910). See also Louis Bignami, "Past and Present Tents," *Westways*, 73 (1981), pp. 34-37.

11 A revealing account of an 1890 trip with packstock in the Sierra Nevada is Joseph N. LeConte, *A Summer of Travel in the High Sierra* (Ashland, Or., 1972).

12 David R. Brower, "Individual

Freedom in Public Wilderness," *Not Man Apart*, 6 (1976), p.2.

13 Colin Fletcher, *Complete Walker* discusses modern equipment. A comparable volume is John Hart, *Walking Softly in the Wilderness: The Sierra Club Guide to Backpacking* (San Francisco, 1977).

14 In this regard see Charles Jones and Klaus Knab, *American Wilderness: A Gousha Weekend Guide to Our Wild Lands and Waters* (San Jose, Ca., 1973).

15 McPhee, *Encounters*, p. 34.

16 Karl Schwenke and Thomas Winnett, *Sierra South: 100 Backcountry Trips in California's Sierra* (Berkeley, 1968). George S. Wells, *Handbook of Wilderness Travel* (Denver, 1968) is nationwide in focus. Step-by-step "how to" books abound as, for instance, Mary Scott Welch, *The Family Wilderness Handbook* (New York, 1973).

17 *Adventure Trip Guide*, ed. Pat Dickman (New York, 1972).

18 A typical contemporary statement is Susan Sands, "Backpacking: 'I Go to the Wilderness to Kick the Man-World Out of Me,'" New York *Times*, May 9, 1971, p. I.

19 "We're Loving our Wilderness to Death," *Audubon*, 75 (1973), III. An excellent examination of crowding of eastern wilderness is contained in Laura and Guy Waterman, *Backwoods Ethics* (Boston, 1979) pp. 158-70.

20 Interview with Ivan Maxwell, February 10, 1973.

21 Interview with Ed Waldapful, U.S. Forest Service Information Officer, October 6, 1978.

22 Edward Hay, "Wilderness Experiment," *American Forests, 80* (1974), 26-29; Jack Quigg, "Our Desert Being Killed with Love," *Santa Barbara [Ca.] News Press*, March 28, 1970; U.S. Department of the Interior, Bureau of Land Management, *The California Desert Conservation Area: Draft Plan Alternatives and Environmental Impact Statement* (Riverside, Ca., 1980).

23 The emphasis on "carnivalism" in the national parks is well covered in Alfred Runte, *National Parks: The American Experience* (Lincoln, Neb., 1979), especially Chapter 8.

24 As quoted on Roderick Nash, "Historical Roots of Wilderness Management" in *Wilderness Management*, ed., John Hendee, George H. Stankey, and Robert Lucas, "U.S. Forest Service Miscellaneous Publication No. 1365" (Washington, D.C., 1978), p.35.

Bibliography and Further Reading

*The authors included in this anthology and their other selected works are
listed below.*

Abbey, Edward. *Beyond the Wall*. New York: Henry Holt and Co., 1984.
    Desert Solitaire. Layton: Gibbs M. Smith, 1981.
    Down the River. New York: E. P. Dutton, 1982.
    Good News. New York: E. P. Dutton, 1980.
    The Journey Home: Some Words in Defense of the American West. New
    York: E. P. Dutton, 1977.
    The Monkey Wrench Gang. Salt Lake City: Dream Garden, 1985.

Austin, Mary Hunter. *The Land of Journey's Ending*. Tucson: The University of
    Arizona Press, 1983
    The Basket. New York: Gordon Press, 1973.
    Earth Horizon. Boston: Houghton Mifflin, 1932. (Out of Print – Check your
    local library).
    The Land of Little Rain. New York: Gordon Press, 1973.
    A Woman of Genius. Salem: Ayer Co. Publishers, 1977.

Back, Mary. *Seven Half Miles From Home*. Boulder; Johnson Books, 1985.

Benét, Stephen Vincent. "The Ballad of William Sycamore," from *The Pocket
    Book of Verse*. New York: Pocket Books, 1956.
    The Beginning of Wisdom. Sharon Hill: Russell Press, 1985.
    The Devil and Daniel Webster and Other Stories. New York: Archway,
    1972.
    James Shore's Daughter. Sharon Hill: Russell Press, 1985.
    John Brown's Body. Cutchogue: Buccaneer Books, 1982.

Berry, Wendell. *The Gift of Good Land*. San Francisco: North Point Press, 1981.
    The Collected Poems of Wendell Berry, 1957-1982. Berkeley: North Point
    Press, 1985.
    Farming: A Hand Book. New York: Harcourt, Brace Jovanovich, 1971.
    The Memory of Old Jack. New York: Harcourt, Brace Jovanovich, 1975.
    A Place on Earth. Berkeley: North Point Press, 1983.
    The Unsettling of America: Culture & Agriculture. San Francisco: Sierra
    Club Books, 1977.

Beston, Henry. *The Outermost House.* New York: Henry Holt and Co., 1956.
    Cape Cod to the St. Lawrence. Lexington: Greene, 1976.
    Especially Maine: The Natural World of Henry Beston, from
    The Book of Gallant Vagabonds: Trelawny, Rimbaud. Darby: Folcroft,
    1978.
    Northern Farm. New York: Ballantine Books, 1972.

Borland, Hal. *High, Wide and Lonesome.* Boston: G. K. Hall, 1984.
    Country Editor's Boy. New York: Harper & Row, 1970.
    A Countryman's Flowers. New York: Knopf, 1981.
    Hal Borland's Book of Days. New York: Bantam, 1972.
    Hal Borland's Twelve Moons of the Year. Boston: G. K. Hall, 1985.
    When the Legends Die. New York: Bantam, 1972.

Brooks, Sara. *You May Plow Here.* Edited by Thordis Simonsen. New York:
    W.W. Norton, 1986.

Brower, David. "Wilderness – Conflict and Conscience," from *Voices for the*
    Wilderness. Edited by William Schwartz. New York: Ballantine Books,
    1969.
    Only a Little Planet. New York: Ballantine, 1975.

Bryant, William Cullen. "To a Waterfowl," from *One Hundred and One Famous*
    Poems. Chicago: Contemporary Books, Inc., 1958.
    The Letters of William Cullen Bryant: 1849-1857, Volume III.
    New York: Fordham, 1981.
    The Letters of William Cullen Bryant: 1858-1864, Volume IV.
    New York: Fordham, 1984.
    The Library of Poetry and Song. Salem: Ayer Co., Publishing.
    Picturesque America: Oh the Land We Live In. Secaucus: Lyle - Stuart,
    1975.

Burnford, Sheila. "Canadian Spring," from *Highlights from 125 Years of the*
    Atlantic. Boston: Atlantic Monthly Press, 1977.
    Fields of Noon. Boston: Little, Brown, 1972.
    The Incredible Journey. New York: Bantam, 1977.
    One Woman's Arctic. Boston: Little, Brown, 1964.

Burroughs, John. "The Summit of My Years," from *Highlights from 125 Years of the Atlantic.* Boston: Atlantic Monthly Press, 1977.
Camping and Tramping with Roosevelt. Salem: Ayer Co. Publishing, 1970.
A River View and Other Hudson Valley Essays. Croton - on - Hudson: North River, 1981.
Ways of Nature. Salem: Ayer Co. Publishing, reprint of 1905 edition.

Carrighar, Sally. *One Day at Teton Marsh.* Lincoln: University of Nebraska Press, 1979.
The Glass Dove. New York: Avon, 1977.
One Day on Beetle Rock. Lincoln: University of Nebraska Press, 1978.

Carson, Rachel. *The Sense of Wonder.* New York: Harper & Row, 1965.
The Edge of Sea. Boston: Houghton Mifflin, 1955.
The Sea Around Us. New York: Oxford University Press, 1961.
Silent Spring. Boston: Houghton Mifflin, 1962.

Cather, Willa. *O Pioneers!* Boston: Houghton Mifflin, 1941.
A Lost Lady. New York: Vintage Books, 1971.
Lucy Gayheart. New York: Vintage Books, 1976.
My Antonia. Boston: Houghton Mifflin, 1977.
Obscure Destinies. New York: Vintage Books, 1974.
One of Ours. New York: Vintage Books, 1971.

Clark, A. Carman. *From the Orange Mailbox.* Gardiner: Harpswell, 1985.

Cooper, James Fenimore. *The Prairie.* New York: New American Library, 1980.
The Deerslayer. Cutchogue: Buccaneer Books, 1984.
The Last of the Mohicans. New York: Bantam, 1981.
Letters and Journals of James Fenimore Cooper. New York: Harper & Row, 1960.
The Pathfinder. Cutchogue: Buccaneer Books, 1984.
The Pioneers. Cutchogue: Buccaneer Books, 1984.

DeVoto, Bernard. *The Course of Empire.* Boston: Houghton Mifflin, 1952.
Across the Wide Missouri. New York: Crown, 1981.
The Easy Chair. Boston: Houghton Mifflin, 1955.
Mark Twain's America. Westport: Greenwood, 1978.
The Year of Decision. Boston: Little, Brown, 1943.

Dickinson, Emily. "Final Harvest," from *Emily Dickinson's Poems*. Boston: Little, Brown, 1961.
    Acts of Light: Emily Dickinson. Boston: New York Graphic Society, 1980.
    The Complete Poems of Emily Dickinson. Boston: Little, Brown, 1960.
    Emily Dickinson: Selected Letters. Boston: Harvard University Press, 1971.
    Selected Poems and Letters. New York: Doubleday Anchor, 1959.

Dillard, Annie. *Pilgrim at Tinker Creek*. New York: Harper & Row, 1974.
    Living by Fiction. New York: Harper & Row, 1983.
    Teaching a Stone to Talk: Expeditions & Encounters. New York: Harper & Row, 1983.
    Tickets for a Prayer Wheel. Columbia: University of Missouri Press, 1974.

Doig, Ivan. *This House of Sky: Landscapes of a Western Mind*. New York: Harcourt, Brace Jovanovich, 1978.
    English Creek. New York: Penguin, 1984.
    Inside This House of Sky. New York: Atheneum, 1983.
    The Sea Runners. New York: Penguin, 1983.
    Winter Brothers: A Season at the Edge of America. New York: Harcourt, Brace Jovanovich, 1982.

Douglas, William O. *Of Men and Mountains*. New York: Harper & Row, 1950.
    Go East Young Man. New York: Random, 1974.
    The Right of the People. Westport: Greenwood, 1980.
    The Three Hundred Year War: A Chronicle of Ecological Disease. New York: Random House, 1972.

Eiseley, Loren. *The Immense Journey*. New York: Vintage Books, 1957.
    All the Strange Hours: The Excavation of a Life. New York: Scribner, 1975.
    The Invisible Pyramid. Magnolia: Peter Smith, 1983.
    The Star Thrower. New York: Times Books, 1978.

Emerson, Ralph Waldo. *The Portable Emerson*. New York: Penguin Books, 1981.
    Nature. Boston: Beacon Press, 1985.
    Ralph Waldo Emerson: Selected Essays. New York: Penguin, 1982.

Frost, Robert. "Prayer in Spring," from *Poetry and Prose*. New York: Holt, Rinehart and Winston, 1969.
  The Collected Poems: Complete and Unabridged. New York: Holt, Rinehart and Winston, 1969.
  In the Clearing. New York: Holt, Rinehart and Winston, 1972.
  The Road Not Taken. New York: Holt, Rinehart and Winston, 1971.

Grey, Zane. "The Thundering Herd," from *Zane Grey, Five Complete Novels*. New York: Avenel Books, 1980.
  The Dude Ranger. New York: Pocket, 1981.
  The Heritage of the Desert. New York: Pocket, 1983.
  Nevada. New York: Bantam, 1986.
  The Rainbow Trail. New York: Pocket, 1961.

Hay, John. *In Defense of Nature*. Boston: Atlantic Monthly Press, 1969.
  The Atlantic Shore, (co-author Peter Farb). Orleans: Parnassus Imprints, 1982.
  The Great Beach. New York: Norton, 1980.
  Nature's Year. New York: Doubleday, 1961.
  The Run. New York: Norton, 1959.

Heat Moon, William Least. *Blue Highways*. Boston: Atlantic-Little Brown, 1982.

Hoagland, Edward. *Walking the Dead Diamond River*. New York: Random House, 1973.
  African Calliope: A Journey to the Sudan. New York: Random House, 1979.
  Notes from the Century Before: A Journal from British Columbia. Berkeley: North Point Press, 1982.
  Red Wolves and Black Bears. New York: Random House, 1976.
  The Tugman's Passage. New York: Penguin, 1983.

Jefferson, Thomas. *Jefferson's Letters*. Eau Claire: E.M. Hale and Co. (no date)
  An Account of Louisiana. Boston: Directory of the Old South works, 1902.
  Autobiography. New York: Capricorn Books, 1959.
  The Portable Thomas Jefferson. New York: Viking Press, 1975.

Jenkins, Peter, and Barbara Jenkins.*The Walk West.* New York: William Morrow, 1981.
  The Road Unseen. Nashville: Thomas Nelson, 1985.

Kavanaugh, James. "I Asked the River," from *Walk Easy on the Earth.* New York: E. P. Dutton, 1979.
  Celebrate the Sun. New York, E. P. Dutton, 1973.
  Laughing Down Lonely Canyons. New York: Harper and Row, 1984.
  Sunshine Days & Foggy Nights. New York: E. P. Dutton, 1975.
  There are Men too Gentle to Live Among Wolves. New York: Harper & Row, 1984.
  Winter Has Lasted Too Long. New York: E. P. Dutton, 1977.

Ketchum, Richard. *Second Cuttings: Letters from the Country.* New York: Viking, 1981.
  The Battle of Bunker Hill. New York: Doubleday, 1962.
  Faces from the Past. New York: American Heritage Press, 1970.
  The World of George Washington. New York: American Heritage Press, 1974.

Krutch, Joseph Wood. *The Desert Year.* Tucson: University of Arizona Press, 1985.
  Grand Canyon: Today and All It's Yesterdays. New York: Morrow Quill, 1958.
  The Great Chain of Life. Boston: Houghton Mifflin, 1978.
  Measure of Man: On Freedom, Human Values, Survival & the Modern Temperment. Magnolia: Peter Smith, (no date).
  The Voice of the Desert. New York: Morrow Quill, 1955.
  The Violence of the Desert: A Naturalist's Interpretation. New York: Morrow, 1971.

Leopold, Aldo. *A Sand County Almanac.* New York: Oxford University Press, 1977.
  Round River. New York: Oxford University Press, 1953, (Out of Print Contact your local library).

Lincoln, Abraham. "Poem," from *The Living Lincoln*. New Brunswick: Rutgers
    University Press, 1955.
    Abraham Lincoln on War and Peace, 1860-64. Boston: edited by
    Lawrence V. Roth, 1918.
    Abraham Lincoln: Selected Speeches, Messages, and Letters,
    edited by T. Harry Williams. New York: Rinehart, 1957.
    The Essential Lincoln, edited by Keith Jennison. New York: F. Watts, 1971.

London, Jack. *The Call of the Wild*. New York: Crown, 1983.
    Martin Eden. New York: Penguin, 1984.
    The Sea Wolf. New York: Bantam, 1986.
    White Fang. New York: Airmont, 1964.

Longfellow, Henry Wadsworth. *Evangeline*. New York: Airmont Publishing,
    1965.
    The Poetical Works of Longfellow. Boston: Houghton Mifflin, 1975.

Lopez, Barry Holstun. *River Notes: The Dance of Herons*. New York: Avon,
    1979.
    Arctic Dreams. New York: Scribner, 1986.
    Desert Notes: Reflections in the Eye of the Raven. Fairway: Andrews,
    McMeel Parker, 1976.
    Winter Count. New York: Scribner, 1982
    Of Wolves and Men. New York: Scribner, 1979.

Lowell, James Russell. "The Moosehead Country in 1853," from *White Pine and
    Blue Water: A State of Maine Reader*. Camden: Down East Magazine, 1950.
    My Study Windows. Darby: Folcroft, 1982.

MacLean, Norman. *A River Runs Through It*. Chicago. University of Chicago,
    1976.

McPhee, John. *Coming Into the Country*. New York: Farrar, Straus, Giroux, 1977.
    The Crofter & the Laird. New York: Farrar, Straus, Giroux, 1970.
    Encounters with the Archdruid. New York: Farrar, Straus, Giroux, 1971.
    The John McPhee Reader. New York: Farrar, Straus, Giroux, 1976.
    The Pine Barrens. New York: Farrar, Straus, Giroux, 1968.

McRae, Wallace. *It's Just Grass and Water*. Spokane: Shaun Higgins, 1979.

Mowat, Farley. *Never Cry Wolf*. Boston: Atlantic-Little, Brown, 1963.
    The Desperate People. Toronto: McClelland & Stewart-Bantam Ltd., 1975.
    Grey Seas Under. New York: Bantam, 1982.
    My Discovery of America. Boston: The Atlantic Monthly Press, 1985.
    People of the Deer. Toronto: McClelland & Stewart-Bantam Ltd., 1952.
    Sea of Slaughter. Boston: Atlantic Monthly, 1984.

Muir, John. *Stickeen*. Berkeley: Heyday Books, 1981.
    My First Summer in the Sierra. Boston: Houghton Mifflin, 1944.
    The Mountains of California. New York: Penguin, 1985.
    A Thousand-Mile Walk to the Gulf. Boston: Houghton Mifflin, 1981.
    Travels in Alaska. Boston: Houghton Mifflin, 1979.

Murie, Margaret E., and Olaus J. Murie. *Two in the Far North*. Anchorage: Alaska Northwest Publishing, 1983.
    Island Between. Fairbanks. University of Alaska Press, 1977.
    Wapiti Wilderness. Boulder: Colorado Associated Press, 1985.

Murray, William Cotter. "Grass," from *American Heritage,* April 1968, Volume IX, Number 3. New York: American Heritage Publishing Co., 1968.

Nash, Roderick. *Wilderness and the American Mind*. 3d ed. New Haven: Yale University, 1982.
    The American Environment: Readings in the History of Conservation. New York: Random House, 1976.
    From These Beginnings: A Biological Approach to American History. New York: Harper & Row, 1984.

Ogburn, Charlton, Jr. *The Winter Beach*. New York: Pocket, 1971.
    The Marauders. New York: Morrow, 1982.
    Railroads: The Great American Adventure. Washington, D. C.: National Geographic, 1977.
    The Southern Appalachians: A Wilderness Quest. New York: Morrow, 1975.

Olson, Sigurd F. *Reflections from the North Country.* New York: Knopf, 1976.
    Listening Point. New York: Knopf, 1958.
    Lonely Land. New York: Knopf, 1961.
    Open Horizons. New York: Knopf, 1963.
    Sigurd F. Olson's Wilderness Days. New York: Knopf, 1972.
    The Singing Wilderness. New York: Knopf, 1956.

Parkman, Francis. *The Oregon Trail.* Boston: Little, Brown, 1882.
    France and England in North America. New York: Literary Classics, 1983.
    La Salle and the Discovery of the Great West. Williamstown: Corner House, 1968.

Powell, John Wesley. *History of the Exploration of the Canyons of the Colorado.* Washington, D. C.: Smithsonian Institution, 1869.
    Selected Prose of John Wesley Powell. Boston: D. R. Godine, 1970.

Richards, Rosalind. " A Northern Countryside," from *White Pine and Blue Water: A State of Maine Reader.* Camden: Down East Magazine, 1950.

Rölvaag, Olie. *Giants of the Earth.* New York: Harper & Row, 1927.
    The Boat of Longing: a Novel. Westport: Greenwood, 1974.
    Peder Victorious: A Tale of the Pioneers 20 Years Later. Lincoln: University of Nebraska Press, 1982.
    Their Father's God. Lincoln: University of Nebraska Press, 1983.

Roosevelt, Theodore. *Ranch Life and the Hunting Trail.* Lincoln: University of Nebraska Press, 1983.
    African Game Trails. New York: Scribner, 1910.
    American Bears: Selection from Writings of Theodore Roosevelt. Boulder: Colorado Associated University Press, 1983.
    The Rough Riders. New York: Scribner, 1902.
    The Winning of the West. New York: Hasting House, 1963.

Sandburg, Carl. *Cornhuskers.* New York: Harcourt Brace Jovanovich, 1918.
    The Complete Poems of Carl Sandburg. New York: Harcourt, Brace, Jovanovich, 1969.
    Honey and Salt. New York: Harcourt Brace Jovanovich, 1963.
    The People, Yes. New York: Harcourt Brace Jovanovich, 1936.

Sandoz, Mari. *Old Jules*. Lincoln: University of Nebraska Press, 1962.
  The Beaver Men. Lincoln: University of Nebraska Press, 1964.
  The Buffalo Hunters. Lincoln: University of Nebraska Press, 1954.
  Love Song to the Plains . Lincoln: University of Nebraska Press, 1961.
  Sandhill Sundays and Other Recollections. Lincoln: University
  of Nebraska Press, 1984.

Service, Robert William. "The Call of the Wild," from *Best Tales of the
  Yukon*. Philadelphia: Running Press, 1983.
  Collected Poems of Robert Service. New York: Dodd, Mead, 1944.

Steinbeck, John. *The Grapes of Wrath*. New York: Penguin, 1985.
  Cannery Row. New York: Bantam, 1985.
  East of Eden. New York: Penguin, 1979.
  Of Mice and Men. New York: Bantam, 1984.
  Travels with Charley. New York: Penguin, 1985.

Stockton, Bill.*Today I Baled Some Hay to Feed the Sheep the Coyotes Eat*.
  Helena: Falcon Press, 1983.

Sutton, George Miksch. "Forever and Ever, Amen." *Audubon,* September 1985,
  Volume 87, #5.
  Bird Student: An Autobiography. Austin: University of Texas Press, 1980.
  Eskimo Year. Norman: University of Oklahoma Press, 1985.
  Iceland Summer: Adventure of a Bird Painter. Norman: University of
  Oklahoma Press, 1980.

Taylor, Bayard, ed.*Wonders of theYellowstone*. New York: Scribner,
  Armstrong, & Company, 1874.
  Journey to Central Africa. Westport: Greenwood, reproduction of 1854
  edition.

Teal, John, and Mildred Teal. *Life and Death of the Salt Marsh*. Boston: Little,
  Brown, 1971.
  Portrait of an Island. Athens: University of Georgia Press, 1981.

Teale, Edwin Way. *North with the Spring.* New York: Dodd, Mead, 1951.
  Autumn Across America. New York: Dodd, Mead, 1981.
  Journey Into Summer. New York: Dodd, Mead, 1981.
  A Waltz Through the Year. New York: Dodd, Mead, 1978.
  Wandering Through Winter. New York: Dodd, Mead, 1981.
  Wilderness World of John Muir. Boston: Houghton Mifflin, 1954.

Ten Bears. "Do Not Ask Us to Give Up the Buffalo for the Sheep," from *Indian Oratory.* Edited by W. C. Vanderwerth. Norman: University of Oklahoma Press, 1972.

Thoreau, Henry David. *The Heart of Thoreau's Journal.* Edited by Odell Shepard. New York: Dover, 1961.
  In the Woods and Fields of Concord:Selections from the Journals of Henry David Thoreau. Salt Lake City: Peregrine Smith, 1982.
  The Variorium Walden. New York: Washingto Square Press, 1962.
  H. D. Thoreau: A Writer's Journal. Edited by Laurence Stapleton. New York: Dover, 1960.
  The Portable Thoreau. New York: Penguin, 1977.
  Thoreau in the Mountains. New York: Farrar, Straus, Giroux, (no date).

Turner, Frederick Jackson. *The Frontier in American History.* Tucson: University of Arizona Press, 1986.
  Frederick Jackson Turner's Legacy: Unpublished Writings in American History. San Marino: Huntington Library, 1965.
  Europe: 1789-1920. Norwood: Norwood Editions, reproduction of 1920 edition.

Twain, Mark. *Roughing It.* New York: The New American Library, 1962.
  The Adventures of Huckleberry Finn. New York: Doubleday, 1985.
  The Adventures of Tom Sawyer. New York: Penguin 1983.
  Innocents Abroad. New York: National American Library, 1980.
  Life on the Mississippi. New York: Bantam, 1985.

Warner, William W. *Beautiful Swimmers.* Boston: Little, Brown, 1976.
  Distant Water: The Fate of the North Atlantic Fisherman. New York: Penguin, 1984.

Whitman, Walt. "Songs of Myself" from *Leaves of Grass*. New York: The Viking Press, 1959.
  Leaves of Grass. New York: Penguin, 1959. ·
  The Portable Whitman. New York: Penguin, 1973.
  Walt Whitman: The Complete Poems. New York: Penguin, 1975.

Wood, Nancy. *Many Winters*. New York: Doubleday, 1974.
  War Cry on a Prayer Feather: Prose & Poetry of the Ute Indians. New York: Doubleday, 1979.

Zwinger, Ann. *Beyond the Aspen Grove*. New York: Harper Colophon, 1981.
  A Desert Country Near the Sea: A Natural History of the Cape Region of Baja California. New York: Harper & Row, 1983.
  Run, River, Run: A Naturalist's Journey Down One of the Great Rivers of the West. Tucson: University of Arizona Press, 1984.
  Wind in the Rock: A Naturalist's Explores the Canyon Country of the Southwest. New York: Harper & Row, 1978.